Anonymous

Buell and Williams' Indianapolis City Directory

and business mirror for 1864

Anonymous

Buell and Williams' Indianapolis City Directory
and business mirror for 1864

ISBN/EAN: 9783337291440

Printed in Europe, USA, Canada, Australia, Japan

Cover: Foto ©Andreas Hilbeck / pixelio.de

More available books at **www.hansebooks.com**

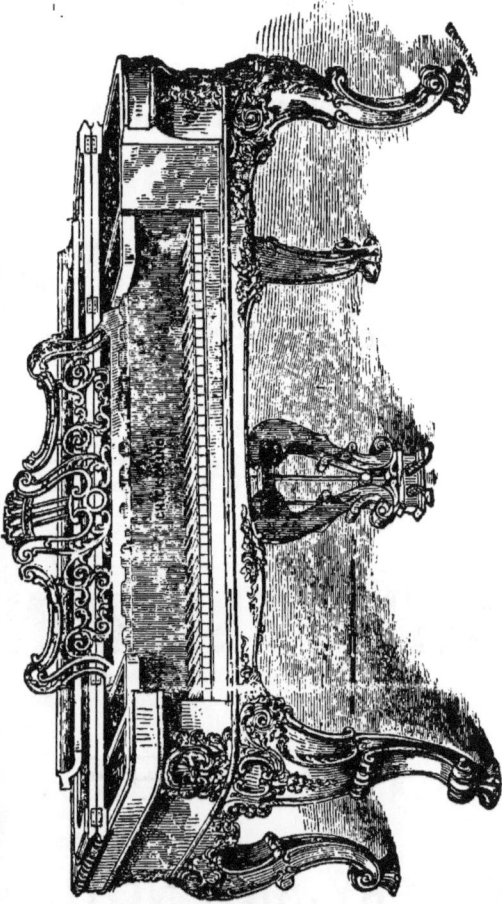

BUELL & WILLIAMS'

INDIANAPOLIS

CITY DIRECTORY

AND

BUSINESS MIRROR,

FOR 1864.

PUBLISHED ANNUALLY.

INDIANAPOLIS, IND.:
BUELL & WILLIAMS, PUBLISHERS.
1864.

TO THE PUBLIC.

The Indianapolis City Directory for 1864, is herewith presented. The Publishers desire to acknowledge the courtesy and liberality which they have experienced at the hands of the merchants and leading citizens, and they offer this result of their labors, in the full confidence that it will be found generally correct and satisfactory.

The attention of advertisers is called to an important improvement, that of referring from the names in the Alphabetical List and Business Mirror to the page containing the cards of the advertisers. This feature has met with general satisfaction wherever it has been introduced.

Respectfully,

BUELL & WILLIAMS.

INDIANAPOLIS, May 18th, 1864.

CONTENTS.

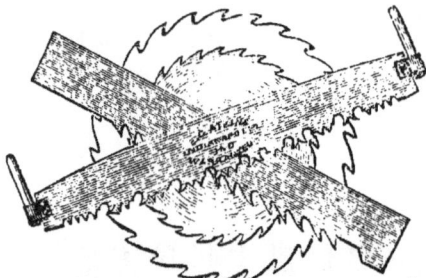

INDEX TO ADVERTISEMENTS.

$1\frac{1}{2}$

NAMES TO LATE FOR

REGULAR INSERTION, REMOVALS, ETC.

Anderson Thomas, res. 84 Indiana ave.

BARNITZ & GRIFFITH, REAL ESTATE AGENTS, 1 s. Meridian. See card, p. 144.

Byrkit Martin, of B. & Beam, res. 68 s. Tennessee.

Cahill Michael, laborer, res. 52 n. Liberty.

Carrington H. B., Col. 18th U. S. Infantry, off. 79 w. Washington.

Chase, Ludington & Cady, boot and shoe store, 19 and 20 e. Washington.

DIXON JAMES W., UNION DYE HOUSE, n. of Washington, near Canal. See card, p. 276.

Finter F., baker, res. 75 Fort Wayne ave.

Hawes & Redfield, publishers State Gazetteers and Directories, 16½ e. Washington.

Hill Rev. James, res. 118 n. West.

McCreery Joseph, queensware, 85 e. Washington, res. 72 n. East.

Stillhorn Fred., res. 86 n. Davidson.

Sthurn Harmon, res. 100 n. Tennessee/

BUELL & WILLIAMS'

Indianapolis City Directory

FOR 1864.

ABREVIATIONS.

Bds , *boards;* cor., *corner;* res., *residence;* col., *colored;* wid., *widow;* opp., *opposite;* bet., *between;* ave., *avenue;* off., *office;* e., w., n., s., *East, West, North, South.* The word *street* is implied. Names in capital letters indicate patrons of this work.

A

Abbett J. M., tinner, bds. Wright's.

Abbett L., physician, 20 Virginia ave. res. same.

Abdill L. B., clerk, Head-quarters Supt. Recruiting Service, bds. 64 Massehusetts ave.

Abeling Gustave, salesman, German Dry Goods Store.

Abrahams John, clerk, res. 71 w. Noble.

Abramit Adolph, clerk, Ætna Ins. office, res. n. Pennsylvania.

Abrams John, clerk, res. 69 n. Noble.

Achenbach A. P., book-keeper, C. E. Geisendorff & Co., res. 272 w. Washington.

Achey H., res. 5 Kentucky ave.

Adams Alexander, boarding house, res. 53 Indiana ave.

ADAMS EXPRESS CO., JOHN H. OHR, AGENT, 12 e. Washington.

Adams G. F., wholesale and retail Furniture, 56 e. Washington, res. 30 n. Delaware.

Adams Geo. H., of Asher & A., res. 20 w. North.

Adams H. S., policeman, res. 61 s. New Jersey.

Adams J. C., brick maker, res. 125 n. Delaware,

Adams J. W., of Mauldin, A. & Co., res. 70 s. Tennessee.

Adams Reuben, deputy sheriff, res. 71 s. New Jersey.

Adams Samuel C., brick maker, res. 125 n. Delaware.

2

Adams Samuel, law student, with J. C. Bufkin, res. 125 n. Delaware.

Adams W. L., of Hume, Lord & Co., res. 60 e. North.

Adams W. M., carpenter, res. 184 n. Illinois.

Adgar Mary A., res. 47 cor. Delaware and Ohio.

Aelschlager John, clerk, res. 188 e. St. Clair.

ÆTNA BUILDING, n. Pennsylvania, bet. Washington and Market.

ÆTNA INS. CO., WM. HENDEBSON, AGENT, office, 13 n. Pennsylvania.

Affantranger S. J., blacksmith, 111 North.

Aftune A., works Rolling Mill.

Arther L., moulder, Washington Foundry.

Alvoy D. L., painter, bds. 68 n. Missouri.

Albert J. W., saddler, 210 n. Alabama.

Albeit S. S., clerk, 210 n. Alabama.

Albertson N. D., clerk, A. & U. S. Express Co., bds. Pyle House.

Albesmyer D., laborer, res. 56 Union.

Albro Henry, moulder, res. 225 s. Delaware.

Aldag A., shoemaker, res. Washington, on alley, bet. Alabama and New Jersey.

Aldag C., boot and shoe dealer, 137 e. Washington.

Aldag C. L., shoemaker, res. 50 n. Liberty.

Aldag Louis, shoemaker, res. 30 n. Liberty.

Aldag L., shoemaker, 30 n. Liberty.

Aldrich Frank, res. 20 n. West.

Aldridge John, carpenter, res. 131 n. Davison.

Alexander A., teamster, res. 130 e. North.

Alexander Christ., teamster, res. 197 Noble.

Alexander Geo. H., painter, res. cor. South and Tennessee.

Alexander G. W., barber, works 145 w. Washington.

Alexander Irvin, teamster, McCord & Wheatly.

Alexander Joseph, carpenter, 91 Huron.

Alford T. G., of A., Talbot & Co., res. 83 n. Alabama.

Alford, Talbot & Co., wholesale grocers, 36 e. Washington.

Alghands Jno., laborer, res. 171 n. Noble.

Algoo Samuel, porter, A. Wallace.

Aligatt Mrs. L., washing, res. 77 n. Noble.

Allaire A., blacksmith, Clinton, bet. New Jersey and East.

Allaire James, brick mason, res. 12 St. Clair.

Allaire Peter, brick mason, res. 101 n. Meridian.

Albright John W., Head-quarters Supt. Recruiting Service, bds 27 s. Delaware.

Allen A. C., minister, res. 38 e. New York.

Allon Alfred, clerk, New York Store, bds. 14 e. Ohio.

Allen C., shoemaker, bds. Bicken House.

ANDREW WALLACE,

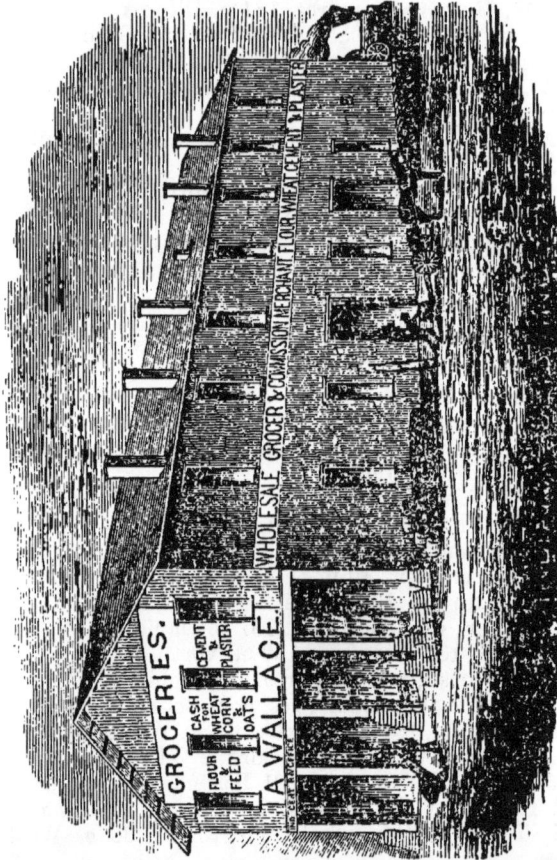

WHOLESALE GROCER!
FORWARDING, PRODUCE & COMMISSION MERCHANT,

No. 38 Virginia Ave. and 51 Delaware St., Indianapolis.

Dealer in Fish, Nails, Cheese, Flaxseed, Grains, Flour, &c. Also, sole Agent for the sale of Lake and Kanawha Salt, Louisville Cement, Jersey City and Newark Lime and Plaster. Sells all kinds of Groceries, except liquors. Particular attention is given to the sale or shipment of Flour and Grain, and liberal advances made on same.

ALLEN HENRY, LIVERY AND SALE STABLES, 12
and 14 e. Pearl, rear Glenn's Block, res. 66 w. Vermont.
See card, page 100.

Allen James, printer, works A. C. Chandler, res. 131 n.
Mississippi.

Allen Mrs. J., res. 8 s. Pennsylvania.

Allen Joseph, (col.) res. 186 North.

Allen T. C., res. 38 e. New York.

Allen W. A., clerk, U. S. mustering office, bds. Littles Hotel.

ALLEN & STEWART, LIVERY AND SALE STABLE,
12 and 14 e. Pearl. See card, page 100.

Allen Wm., foreman, Western Machine Shops, res. 105 Meek.

Allred G. W., sexton, res. 137 w. South.

Altland Samuel, carpenter, res. 122 n. East.

Altman H., Moulder's Saloon, 67 s. Illinois, res. same.

Alvert J. A., plasterer, bds. 210 n. Alabama.

Alvert S. S., clerk, bds. 210 n. Alabama.

Alvert J. W., saddler, res. 210 n. Alabama.

Alvey J. H., with Donaldson & Carr. res. cor. First and
Tennessee.

Alvord, Caldwell & Alvord, wholesale grocers, 68 e. Washington.

Alvord E. B., of A., Caldwell & Alvord, res. 141 n. Illinois.

Alvord E. S., res. 54 n. Pennsylvania.

Alvord H. B., of Alvord, Caldwell & Alvord, bds. Bates
House.

Alvord J. C., clerk, res. 54 n. Pennsylvania.

Alward Samuel, clerk, res. Vermont, e. of Delaware.

Alward Samuel, clerk, res. cor. Fort Wayne Ave. and Walnut.

American Express Co., J. Butterfield, agent, cor. Meridian
and Washington.

Ames J., of Benham & Co., res, Blakes' Block, third floor.

Amos J., spinner, res. Washington, near tole gate.

Amos Mrs. Nancy, res. 143 n. Noble.

Anderson Alexander, res. 12 e. Huron.

Anderson Cinthia, (wid.) res. 53 e. Market.

Anderson David, carpenter, res. 52 Indiana ave.

ANDERSON GEO P., VARIETY STORE AND INS.
AGENT, 25 s. Illinois, res. 175 e. South. See card,
page 100.

Anderson Geo., carpenter, res. 53 e. Market.

Anderson G. T., toy store and Ins. agent, res. 175 e. South.

Anderson J. W., messenger, American Express Co.

Anderson James, works Exchange Stable.

Anderson James, teamster, bds. Ohio House.

Anderson James, laborer, res. New York, bet. Illinois and
Meridian.

B. F. HAUGH.   F. E. SCHOWE.

HAUGH & SCHOWE,

MAKERS OF

ORNAMENTAL IRON WORK!

IRON RAILING,

VERANDAHS,

BANK VAULTS!

AND JAIL WORK,

BRIDGE BOLTS, &c., &c.

ALSO,

BUILDERS OF E. MAY'S

PATENT JAIL!

We would call special attention to County Commissioners, Architects and individuals requiring work in our line, would do well to confer with us.

No. 2 NORTH DELAWARE STREET,

Opposite the Court House,

INDIANAPOLIS, IND.

Anderson Jerome S., clerk, City Grocery, res. 42 Mississippi.

Anderson J. W., express messenger, res. 82 n. East.

Anderson L., boiler maker, Washington Foundry.

Anderson R. J., brick mason, res. 156 n. Delaware.

Anderson S., (col.) laborer, res. 34 c. Maryland.

Andes R., carpenter, bds. 59 n. Noble.

Andra John, of J. A. & Co., res. 152 e. New York.

ANDRA JOHN & CO., SADDLERS AND HARNESS MAKERS, 169 c. Washington. See card, page 62.

Andre John, saddler, 152 e. New York.

Andrews J., works Rolling Mill.

Andrews Robert, res. Missouri, bet. South and Merrill.

Andrews S. B., photographer, 32 opp. Union Depot, bds. Spencer House.

Andrews L. N., gen. freight agent, Peru & Indianapolis R. R., res. 258 n. Tennessee.

Andy Jacob, blacksmith, res. 178 s. Alabama.

Angle John, machinist, bds. 163 c. Ohio.

Angle Sandy, machinist, bds. 163 c. Ohio.

Anheier A., bar-keeper, res. 85 s. Illinois.

Anner Louis, butcher, res. 223 n. Noble.

Anner Wm., varnisher, res. 225 n. Noble.

Annis Philip, grocery, res. 229 n. Noble.

Anspach A., shoemaker, works 138 w. Washington.

Anta Jacob, finisher, Eagle Foundry.

Anthes Jacob, gas lighter, res. 24 e. Maryland.

Anthony David, carpenter, res. 36 East.

Antles Mrs. E. A., res. 50 n. East.

Apple G. W., of Apple & Thorn, bds. S. Beck's.

Apple G. W. & Co., boot and shoe store, 86 c. Washington.

Apple & Thorn, photographic artists, 84 and 86 c. Washington.

Applegate Bery, of A. & H. Schnull.

Appleton J. R., with of Dodd & Co., res. 100 w. Vermont.

Arbanckel Samuel, teamster, res. North, bet. East and Liberty.

Arbetsmeyer Henry, laborer, res. 152 n. Noble.

Armbruster J. J., works 137 w. Maryland, res. 47 West.

Armendroubt ———, res. bet. Alabama and Delaware.

Armington A., law student, with Wm. Henderson.

Armstrong J., works Rolling Mill.

Armstrong James, merchant, res. 83 n. Illinois.

Armstrong Rev. Wm., agent American Bible Society, 4 Talbott & New's Block, res. 110 n. Meridian.

Armstrong Wm. S., cashier, 17 w. Washington, res. 110 n. Meridian.

Arnhoelter H., of John Andra & Co., bds. 152 c. New York.

Arnhoelter W., harness maker, bds. 152 e. New York.
Arnold A. H., clerk, res. 145 Virginia ave.
Arnold Emma, res. 59 Massachusetts ave.
Aron A., clerk, res. 62 n. Delaware.
Arrington S. B., M. D., res. 11 Mississippi.
Arthur Thos., moulder, res. 117 s. Tennessee.
Arthur Thos., foreman, Washington foundry, res. 117 s.
    Tennessee.
Arthur W., moulder, Washington foundry.
Arthur W. A., moulder, res. 117 s. Tennessee.
Arthur Wm., stone cutter, res. 7 e. New York.
Asberry Chappel, New Jersey, bet. South and Virginia
    ave.
Ash Richard, laborer, res. 16 Georgia.
Asher J. R., of A. & Adams, res. 105 s. New Jersey.
Asher & Adams, book and map publishers and wholesale
    booksellers, 4 Odd Fellows Hall.
Asmus F., works Rolling Mill.
Assmus Fred., laborer, 74 Michigan.
Athon Dr. J. S., Secretary of State, 11 Kentucky ave. res.
    82 n. New Jersey.
Athon Thos., painter, res. 11 Massachusetts ave.
ATKINS E. C., SHEFFIELD SAW WORKS, 155 s. Illinois,
    res. 141 e. South. See card, opp. table of contents.
Atlantic Saloon, J. E. Gridley, prop'r, Palmer House cor.
Atwood T. Frank, penman at Purdy's Commercial College,
    bds. Palmer House.
Auch F , works Express Co., res. 23 Union.
Auerweck D., shoemaker, bds. Lafayette House.
Aue G., laborer, res. 51 Union.
Aufderheet Fred., painter, res. 150 n. Davison.
Aufderheet Henry, shoemaker, res. 126 n. Davison.
Aufderheet Henry, drayman, wks. Union Cabinet Factory.
Aufderheet William, drayman, works Union Cabinet Fac-
    tory.
Augall I., hack driver, 280 Indiana ave.
Aughinbangh C. R., money and freight bill clerk, Adams
    Express Co.
Aughinbaugh E., clerk, Browning & Sloan.
Augstein Charley, bds. East Street House.
Auholder Henry, saddler, res. 152 e. New York.
Aunckbrook Henry, drayman, res. 269 s. Delaware.
Austin Mrs. H., 20 s. Meridian.
Austin John, gardner, res. 23 Georgia.
Avers Mrs. M., res. 275 s. Delaware.
Avens Joseph, expressman, res. 259 s. Pennsylvania.
Avery J. L., carpenter, res. 104 n. Alabama.
Ayers Jos., works Rolling Mill.

Ayres G. W., blacksmith, bds. East Street House.
Ayers W. S., carpenter, res. First, bet. Tennessee and Illinois.

B

Babbs W., tailor, bds. Calafornia House.
Backesto J. P., M. D., off. 23½ n. Mississippi, res. 26 n. Mississippi.
Backett Thomas, engineer, bds. 120 n. Noble.
Bacon Daniel, prop'r Exchange Saloon, 19 and 21 n. Illinois.
Bacon E. H., M. D., off. s. w. cor. Meridian and Washington.
Bacon J , blacksmith, res. 131 n. Alabama.
Bacon Robert D., printer, bds. 39 n. Pennsylvania.
Bacon T. S., clerk, bds. 59 e. New York.
Bade Anthony, laborer, res. 129 s. Alabama.
Bade Wm., with Frese & Kropp.
Bader H., currier, works with Mooney & Co.
Baggett Pat., porter, 74 w. Washington.
Baggs Fred., cashier, 70 e. Washington, res. 59 e. Ohio.
Bah C., laborer, res. Garden, bet. Illinois and Tennessee.
Bahenmier Henry, laborer, res. 340 Virginia ave.
Bahler Ludwig, grocer, res. 142 e. Market.
Bailey J. C., clerk, bds. Little House.
Bailey Julius, carpenter, res. 8, cor. Bates and Noble.
Bailey M. N., hackman, res. 74 n. Illinois.
Baird Wm., cooper, res. 63 w. New York.
Bakeman Peter, carpenter, res. 249 s. Delaware.
Baker Mrs. A. & Co., millinery, 24 s. Illinois.
Baker C., bar keeper, bds. 81 s. Meridian.
Baker Conrad, Col. 1st Ind. Cavalry, A. A. P. M. Gen. for Ind., and Supt. recruiting, off. Blackford Block, bds. 132 n. Tennessee.
Baker Chas., barber, bds. Georgia, bet. Illinois and Meridian.
Baker H., wagon maker, 99 Bluff Road.
Baker Jesse, hatter, res. 26 s. Illinois.
Baker John, blacksmith, res. 131 n. Alabama.
Baker J. M., of B. & McIver, res. 24 s. Illinois.
Baker R. M., clerk, bds. S. Beck's.
Baker W. M., painter, res. bet. Alabama and New Jersey.
BAKER & McIVER, HAT STORE, 22 e. Washington.
Baldwick Fred., fruit stand, opp. Union Depot, res. same.
Baldwin Alexander, book-keeper, in National Bank, bds. Littles Hotel.
Baldwin J. H., Fancy Bazaar, 6 e. Washington, res. 105 n. Meridian.
Baldwin Mrs. Mary, res. 176 n. East.

Bales Oliver H., prof. at Bryant & Spencer's Commercial College, res. 102½ n. Meridian.

Balke C., saloon, 175 e. Washington, res. same.

Ball A., bakery, 132 s. Illinois, res. 134 s. Illinois.

Ball H., blacksmith, bds. 26 Massachusetts ave.

Ball Wm., res. 83 w. Maryland.

Ballard Austin, seal engraver, res. 5 Circle.

Ballard H. W., teacher at Institute for the blind.

Ballard Charles, painter, res. 5 Circle.

Ballinger L. M., carpenter, bds. 100 Fort Wayne ave.

Ballman Herman, res. 114 w. Vermont.

Ballweg Ambrose, machinist, res. 57 Madison ave.

Bals Charles, of Raschaupt & B., res. 56 e. St. Joseph.

Bals Christian, clerk, bds. 120 e. Market.

Balton J. T., yard master, Bellefontaine R. R.

BAMBERGER H., HATTER, (also of Rice & B.,) 16 e. Washington, res. 119 e. Ohio.

Bamberger Isaac, clerk, 6 Bates House.

Bamberger Solomon, clerk, with H. Bamberger, bds. 119 e. Ohio.

Ban D., works Rolling Mill.

Baner Henry, cabinet maker, wks. Union Cabinet Factory.

Banfeldt George, wholesale merchant, bds. 88 Virginia ave.

Banister Mrs. Sarah, res. 167 e. Ohio.

Bank of State, cor. Illinois and Kentucky ave.

Bannister E., boot fitter, with A. Lintz.

Bannon J., laborer, works with Wm. Hinesley.

Bannworth B., boots and shoes, Washington, bet. East and Liberty, res. same.

Bar G. L., cabinet maker, res. 253 s. Delaware.

Barble Sampson, res. bet. Michigan and e. Washington.

Barbour Lucian, of B. & Howland, res. 107 n. Alabama.

Barbour Samuel, laborer, res. 126 n. West.

Barbour Samuel, steward, Palmer House.

Barbour T. O., with Dodd & Co., res. 126 n. West.

BARBOUR & HOWLAND, ATTORNEYS AT LAW, 4½ w. Washington.

Bardihop Dick, watch maker, Terre Haute Depot, res. 172 Virginia ave.

Bargh George, res. 198 Virginia ave.

BARKER THOS. D., REAL ESTATE AND CLAIM AGENT, 5 Blackford Block, res. 113 e. New York. See card, page 66.

Barker S., res. 168 n. Alabama.

Barker Wm., bds. 115 w. Washington.

Barkes Wm., mason, res. 149 n. West.

Barnes A., printer, res. 115 n. East.

GEORGE FELLER,

DEALER IN

WATCHES!

CLOCKS,

AND JEWELRY,

No. 107 East Washington Street,

(Opposite the Court House.)

INDIANAPOLIS, IND.

GOLD AND SILVER PLATING!

EXECUTED IN THE BEST STYLE.

☞ Particular attention given to the Repairing of all kinds of Watches, Clocks and Jewelry.

Barnes Alphonso, American Express office, res. 111 Virginia ave.

Barnes Dr. H. F., off. 1 Blakes building, res. 91 n. Alabama.

Barnes J., (col.) cook, Mason House.

Barneclo Lorenzo, machinist, res. 102 s. Noble.

Barnes L. N., works Union Depot, res. 59 Louisiana.

Barnes W., boarding house, 72 s. Illinois.

Barnich L., machinist, works I. & C. R. R. machine shop.

Harnicle Mrs. Rebecca, res. cor. Bates and Benton.

Barnitt Thos., res. 83 e. Market.

Barnitz Chas., of B. & Griffith, res. 119 s. Noble.

BARNITZ & GRIFFITH, REAL ESTATE AGENTS, 38½ w. Washington.

Barns E., city printer, res. 118 n. East.

Barns J., machinist, works I. & C. machine shop, res. 167 s. Noble.

Barr Jacob, carpenter, res. 172 n. Delaware.

Barr L. D., res. 49 w. South.

Barr Wm. A., fireman, on railroad, res. 176 n. Delaware.

BARRETT E. G., GEN. AGT. BOOKS AND GAS BURNERS, 6 Blakes Block, res. cor. Third and Mississippi.

Barrett Pat., laborer, res. Meek.

Barritt Zelotes, yard master, Indiana Central, e. Washington, near corporation line.

Barrick S. J., cabinet maker, res. 160 w. Maryland.

Barrie Mike., stone cutter, res. 46 n. Spring.

Barrows David, book-keeper, C. E. Geisendorff & Co.

Barrows H. W., of Springer, B. & King, res. 133 w. Maryland.

Barrows T., clerk, bds. Pyle House.

Barry E. H., Secy. Grand Lodge I. O. O. F., off. 2 Odd Fellows Hall, res. cor. First and n. Tennessee.

Barry T G., of Stewart & Morgan, res. cor. Massachusetts ave. and Pennsylvania.

Barry Thos. G., druggist, bds. 53 n. Pennsylvania.

Bartelsman Mrs. Lisette, res. 108 n. Noble.

Barthels F., clerk, bds. Union Hall.

Bartholomew Thos., cooper, bds. 204 n. Mississippi.

Bartlett Joseph L., of Bartlett & Richardson, res. 121 s. Tenn.

BARTLETT & RICHARDSON, DEALERS IN CONFECTIONERIES, FRUITS, NUTS AND FANCY GROCERIES, Louisiana, opp. Union Depot.

Bartlow J., carpenter, Washington Foundry.

Base Ernst, laborer, res. 28 s. Liberty.

Barer Fred., saloon, res. Vermont, bet. Noble and Liberty.

Bass S., saloon, cor. Meridian and Washington, res. 22, cor. Bates & Benton.

Bass Wm., works Rolling Mill.

CITY

INTELLIGENCE

AND

GENER'L INFORMATION

OFFICE,

No. 63 EAST WASHINGTON STREET

(Over Dury & Cox's Boot and Shoe Store,)

INDIANAPOLIS, IND.

At this office information will be given to all wishing to hire help, either male or female. To girls or men who want situations of any kind, those wanting to Buy or Sell Business, such as Saloons, Stores, &c. All wishing Partners or wanting to enter into Partnership.

Also, a Register will be kept for the Renting of Houses, Stores, &c., as well as for those wishing Boarding or Boarders.

PERSONS desiring the benefit of the above office will be required to pay the sum of $1.00 for the Register of their names and business, for which they will have the full benefit of said office for one month, in which time the Proprietor will do his best to please his customers, but no money will be refunded if the parties can not be satisfied. All business will be transacted in a fair and honorable manner.

W. B. WALLACE,
PROPRIETOR.

Bassett Mrs. Amanda, res. c. Ohio.

Bassett Frank, works I. C. R. R. machine shop.

Bassett H., works Delzell & Jones, res. n. w. cor. Pennsylvania and Ohio.

Baster Edward, carpenter, Orient, near Washington.

Basto James, works Indiana Central R. R. machine shop.

Bates H., sr., res. 66 c. Market.

Bates Henry, jr.. res. 73 n. Delaware.

BATES HOUSE, J. L. HOLTON, prop'r, cor. Illinois and Washington. See card, page 128.

Baty E. H., paper maker, with Wm. Sheets, res. 116 N. York.

Bauer Mrs. Mary, res. 63 n. Illinois.

Baumann Andrew, res. 31 Elizabeth.

BAXTER P. D., OF J. L. KNOX & CO., res. 181 w. Washington.

Bayless G. A., clerk, Qr. Dep. U. S. A.

Baymiller C. P., local editor, Sentinel office, res. 90 Massachusetts ave.

Beace C. H., machinist, works I. & C. R. R. machine shop.

Beach Nelson, carpenter, res. 132 c. St. Clair.

Beach W. B., clerk, Sinking Fund, res. 106 n. West.

Beal John A., attorney, 15½ c. Washington.

Beal Joshua, painter, res. 32 Michigan Road.

Beal S., gunsmith, alley, Washington, bet. New Jersey and East.

Beale J., house and sign painter, room 12 old post-office building.

Beall A. C., watch maker, bds. Bates House.

Beam David, of Byrket & B., res. 125 s. Tennessee.

Beaman A., shoemaker, res. 79 c. Washington, up stairs.

Beans T., carpenter, bds. 163 c. Ohio.

Beard A., plow maker, with Case & Marsh, res. 67 Tenn.

Beard S., clerk, res. 58 w. Vermont.

Bearss C. W., saloon, 13 Kentucky ave.

Beasley J. A., shoemaker, 105 n. Tennessee.

Beasley John E., res. 105 n. Tennessee.

Beatty E., works Paper Mill, res. 116 w. New York.

Beaty D. S., Gen. Agency, 3 Browns Block, res. 80 New Jersey.

Beaty D. S., jr.. clerk, res. 80 c. Michigan.

Beaver Thos., teamster, res. 144 c. Walnut.

Beck A., res. 69 w. South.

Beck C., gunsmith, res. 80 w. New Jersey.

BECK E., CRYSTAL PALACE SALOON, 44 w. Washington, res. 19 Maryland. See card.

Beck F., meat market, cor. McCarty and Bluff Road, res. same.

3

Beck Jacob, soldier, res. 186 n. New Jersey.
Beck Martin, soap maker, res. s. Illinois.
Beck S., gunsmith, 21 s. Delaware, res. same.
Beck Samuel, with C. A. Ferguson.
Becker H., trunk maker, 30 w. Washington.
BECKER JACOB, CLOTHIER AND MERCHANT TAI-
LOR, 103 e. Washington, res. 85 e. New York.
Beckle Y., laborer, res. 184 s. Delaware.
Beckman Wm., laborer, res. 208 s. Alabama.
Beckner L. H., clerk, bds. 34 e. Ohio.
Beckner S. H., notary public, with R. L. Walpole.
Beeber Geo. P., bridge builder, res. 25 Meek.
Beebe R., Empire Saloon, 23 w. Washington.
Behmer Augustus. shoemaker, res. 79½ e. Washington.
BEHRISCH B., CLOTHIER, Spencer House Block. See
card, page 80.
Behrs J., machinist, Washington Foundry.
BEHYMER D., MANUFACTURER OF DOORS, SASH,
BLINDS AND MOULDINGS, cor. Benton and Mar-
ket, res. 172 e. Ohio. See card, page 130.
BEHYMER S., SASH, DOORS, BLINDS AND MOULD-
INGS. 47 e. South. See card, page 114.
Behymer S., of S. B. & Noe, res. 138 e. South.
Behrisch B., clothier, 15 w. Washington, res. 119 w. Wash-
ington.
Behymer S. E. B., carpenter, res. 138 e. South.
Beihammer, Daniel, carpenter, res. 174 e. Ohio.
Beilstem Ernst, painter, res. 144 e. Ohio.
Beini Henry, laborer, res. 227 n. Alabama.
Belcher Wm., teamster, res. Water.
Bell Alfred R., printer, Journal office.
Bell Chas., house and sign painter, res. Ramsey's Block.
Bell Milton, law student, with McDonald & Roache.
Bell Wm., city expressman, res. 74 Blackford.
Belles J. T., res. 119 s. New Jersey.
BELLIS S., AGENT FLORENCE SEWING MACHINE,
17 n. Pennsylvania, res. 110 n. Pennsylvania.
Bellows E., blacksmith, res. 173 n. Alabama.
Belzer Geo., laborer, res. 213 n. Alabama.
Belzer G., machinist, Washington Foundry.
Bender David, proprietor National Hotel, 217 w. Wash-
ington.
Bender S., laborer, res. 131 e. Market.
Benham H. L., clerk. with Benham & Co., bds. Pyle House.
Benham A. M., of B. & Co., bds. Macy House.

BENHAM A. M. & CO., MUSIC DEALERS, cor. Illinois and Washington.
Benjamin D. O., res. Meridian, bet. Merill and McCarty.
Benjamin L., clerk, 15 w. Washington.
Benner Gottlieb, laborer, res. 90 n. Davison.
Benner Samuel, clerk, 10 w. Washington.
Bennett H. W., pattern maker, res. 124 s. Noble.
Bennett J. B., porter, Littles Hotel.
Benninger Philip, res. 72 n. Noble.
Benson John A., tole gate keeper, National Road, foot of Washington.
Benton H. S., boiler maker, works I. & C. machine shop.
Bentson Henry, res. 51 Benton.
Beohlen D. A., architect, res. 87 Indiana ave.
Berands J., cabinet maker, 4 s. Pennsylvania.
Berg Geo., feed boy, Journal office.
Berg Henry, carpenter, res. 156 s. Tennessee.
Bergart Andy, cabinet maker, res. 272 s. Delaware.
Berget John, carpenter, res. Norwood, bet. Illinois and Tennessee.
Bergner G., book-keeper, Indianapolis Branch Banking Co.
Bergner John, stone mason, res. 17 Nathan.
Bermaner Joseph, laborer, res. 52 Huron.
Berner C., clerk, res. 11 Elsworth.
Bernhammer Wm., brick mason, res. cor. Michigan and West.
Bernhart C., clerk, res. 81 s. Illinois.
Bernstein Samuel, clerk, with Rice & Bamberger.
Bernhardt Wm., laborer, res. 91 e. St. Joseph.
Berry Edward, cabinet maker, res. 306 s. Delaware.
Berryman John, blacksmith, res. 50 s. Noble.
Berry John, res. 137 n. Mississippi.
BERRY J. R., SECY. MISSISSIPPI INS. CO., bds. 21 s. Delaware. See card, page 88.
Berry Mrs. Mary, res. 212 e. St. Clair.
Bertling H., of Zunmer & Co., res. 138 e. Washington.
Bese Ernst, laborer, with Voegtle & Metzger.
BESSONIES REV. AUGUSTUS, res. Georgia, bet. Illinois and Tennessee.
Bettis G. W., orderly sergeant, bds. 27 s. Delaware.
Bettis W. H., clerk, res. 24 Massachusett ave.
Beunerchics Carl, machinist, bds. Mechanics House.
Bevington Albert, plasterer, res. bet. Alabama and New Jersey.
Bieker J., marble polisher, 57 St. Joseph.

Biden Mrs. E. E. J., dress maker, 139 c. Washington.
Biddleman Silas, shoemaker, res. 34 c. Georgia.
Bidwell Chas. L., agent, bds. Littles Hotel.
Biedemeister Chas. Gustave, res. 59 n. East.
Bieler J. L., harness maker, with John C. Hereth.
Bierman John, laborer, res. 114 s. Noble.
Biesamber John, carpenter, res. 148 n. Liberty.
Biggs L. R., res. cor. South and Missouri.
Biglow I. S., Deputy U. S. Marshall, res. 100 w. Michigan.
Bilger Joseph, carpenter, res. 154 c. New York.
Billings Henry, painter, res. Water.
Bilstein Ernst, res. 144 E. Ohio.
Bingham J. J., editor State Sentinel, res. 88 W. Maryland.
Bingham James, stone cutter, res. Orient bet. Michigan road
    and Washington.
Bingham W. P. & Co., dealers in watches, clocks and jew-
    elry, 50 c. Washington, res. 53 n. Meridian.
Binkley Sam'l, jr., wks. Western Agricultural Works.
Binkley Sam'l, of Goolman, Morris & Co., res. s. Illinois in
    rear of Agricultural Works.
Binnamon Henry, orderly sergeant, bds. 27 s. Delaware.
Bippus Frederick, porter, C. E. Hawthorn, res. 79½ c. Wash-
    ington.
Bippus John, tailor, 18 n. Pennsylvania, bds. 93 c. Wash-
    ington.
Bicket Chas. W., tailor, res. 11 Huron.
Bird Abram, res. 95 n. Illinois.
Birney P., shoemaker, with A. Lintz.
Bisbing Jacob J., police, res. 124 n. West.
BISBING J. J. & CO., INDEPENDENT DETECTIVE
    POLICE, cor. Illinois and Louisiana, 2d floor.
Bishop A., painter, Washington Foundry.
Bishop John L., bookkeeper, res. cor. Winston and New
    York.
Bishop Wm., wks. Rolling Mill, res. cor. McCarty and
    Tennessee.
Bisplinghoff C., laborer, res. 142 c. McCarty.
Bissett Wm., clerk, 14 Illinois.
Black Davidson, 107 Ohio.
Black George H., carpenter, res. 22 s. East.
Black John, clerk, Oriental House.
Black Wm. M., eating house, cor. St. Clair and Indiana ave.
Blackwell Henry, res. 168 s. Illinois.
Blackwell T., wks. Rolling Mill, bds. Wm. Johnson.
BLAES NICHOLAS, SALOON, 48 s. Delaware, res. same.

Blain T. M., sr., heater, Washington Foundry.
Blain T. M., jr., apprentice, Washington Foundry.
Blain Thomas, wks. Washington Foundry, res. 95 w. New York.
Blaine Thos., clerk O. B. Stout & Bro., bds. 95 w. New York.
BLAIR J. M., HARNESS AND COLLAR MAKER, 198 W. WASHINGTON, RES. SAME. See card, p 136.
Blake A., buss driver Little's Hotel.
Blake J. R., clerk Indiana Rolling Mill.
Blake James, res. 186 n. Tennessee.
Blake James R., weigh master Rolling Mill, res. 186 n. Tennessee.
Blake J. P., wks. Rolling Mill.
Blake Capt. O., bds Oriental House.
Blake Wm., assistant quartermaster, res. 201 n. Tennessee.
Blanc J. D., res. 91 Indiana ave.
Bland Hiram, carpenter, res. 166 s. New Jersey.
Blanc James W., express, res. 61 n. Spring.
Blank A., clerk, res. 142 e. Washington.
Blank Fred., tinner, wks. with Munson & Johnson.
Blase Henry, shoemaker, bds. 179 s. Delaware.
Blaswick Christ., cabinet maker, res. 206 n. Alabama.
Blauvelt D., transfer clerk Adams Express Co., res. w. Market.
Bledwe Mrs. N., res. 140 e. Market.
Bless Eli, res. 168 n. New Jersey.
Blight John, horse buyer, res. 119 e. Market.
BLIND ASYLUM, W. H. Churchman, superintendent, North bet. Pennsylania and Meridian.
Bliss John, carpenter, 137 w. New York.
Blithe Wm., engineer, res. Bates near Cady.
Blockstett H., stonemason, res. 62 n. Noble.
Blode John, cabinet maker, res. 27 n. East.
Bloome I., wks. Rolling Mill.
Bloom S., bookkeeper, 3 e. Washington, bds. 115 w. Maryland.
Bloomer Frank, cashier Bee Hive Store, bds. Macy House.
Bloomer Isaac L., lawyer, bds 74 n. East.
Bloomfield A. R., student, with S. C. Frink.
Blotts J., laborer, 43 w. McCarty.
Blue C. B., carpenter, res. 153 n. East.
Bly John ships horses for government, res. 277 s. East.
Bly O. H. P., trader, res. 18 n New Jersey.
Bly Perry, brickmaker, res. 18 s. New Jersey.

Blythe Samuel, machinist, res. 115 s. Alabama.
Boardingkerger A., laborer, bds. 67 n. New Jersey.
Boarf Mrs. Naomi, res. 20 w. North.
Boaz W. T., res. 261 s. Pennsylvania
Bobbs J. S., M. D., 3d floor Harrison's Block, res. Michigan road.
Bockerman Henry, shoemaker, res. 59 St. Mary.
Bockstabur Martin, res. 283 Virginia ave.
Bodenmiller L., blacksmith, res. St. Mary, bet. Alabama and Delaware.
Bodman E., M. D., res. 144 n. Illinois.
Boger J. A., salesman New York Store, bds. California House.
Boggs Alexander, bds. 154 e. North.
Bogle R. D., of Hyde & B., res. cor. Alabama and St. Clair.
Bogle Repp, livery stable, res. 76 e. St. Clair.
Boerum Joseph S., mail agent Bellefontaine R. R., res. 200 n. Illinois.
Boetticher Julius, editor Indiana Volksblatt, res. 132 e. Washington.
Boetticher O., printer, bds. 132 e. Washington.
Bohart F., coppersmith, res. 232 e. Washington.
BOHLEN D. A., ARCHITECT, office 3d story ÆTNA BUILDING, res. 85 Indiana ave.
Bohsey Gottlieb, laborer, res. 47 n. Liberty.
Bohtenmiller Leonhardt, blacksmith, res. 70 e. St. Mary.
Boinhefer H. W., carpenter, res. 236 Madison R. R. ave.
Bok Christian, carpenter, bds. 214 n. Alabama.
Bolan Michael, wks. Rolling Mill, res. 39 Henry.
Bolander Jacob, res. 71 Bright.
BOLLMANN FRED., CINCINNATI BAKERY, Washington bet. Delaware and Alabama, res. same.
Boman Henry, laborer, res. 74 s. Noble.
Bombarger David, carpenter, res. 207 Indiana ave.
Bond Abraham, shoemaker, res. 35 w. New York.
Bond E., teamster, res. 144 n. Mississippi.
Bond Mrs. Caroline, res. 144 n. Mississippi.
Bond J., res. 55 e. Ohio.
Bond S. S., barber, with W. H. Franklin.
Bond W. A., harnessmaker, with A. J. Hinesley & Co.
Boobs Elizabeth, res. 81 n. Pennsylvania.
Bookter Geo., weaver, res. w. Maryland.
Boor Philip, cooper, 134 Indiana ave., bds. 107 Indiana ave.
Boorhes Wm., soldier, res. bet. Alabama and Delaware.
Booso H., machinist, Washington Foundry.

Boring E., plasterer, res. 64 Massachusetts ave.
Bornstim A., clothier, res. 89 s. Tennessee.
Bornstein A., clerk, bds. Commercial Hotel.
BORST F. & CO., MEAT MARKET, 16 n. Illinois.
Borth L. A., clerk, J. C. Mayhew & Co.
Bosch George, laborer, res. 66 e. Merrill.
Bost John, basketmaker, res. 178 e. Market.
Botenmiler L., blacksmith, cor. Kentucky ave. and Georgia.
Bothwell H., barkeeper, res. 47 w. McCarty.
Bourgoune S., cigarmaker, bds. California House.
Bourier Wm., whitewasher. res. 53 w. Georgia.
Bouse David W., carpenter, res. 62 e. New York.
Bouoy Adrian, turner, res. 264 s. Delaware.
Bovey C. W., bricklayer. res. 152 e. North.
Bovey E., tinner, 264 s. Delaware.
Bovey G. C., with T. D. Barker. res. 152 e. North.
BOWEN FRANK W., SUPERINTENDENT JEFFER-
     SONVILLE R. R., res. Jeffersonville.
Bowen John, brickmason, res. 169 s. Delaware.
BOWEN, STEWART & CO., BOOKSELLERS AND
     STATIONERS, 18 w. Washington. See card page 66.
Bowser Levi C., laborer, res. 167 s. Noble.
Bowen Lucien B., clerk, 18 w. Washington, bds. 8 Virginia
     ave.
Bowen Silas T., of B., Stewart & Co.. res. 126 n. Illinois.
BOWLES THOMAS H., ATTORNEY, No. 3 Talbott &
     News' Block, res. 108 n. Meridian.
Bowles Geo. A., bookkeeper. bds. 44 s. Pennsylvania.
Bowman Henry, barkeeper Franklin House.
Bowman John, tobacconist, bds. Palmer House.
Bowman Wm., carpenter, res. 68 Bluff road.
Boyd D. M., city wood measurer, res. 37 s. Meridian.
Boyd D. M., jr., ticket clerk Bellefontaine R. R. office, res.
     37 s. Meridian.
Boyd Frank. A., bds 20 Virginia ave.
Boyd James, res. 118 n. Alabama.
Boyd J. T., physician, office 40 n. Pennsylvania, res. 85
     Massachusetts ave.
Boyd W. H., telegraph operator T. H. & R. R. R.
Boykink C., drayman, res. 27 Union.
Boyle M. W., salesman, res. 40 e. New York.
Brachlan Tim, wks. Rolling Mill.
Brackebush Mrs., widow, res. 254 n. Tennessee.
Brackebush C. J., of Lukens & B., res. 254 n. Tennessee.
Brackebush Otto, salesman, New York Bazaar.

New York Bazaar!

NO. 37½ EAST WASHINGTON ST.,
INDIANAPOLIS, IND.

EMIL KLOTZ, - - PROPRIETOR.

ALL KINDS OF

Notions and Fancy Goods!

CHILDREN'S CABS & CARRIAGES,
MILITARY GOODS,

FIRE - ARMS AND AMUNITION,
WHOLESALE AND RETAIL.

J. M. SPURGIN.E. C. LONG.

SPURGIN & LONG,

HOUSE, SIGN & ORNAMENTAL

PAINTERS,

NO. 6 MERIDIAN STREET,
Opposite Old Post Office,

INDIANAPOLIS, IND.

Graining, Gilding, Bronzing and Varnishing done in the Neatest Manner.

ORDERS PROMPTLY ATTENDED TO.

Brackin Thos. E., of Isgrigg & Brackin, res. cor. St. Joseph and Illinois.

Brademier Charles, teamster, res. 102 c. Market.

Brademeier Christ., laborer, res. 150 n. Davison.

Brademier J. F., teamster, res. Washington bet. New Jersey and East.

Bradon Capt. D., provost marshal, office Blackford's building, res. 41 c. Michigan.

Bradon Jas., bds. with W. Bradon.

Bradon William, stationer and blank book manufacturer, 24 w. Washington.

Bradley Jepthey, policeman, res. 69 Benton.

Bradley J. H., R. R. agent, res. 69 n. Pennsylvania.

Brado C., silversmith, with Zumbush.

Brado Jos., salesman, with M. H. Good.

Brado Thomas, groceries, cor. South and East, res. same.

Bradshaw George, cooper, res. Michigan road near Central R. R.

Bradshaw Capt. James, res. 173 w. Pennsylvania.

Bradshaw John A., mule dealer, res. 12 c. Vermont.

Bradshaw J. W., of W. A. Bradshaw & Son, res. 70 n. East.

Bradshaw O., machinist, wks. Indianapolis and Cincinnati Machine Shop.

Bradshaw W. A., of B. & Son, internal revenue assessor to the district, res. 70 n. East.

Bradshaw W. A. & Son, grain, flour and produce dealers, 5 s. Delaware.

Brady Michael, brickmason, res. Illinois n. of Third.

Brarnard John, cooper, res. w. Washington opp. Ætna Mills.

Brah Leopold, bakery and confectionery, res. 46 Ft. Wayne ave.

Braman A. C., grocer, cor. North and Alabama, bds. 119 n. Alabama.

Bramdige Edward, shoemaker, res. 167 c. Market.

Bramwell J. M., with Browning & Sloan, res. 48 s. Mississippi.

Bramwell Z. F., engineer, res. 66 c. Merrill.

BRANCH OF THE BANK OF THE STATE OF INDIANA, cor. Washington and Meridian.

Brandon A., wks. Rolling Mill, res. 182 s. Mississippi.

Brandt C. & H., c. Washington near Corporation line.

Branham McClure, agent I. & M. R. R., bds. Ray House.

Branham Orlando, Western Union telegraph, res. Vernon, Jenning's Co. Ind.

F. P. CUNNINGHAM,
BAKERY, CONFECTIONERY!
AND
LADIES OYSTER AND ICE CREAM SALOON,
Cor. Market & Illinois St.

Opposite Governor's Mansion.

Keeps constantly on hand every variety
of Candies, Taffys, also celebrated
Ice Cream Candy and Pine
Apple Rock.

OYSTERS, PIGS FEET, HAM AND EGGS!

Chickens and Game in Season,

Meals served at the Saloon or any part of the City.

Weddings and other Parties sup
plied with the best articles and most reasonable terms. Refreshments can also be
had at the Theater Saloon.

H. C. CHANDLER & CO.,
CARD, JOB AND ORNAMENTAL
PRINTERS!

S. W. Cor. Washington & Meridian Sts.,

HUBBARD'S BLOCK,

INDIANAPOLIS, IND.

Every description of Printing executed in the neatest manner at short
notice and reasonable terms.

WOOD ENGRAVING
EXECUTED TO ORDER.

Brannan Thos., sheet iron worker, bds. Cincinnati House.
Brannan Thos., shoemaker, bds. Mrs. S. Kelly's Boarding House.
Brannger Fred., laborer, res. Davison bet. Vermont and Michigan.
Branning Ernst, shoemaker, bds. Pearidge House.
Brans Thomas, carpenter, bds. cor. North and Delaware.
Beargan A., wks. Rolling Mill.
Brason Mrs. Julian, res. 24 n. Liberty.
Brattain W. J., soldier, res. 56 Massachusetts ave.
Bray John S., policeman, res. 104 n. East.
Breckway T., cooper, res. 89 Bluff road.
Breis John, shoemaker, res. 71 n. East.
Bremuman Frederick, carriage maker, res. 140 n. Alabama.
Bremmerman C., carriage maker, res. 148 n. Delaware.
Brenan John, laborer, res. 356 Virginia ave.
Brennig Rev. G. A., of the German Episcopal Church, res. Ohio bet. New Jersey and East.
Brenning Mollie E., teacher of vocal and instrumental music, res. Ohio bet. New Jersey and East.
Brett M. L., state treasurer, 13 Kentucky ave., Sinking Fund Building.
Brett Tom, wks. Rolling Mill.
Bretz Adam, grocer, 40 Louisiana, res. Illinois bet. Louisiana and Georgia.
Brentholts L., boiler maker, Washington Foundry.
BREUNNINGER A., GROCER, cor. Washington and Missouri, res. same. See card, p. 70.
Brewer Edward, (col.) barber, res. Douglas.
Brewer & Bird, borbours, 48 s. Illinois.
Brickett Mrs. D. A., res. 135 w. Market.
Bridge Albert, res. 166 s. Illinois.
Briggs C. H., engineer, res. 136 n. Alabama.
Briggs Mrs. E., res. 280 Indiana ave.
Briggs W., carpenter, res. Tennessee near cor. McCarty.
Brigham Chas. E., printer, 24 w. Washington, res. 148 New Jersey below South.
Bright Amos, printer, with Dodd & Co., res. 45 n. Pennsylvania.
Bright Mrs. C., artist, res. n. Illinois near First.
Bright Eliza, boarding, res. 45 n. Pennsylvania.
Brill John, carpenter, res. 188 s. Delaware.
Brill J., wks. Rolling Mill.
Brinner Jacob, carpenter, res. 36 n. Spring.
Brinneman Caston, carriage maker, res. 148 n. Delaware.
Brinmerman F., wagonmaker, with Case & Marsh.
Briniger John, cooper, res. 19 Willard.

4

Brink Cad, clerk, 29 w. Washington, bds. Palmer House.
Brink Fred., teamster, res. 184 e. Vermont.
Brink T., laborer, 182 e. Vermont.
Brinker August, grocery store, 94 New York.
Brinker Wm., cooper, res. 169 n. New Jersey.
Brinkman C., of B. & Ruschhaupt, 67 n. New Jersey.
Brinkmann John F., carpenter, res. 212 n. Noble.
Brinkman W., shoemaker, bds. Farmers' Hotel.
BRINKMAN & RUSCHHAUPT, livery stable, 17 s. Delaware.
Brinkmier Charles, lawyer, res. 152 n. Liberty.
Brinkmier Fred., laborer, res. 127 n. Davison.
Brinkmeier G., res. 129 n. Davison.
Brinkmeyer F., with J. C. B. & Co., 82 w. Washington, res. 127 Davison.
Brinkmeyer Geo., with J. C. B. & Co., res. 129 Davison.
Brinkmeyer J. C., of J. C. B. & Co., res. 152 n. Liberty.
Brinkmeyer J. C. & Co., importers and wholesale dealers in foreign and domestic liquors, 82 w. Washington.
Bristol A. I., bookkeeper, 14 w. Washington, res. 59 e. Market.
Bristol A. R., druggist, res. 59 e. Market.
Bristol W. M., clerk Jeffersonville R. R. freight depot, res. 59 e. Market.
Bristor S. M., carriagemaker, res. 51 n. Delaware.
Britt Thos., wks. Rolling Mill, res. 45 s. Illinois.
Brittingham A., wks. Rolling Mill.
BRITTON J. G., BARBER, 145 w. Washington, res. same.
Brock Robert, carpenter, 86 Huron.
Brocksmith Henry, blacksmith, res 44 Huron.
Brodan James, cast iron worker, res. 119 e. New York.
Brodan Michael, printer, res. 117 e. New York.
Broden J., moulder, wks. with D. Root & Co.
Broden J., turner, res. 119 e. New York.
Broden J., machinist, res. 21 Willard.
Broden Jas., machinist, res. Willard bet. Mississippi and Tennessee.
Broden Patrick, moulder, res. Mississippi bet. South and Henry.
Broderick Mrs. Mary, 104 Indiana ave.
Brolan M. J., wks. Rolling Mill.
Brommer Fred., barkeeper, res. 119 e. Washington.
Broniken Joseph, baker, wks. Cincinnati Bakery.
Bronner R., finisher, res. McCarty.
Bronson R. T., carpenter, res. 103 n. Alabama.
Brooks Mrs. Ellen, res. 14 s. New Jersey.
Brooks J. C., clerk, bds. 118 n. Pennsylvania.

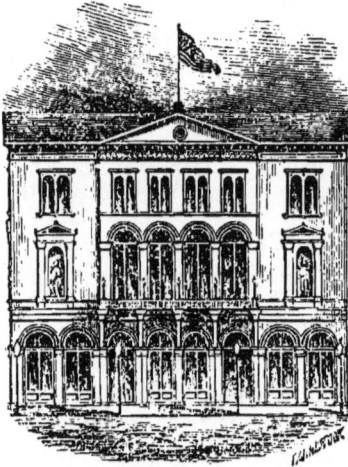

Brooksmith H., blacksmith, Washington Foundry.
Brooksmith L., rivet heater, Washington Foundry.
Broomen N., teamster, res. 123 e. St. Clair.
Brother John, blacksmith, res. e. Washington.
Brothers W. H., of B. & Schroy, bds. Palmer House.
Brothers & Schroy, photograph gallery, cor. Washington and Meridian.
Brough George, laborer, res. Central R. R. bet. East and Liberty.
Brough G. W., clerk Bellefontaine freight house, res. 217 s. Alabama.
Brouse Andrew, carpenter, res. 60 e. New York.
Brouse D. W., carpenter, bds. 60. e. New York.
Brouse J. A., chaplain Army, res. 38 e. Market.
Brown A., of A. B. & Co., bds. Little's Hotel.
Brown A. C., carpenter, bds. 141 w. Market.
Brown A. H., clerk, res. Meridian near Merrill.
Brown Albert, laborer, res. Wyoming, bet. Delaware and High
Brown A. R., moulder, bds. Ray House.
Brown A. & Co., Globe Saloon, 103 e. Washington.
Brown C., blacksmith, wks. with D. Root & Co.
Brown C. H., carpenter, res. 217 Indiana ave.
Brown E., painter, 9 Virginia ave.
Brown E. W., carpenter, res. 17 w. Georgia.
Brown Ezra W., teacher, deaf and dumb asylum.
Brown Ellison, painter, res. cor. Illinois and Second.
Brown F. M., book keeper, res. 119 Massachusetts ave.
Brown Geo. P. C., machinist, wks. Western Machine Works, res. 167 n. Alabama.
Brown H. C., carpenter, res. 47 n. Noble.
Brown John, plasterer, res. 182 n. Liberty.
Brown I., salesman, res. 151 e. South.
Brown J. H., druggist, res. 64 e. New York.
Brown J., (col.) fireman, Mason House.
Brown J., carpenter, res. 268 Madison R. R. ave.
Brown I., attorney at law, res. 151 e. South.
Brown James B., paper hanger, res. bet. Alabama and Delaware.
Brown J. B., machinist, Washington Foundry.
Brown John H. F., tinner, bds. 103 n. Alabama.
Brown Jerry, (col.) engineer, res. 151 n. Alabama.
Brown Jesse B., machinist, res. 13 Henry.
Brown J. F., carpenter, res. cor. Ohio and West.
Brown J. F., tinner, res. 168 n. Alabama.
Brown J. G., grocer, 150 n. New Jersey, res. 144 n. New Jersey.
Brown J. H., clerk, Vickers' Drug Store.

Brown J. W., res. 22 n. Meridian.
Brown J. W., baker, 150 n. New Jersey, res. same.
Brown L. W., tinner, res. 25 Bluff road.
Brown Mrs. Laurie, res. 193 n. New Jersey.
Brown Mrs. Mary, widow, res. 144 n. New Jersey.
Brown M. H., messenger, American Express Co.
Brown P. A., attorney and treasurer of Farmers' and Merchants' Insurance Co., office Blackford's Building, res. 130 n. New Jersey.
Brown Pat, laborer, res. 176 s. Alabama.
Brown R., wks. Last Factory, res. Eddy.
Brown R. D., wks. Rolling Mill.
Brown R. T., R. R. agent, bds. 48 n. East.
Brown R. T., of B. & McNab, res. n. e. end Fort Wayne ave.
Brown S. W., tinner, with R. L. & A. W. McOuat.
Brown Wm., express messenger, res. 101 w. New York.
Brown Willis, (col.) hackman, res. 116 w. Georgia.
Brown W. P., hatter, 20 Kentucky ave., res. same.
Brown & McNab, physicians and surgeons, 7 New & Talbott's Block.
Browning C. O., works, 84 w. Washington.
Browning Edmund, register land office, res. 88 Virginia ave.
Browning Fred., drayman, res. 69 Bluff road.
Browning Gordon, clerk, Post Office.
Browning Geo. T., assistant quartermaster U. S. A. off., cor. New Jersey and Washington, bds. 8 Virginia ave.
Browning Robert, of B. & Sloan, res. 102 n. Illinois.
Browning Wm. H., works, 84 w. Washington.
BROWNING & SLOAN, WHOLESALE AND RETAIL DRUGGISTS, 22 w. Washington. See card, p. 130
Brorfles Moses, (col.) school teacher, res. Missouri.
Brubaker H. W., clerk, res. 31 Kentucky ave.
Bruening E., of E. & J. B., res. 6 e. Washington.
Bruening E. & J., photograph gallery, 6 e. Washington.
Bruening J., of E. & J. B., res. 6 e. Washington.
Bruggmann Wm., tailor, res. 192 e. Ohio.
Brumick Thos., works Rolling Mill.
Brummer Prof. C., music teacher at Indianapolis Female College, res. 79 e. Washington, up stairs.
Brummer ——, foreman, C. F. Schmidt's Brewery.
Brunnanur Wm. F., day police, Douglas.
BRUNDAGE E. C., of M. Hunter & Co., res. 167 e. Market.
Bruner Charles, res. 112 s. New Jersey.
Bruner R., machinist, Washington Foundry.
Brunner John, gardner, res. 43 e. St. Mary.
Bruns Henry, teamster, res. 186 n. New Jersey.
Bruns Mrs. L., res. 168 n. Noble.
Brunson James G., res. 15 n. Illinois.

Brurkink Richard, drayman, res. Wyoming, bet. Delaware and High.

Bryan F. A., clerk, bds. Spencer House.

Bryan Joseph, laborer, res. 14 Michigan Road.

Bryan G. W., druggist, 3 Spencer House Block, bds. Spencer House.

Bryant A. C., master transportation, Bellefontaine R. R., bds. Littles Hotel.

Bryant E. R., Supt. Telegraph, T. H. & R. R. R.

Bryant J. B., book agent, bds. 44 s. Pennsylvania.

Bryant J. S., railroader, res. Henry, bet. Canal and Miss.

Bryant J. W. C., tallyman, Bellefontaine freight depot, res. cor. Massachusetts ave. and Peru R. R.

Bryant J. Z., tallyman, Bellefontaine freight depot, bds. Littles Hotel.

Bryant Thos. J., of B. & Spencer, principal, Commercial college, res. 33 n. Delaware.

BRYANT & SPENCER, COMMERCIAL COLLEGE, 30 w. Washington.   See card, inside front cover.

Buchanan Andrew, laborer, res. 83 Huron.

Buchanan J. H., clerk, Post-office, res. 26 s. Mississippi.

Buchanan A., peddler, res. 218 s. Alabama.

Buchanan Mrs. Catharine, res. 262 e. Washington.

Buchanan S. A., clerk, Post-office.

Buche F., shoemaker, McCarty, bet. Illinois and Bluff Road.

Buckley John, works Rolling Mill, res. 20 Lord.

Buckhorn W., chair maker, bds. cor. Ohio and Davidson.

Buckley J. M., porter, New York Store.

Buckley T., railroader, res. 45 s. East.

Buckley John, works Rolling Mill.

Buckset Wm., trader, res. 56 s. Pennsylvania.

Budd John, brick maker, res. Orient, bet. Michigan Road and Washington.

Buddenbaum Geo. H., res. cor. Davidson and Ohio.

Buddenbaum H., laborer, res. Davidson, bet. Ohio and New York.

Budence H., tailor, res. 160 s. Pennsylvania.

Buchrig H., res. 21 w. South.

Buell C. H., of Frost & B., res. 105 Virginia ave.

Buell Chas. L., of B. & Williams, bds. Bates House.

BUELL & WILLIAMS, publishers of City, County and Railroad Directories, 39 e. Washington, 2d floor.

Butkin J. C., attorney, College Hall building, over German dry goods store.

Bugby P., fireman, res. 7 w. Railroad.

Buhhorn Cris, wagon maker, works with C. Wehling.

Buhof Wm., works Rolling Mill.

Buist Thos., iron merchant, res. cor. Calafornia and Virginia ave.

Bulach S., bar-keeper, bds. 91 e. Wsshington.

Bullard Mrs. K., (wid.) res. 87 e. Ohio.

Bullard W. R., physician, 23 s. Meridian.

Bullard Chas., cabinet maker, res. 145 n. Alabama.

Bullin W. S., carriage trimmer, res. 98 Massachusetts ave.

Bult H., laborer, with J. Fishback.

Bundy E., clerk, Paymaster U. S. A., bds. 21 s. Delaware.

Bundy Major M. L., Post Pay-master, U. S. A., 8 e. Washington, bds. Bates House.

Burbidge Thos., works Union Steam Bakery.

Burdt Geo., tanner, res. cor. Bansin and Washington.

Burdin T., tailor, res. 19 Kentucky ave.

BURDICK WM. P., WHOLESALE JEWELER, 8 n. Meridian, res. 10 w. North. See card, page 84.

Burden Thos., tailor, 59 Kentucky ave.

Burdick Wm., jeweler, res. 10 w. North.

Burgess C. C., dentist, 1 Odd Fellows Hall, res. n. Penn.

Burgess C. N., printer, Journal office, res. 129 Mass. ave.

Burgess John W., res. 66 n. Mississippi.

Burgess L. A., saddler, res. w. St. Clair.

Burgess O. A., minister, Christian Church, res. 115 n. East.

Burhgraf H., works State Armory, res. 243 s. Peru.

Burk A., bar keeper, Empire Saloon.

Burk Geo., res. 104 s. New Jersey.

Burk J., clerk. 15 w. Washington.

Burk J. J., clerk, 104 s. New Jersey.

Burk John, coal dealer, res. 148 n. Tennessee.

Burk L., laborer, res. Tennessee, bet. McCarty and South.

Burk Thos., res. 61 s. West.

Burk M., machinist, Washington Foundry.

Burk Thos., works Rolling Mill.

Burk L., res. 266 Madison Railroad ave.

Burk W. C., of Sloan & B., res. 148 n. Tennessee.

Burk & Shaffer, prop's Burks Saloon, 13 w. Washington.

Burke Henry, stone mason, res. 274 s. Delaware.

Burkhart A. J., ice dealer, res. 146 n. Mississippi.

Burks' Saloon, 13 w. Washington.

Burne Wm., res. West, bet. Merrill and South.

Burns Mrs. Margret, res. 37 s. Noble.

Burnes M., sheet-iron worker, bds. Cincinnati House.

Burnes P., res. 1 Willard.

Burnet John, conductor, Madison R. R., bds. 223 s. Delaware.

Burnett J. C., Secy. Union Central Committee, res. 22 s. Meridian.

Burnham N. G., M. D., off. and res. 10 e. Market.

Burnes James, R. R. engineer, res. 77 n. East.
Burns John, Brilliant saloon, 63 s. Illinois, res. same.
Burns M., of J. & M. Burns, res. 63 s. Illinois.
Burns Michael, laborer, res. 44 Mass. ave.
BURNS J. & M., SALOON, 63 s. Illinois, res. same.
Burns P., works Gas Factory, res. 243 s. Pennsylvania.
Burns T., actor, Metropolitan Hall, bds. Littles Hotel.
Burpee F. L., carpenter, res. 135 n. Mississippi.
Burris J. M., plasterer, res. 180 s. Tennessee.
Burrows G. W., livery stable, 14 n. Pennsylvania, res. 142
    Virginia ave.
Burrows S. A., engineer, works Hill & Wingate.
Burrows & Edwards, cloaks and mantillas, 22 s. Illinois.
Burt A. G., of B. & Cowger, res. Winson, bet. Michigan and
    New York.
Burt A. S., res. 56 Indiana ave.
Burt & Cowger, saddlers and harness makers, 254 e. Wash-
    ington.
Burton J. C., res 221 n. New Jersey.
Burton Daniel, cooper, 134 Indiana ave., bds. Mrs. Webb's
Burton G. H., cooper, res. 78 n. Mississippi.
Burton Martin, of B. & Shilling, res. 202 n. Illinois.
BURTON & SHILLING, TRUNK MANUFACTURERS,
    13 s. Illinois. See card, page 86.
Busboy Wm., brick mason, res. 196 e. St. Clair.
Busch Christian, boot and shoemaker, 138 w. Washington.
Buscher Henry, saloon, 51 e. South, res. same.
Buser Jacob, 30th Idiana Battery, res. 116 s. Illinois.
Buser Samuel, policeman, res. 60 Louisiana.
Bursew H., machinist, res. 122 e. Market.
Bush A., carpenter, res. 188 n. Illinois.
Bush G. M., Oriental Saloon, Oriental House, res. same.
Bush Jacob, saloon, 162 w. Washington, res. 250 e. Wash-
    ington.
Busher H., brewery, 14 s. Alabama.
Bushey Jacob, switchman, res. Water.
Bushkel W., res. Orient, near e. Washington.
Bushmann Wm., of B., Severy & Co., res. 111 e. St. Mary.
Bushnell J. H., artist, 39 e. Washington.
Busking Christ., laborer, res. 58 Huron.
Busking Christ., res. 60 Huron.
Busking H., apprentice, Washington Foundry.
Bussell Dr. E. T., res 152 n. Tennessee.
Bussell Reuben, printer, bds. 152 n. Tennessee.
Bussell W. M., clerk, bds. 152 n. Tennessee.
Bussert John, bakery, 54 Bluff Road, res. same.
Bussey John, prop'r Palmer House, cor. Washington and
    Illinois, res. same.

BUSSEY JOHN & CO., VERANDA SALOON, 36 Louisiana, opp. Union Depot.

Buswell J., carpenter, res. cor. Buchanan and Wright.

Butsch G. M., res. 173 s. Delaware.

BUTSCH JOS., ICE DEALER, res. 48 w. South. See card, page 100.

BUTSCH VALENTINE, PROP'R AND MANAGER METROPOLITAN THEATER AND DEALER IN COAL, LIME AND CEMENT, off. e. South, opp. Madison railroad offices, res. 73 w. South. See cards, pages 52 and 54.

Butten Louis, tailor, res. 197 n. Alabama.

BUTTERFIELD C. S., CITY CLERK. res. w. Ohio, n. side, bet. Mississippi and Missouri.

BUTTERFIELD J., AGENT, AMERICAN AND U. S. EXPRESS CO.'S, cor. Meridian and Washington. res. 103 n. Tennessee. See card, page 4.

Butterfield James A., with A. M. Benham & Co., res. 14 e. Walnut.

Butterfield Jeremiah, expressman, res. 103 n. Tenn.

Butterfield J. W., foreman press room, Journal office.

Butterfield S. A., physician, res. 162 n. East.

Byfield C., salesman, 76 w. Washington, bds. Bates House.

Byram N. S., of Tousey & B., res. 84 e. Ohio.

Byrkit A., works Rolling Mill.

Byrkit J. W., book-keeper, Byrkit & Beam, res. Norwood.

Byrkit Philip, carpenter, res 81 n. New Jersey.

Byrkit & Beam, sash, door and blind factory, cor. Georgia, and Tennessee.

Bywater Edward, grocer, 226 e. Washington, res. same.

Bywater Pat., contractor, res. 226 e. Washington.

C

CABINET MAKERS, UNION, 97 e. Washington. See card, p. 74.

Cady Mrs. C. W., res. 4 Circle.

Cady D., of Chase & Co.

Caffrey John, machinist, wks. Western Machine Works.

Cahalin Patrick, night watch, Great Central R. W. line.

Cahill J. B., apprentice, with Dodd & Co., res. 66 Bluff road.

Cahill Mrs. Mary, res. 231 w. Washington.

Cahn A., salesman, with Feibelman & Rauh.

Cahn J., clerk, with D. Manhenner.

Cain M., apprentice, Eagle Foundry.

Caine John, lumber dealer, res. 141 n. East.

Caison M., wks. Rolling Mill.

Calahan D., wks. Central Freight House, res. Missouri near Canal.

Calahan Mike, res. 278 s. Delaware.
Caldwell J. M., of Alvord C. & Caldwell, res. 148 n. Illinois.
Calchan Michiel, laborer, res. 22 Lord.
CALIFORNIA HOUSE, ADAM KISTNER, PROPRIE-
TOR, 136 s. Illinois. See card, p. 90.
Callaghan M., blacksmith, with Case & Marsh.
Callahan J. P., wks. with T. B. Elliott, res. 103 c. South.
Callahan Michael, laborer, 27 Ellsworth.
Callahan Pat., laborer, res. 82 s. Noble.
Callinan D. J., dry goods, 28 c. Washington, res. Ohio, bet.
Illinois and Tennessee.
Calog A. V., engineer, res. Davidson, bet. Ohio and Market.
Cambron J. J., student, with J. S. Bobbs, bds. same.
Camer Washington W. G., 1st regiment Indiana Siege Ar-
tillery, res. Georgia, bet. Missouri and West.
Camp C. M., messenger U. S. Express Co.
Campaign Joseph, laborer, res. 42 Huron.
Campaign Lewis, carpenter, res. 42 Huron.
Campbell A., tailor, wks. 8 s. Pennsylvania, up stairs, res.
16 West.
Campbell Chas. C., res. 2 w. North.
Campbell J. D., (col.) barber, rc. East.
Campbell J. D., canvasser for H. H. Dodd & Co.
Campbell H., carpenter, res. 194 s. Delaware.
Campbell Sam'l L., book binder, with Dodd & Co., res. 2
cor. n. Meridan.
CAMPBELL W. H., PROPRIETOR MACY HOUSE, cor.
Illinois and Market.
Cameron Geo., brick yard, res. 285 s. East.
Cameron W. S., book and job printer, 8 c. Pearl, res. 116 n.
Alabama.
Campion Daniel, carpenter, res. 203 n. Noble.
CANAN J. W., PROPRIETOR SPENCER HOUSE, cor.
Illinois and Louisiana. See card, p. 120.
Cannon W. B., bookkeeper, bds. Palmer House.
Cantwell Michael, pattern maker, Sinker & Co.
Capitol Mills, J. P. Evans & Co., proprietors, cor. Market
and Canal.
Caray H. G., res. 71 n. Meridian.
Cardel Michael, res. 39 Henry.
Carey J., moulder, wks. with D. Root & Co.
Carey J. S., of C. & Dills, res. — Vermont.
Carey & Dills, barrel and box factory, w. of Soldiers' Home,
bet. Georgia and Terre Haute and Richmond R. R.
Carico James, carpenter, res. 68 Michigan.
Carle Washington, grocer, res. 128 n. Alabama.
Carleton James M., speculator, 108 Indiana ave.
5

Carlisle Mrs. A. M., res. 67 n. Mississippi.
Carlisle Daniel, contractor, res. 46 cor. Walnut and Tennessee.
Carlisle D. W., contracting agent Bellefontaine R. R., office cor. Washington and Delaware. res. cor. Mississippi and Walnut.
Carlisle H., miller, res. Market, bet. California and West.
Carlisle John, miller, res. 204 w. Washington.
Carlisle's Model Mills, w. Washington, bet. Blake and West.
Carmichael J. D., of Todd & C., res. 123 n. Meridian.
Carr Henry, shoemaker, bds. Ohio House.
Carr L. H., salesman, 17 w. Washington.
Carr M., shoemaker, with A. Lintz.
Carr R. S., of Donaldson & C., res. 131 n. Meridian.
Carr Thos., laborer, res. cor. Merrill and Missouri.
Carrigan T., Ostler, wks. with Orlopp & Taylor.
Carrington Gen. H. B., res. 115 n. New Jersey.
Carrington Robt., grocer, res. 45 e. Georgia.
Carroll Washington, grocer, res. 128 Alabama.
Carson J. L., clerk, bds. Corvin's.
Carter A., barber, bds. 145 Washington.
Carton A., wks. Rolling Mill.
Carter Chas. E., res. 89 n. Illinois.
Carter D. E., physician, cor. Tennessee and Washington, res. 79 n. Illinois.
Carter E. B., carpenter, res. 11 w. Market.
Carter Geo., of Leathers & C., res. 113 n. Alabama.
Carter Henry C., carpenter, res. Illinois, below McCarty.
Carter Joel, carpenter, res. 125 n. Delaware.
Carter John, carpenter, res. 197 n. East.
Carter Robt., (col.) res. cor. Howard and First.
Carter S. A., R. R. engineer, res. 227 s. Delaware.
Carter Thos., cutter, with Louis Scholtz.
Cartwright W., machinist, wks. with D. Root & Co.
CARVIN J. M., GROCER, 268 e. Washington, res. 5 n. Noble.
CARVIN & RUBLE, EAGLE GROCERY, WHOLESALE AND RETAIL, cor. Illinois and Indiana av. See card, p. 44.
Cary James, moulder, res. Tennessee, bet. McCarty and South.
Casanova B., laborer, res. cor. Vermont and Davidson.
Case E. E., of C. & Marsh, res. 59 n. Meridian.
Case Jno. L., wks. Indiana Central R. R. Machine Shop, res. 43 e. Georgia.
Case Mike, tailor, res. 270 s. Delaware.

CASE & MARSH, MANUFACTURERS OF PLOWS AND
WAGONS, 86 w. Washington.
Casey G. Maurice, res. 82 w. Maryland.
Casey Patrick, laborer, res. 41 Orsbrook.
Casey T., laborer, Washington Foundry.
Casin J. H., real estate and U. S. claim agent, 8 w. Wash-
ington, bds. Bates House.
Cass Lewis, vice president Farmers' and Merchants' Insur-
ance Co., off. in Blackford's Building.
Cassin M., laborer, res. Wyoming, bet. Delaware and High.
Cathcart A., engineer, 162 s. New Jersey.
Catlin Mrs. M., res. Market, near California.
Catterson Abel F., policeman, res. 56 s. Noble.
Catterson C. W., street contractor, res. 176 e. South.
Catterson Miss Emma, school teacher, 197 Indiana ave.
Catterson James, res. 241 Indiana ave.
Catterson R. F., turner, bds. Pyle House.
Caufield J., laborer, bds. Knight's.
Cavanaugh Laurance, laborer, res. 211 s. Alabama.
Cavanaugh L., blacksmith, res. 213 s. Alabama.
CAVIN JOHN, MAYOR, off. Glenn's Block.
Caven & Sulgrove, attorneys, 15½ e. Washington.
Cavener P., blacksmith, with Case & Marsh.
Caylor Anthony, potter, res. 158 n. Noble.
Caylor O., express driver, res. 125 n. Railroad.
Celleg Barnard, res. 63 Orsbrook.
Central House, T. Graven, proprietor, 44 s. Meridan.
Chadwick L. W., clerk, 3 Blackford's Building, bds. 38 w.
Market.
Chambers A., engineer, res. cor. Illinois and Morrill.
Chambers C. S., clerk, bds. Macy House.
Champane Mrs. C., dress maker, res. 79 e. Washington.
Champion Wm., pressman, with Dodd & Co., res. 165 s.
Tennessee.
Chandler France, general ticket agent, Great Central R. W.
line, bds. 67 n. Pennsylvania.
Chandler G. R., printer, 72 w. Maryland.
Chandler Geo. R., printer, Journal off., res. 72 Maryland.
CHANDLER H. C., JOB PRINTING ESTABLISH-
MENT, Hubbard's Block, cor. Washington and Meri-
dian, res. — California. See card, p. 48.
Chandler T. E., of Wiggins & C., res. 22 California.
Chapman Allwood, painter, res. 210 n. New Jersey.
Chapman A. F., saloon, 32 s. Illinois, res. same.
Chapman Saml., dry goods, res. 19 e. Bates.
Chapman G. R., train master, Jeffersonville R. R., bds.
Alvord's Block.
Chapman Mrs. J. P., res. Louis' Block, Ohio.

Chapman S. S., carpenter, res. 27 n. James.
Chappel R., res. Madison R. R., opp. depot.
Charles D., clerk, Post Office, res. 13 e. Michigan.
Charles D. B., clerk, Post Office.
Charles Thomas, hackman, res. 65 s. Noble.
Charles J., wks. Rolling Mill.
Charters Wm., wks. Rolling Mill.
Chase Andrew, mail agent, bds. 99 Virginia ave.
Chase D. H., of C. & Cady, res. 159 Virginia ave.
Chase J. W., railroader, res. 223 s. Delaware.
CHASE & CADY, LADIES' SHOE STORE, 20 e. Washington.
Chatten D. C., photographer, bds. 20 n. Delaware.
Cheek E. C., res. e. Washington, e. of Corporation line.
Cheek Omer T., clerk, res. Michigan road, near Central R. R.
Cherry A. O., carpenter, bds. 60 e. New York.
Chester G., student, bds. 38 s. Pennsylvania.
Chesnut William, brick mason, res. 220 e. Washington.
Chetester W. G., moulder, Eagle Foundry.
Childers Mrs. E. J., res. 151 s. Noble.
Childers Joshua, wks. with McCord & Wheatley.
Childers J. R., pump maker, 68 s. Delaware.
Childers Mrs. L., res. 19 Willard.
Chisley C., res. Madison ave.
Chism Mrs. M., res. 190 North.
Chipman Leander, res. 128 n. Tennessee.
Chittenden Mrs. R., res. North, bet. Noble and Liberty.
Chives E. B., shoemaker, res. 177 Railroad.
Chives George W., wagon maker, res. 177 Railroad.
Chmitt George, grocer, 70 s. Delaware, res. same.
Choff C., baker, wks. Cincinnati Bakery.
Cholett J. H., clerk U. S. commissary department, res. 22 n. Mississippi.
Christian Church, cor. Delaware and Ohio.
Christian Fred., wks. Rolling Mill.
Christian Mortz, wks. Rolling Mill.
Christian Record, E. Goodwin, editor and proprietor, Journal building.
Chritmann John, res. 19 Maryland.
CHRISTY ALBERT, UNION SALOON, opp. Union Depot, 55 w. South.
Church George, assistant superintendent Jeffersonville R. R., res. 48 s. Pennsylvania.
Church George, master transportation Jeffersonville R. R.
Church Joseph, miller, res. 35 s. Noble.
Churchman F. M., of S. A. Fletcher & Co., res. 56 n. Alabama.

Churchman W. H., superintendent Institute for the Blind, res. at Institute.
Cincinnati House, 124 s. Delaware.
Cinane M., clothing, res. 173 e. Ohio.
CITY BANK, PETTIBONE, MANSUR & CO., 3 w. Washington.
City Brewery, 26, 27 and 28 s. Pennsylvania.
CITY HOTEL, s. Illinois. See card, page 60.
CITY GROCERY, C. L. HOLMES, 31 w. Washington.
City Saloon, 53 s. Illinois.
City Council Chamber, 4, 3d floor, Glenn's Block.
City Police Office, 1, 2d floor, Glenn's Block.
Claffey Fred., carpenter, res. 96 e. McCarty.
CLAFLIN C. C., AGENT, WHEELER & WILSON'S SEWING MACHINES, res. 106 n. Meridian. See card, opp business mirror.
Clam W. F., clerk, res. 110 n. Alabama.
Clark Chas., telegraph repairer, res. Hendricks Co., bds. Bicking House.
Clark E. W., editor Witness, Journal building.
CLARK EDMUND, PREST. AND AGT. INDIANA AND ILLINOIS CENTRAL R. R. CO., office, 24½ e. Washington, res. 36 n. Delaware.
Clark F. D., M. D., off. 24½ e. Washington, res. 55 n. Liberty.
Clark Amond, Prest. Ch. R. R. Co., res. 36 n. Delaware.
Clark H., wagon maker, res. 35 e. St. Clair.
Clark Isaac N., minister, res. 127 n. Pennsylvania.
Clark J. S., student w. J. F. Johnston, 11 n. Maryland.
Clark Mrs. Maria, res. 95 w. Vermont.
CLARK PHILO M., MANUFACTURER OF SODA WATER, 209 e. Washington. See card, page 64.
Clark Reuben O., carpenter, res. 98 w. Michigan.
Clark S. A., carriage trimmer, bds. Littles Hotel.
Clark Wm., merchant tailor, 28 n. Illinois, res. 175 e. Ohio.
Clark W. F., agent, Merchants Dispatch, cor. Virginia ave. and Alabama, res. 17 Loukebee.
Clarke A. D., of Bowen, Stewart & Co., 67 n. Mississippi.
Clarke E. R., clerk, 8 w. Washington, res. cor. New York and Delaware.
Clarke Hampton, machinist, res. 215 Indiana ave.
Clarke W. B., teacher at Institute for the blind.
Clary Pat., porter, Palmer House.
Clary Robert, works Indiana Central R. R. machine shop.
CLASICAL INSTITUTE, L. H. CROLL, PRINCIPAL cor. New York and Alabama.
CLAY HILARY, RECEIVER, SINKING FUND, res. rear Sinking Fund office.

Clayton Chas., carpenter, res. 3 Willard.
Clem Aaron, grocery keeper, res. 113 Massachusetts ave.
Clement John, carpenter, res. 235 Indiana ave.
Cleppinger J. W., doctor, res. 112 n. Delaware.
Clines Peter, carprnter, works Hill & Wingate.
Clingenpeel W., clerk, res. Madison ave.
Clipton W. R., of Elliott & C., res. 29 n. Noble.
Clipton J. B., teamster, res. 174 n. New Jersey.
Cloffee Conrad, laborer, res. 7 Huron.
Close Wm. H., salesman, Bee Hive Store, bds. Macy House.
Close W. H., (col.) barber, with W. Franklin, res. 56 Massachusetts ave.
Cloud J., (col.) barber, res. 91 Tennessee.
Cloud John, painter, bds. 118 n. Alabama.
Cluck Wm. C., laborer, res. 129 Blake.
Clutter J., works with Jordon & Spotts.
Cutter J. A., clerk, 88 Winson.
Coats Balis, stewart, Littles Hotel.
Cobben Jesse, carpenter, res. 128 e. Market.
Coburn Mrs. Annie, res. 159 n. Noble.
Coburn Fred., machinist, res. 184 Virginia ave.
Coburn H., of C. & Jones, res. 57 bet. Delaware and Ala.
Couburn J. C., res. 79½ up stairs.
Coburn J. F., machinist, res. 184 Virginia ave.
Coburn S., res. 47 cor. Delaware and Ohio.
COBURN'S SALOON, COBURN, TURNER & CO., PROPR'S, 15 n. Illinois, opp. Bates House, C. T. & Co., bds. Palmer House. See card, page 50.
Coburn & Jones, lumber yard, cor. Delaware and New York.
Cochran W. A., carpenter, res. 3 Eddy.
Coen J., boarding house, 107 s. Tennessee.
Coffeen M. D., law student, w. J. C. Dye, bds. 45 n. Penn.
Coffin E., of C. & Reynolds & Co., res. New York, bet. Noble and Spring.
Coffin Stephen, pork merchant, res. cor. Michigan and Delaware.
Coffin B. & Co., pork and beef packers, 14 s. Meridian.
Coffin Stephen, of B. C. & Co., res. cor. Michigan and Delaware.
Coffin Wm. J., cigar maker, res. New York, bet. Noble and Spring.
Coffman Jacob, carpenter, res. 165 s. New Jersey.
Coffman & Morton, pork house, Blake, near Washington.
Cogill John, teamster, res. 89 s. New Jersey.
Cogill John, laborer, works, Hill & Wingate.
Cogle Wm., res. 186 Virginia ave.
Cogswell W. J., actor, Metropolitan Hall.

Cohen J., clerk, 10 w. Washington.
Cokely Mike, Watchman, 52 e. South.
Colby Henry, (col.) laborer, res. 119 n. Missouri.
Cole J. C., brick mason, res. 69 St. Mary.
COLERICK JOHN, ATTORNEY, off. 16½ e. Washington, room 3, bds. Oriental House.
Colestock Hiram, carpenter and builder, res. 150 n. Illinois.
Colsby L., (col.) res. 125 Indiana ave.
Coll Dennis, res. 123 w. Maryland.
Callahan J. P., clerk, res. 103 e. South.
Colley S. A., attorney, 10 s. Meridian, res. 164 n. New Jersey.
Collier Wm., saloon, res. 81 s. New Jersey.
Collins Cornelius, laborer, res. 180 s. Alabama.
Collins E. J., Lieut. 26th Ind. Vols., res. 148 e. New York.
Collins Jerry, machinist, works, I. & C. R. R. machine shop.
Collins John, carpenter, res. 37 s. Illinois.
Collmann Chas., butcher, res. 118 e. Michigan.
Colman H. C., laborer, res. 66 Indiana ave.
Colton Wm., inspector, 16 e. Washington.
Comegis Levi, house mover, res. 62 n. Delaware.
Commel Geo., hatter, res. 23 Chapman.
COMMERCIAL COLLEGE, BRYANT & SPENCER, Temperance Hall, w. Washington.
Commercial College. Purdy's, Ætna building, n. Penn.
COMMERCIAL HOTEL, cor. Georgia and Illinois.
Compayne J., laborer, works with D. Root & Co.
Compton W. N., clerk, U. S. Acct Dept., bds, 21 s. Delaware.
Conatey J. B., bleacher, 22 s. Illinois.
Conde Chas. A., pattern maker, Western Machine Works.
Condell James, blacksmith, res. Bates, near Cady.
Condit J. D., office, 1 Blackfords Block, 2d floor, res. s. of city, near Madison road.
Condo Geo. W., messenger American Express.
Cone W. S., clerk, I. & M. R. R. Freight Depot, bds. Ray House.
Conkle J., laborer, res. 30 Union.
Conklin J., railroader, res. 98 s. Pennsylvania.
Conklin H. N., of C. & Redman, res. cor. Mississippi and Michigan.
CONKLIN & REDMOND, WHOLESALE DEALERS IN FOREIGN AND DOMESTIC LIQUORS, 140 w. Washington. See card, page 18.
Conlen Michael, res. 247 Indiana ave.
Conlon C., attorney at law, res. Pearl, bet. Alabama and Delaware.
Conly J., works Rolling Mill.

CONNER A. H., POST MASTER, res. 90 e. Market.
Conner Thomas, shoemaker, res. 208 s. Delaware.
Conners T., laborer, Gas Works.
Conner Thos., laborer, res. 204 s. Delaware.
Connolly G., boiler maker. Washington Foundry.
Connolly H., laborer, Washington Foundry.
Connor Mrs. Mary, res. 28 Willard. *
Connor Michael, res. 99 e. Louisiana.
Connor Thos., engineer, res. 36 n. Illinois.
Conor John, laborer, res. 41 Orsbrook.
Conroy P., tailor, res. West, bet. Georgia and Maryland.
Converse Joseph, soldier, res. 157 n. East.
Cook ———, res. 31 Meek.
Cook A. S., carriage trimmer. res. alley, bet. East and Liberty.
Cook Bawlebrow, carpenter, res. 164 n. Delaware.
Cook Mrs. Carrie, music teacher, res. 20 Spring, bet. New Albany and Indiana ave.
Cook F., sr., merchant, res. 36 s. Liberty.
Cook Fred., jr., laborer, res. 36 s. Liberty.
Cook P., shoemaker, with C. Aldag.
Cook Henry, laborer, res. 36 s. Liberty.
Cook J., machinist, Western Agricultural Works.
Cook J., machinist, Washington Foundry.
Cook John, collar maker, 201 s. Pennsylvania.
Cook Mrs. Julia, res. 59 w. New York.
Cook Mrs. Lucinda, res. 195 Indiana ave.
Cook M. R., painter, 318 Meridian, res. 75 w. Maryland.
Cook N. L., printer, Journal office.
Cook Wm., dry goods and groceries, 186 w. Washington.
Coonay Pat., laborer, res. cor. Pine and Forest ave.
Coney D., moulder, Washington Foundry.
Cooney Dennis, laborer, res. 9 n. East.
Cooney Pat., works Western Machine Works.
Cooney Thos., apprentice machinist, res, 31 Fletcher's ave.
Cooper Albert, works Indiana Central machine shop.
Casper Allen, machinist, res. 46 Benton.
Cooper Chas. A., res. 155 Virginia ave.
Cooper Mrs. Frank, res. 114 n. Missouri.
Cooper J., machinist. Washington Foundry.
Cooper J. J., speculator, res. 236 n. Illinois.
Cooper Mrs. J., res. Market, bet. California and West.
Cooper John, foundryman, res. 229 s. Delaware.
Cooper Joshua, shoemaker, res. 81 n. Alabama.
Copeland H. E., clerk, 72 w. Washington, bds. 46 s. Pennsylvania.
Copeland J., of Eden & C., res. 128 e. Market.

THE NEW YORK BRANCH.

Wholesale and Retail

CLOTHING STORE!

No. 15 West Washington Street,
INDIANAPOLIS, IND.

B. BEHRISCH, Prop'r.

Latest styles of Clothing, together with a splendid supply of Gent's Furnishing Goods, will be constantly kept on hand at the lowest prices.

JOSEPH KOHN.
Dealer in
CLOTHING!
And Gent's Furnishing Goods,
No. 80 WEST WASHINGTON STREET,
(Nearly opposite Masonic Hall,)
INDIANAPOLIS, IND.

☞Military Goods constantly on hand.

EAGLE CLOTHING STORE!
M. DERNHAM,
Dealer in
CLOTHING
GENT'S FURNISHING GOODS,
HATS, TRUNKS AND VALISES.
No. 1 South-West Cor. Washington and Meridian Streets,
INDIANAPOLIS, IND.

J. D. MYERS,
COMMISSION MERCHANT!
And Wholesale and Retail Dealer in
CHOICE FAMILY FLOUR,
BUCKWHEAT AND RYE FLOUR, CORN MEAL AND ALL KINDS OF FEED.
No. 8 & 12 South PENNSYLVANIA STREET,
Few doors below Sharpe & Fletcher's Bank, Indianapolis.

Copeland J. W., millinery, 8 e. Washington, res. 97 n. Meridian.

Coplin Gideon. miller, res. cor. New York and Bright.

Corbeley Saml., book-keeper, with Spiegel, Thoms & Co.

Corliss Dr. C. T., homœopathic physician, res. 106 n. Pennsylvania.

Cornelius Casius, plasterer, res. 166 s. Alabama.

Cornelius Edward, laborer, res. 166 s. Alabama.

Cornelius Louis, bar-keeper, Capital Garden.

Cosby R. M., carpenter, res. 183 n. East.

Cosler D. W., carpenter, 79 n. Davidson.

Costigan Frank, clerk, bds. 107 Virginia ave.

Costillo John, machinist, res. 153 w. Maryland.

Costlo John, finisher, res. 52 w. Maryland.

Cottman Mrs., res. 159 w. Vermont.

Cottrell Thomas, of C. & Knight, res. 102 s. New Jersey.

Cottrell & Knight, coppersmiths and gas-fitters, 94 s. Delaware.

Coughlan Wm., of Merrill & C., res. 154 w. New York.

Council Chamber, Glenn's Block.

Council J. F., of W. R. Hogshire & Co., res. 80 w. Georgia.

County Offices, Court House square, Washington, bet. Delaware and Alabama.

Court House, Washington, bet. Alabama and Delaware.

Courtney P., wks. with McCord & Wheatley.

Courtney Wm., hackman, res. cor. Blake and North.

Cousins W., (col.) minister, res. 151 w. Washington.

Covat Frederick, wood-sawyer, Michigan.

Cover Mrs. Annie, res. 157 e. Ohio.

Covert W. T., police, res. 74 Bluff road.

Covington Mrs. Susan, res. 140 w. Market.

Cowger A. H., of Burt & C., res. Winsor, bet. Vermont and New York.

Cowten John, carpenter, res. 83 n. New Jersey.

Coylor Jacob, horse-dealer, res. cor. Katies & Washington.

Coyner Martin L., res. 209 e. St. Clair.

Cox Andrew, shoe merchant, res. 145 n. New Jersey.

Cox A. J., of Dury & C., res. 45 n. New Jersey.

Cox Charles, of C., Lord & Peck, res. 43 s. Meridian.

Cox G., salesman, 21 w. Washington, res. 41 s. Meridian.

Cox Henry C., Carpenter, res. 184 w. Washington.

Cox J., carpenter, res. old Post Office building.

Cox Jacob, artist, res. 41 s. Meridian.

Cox, Lord & Peck, Hoosier State Foundry and Stove Works, 103 s. Delaware.

Cox Mrs. Sophia, res. 148 w. Market.

Cox W. A., printer, res. 135 e. New York.

6

Cox W. C., of Tomlinson & C., res. 40 w. Ohio.
Cozad Justis, engineer Bellefontaine R. R., res. 83 e. South.
Craft Frost, messenger Branch Bank State of Indiana, bds. 80 n. Meridian.
Craft Smith, blacksmith, res. 210 Indiana ave.
Craft W. H., jeweler, 2 Odd Fellows' Hall, res. 79 n. Alabama.
Craft Wm., wks. Rolling Mill.
Crago Wm., boarding house, 116 n. Missouri.
Craig David P., carpenter, res. cor. Vermont and Davidson.
Craig W. M., teacher, bds. 109 s. Alabama.
Craig Wm. R., book-keeper, 24 w. Washington, res. Fletcher's ave.
Craighead D., res. 18 w. Maryland.
Crake Thos., wks. Rolling Mill.
Crane D., porter Spencer House.
Crane Dennis, wks. Spencer House, res. 182 s. Tennessee.
Crane J. D., photograph gallery, 19 w. Washington, 3d floor, res. 103 n. South.
Crancy A. C., salesman, with Feibelman & Rauh.
Crapo R. C., dealer in photographic materials, 17 w. Washington, res. same.
Craven James, laborer, res. Ann, near Rolling Mill.
Crawford Eli, moulder, res. 250 s. Delaware.
Crawford James, moulder, bds. 65 s. Pennsylvania.
Crawford J. P., res. 65 s. Pennsylvania.
Crawmer Philip, clerk, 138 s. Illinois, bds. California House.
Craymer W. W., wks. Post, Helwig & Co.'s Planing Mill.
Creden J., fireman Gas Works.
Cress Geo., porter, A. & U. S. Express.
Cruger Joseph, cistern moulder, res. 115 e. Market.
Crist B., laborer, res. cor. McCarty and Tennessee.
Crist Mrs. N., res. 112 Virginia ave.
Criqui M., clothier, 84 e. Washington, res. 173 e. Ohio.
Criswelld Joseph, clerk, res. 27 n. East.
Crouch Wesley, artist, res. 114 n. Missouri.
Croffut H. P., actuary Farmers' and Merchants' Insurance Co., Blackford's Building, res. n. Delaware.
Crofts M., wks. Rolling Mill, res. Meridian, bet. Merrill and McCarty.
Crop Henry, res. Washington, near Orient.
Cropper Roland, railroader, res. 168 s. New Jersey.
Cropsey J. E., piano-maker, res. Ohio, bet. Mississippi and Missouri.
Cropsey J. E., cabinet-maker, res. 99 Ohio.
Crosby A. T., driver A. & U. S. Express.
Crosby Mrs. Elizabeth, seamster, res. Liberty, bet New York and Vermont.

Crosen Henry, cooper, res. near Cornell, West.
Crosir Geo., watchman, New York Store.
Crossland J. A., of C. & Pee, res. 224 n. Illinois.
Crossland & Pee, wholesale dry goods, 42 s. Meridian,
    Schnull's Block.
Crossley T. B., saddler, bds. Patterson House.
Crossman T., porter Oriental House.
Crouch J., laborer, res. 11 Virginia ave.
Crouch Jeptha, res. 140 Virginia ave.
Crouch Wesley, artist, res. 190 n. Illinois.
Crowford E., moulder, Eagle Foundry.
Crozier George, New York Store, res. 89 n. Meridian.
Crull David, carpenter, res. Crull, bet. New Jersey and East.
Crull Jacob, Teamster, res. 139 w. South.
Crum John, of J. W. Davis & Co., res. Louisiana, bet. New
    York and East.
Cruse J. P., brick-mason, res. 270 e. Washington.
CRUSIUS MISS CARRIE M., LONDON ART GAL-
    LERY, 39 e. Washington. See card, p. 82.
Culley Daniel, book-keeper, res. 156 n. Pennsylvania.
Culley Dava, superintendent city schools, res. 9 e. Ohio.
Culley Wm., shoemaker, res. 119 s. Tennessee.
Cullum Eberle, printer, 24 w. Washington, bds. Pyle House.
Cully D. B., book-keeper, res. 156 n. Pennsylvania.
Culon Chas., attorney-at-law, off. 97 e. Washington, res.
    Cumberland, near Alabama.
Culver E., res. 56 w. New York.
Cuwan Pat., yard master, Little's Hotel.
CUNNINGHAM FRANK, DEP'T AUDITOR STATE,
    res. 11 w. Ohio.
CUNNINGHAM F. P., BAKERY, CONFECTIONERY,
    LADIES' OYSTER AND ICE CREAM SALOON,
    cor. Illinois and Market. See card, p. 48.
Cunningham Hugh, laborer, res. 16 Georgia.
Cunlen T., cabinet-maker, res. 21 s. Meridian.
Cunirg Wm., laborer, res. 46 Orsbrook.
Curan Patrick, laborer, res. 6 e. Huron.
Curtis A., squire, res. 11 Fort Wayne ave.
Curtis C. E., engineer, res. 56 n. Delaware.
Curtis J., (col.) cook, res. cor. North and Missouri.
Curran David, printer, Journal off., res. 6 Huron.
CURRY J. H., BARBER, cor. Washington and Pennsyl-
    vania. See card, p. 84.
Curzon Joseph, architect, off. Journal Building, res. 218 n.
    Illinois,
Cusick John, res. 41 West.

D

Daccon John, engineer, res. Meek, near Benton.
Dafoe Elizabeth, res. 143 n. Liberty.
Daggett W., of D. & Co., bds. cor. Meridian and Penn.
Daggett & Co., manufacturers of candies and dealers in
 teas, foreign fruits, &c., 22 s. Meridian.
Daily C., hatter, res. 144 n. New Jersey.
Daily Eugene, laborer, res. 217 s. Delaware.
Dain Robert C., paper hanger, res. 106 n. East.
Dain Thos., painter, res. 18 Michigan road.
Daisie Pat., laborer, res. 230 c. Washington, 2d floor.
Dale Peter, laborer, res. 97 c. McCarty.
Dallart C., clerk, bds. East Street House.
Dalton Thos., laborer, works Sinker & Co.'s machine works,
 res. 178 s. Tennessee.
Dame Jason, dealer in marble, 67 c. Washington, res. 70 s.
 East.
Damme Frank, pattern maker, res. 184 s. Alabama.
Dana Mrs. E. S., res. 67 n. Pennsylvania.
Danforth A. J., grocer, res 112 n. Pennsylvania.
Daniels Mrs. C. F., dress maker, res. 60 n. Delaware.
Daniel Cornelius, clerk, with Rice & Bamberger.
Daniel S. P., res. 63 s. New Jersey.
Danforth A. J., of D. & Simpson, res. 112 n. Penn.
Danforth & Simpson, grocers, 3 Pennsylvania, under Odd
 Fellows Hall.
Daragh Wm., tailor, res. 200 s. Delaware.
Darby J., clerk, res. 189 s. New Jersey.
Darnell C. F., carpenter, res. Illinois, n. of Third.
Darnell Wm. W., Col. 11th Ind. Vols., res. New York, bet.
 Noble and Liberty.
Darow Benj. C., boot and shoemaker, res. 146 n. Illinois.
Darrow Geo., printer, res. 176 New Jersey.
Darrow James, sutler, res. 176 n. New Jersey.
Dater Wm., drayman, res. Michigan road, near Washington.
Daubenspeck N., miller, res. 84 Mass. ave.
Dauget Albert, foreman, Eagle Foundry.
Daugherty H. H., law student, bds. 148 n. Pennsylvania.
Daugherty J. F., clerk, Post-office.
Daugherty James, bds. 1 Willard.
Daumont H. & Co., clock store, 17 n. Pennsylvania, also 80
 c. Washington.
DAUMONT P. A., JEWELER, 9 s. Meridian, res. same.
 See card, page 74.
Davenport John, engineer, Planing Mill, res. 67 West.
Daven Peter, laborer, res. 55 Huron.
Davenish John, iron moulder, res. 140 c. New York.

Davidge C. H., clerk, res. 44 s. Meridian.
DAVIES THOS. J., DAVIES & MERRITT, 26 and 28 w. Washington.
DAVIES & MERRITT, FINE ART GALLERY, 26 and 28 w. Washington. See card, page 108.
Davis Allen, conductor, res. Michigan road, near Washington.
Davis Mrs. Annie, res. 119 e. Market.
Davis Benj., res. 51 cor. East and Market.
Davis B., teamster, bds. 135 w. Allan.
Davis Miss C., Union Steam Bakery.
Davis Chas. E., salesman. Hume, Lord & Co.
DAVIS C. B., INSURANCE AGENT, 6 Odd Fellows Hall, res. 137 n. Pennsylvania.
Davis E., butcher, res. 156 e. New York.
DAVIS E. A., ATTORNEY AND U. S. COMMISSIONER, 3 Talbott & News Block, bds. Bates House. See card, page 84.
Davis F., boiler maker, Washington Foundry.
Davis F. A. W., teller, Indianapolis Branch Banking Co.
Davis Geo., blacksmith, res. 179 e. Market.
Davis Geo., boot and shoemaker, res. 92 Meridian.
Davis Haldon, hack driver, res. 150 n. Delaware.
Davis H., butcher, res. 156 e. Few York.
Davis H. C., machinist, works I. & C. R. R. machine shop.
Davis Ira, res. cor. Illinois and First.
DAVIS ISAAC, HAT STORE, 15 n. Pennsylvania, bds. Bates House. See card, outside back cover.
Davis James, soldier, res. 221 n. Noble.
Davis James, res. 135 n. Alabama.
Davis James, shoemaker, res. Orient, bet. Michigan road and Washington.
Davis James, shoemaker, 187 e. Wascington, res. Deaf and Dumb Assylum.
Davis Miss Jennie, res. 66 e. Meek.
Davis John, carpenter, res. 172 n. Liberty.
Davis J. H., shoemaker, with James Davis.
Davis J. W., of J. W. D. & Co., res. 129 Virginia ave.
DAVIS J. W. & CO., BRASS FOUNDRY, GAS AND STEAM FITTERS, 96 s. Delaware. See card, p. 106.
Davis L. L., res. 55 e. Ohio.
Davis D., laborer, res. 25 e. Ohio.
Davis Monroe, blacksmith, 130 Indiana ave.
Davis M., carpenter, res. 27 McCarty.
Davis Matty, cash boy, New York Store.
Davis S., meat shop, 59 e. Washington, res. 156 e. New York.
Davis S. A., pump maker, bds. 31 w. Market.

Davis Wesley, carriage trimmer, res. cor. Pennsylvania and Sinker.

Davis W. W., engineer, res. Davidson, bet. Ohio and Market.

Davis Wm., pump maker, res. First, near Miss.

Davis Wm., clerk, Fletcher's Bank, res. cor. Ohio and Meridian.

Davis Wm. M., dry goods, res. 138 n. Alabama.

Davis Wm. M., of Jones, Hess & D., res. 208 n. New Jersey.

Davison J. W., broom maker, res. 35 Orsbrook.

Davison J., collector, Journal office, res. 85 n. Davidson.

Davison R., carpenter, res. Blackford, bet. Vermont and New York.

Dawes A. C., of D., Evans & McMillin, bds, Louis Lang's Restaurant.

DAWES, EVANS & McMILLIN, WHOLESALE BOOT AND SHOE HOUSE, 75 w. Washington. See card, page 38.

Dawson D., blacksmith, res. 43 e. McCarty.

Dawson Riley, salesman, res. e. St. Clair.

Dawson F. L., machinist, Washington Foundry.

Dawson Wm. P., fire department, res. 50 n. Delaware.

Day Elisha, laborer, res. 194 Indiana ave.

Day Miss Georgia L., clerk, 48 e. Washington, res. 32 e. New York.

Day Green, laborer, res. Indiana ave, near Missouri.

Day Rev. Henry, res. 60 North.

Day J., laborer, res. 67 n. East.

Day John, (col.) laborer, res. w. Vermont.

Day John E., carpenter, res. 154 n. Noble.

Day J. H., carpenter, res. 55 s. noble.

Day M. D. L, clerk, 22 w. Washington.

Day Wm., butcher, res. 198 e. St. Clair.

Dayley Mrs. Jennie, res. 71 cor. Market and New Jersey.

Dayton Wm., moulder, wks. Wiggins & Chandler, bds. 258 w. Washington.

Deaf and Dumb Asylum, National Road, one and half miles east of city.

Deal Thos. J., clerk Equitable Fire Insurance Co., bds. 75 n. New Jersey.

Dean Hugh, 2d clerk Little's Hotel.

Dean J., clerk New York Store, bds. Patterson House.

Dearinger David, carpenter, res. Mississippi, bet. 1st and 2d.

Dearinger S., plasterer, res. 17 e. Georgia.

Deaver Geo., res. 140 n. Illinois.

Debenish John, moulder, Eagle Foundry.

Decheo Conrad, blacksmith, res. 146 n. Davidson.

Deckembrock W., laborer, res. 75 Bluff road.

Deem J. F., clerk, res. 59 n. Pennsylvania.

LOUIS SCHOLTZ,

FASHIONABLE

MERCHANT TAILOR!

PENNSYLVANIA STREET,

Two doors South of the Post Office,

INDIANAPOLIS, INDIANA.

☞ Particular attention paid to Military Clothing. ☜

Deerberg Christian, res. 129 e. McCarty.
Defors V., wood-sawyer, res. 193 n. New Jersey.
Dehart Austin, laborer, res., n. Missouri, near Indiana ave.
Dehart David, laborer, res. n. Meridian, n. of Third.
Dehart Tolleson, watch-maker and jeweler, res. 18 e. Market.
Deitrich William, clerk, Post Office.
Delany M., wks. Rolling Mill.
Delany M., laborer, res. 70 n. Noble.
Delany Pat., wks. Rolling Mill.
Delany Peter, wks. Rolling Mill.
Delany Wm., wks. Rolling Mill.
Dell John, gardener, res. Meridian, near First.
Deller Fred., house and sign painter, res. 102 n. Noble.
Dellhoen Crist, carpenter, res. 176 e. North.
Delong J. S., laborer, wks. Hill & Wingate.
Delvans Eugene, stone-cutter, res. n. Orsbrook.
Delvan J., apprentice, Washington Foundry.
Delzell Hugh, feed stables, 32 e. Maryland.
Delzell Samuel, of D. & Jones, res. 87 n. Alabama.
Delzell & Jones, real estate agents, 37 e. Washington.
Demmerd Wm., varnisher, wks. Union Cabinet Factory.
Demmy Martin, harness-maker, res. 129 n. West.
Demoss L., check agent, res. 103 s. Tennessee.
Demotte W. H., instructor Deaf and Dumb Asylum, res. Washington, near Orient.
Demme Frank, pattern-maker, Eagle Foundry.
Deneen A., widow, res. 157 n. Alabama.
Deneen J. M., tailor, res. 157 n. Alabama.
Dennis C. C., clerk, res. 31 Ellsworth.
Dennis Mrs. E. K., res. 31 Ellsworth.
Denniston Mrs. E. A., res. 73 Missouri.
Dennot R., machinist, wks. I. & C. R. R. Machine Shop.
Denny Rev. Robert, res. 12 e. Bates.
Deppel John, carpenter, res. 63 e. Michigan.
Deppel L., cabinet-maker, res. Wyoming, bet. Delaware and High.
DERNHAM M., CLOTHIER, cor. Meridian and Washington. See card, p. 80.
Deer Philip, laborer, res. 135 n. Davidson.
Deschler Joseph, saloon, 9 n. Pennsylvania.
DESCHLER & SCHLOER, ASTOR SALOON, 9 n. Pennsylvania.
Deshlar John, cabinet-maker, res. 239 s. Delaware.
Deshong Hiram, carpenter, res. Georgia, near Cady.
Despa Ernst, painter, res. cor. Loukbee and Liberty.
Dessar Adolphus, of D., Bro. & Co., res. 135 n. Illinois.

DESSAR, BRO. & CO., WHOLESALE DEALERS IN CLOTHING, PIECE GOODS AND FURNISHING GOODS, Schnull's Block, cor. Meridian and Maryland. See card, p. 94.

Dessar Joseph B., of D., Bro. & Co., res. 113 e. Ohio.

Dessar David, of D. & Bro., res. Mississippi, bet. West and Market.

Dessar L., salesman, bds. 131 Ohio.

Dessar O. H., saloon, 212 w. Washington, res. same.

DESSAR & BROS., MERCHANT TAILORS AND CLOTHIERS, 4 e. Washington.

Dessaner Levi, salesman, with M. Dernham, bds. Bates House.

Dessel W., porter, with Jay, Cox & Fitzhugh.

Desser David, clothing store, res. cor. Mississippi and Market.

Dessy pat., wks. Rolling Mill.

De Stugner Emanuel, dentist, with G. A. Urees.

Detterich Christ., cabinet-maker, bds. Georgia, bet. Illinois and Meridian.

Devennish Solomon, tailor, res. 139 e. South.

Dever Charles, laborer, bds. 44 Massachusetts ave.

Devine Wm., tailor, res. 53 w. South.

Dernish S., stove-filer, Eagle Foundry.

Devolviss Mrs. E., res. Ramsey's Block.

Dewald M., porter, with J. W. Holland & Son,

Dewald Martin, clerk, res. 73 n. Davidson.

Dewire J., fireman, Gas Vorks.

Dibel John Peter, hack-driver, res. 55 n. Liberty.

Dicker Jacob, cabinet-maker, wks. Union Cabinet Factory.

Dickinson J. C., butcher, res. 109 s. Alabama.

Dickinson James, physician, res. 267 s. East.

Dickman Fred., carpenter, res. 41 n. East.

Dickson Carlos, book-keeper, Hume, Lord & Co., bds. 38 n. Market.

Dickson G., cook, res. 122 w. Ohio.

Dickson J., clerk, res. cor. Tennessee and South.

Dickson James, lime and coal, res. 139 s. Tennessee.

Dickson William, clerk, res. 139 s. Tennessee.

Dietch John, painter, res. 228 n. Alabama.

Dieter Ernest, shoemaker, res. 133 n. Railroad.

Dieter John, tinner, with Voegtle & Metzger.

Dieter Ernst, shoemaker, res. 133 Railroad.

Dietes Peter, watchman, res. 181 Blake.

Dietrichs Mrs., milliner, 63 e. Washington, res. same.

Dietrichs W., clerk, Post Office, res. 63 e. Washington.

Diets F., tinner, res. Market, bet. Noble and Davidson.

Dietz Adam, saloon-keeper, res. 68 Fort Wayne ave.

Dietz Henry, candle-manufacturer, res. 26 n. Noble.
Dietzel Adam, expressman, res. 77 n. Davidson.
Dill Clay, real estate agent, with Wm. Love, bds. North, 1
    door w. Pennsylvania.
Dill Ezkiel, blacksmith, res. 101 n. Meridian.
Dill Mrs. Gertmell, res. 15 e. North.
Dills H. W., grocery-keeper, res. 3 Massachusetts ave.
Dills W. R., cooper, res. 208 n. Illinois.
Dilley John, res. Norwood, bet. Illinois and Tennessee.
Dills W. R., of Carey & D., res. 208 n. Illinois.
Dillon Daniel, res. Ann, bet. Mississippi and Tennessee.
Dillon P., apprentice, Washington Foundry.
Dillon Mrs. S., res. 30 Willard.
Dippel H., varnisher, with Spiegel, Thomas & Co.
Dippel H., carpenter, res. 95 n. Davidson.
Dippel John, carpenter, res. 170 e. Michigan.
Dippel John, J., baker, res. 107 n. Noble.
Dinnin S. E., clerk, quartermaster department U. S. A.
Dirr John, laborer. res. 230 n. Alabama.
Ditsel Charles, express-driver, res. 151 n. Liberty.
Dixon G. W., with J. D. Crane.
Dixon J. W., res. Missouri, bet. South and Merrill.
Dinmy Martin, saddler, res. 129 West.
Doarr G., bar-keeper, Spencer House Saloon.
Dobson Mrs. T., res. 170 w. Market.
Dodd H. H., of Dodd & Co., printer, res. 168 w. New York.
Dodd H. H. & Co., book and job printers, book-binders and
    stereotypers, 16½ e. Washington.
Dodd Capt. J. W., res. 128 n. Illinois.
Dodds W. H., conductor, Indiana Central R. R., res. 41 w.
    Michigan.
Dodson James, engineer, T. H. & R. R. R., res. 109 n.
    South.
Doerr Geo., wks. Spencer House, res. 34 s. Illinois.
Doffer J., wks. Rolling Mill, res. 180 s. Mississippi.
Doggett W. F., auditor, Indiana Central R. R., res. 40 n.
    New Jersey.
Dogget John, clerk, res. 40 n. New Jersey.
Dogherty Charles, laborer, res. 247 s. Delaware.
Dohn Philip, cabinet shop, 21 s. Meridian, res. same.
Doll Peter, wks. Western Machine Works.
Dolon James, laborer, wks. with D. Root & Co.
Domon Emil, grocer, 138 s. Illinois, bds. California House.
Domon Jacob, grocer, 138 s. Illinois.
Dourphey H., bridge-builder, bds. 179 e. Market.
Doumont H., clock maker, res. 10 Fort Wayne ave.
Donald Mrs. E., res. 12 Willard.
7

Donaldson C. S., of D. & Carr, res. 222 n. Illinois.
DONALDSON & CARR, WHOLESALE DEALERS IN
HATS, CAPS, AND STRAW GOODS, 38 s. Meridian,
Schnulls Block.
Donavan Robert, ice dealer, res. 130 Mass. ave.
Donenberg Louis, carpenter, 27 s. Liberty.
Donnally Francis, grocer, res. 24 Henry.
Donnan Mrs. B., res. 74 n. Tennessee.
Donnell S., sculptor, bds. Pyle House.
Donnelly Francis, grocer, 265 s. Delaware, res. same.
Donough Daniel, clerk, res. 101 s. New Jersey.
Donoran James, drayman, 194 North.
Donvoen E., carpenter, res. 184 n. East.
Dorbecker John, barber, res. 41 n. New Jersey.
Dorfer J., works Rolling Mill.
Dorsey Dr. N. J., res. 46 n. Penn.
Doty James, Magnolia Saloon, 9 s. Illinois, res. cor. Ohio
and Missouri.
Doty D., saloon, res. 12 s. Mississippi.
Doty & Lee, saloon, 107 w. Washington.
Dougherty J. F., clerk, Post-office.
Dougherty Z., M. D., res. Calafornia, bet. Washington and
Market.
Douglas Mrs. ———, res. 130 w. New York.
Douglas B. W., laborer, res. 40 Orsbrook.
Douglas James G., book binder and blank book mannfac-
turer, Journal building, res. 130 w. New York.
Douglas S. M., baggage master, Union Depot, res. 130 w.
New York.
Doughty Lafayette, brick moulder, res. 5 Huron.
Doughty J. G., res. 21 Indiana ave.
Dow Ely, works Indiana Central Railroad machine shop.
Dow E. S., machinist, res. 120 n. Noble.
Dowling Jas., laborer, res. 107 s. West.
Dowling W. W., asst. editor, Christian Record, Journal
building.
Down Wm., barber, bds. 54 Blackford.
Downey B., blacksmith, Eagle Foundry.
Downney J. W., printer, bds. 34 e. Market.
Downey J., with M. Downey.
Downey M., marble shop, 127 e. Washington, res. same.
Downey James E., job printer, Talbott & New's Block.
Downey John, works Hill & Wingate.
Downey John, stone cutter, res. 11 e. Georgia.
Downie Mrs. M. E., res. 43 n. Penn.
Downing B., blacksmith, res. cor. Market and Calafornia.
Downing Mrs. Francis, res. 190 North.
Downing J., laborer, bds. Sullivan's.

Downing Jerry, brick layer, bds. 190 Virginia ave.
Downs Wm., (col.,) barber, res. 54 Blackford.
Doyle Miss J., millinery, 18 s. Illinois.
Doyle Lane, laborer, res. 194 s. Delaware.
Doyle Lawrence, works Western Machine Works.
Drage Wm., baker, works Cincinnati Bakery.
Drager Chas., watch maker, res. e. Washington.
Drake A. B., manufacturer of paint, res. 88 n. Alabama.
Drake E. B., of D. & Merrymon, res. 88 n. Alabama.
Drake Robert, book binder, with J. G. Douglas.
DRAKE & MERRYMON, WHITE LEAD AND COLOR
    WORKS, 47 e. South. See card, page 58.
Draper G. W., of D. & Tarlton, res. 27 n. Illinois.
Draper J. F., carpenter, res. 31 Indiana ave.
Draper Jos., carpenter, res. s. Tennessee, near city limits.
Draper & Tarlton, grocers, 32 n. Illinois.
Drechsel G., plow stocker, bds. East Street House.
Dreher Mathias, clerk, with Tousey & Bryam.
Dressar A., clothing store, res. 135 n. Illinois.
Drescole Mrs. E., res. 18 Willard.
Drew J. A., foreman, livery stable, res. 76 n. Tenn.
Drew John, laborer, res. 76 n. Tennessee.
Drew S. W., of D. & Shaw, res. 68 Massachusetts ave.
DREW & SHAW, CARRIAGE MANUFACTURERS, e.
    Market Square. See card, page 60.
Dricol J., works Rolling Mill.
Driggs N., clerk, 22 w. Washington.
Drinkot Wm., watchman, res. 50 s. East.
Driscol J., works Rolling Mill, res. 26 Williard.
Drum Geo., carpenter, res. 111 s. New Jersey.
Drum Mrs. J. J., res. 144 n. Penn.
Drum Robert, soldier, res. 142 e. New York.
Drum W. H., of D. & Ramsey, res. 238 s. Alabama.
Drum & Ramsey, saloon, 121 e. Washington.
Duckey Chas., cooper, res. 27 n. Spring.
Ducker Mrs. Louisa, res. 7 s. New Jersey.
Dudley Steele, West, D. & Co., res. 119 n. Penn.
Duffy John, tailor, res. cor. Maryland and California.
Duffy M., tailor, res. Kuloy's Row, bet. New Jersey and
    East.
Dugan H., blacksmith, bds. East Street House.
Dugan N., porter, Adams Express.
Dugan N., laborer, res. Keeley's Block, bet. New Jersey
    and East.
Dugan Thos., shoemaker, res. 42 Mass. ave.
Duggins Mrs. Louisa, res. 76 Kentucky ave.
Duke James, of J. D. & Co., res. 181 Indiana ave.

Duke James & Co., real estate and commercial brokers, Sentinel building.

Dulhere James, laborer, res. 39 Huron.

Dull C. C., carpenter, res. 137 n. West.

Dulop John, res. 72 n. Meridian.

Dummyer C., boarding house, Illinois, s. depot.

Dumon Geo., res, 75 s. Noble.

Dumont Gen. E., res. 149 n. Illinois.

Dunmeir Chas., drayman, res. 146 e. Ohio.

Dunmeir Fred., drayman, res. 146 e. Ohio.

Dumton W. B., iron dealer, res. 159 n. Penn.

Dunbar M., mason, res. 178 s. Pennsylvania.

Duncan Daniel, grocer, res. 86 n. Meridian.

Duncan J. & D., wholesale liquors, 22 s. Illinois.

Duncan R. B., attorney, 3 Brown's Block, res. Fort Wayne road.

Dunkel J., cigar maker, bds. Chicago House.

Dunlea C., driver, Adams Express Co.

Dunlap Mrs. D., res. 12 Virginia ave.

Dunlap Robert, laborer, res. 86 Huron.

Dunlap W., wagon maker, with Case & Marsh.

DUNLAP JNO. S., FIRE AND LIFE INS. AGT., 7 n. Meridian, res. 116 n. Penn.

Dunn Edward, works Rolling Mill, res. 8 Willard.

Dunn Jas., works Rolling Mill.

Dunn J. C., of J. C. D. & Co., res. cor. Mississippi and First.

DUNN J. C. & CO., PLUMBING AND GAS FITTING, 24 and 26 Kentucky ave.

Dunn John, brick mason, res. Market, near cor. California.

Dunn J. P., res. cor. St. Clair and Tennessee.

DUNN J. T., COMMISSION MERCHANT AND WHOLESALE AND RETAIL DEALER IN CHOICE FAMILY FLOUR, FEED, &C., 12 s. Pennsylvania, res. n. e. cor. Alabama and Walnut.

Dunn Mrs. Maggie, res. 5 n. Meridian.

Dunn Peter, works Rolling Mill.

Dunn Wm., clerk, with Tarlton & Keehn.

Dunning Thos., carpenter, res. cor. Vermont and Ellsworth.

Durnin M. J., clerk, bds. Patterson House.

Dury John, of D. & Cox, res. 136 Mass. ave.

Dury & Cox, boot and shoe dealers, 63 e. Washington.

Dusback C. H., clerk, A. and U. S. Express Co.

Duschey Chas., confectioner, res. 93 n. Railroad.

Dutcher Jacob, salesman, 38 w. Washington, bds. Union Hall.

Dutton G., machinist, Gas Works.

Dutton Isaac, miller, res. 13 s. Mississippi.

Duvall D. C., clerk, res. 113 n. Illinois.

Duvall E. C., clerk, res. 113 n. Illinois.
Duvall Ely, teamster, bds. 223 s. Alabama.
Duvall J., policeman, res. 260 Madison R. R. ave.
Duvall Mrs. Sarah, res. 223 s. Alabama.
Duzan J. H., printer, w. H. C. Chandler, bds. 64 n. Meridian.
Duzan W. N., of D. & Parr, res. 250 n. Tennessee.
Duzan Wm., cabinet maker, res. 64 n. Meridian.
Duzan & Parr, physicians, 16 Virginia ave.
Diver James, grocer, 245 s. Delaware, res. same.
Dwiar Wm., laborer, res. Wyoming, bet. Delaware and High.
Dwyer Thos., works Rolling Mill.
Dwyer Wm., works Rolling Mill.
Dyaar E., laborer, res. 263 s. Delaware.
DYE B. E., res. 209 e. Washington.
Dye J. T., attorney and notary public, 6 New & Talbott's Block, res. 111 w. South.
Dyer Mary A., teacher, at Institute for the Blind.

E

Eagen Patrick, laborer, res. 8 Michigan road.
Eagle Fred., messenger, Adams Express Co.
EAGLE FOUNDRY, D. ROOT & CO., 130 s. Pennsylvania.
Eagle J. D., printer, Journal office.
Eagle John H., printer, Journal office, res. 142 n. Alabama.
Earl Mrs. M., res. Eddy.
Earl Wm. E., harness-maker, bds. Soldiers' Home.
Early Mrs., res. 157 s. Tennessee.
Early Pat., hackman, res. cor. North and Bright.
Early Peter, wks. Rolling Mill, res. Meridian, bet. Merrill and McCarty.
Earmin C., shoemaker, with C. Rehling, 176 e. Washington.
East J. H., of Roberts & E., bds. Pyle House.
East Street House, Henry Hahn, proprietor, s. East, bet. Washington and Georgia.
Eastman F. M., harness-maker, bds. Jack's boarding house.
Eastman Henry, res. 191 s. Delaware.
Eastwood H. H., salesman, bds. Macy House.
Eaton J. H., of E. & Furgason, bds. Mrs. Igon.
Eaton L., student, res. 149 n. Liberty.
EATON & FURGASON, PEARL GROCERY, 18 s. Meridian. See card, p. 36.
Ebert Chas., tailor, res. 3 s. New Jersey.
Ebert John, carpenter, 32 Kentucky ave., res. 135 w. South.
Eccles Wm., salesman, Hume, Lord & Co.
Eck I., wks. Rolling Mill.

Eckhart W. H., salesman, 19 w. Washington.
Eden Asa, bricklayer, res. 190 Virginia ave.
Eden Carlton, of E. & Copeland, res. 86 e. Ohio.
Eden S. C., clerk, bds. 19 Circle.
Eden & Copeland, manufacturers blinds, sash, &c., 27 e.
    Market.
Eddy Rev. Augustus, chaplain Indianapolis Hospital, res.
    Tennessee, bet. First and Second.
Eddy M. R., clerk, quartermaster department U. S. A.,
    bds. 156 n. Tennessee.
Edmunds Wm., of Hendricks, E. & Co., res. —— Meridian.
Edson Rev. H. A., res. 87 n. Pennsylvania.
Edwards E., harness-maker, bds. Bicking House.
Edwards J. F., of Burrows & E., res. cor. Illinois and Mary-
    land.
EDWARDS LOUIS, PROPRIETOR EDWARDS' HOUSE,
    53 s. Illinois. See card, p. 112.
Eggerstedt Jacob, bds. 107 e. Ohio.
Egner F., of E. & Wocher.
EGNER & WOCHER, DRUGGISTS, 85 e. Washington.
    See card, p. 70.
Ehardt A. H. ,res. 155 n. Railroad.
Ehrlich J., clerk, with M. Marks.
Ehrenslierger Ernst, clerk, res. 117 n. East.
Ehrensperger Frank, clerk, J. C. Mayhew & Co.
Eichman C., clerk, res. 69 n. Davidson.
Eighth Ward School House, cor. Virginia ave. and Huron.
Eiler Mrs. Margaret, res. 101 n. Railroad.
Einatz Anthony, bakery wagon driver, res. 14 s. West.
Elder E. A., chief clerk, Post Office, res. 98 West.
Elder, Harkness & Bingham, proprietors State Sentinel.
Elder John R., of E., Harkness & Bingham, res. 78 n. New
    Jersey.
Elder Wm., res. 63 n. Illinois.
Elder Wm. E., clerk, res. 118 n. Alabama.
Elder W. G., wks. 84 w. Washington.
Eldridge Issac, messenger, American Express Co.
Eldridge A. M., book-keeper, bds. Macy House.
ELDRIDGE JACOB, REAL ESTATE AND COMMER-
    CIAL BROKER, 31½ w. Washington, res. 50 s. Missis-
    sippi. See card, p. 50.
Elff Frank, barber, 81 e. Washington, res. 175 s. New Jersey.
Ellbow E. M., salesman, 2 Palmer House, bds. Bates House.
Elley R., speculator, bds. Ray House.
Elliott B. K., attorney at law, 24½ e. Washington, res. 16
    California.
Elliott C. A., of C. A. E. & Co., res. 76 n. Illinois.
Elliott C. A. & Co., wholesale liquors, 32 s. Meridian.

Elliott John, feed store, res. 31 n. Noble.
Elliott J., of E. & Clinton, res. 51 n. Noble.
Elliott J., photographist, res. 1 e. South.
Elliott J., laborer, wks. with D. Root & Co.
Elliott John F., agent Singer Sewing Machines, 48 e. Washington.
ELLIOTT J. PERRY, PHOTOGRAPH GALLERY, 8 and 10 e. Washington, res. cor. Meridian and South. See card, p. 24.
ELLIOTT T. B., DEALER IN FLOUR, GRAIN AND PRODUCE, cor. Alabama and I. & C. R. R. track, res. w. end Michigan.
Elliott W. J., county recorder, res. 89 e. Ohio.
ELLIOTT & CLINTON, FEED STORE, 19 s. East.
Ellis D., blacksmith, with Case & Marsh.
Ellis Frank, clerk, Capt. Blake, res. 131 w. Vermont.
Ellis Thos., wks. Western Machine Works
Ellostrod Henry, cabinet-maker, res. s. Liberty, near R. R.
Ellsworth Henry W., attorney, res. 88 n. Meridian.
Elmer John, res. 140 e. McCarty.
Elmer J. W., clerk, 140 e. McCarty.
Elstrod H., machinist, wks. Union Cabinet Factory.
Elvin Gardener, railroader, res. 170 s. Alabama.
Elvin G. W., fireman, I. & M. R. R.
Elwood Kirk, baggage master, Jeffersonville R. R., bds. Ray House.
Embers T., (col.) barber, cor. Washington and Kentucky ave.
EMERICH NICHOLAS, CLERK, bds. with J. P. Mauer.
EMERSON R. B., CARPENTER AND BUILDER, shop in rear near West, res. 141 w. Market.
Emett Robert, laborer, res. 7 e. New York.
Emmeneger M., saloon, opp. Court House, res. same.
Emmit R., laborer, res. 7 e. New York.
Emmuch H., book-keeper, res. 85 e. New York.
Emmons Wm., res. 26 Huron.
Emolle M., painter.
Emrich Miss Mollie, school teacher, bds. Ohio, bet. New Jersey and East.
Ender A. M., Washington House, 83 s. Meridian.
Endicut Isom, res. Missouri, bet. Vermont and Indiana ave.
Engel J., res. e. Washington.
Engreess H., clothier, cor. West and Maryland.
Engle John, carpenter, res. cor. Cady and Bates.
Enggass H., tailor, 182 e. Washington.
Engle S., machinist, bds. 163 e. Ohio.
Engleking F., laborer, wks. res. 73 Bluff road.
English J. K., city treasurer, res. 113 n. East.

INDIANA FIRE INSURANCE COMPANY!

INDIANAPOLIS, IND.

Office, No. 5 Odd Fellows' Hall, (Up Stairs.)

Capital----One Hundred and Eighty Thousand Dollars!

Insures Dwellings, Household Furniture, Barns, Hay, Grain and Live Stock therein, against Loss and Damage by Fire, for the term of Five or Seven Years.

DIRECTORS:

J. S. HARVEY, Indianapolis. | JNO. H. HUTTON, Richmond. | C. C. OLIN, Indianapolis.
FREDERICK BAGGS, " | | WM. T. GIBSON, "

OFFICERS:

J. S. HARVEY, President.   FREDERICK BAGGS, Treasurer.
FREDERICK BAGGS, Vice President.   WM. T. GIBSON, Secretary.
C. C OLIN, General Agent.

REFERENCES:

Wm. A. Peelle, Ex. Sec. State, Centerville. | J. E. McDonald, Att'y at Law, Indianapolis.
Andrew Wallace, Esq., Merch't Indianapolis. | Josiah Locke, of Locke & Bro , "
Jas. M. Ray, Cash'r Bank of State, " | O. W. Hill, Esq., Pittsboro,
H. A. Fletcher, Esq , Merchant, " | Harvey D. Scott, Esq., Terre Haute.
John Peterson, Esq., Richmond, | M. C Culver, Esq., Tippecanoe.
D. E. Williamson, Att'y at Law, Greencastle. | Stephen R. Wiggins, Merchant, Richmond.
E. J. Peck, Esq., President T. H. & I. Railroad Co., Indianapolis.

EQUITABLE FIRE INSURANCE COMPANY!

Office, New's Block, First Building South of P. O.,

UP STAIRS, INDIANAPOLIS, IND.

Insures Dwellings, Farm Barns and their contents. Also, Churches, School Houses, Stores, Merchandise, and other Property, against loss or damage by Fire for Three or Five Years.

OFFICERS:

WM. A. PEELLE, President. | N. B. HAMILTON, Secretary and Treasurer.
WM. T. GIBSON Vice President. | C. C. OLIN, General Agent.

DIRECTORS:

WM. A. PEELLE. | | WM. T. GIBSON.
J. J. SMITH. | C. C. OEIN. | E. T. SINKER.

REFERENCES:

Hon. J. S. Harvey, Ex-Treas. State, Ind'polis. | Asher & Adams, Publishers, Indianapolis.
Hon. M. C. Culver, Culver Station, Ind. | J. M. Tilford, President Journal Co., "
Hon. A. H. Connor, Post Master, Indianapolis. | John Peterson, Esq., Richmond.
Wm. R. Nofsinger, Cash'r First Nat'l B'k. " | D. E. Williamson, Att'y at Law, Greencastle.
E. H. Berry, Grand Sec'y I. O. of O. F., " | H. B. Pritchard, Esq., Jonesville.
Newcomb & Tarkington, Attorneys at Law, Indianapolis.

English King, res. 113 n. East.
ENGLISH WM. H., PRESIDENT, First National Bank.
  3 n. Pennsylvania.
Enners Louis, butcher, res. 223 Noble.
Ennor Benjamin, carpenter, res. 166 e. Ohio.
EQUITABLE FIRE INS. CO., off. 16 Talbott & News'
  Block. See card, p. 110.
Erghman P., laborer, res. 69 n. Davidson.
Ervin C. A., res. Bickner, bet. Delaware and High.
Ervin Tom, wks. Rolling Mill.
Esaka R., butcher, res. 42 South.
Eska Christopher, laborer.
Espy Mrs. M. F., res. 85 s. Tennessee.
Etherton Samuel, carpenter, res. n. Meridian, n. of Third.
Etsler Loyd, wagon-maker, res. 156 n. East.
Ettinger Gustave, saloon, 168 e Washington, res. same.
Eudaly Elisha, res. 113 n. Tennessee.
Eurich John, saloon, res. 25 Bluff road.
Eurich J. L., of E. & Schoffer, res. 25 s. Illinois.
Eurich & Schoffer, saloon, 7 n. Illinois.
Evans Mrs., res. 112 Virginia ave.
Evans A. J., carpenter, bds. 20 n. Delaware.
Evans D. B., wks. Rolling Mill.
Evans G. T., of J. P. E. & Co., bds. Macy House.
Evans J. H., wks. Rolling Mill.
Evans John, shoemaker, res. 65 South.
Evans John, candy-maker, bds. Macy House.
Evans Joseph R, book-keeper, Capital Mills.
Evans J. P., of J. P. E. & Co., res. Richmond, Ind.
Evans J. P. & Co., proprietors Capital Mills, cor. Market
  and Canal.
Evans J. P. & Co., grain and flaxseed dealers, 98 s Dela-
  ware.
Evans Robert, brick-mason, res. 129 n. Meridian.
Evans Thomas, minister, res. 27 n. Liberty.
Evans W. N., of Dawes, E. & McMillin, bds. Macy House.
Evens H. W., carpenter, wks. I. & C. Machine Shop.
Everett R., laborer, res. 39 s. Illinois.
Everhart Geo., saloon, 278 e. Washington, res same.
Everist S. A., carpenter, res 93 St. Joseph.
Everitt R., wks. Rolling Mill.
Eversale H., silversmith, bds. 45 n. Pennsylvania.
Everson E., clerk, res. 42 e. Maryland.
Everson Mrs. M., res. 53 e. Maryland.
Ewald Robert, clerk, U. S. account department, res. cor.
  New Jersey and St. Clair.
Ewing D., physician, 18 Virginia ave., bds. 44. n. Pennsyl-
  vania.

JOHN HAUCK,

Dealer in

Fruits, Nuts, Confectionery,

CIGARS AND TOBACCO,

OYSTERS AND COFFEE, &c,

OPPOSITE THE UNION DEPOT.

EDWARDS' HOUSE,

No. 53 South Illinois St.,

ONE SQUARE FROM UNION DEPOT,

INDIANAPOLIS, IND.

L. EDWARDS, - - - - Prop'r.

HOOSIER GROCERY.

JOSEPH ILIFF,

Dealer in

GROCERIES & PRODUCE, FLOUR, FEED, &C,

No. 250 East Washington St.,

INDIANAPOLIS, IND.

Cash paid for all kinds of Grain and Produce.

MRS. H. N. QUIMBY,

Fashionable Millinery,

DRESS AND CLOAK MAKING,

Bleaching, Pressing and Coloring,

STAMPING & BRAIDING.

Ewry Joseph, wks. Union Steam Bakery.
Exchange Saloon, D. Bacon, proprietor, 19 and 21 n. Illinois.

F

Faber Mrs. E., res. 99 e. Louisiana.
Fack Fred., stone-cutter, res. 68 w. Ohio.
Faharty Pat., laborer, res. 35 s. Liberty.
Fahnestock O., commission merchant, res. 42 w. Maryland.
Fahnestock Dr. Samuel, res. 28 n. East.
Fahrbach P., of F. & Co., res. 42 South.
FAHRBACH PHILIP & CO., PROPRIETORS WASH-
    INGTON HALL, 78 and 80 w. Washington. See card,
    p. 54.
Fairbank A., wks. with T. B. Elliott, res. 146 s. New Jersey.
Fairbank Philip, whitewasher, res. 148 s. New Jersey.
Fairbairn Richard, printer, with S. F. Wetmore.
Falch O., printer, bds. City Hotel.
Fald G., painter, res. Pearl, bet. Alabama and Delaware.
Fanes R., machinist, wks. I. & C. Machine Shop.
Farall F., laborer, res. 39 St. Clair.
Farion Christ, soldier, res. Michigan, bet. Noble and Liberty.
Fares Mrs. M. A., res. 65 n. Noble.
Farley Henry, engineer, res. 69 e. Merrill.
FARMERS' & MERCHANTS' INSURGNCE COMPANY,
    general office Blackford's Building, cor. Meridian and
    Washington. See card, outside cover.
Farnsworth C. O., local editor Indianapolis Daily Gazette,
    bds. Patterson House.
Farrall Richard, laborer, res. cor. First and Canal.
Farrell Mrs. Mary, res. 82 n. Davidson.
Farrell Fargus, packer, with Crossland & Pee, res. 39 w.
    St. Clair.
Farrell J., bar-keeper, res. 53 s. Illinois.
Farris Wm., steward Bates House.
Fasold Eli, clerk, 48 e. Washington.
Fatout M. K., carpenter, res. 136 n. West.
Fatherling D., laborer, res. 186 Massachusetts ave.
Fatherling Wm., laborer, res. 186 Massachusetts ave.
Fawcett A. H., machinist, Wiggins & Chandler's, bds. 258
    w. Washington.
Faught W. H., of F. & Woodward, res. 100 s. New Jersey.
Faught & Woodward, grocers, 79 e. Washington.
Faulkner I. B., clerk, with Wm. Sheets, res. 37 e. Michigan.
Faut W. O., saddler, bds. 168 n. New Jersey.
FAY B. F., SECRETARY HOME MUTUAL FIRE IN-
    SURANCE CO., bds. cor. New Jersey and Mass. ave.
Fay Owen, engineer, res. 54 s. Benton.
    8

Fearniley John, carpenter, res. 22 Indiana ave.

Feary H., printer, Gazette off.

Feary J. E., carpenter, res. 154 e. North.

Featherson Wm. E., auctioneer, res. 115 Massachusetts ave.

Feguron Robt., plasterer, res. n. Meridian, n. of First.

Feibleman ---., clothier, 6 Spencer House Square, res. 17 s. Alabama.

Feibelman L., clothier, res. 17 s. Alabama.

FEIBELMAN & RAUH, CLOTHIERS, Palmer House corner. See card, p. 132.

Feil John, grocer, 50 Bluff road, res. same.

FELLER GEORGE, WATCH-MAKER, JEWELER AND PLATER, 107 e. Washington, res. 172 n. Tennessee. See card, p. 30.

Fellink Fred., clerk, res. 125 s. New Jersey.

Fellkamp Mrs. Mary, res. 150 s. New Jersey.

Feltbush John, brick-mason, res. 83 n. Davidson.

Fenton F., wks. Sheffield Saw Works, res. 141 e. South.

Ferguson C., pork-packer, res. 28 n. Meridian.

FERGUSON C. A., DEALER IN WATCHES, CLOCKS AND JEWELRY, 7 w. Washington, res. cor. Meridian and Seventh. See card, p. 144.

Ferguson E. H., brick-mason, res. 96 n. Meridian.

Ferguson Kilby, res. cor. East and McCarty.

Ferguson J. A., book-binder, bds. Pennsylvania, bet. Market and Ohio.

FERGUSON J. C., PORK PACKER AND COMMISSION MERCHANT, opp. Madison Depot, res. 28 n. Meridian.

Ferguson Norvel, cutter, with Dessar, Bro. & Co.

Ferguson Rezin, tailor, res. 272 n. Illinois.

Ferli George, res. 96 Maryland.

Fern L., finisher, wks. with D. Root & Co.

Fernley John, carpenter and builder, 18 Circle, res. 22 Indiana ave.

Ferree Jared D., printer, res. 138 e. Ohio.

Ferriter Morris, school teacher, res. 78 Bluff road.

Ferriter Thomas, laborer, res. 3 e. Bates.

Ferry Jas. M., messenger Adams Express Co., res. 68 w. Vermont.

Ferry Mrs. Jane, res. 71 n. Alabama.

Fertig Frank, painter, 6 e. Washington, up stairs, res. 41 w. South.

Fescher B., barber, res. Mississippi, bet. South and Henry.

Fesler Wm. B., carpenter, res. 86 e. Louisiana.

Fesman Fred., baker, bds. 64 n. East.

Fetrow Alexander, carpenter, res. 74 s. East.

Fetrow A., carpenter, wks. Hill & Wingate.
Fette Charles, machinist, res. 164 s. Alabama.
Fettes C., tailor, wks. with G. Hotz & Co.
Fetty C., machinist, Washington Foundry.
Fex Nicholas, laborer, res. 225 s. East.
Fey John, teamster, res. 153 n. Liberty.
Fey Randolph, saloon, 85 e. Washington, res. same.
Feyh Henry, agent, bds. 113 n. Noble.
Fibelimein L., clothier, res. 17 s. Alabama.
Fichtner G., res. 101 w. South.
Fiddick J. J., tinner, bds. 83 s. Illinois.
Fieber William, clerk, Schmidt's Brewery.
Fields A., American Express off.
Field E. S., clerk, bds. Little's Hotel.
Fiel A. J., porter, A. & U. S. Express.
Fifth Ward School House, Maryland, bet. Mississippi and
    Canal.
Fike P., teamster, res. 53 Madison ave.
Finch H. B., bds. Palmer House.
Finchtenicht Ernst, cabinet-maker, res. 279 Virginia ave.
Finley John, railroader, res. Garden, bet. Tennessee and
    Illinois.
Findling Valentine, plasterer, res. bet. Walnut and St.
    Clair.
Fink Daniel, res. North, near Blackford.
Fink Mrs. M., res. cor. Winson and McCarty.
Finn Bridget, res. 101 e. South.
Finn J., cooper, res. 14 Winson.
Finnell John, machinist, bds. Powell's boarding house.
Finney J., clerk, with J. S. Sawyer.
Firchtenicht Ernst, cabinet-maker, wks. Union Cabinet
    Factory.
Fire Mrs. Caroline, res. 65 n. Noble.
FIRST NATIONAL BANK OF INDIANAPOLIS, WM.
    H. ENGLISH, PRESIDENT, 3 Pennsylvania, under
    Odd Fellows' Hall. See card, p. 146.
Fish Mrs. E. L., res. 116 n. Mississippi.
Fish J. L., clerk, Post Office.
Fish John L., real estate agent, res. 38 e. Pratt.
Fish Mrs. O. M., res. 32 s. Meridian.
Fish S. W., printer, Journal off.
Fishback Charles, tailor, bds. 148 s. New Jersey.
Fishback J., leather store, 28 s. Meridian.
Fishback O. T., student, bds. 91 n. Meridian.
Fishback W. P., attorney at law, 62½ e. Washington, res.
    91 n. Meridian.

Fisher Mrs., 121 e. Washington, up stairs.
Fisher A., shoemaker, bds. East House.
Fisher A., clerk, with G. F. Adams.
Fisher Adam, laborer, res. 54 Bluff road.
FISHER BENEDICT, BARBER, cor. Illinois and Louisi-
ana. Res. 147 s. Mississippi.
Fisher Charles, cooper, res. 37 n. Spring.
Fisher Chas., justice of the Peace, Yohn's Block, res. 16 w.
North.
Fisher George, shoemaker, res. 79 Fort Wayne ave.
Fisher Jesse, switchman, Bellefontaine R. R.
Fisher John, bar-keeper, Washington Hall.
Fisher Martin, shoemaker, res. 56 Bluff road.
Fisher S., paymaster Indiana Legion, off. 9 Bates House,
up stairs, bds. Bates House.
Fisher Wm. J., shoemaker, with Joseph Wert, 4 s. Penn-
sylvania.
Fisher Wilson, teamster, res. 120 New York.
Fisk H., blacksmith, res. 207 n. Noble.
Fisk W. B., carpenter, res. 207 n. Noble.
Fitch Wm. H., cabinet-maker, res. 240 w. Washington.
FITCHEY M. G., of F & Sherwood, res. 78 w. Vermont.
FITCHEY & SHERWOOD, CARPENTERS AND BUILD-
ERS, Market, bet. Mississippi and Canal.
Fitzgerald Isaac, clerk, Ohio House.
Fitzgerald J., tinner, wks. with Munson & Johnson.
Fitzgerald N. W., student, bds. Pyle House.
Fitzgerald W., laborer, res. Maple.
Fitzgerald Wm., wks. Rolling Mill.
Fitzhugh L. M., of Jaycox & F., bds. E. Browning.
Flagg W. H., wks. Rolling Mill.
Flaherty Johnson, laborer, res. Illinois, n. of Third.
Flattey B. T., porter, res. cor. Maryland and West.
Fleming J., laborer, with Munson & Johnson.
Flertz C., blacksmith, 99 Bluff road.
Fletcher B., wks. Rolling Mill.
FLETCHER'S BANK, 30 e. Washington.
Fletcher Calvin, sr., of F. & Sharpe, bankers, res. outside
Corporation, continuation n. Pennsylvania.
Fletcher Mrs. E., res. 330 s. Delaware.
Fletcher Rev. E. T., res. 64 Pennsylvania.
Fletcher H. F., messenger American Express Co.
Fletcher Ingram, assistant teller Branch banking Co.
Fletcher Miss Kate, actress, Metropolitan Hall.
Fletcher Mrs. Mary, res. 3 s. Elm.
Fletcher P., wks. Rolling Mill.

Fletcher S. A., sr., farmer, off. Fletcher's Bank, res. 88 c. Ohio.

Fletcher S. A., jr., of S. A. F. & Co., res. 187 Virginia ave.

FLETCHER S. A. & CO., FLETCHER'S BANK, 30 c. Washington.

Fletcher T. R., of F., Vajen & Co., bds. Palmer House.

FLETCHER, VAJEN & CO.'S BANK, 6. n. Meridian.

Fletcher Dr. W. B., res. 77 n. Delaware.

Fletcher Dr. Wm., off. 67 n. Alabama.

Fletcher Wm., res. 267 Virginia ave.

Fletcher W., wks. Rolling Mill.

Fletcher Zachariah, cabinet-maker, res. 64 w. Vermont.

Fletcher & Sharpe, Indianapolis Branch Banking Co., s. w. cor. Pennsylvania and Washington.

Fliming Daniel, city express, res. 99 c. Louisiana.

Flinn T., works Rolling Mill.

FLORENCE SEWING MACHINE CO., S. BELLIS, AGT., 17 n. Pennsylvania.

Flowers A. B. J., manufacturer portable drag saws, cor. Mississippi and Kentucky ave.

Flowers A. B. J., carpenter, res. 98 Maryland.

Flowers C. L., Lieut. and Aid-decamp Gen. Carington's Staff, bds. 8 Virginia ave.

Flowers W., machinist, res. 146 w. Market.

Flowers Mrs. R. E., res. 79 n. New Jersey.

Flowers Samuel, carpenter, res. California, bet. Washington and Market.

Flowers Washington, machinist, res. 146 w. Market.

Foley H., engineer, Washington Foundry.

Foley J. P., laborer, res. 39 s. Meridian.

Foley M., laborer, res. 208 s. Delaware.

Foley Michael, soldier, res. 82 n. Davidson.

Foley Pat., res. 78 c. Louisiana.

Foley T., blacksmith, works Bellefontaine car shop.

Folkening C. H., salesman, McCord & Wheatly.

Follett J. B., attorney, res. 96 n. East.

Follis C., printer, works W. S. Cameron.

Foltz H. M., salesman, bds. 113 n. Alabama.

Foot Jeremiah, notary public, c. Washington, res. 10 Michigan.

Foote O., clerk, res. 89 n. Tennessee.

Forbes Andrew, moulder, Western Machine Works.

Ford Henry, res. 113 w. Michigan.

Ford James, works Rolling Mill, bds. Wm. Johnson.

Ford John, grain buyer, res. 23 w. Michigan.

Ford John, watchman, Post-office.

LEE'S
DRUG STORE!

No. 12 BATES' BLOCK,

(ILLINOIS STREET SIDE,)

INDIANAPOLIS, IND.

We are now prepared to fill all orders for

DRUGS, CHEMICALS!

PERFUMERY,

BRUSHES, SOAPS,

And all articles usually kept by

FIRST CLASS DRUGGISTS.

Having bought our stock from the Importers previous to the recent raise, and continually receiving goods from the best houses east, we can offer inducements to all wishing pure reliable goods. We pledge ourselves to sell pure reliable goods as low or lower than any other house in the city. Orders received by mail will receive prompt attention.
☞Physicians and others are respectfully requested to call and inspect before purchasing elsewhere.

H. H. LEE, Druggist,

No. 12 BATES HOUSE BLOCK,

ILLINOIS ST. SIDE, INDIANAPOLIS.

Foreshee G. W., blacksmith, Tennessee, bet. Washington and Kentucky ave.

Forshee Wm., blacksmith, res. 168 s. New Jersey.

Fosdick B. F., salesman, Hume, Lord & Co., res. 204 Massachusetts ave.

Foster Alfred, boiler maker, res. 14 e. South.

Foster Rev. B. F., res. 148 n. Illinois.

Foster Capt. Thos., Commissary Subsistence U. S. A., office, cor. Mississippi and Washington, res. 58 e. Tenn.

Foster Wm. J., sergeant 6th Ind. Cavalry, res. 116 n. East.

Foster Wm. R., stewart, Deaf and Dumb Asylum.

Foster W. L., carpenter, bds. 145 w. Market.

Foster Joseph, res. 204 Mass. ave.

Foudray J. E., of Wood & F., res. 109 n. New Jersey.

Foust Mrs. Eliza J., res. 85 n. Illinois.

Fowler J. P., carpenter, res. 260 e. Washington.

Fowler & Mount, carpenters, 21 s. East.

Fox Banhot, laborer, res. 66 Orsbrook.

Fox M., waiter, bds. 14 e. Washington.

Fox Geo., engineer, res. 100 e. Louisiana.

Fox Solomon, of F. & Myer, bds. Spencer House.

Fox & Myer, dealers in men's and boy's clothing, 38 w. Washington.

Fracee J. W., laborer, res. 127 n. Delaware.

Frailey Joseph, baggage master, T. H. & R. R. R.

Francis Wm., baggage master, I. & C. R. R., res. 100 Bates.

Franco D., last maker, res. 25 Bluff road.

Franco M., last maker, res. 25 Bluff road.

Franco Mrs. Sarah, res. 5 n. Meridian.

FRANCO & DUNN, MILLINERY GOODS, 5 n. Meridian. See card, page 76.

Franco Rudolph, turner, res. 112 n. Noble.

Franka A., porter, Union depot, res. 60 Union.

Frank A., of R. Schmidt & Co., res. 24 s. Alabama.

Frank Henry, furniture, res. 180 e. Vermont.

Frank James, clerk, Mitzger & Striblin, res. e. Washington, bet. Liberty and Noble.

Frank S., clerk, with Manheimer, 77 w. Washington.

Frankem J., of Frankem & Co., res. 165 n. Illinois.

Frankem J. L., of F. & Co., bds. 155 n. Illinois.

Frankem J. M., clerk, bds. 155 n. Illinois.

Frankem & Co., tin and stove dealers, 49 and 51 e. Washington.

Frankenstein G., barber, Mason House.

Frankenstein Jacob, barber, res. 258 s. Delaware.

Frankin Jonathan, hardware, res. 155 n. Illinois.

WM. H. TURNER,

General Commission Merchant

AND DEALER IN

Agricultural Implements,

DRAIN TILE,

Sewing Machines, Grain, Flax Seed, &c.,

84 West Washington Street,

Metropolitan Theater Building, and opposite East end Union Depot,

INDIANAPOLIS, IND.

FRUIT TREES & NURSERY STOCK.

Fire and Burglar Proof Safes.

FLAX SEED

Loaned, and proceeds contracted for at highest market price.

Dealer in

GROVER & BAKER'S SEWING MACHINES,

Furnish Double Lock, or Single Lock Stitch.

Six kinds of the best Reapers and Mowers in use; the best Grain Drills in use; the best Sugar Mills and Evaporators in use. Grain Tile. Howe's celebrated Standard Scales, stock, platform and counter. All Scales warranted.

The best Threshers and Separators in use.

FRANKLIN W. H., Sr., BARBER, cor. Washington and Meridian, res. 126 w. Ohio. See card, page 102.

Franklin Wm., white washer, res. 119 Indiana ave.

Franks J. J., laborer, res. 9 e. South.

Franz P., res. 122 n. Noble.

Franzman A., freight clerk, Adams Express, res. 107 e. Vermont.

Frary J. C., printer, bds. Macy House.

Franer J., druggist, 185 e. Washington, res. same.

Franer R., turner, res. 112 n. Noble.

Frazee Aaron, brick layer, 172 Blake.

Fraze Frank, pump maker, res. 53 Benton.

Frazee Samuel E., cashier, Post-office, res. 104 n. Illinois.

Frazeir John H., carpenter, res. 22 Loukabee.

Frea F., res. 171 e. Washington.

Frecker F., res. 81 n. Davidson.

Freeman N. B., salesman, res. Illinois, bet. South and McCarty.

Fredricks G., laborer, res. 41 s. Illinois.

Fredricks G., laborer, Eagle Foundry.

Fredricks G., laborer, works with D. Root & Co.

Frederick John, shoemaker, works 150 w. Washington.

Freeman N. B., clerk, shoe store, res. 102 e. New York.

Freeman John, (col.) painter, res. Meridian. near, First.

Freitay Michael, carpenter, res. 167 n. Noble.

French C. G., jeweler, 37 w. Washington.

French Wm. M., teacher, Deaf and Dumb Asylum.

French R. H., freight clerk, Adams Express Co.

Frenkenstein Geo., barber, 60 Bluff road, res. same.

Frenzel J. T., saloon, 85 s. Illinois, res. same.

Fres M., laborer, res. 30 Union.

Frese Chas., of F. & Kroff, bds. Union Hall.

FRESE & KROFF, WHOLESALE AND RETAIL DEALERS IN HARDWARE, &c., 11 w. Washington. See card, page 142.

Fretz Daniel B., miller, works Capital Mills.

Frick J., Commercial Hotel Saloon.

Frick H., porter, Maguire, Jones & Co.

Frick Philip, tinner, res. cor. Liberty and Central R. R.

Fricke Rev. Chas., res. 13 n. East.

Fridley W. K., clerk, 8 w. Washington, res. 8 Meridian.

Frie Henry, laborer, res. 51 w. South.

Friedgen C., boots and shoes, 126 e. Washington, res. 113 e. Market.

Fries Martin, works Union Steam Bakery.

Frink E. O., dentist, 4 Yohn's Block, bds. 118 n. Penn.

BATES HOUSE!

Cor. Washington & Illinois Sts.,

INDIANAPOLIS, IND.

J. L. HOLTON,   -   -   PROPRIETOR.

FRINK S. C., F. & WELLS, DENTIST, 4 Yohn's Block, res. 118 n. Penn. See card, page 132.

FRINK & WELLS, DENTISTS, 4 Yohn's Block. See card, page 132.

Friffin T., bar-keeper, Magnolia Saloon.

Frisbie H., machinist, res. 46 s. Noble.

Frisbie H. F., book-keeper, bds. 71 Indiana ave.

Fritz J., currier, works with Mooney & Co.

Frizzell A., carpenter, res. 2 w. Miss.

Froelking J. T., machinist, Bellefontaine depot, res. 253 s. Pennsylvania.

Frommeyer Henry, clerk, 16 w. Washington, bds. 70 n. Mississippi.

Fromhold P., coppersmith helper, res. 39 Bluff road.

Frost J. M., patent medicine, res. 150 n. Penn.

Frost & Buell, manufacturers Dr. Frost's medicine, res. cor. Delaware & Maryland.

Frotz Emanuel, file cutter, res. 153 n. Liberty.

Frower A., varnisher, 30 n. East.

Frumholt ———, cooper, res. 89 Bluff road.

Erushhower C., stone mason, res. 146 s. New Jersey.

Fry Albert, (col.) hostler, res. 76 Douglas.

Fry A., (col.) hostler, 5 West alley.

Fry Miss R. N., boarding house, res. 122 n. Illinois.

Fry W. H., of Pomeroy, F. & Co., bds. Bates House.

Fucks J., bar-keeper, 206 e. Washington.

Fugate James L., salesman, 21 w. Washington, res. cor. Vermont and Tennessee.

Fuller A., (col.) barber, res. 57 w. Georgia.

Fulton H. H., clerk, bds. 258 n. Tennessee.

Fulton Hance, clerk, New York Store, bds. 14 e. Ohio.

Fullerton J. E., clerk. Commissary U. S. A., res. cor. Mississippi and Maryland.

Fulsom Mrs. E., res. 127 s. Illinois.

Fulton Homer, clerk, 18 w. Washington.

Fulton J. H., trunk maker, bds. Mrs. Simpson's.

Fultz J., works Rolling Mill.

Funkhouser D., of Jameson & F., bds. Bates House.

Fuqua Mrs L. D., 11 n. West.

Furgason J. A., of W. J. Holiday & Co., 160 n. Tenn.

Furgason F. M., of Eaton & F., bds. Mrs. Igan.

Furgason L. A., clerk, bds. 75 n. Miss.

G

Gagg R., of G. & Co., res. 26 s. Pennsylvania.

GAGG & CO., CITY BREWERY, 26, 27 and 28 s. Penn.

Galagher Pat., works Rolling Mill.

9

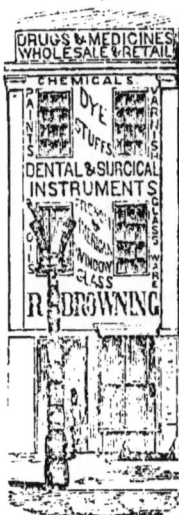

Gale John, laborer, res. cor. Maryland and Penn.
Gall A. D., physician, 22 Virginia ave., res. 37 n. N. Jersey.
Gallag Mrs. M., washer, res. 33 e. Market.
Gallagher F., painter, res. 42 Massachusetts ave.
Gallagher P., bds. Wm. Johnson's.
Gallaher Joseph, gas-fitter, for Gas Works.
Gallaway Mrs. C., res. 110 w. Vermont.
Gallahuse P. M., book-keeper, res. 270 e. Washington.
Galloim M., laborer, 25 Henry.
Gallup E. P., of W. P. & E. P. G., bds. Palmer House.
Gallup W. P., of W. P. & E. P. G., bds. Palmer House.
Gallup W. P. & E. P., dealers in grain and agents Fairbank's Scales, 74 w. Washington.
Gambel M., clerk, res. Market, bet. Noble and Davidson.
Gamerdinger Jacob, blacksmith, works Bellefontaine car shop.
Ganter C., confectionery, 181 e. Washington, res. same.
Ganter D., railroader, res. 181 e. Washington.
Gandolfo P., of J. C. Dunn & Co., bds. National Hotel.
Gardner C., meat market, 5 n. Illinois.
Gardner John T., harness maker, bds. 66 n. Illinois.
Gardner J., tinner, res. 124 n. Mississippi.
Gardner T., laborer, res. 35 w. McCarty.
Gardner Wendel, grocer, 183 Indiana ave., res. same.
Garity M., clerk, Adams Express Co.
Garlick H. M., clerk, A. and U. S. Express Co., bds. Pyle House.
Garner H. S., (Pink,) printer, with Dood & Co., bds. Spencer House.
Garner L. W., watch maker, bds. Spencer House.
Garratt Joseph, Phœnix Bell and Brass Foundry, half square e. Union Depot, res. 209 s. East.
Garrett David, carpenter, res. 91 e. Market.
Gas Works, s. Pennsylvania.
Gaskill David, res. 146 cor. West and Michigan.
Gass Andrew, butcher, res. 60 e. St. Joseph.
Gass Henry, laborer, res. 64 e. St. Joseph.
Gass Margretta, res. 74 e. St. Joseph.
Gasteter Fred., teamster, res. 217 n. New Jersey.
Gaston E., carriage maker, res. cor. Maryland and Kentucky ave.
Gaston H., carriage maker, res. 26 Kentucky ave.
Gaston H. R., carriage maker, cor. Kentucky ave. and Georgia.
Gaston Dr. John M., off. 22 e. Market, res. 77 n. New Jersey.

Gaston S., 9th Indiana Cavalry, bds. 11 n. Alabama.
Gaston Simpson B., res. 11 n. Alabama.
Gates B., of G., **Pray & Co.,** res. 191 n. Illinois.
Gates Daniel, blacksmith, res. 84 s. East.
Gates D. S., blacksmith, 43 Virginia ave., res. 86 s. East.
Gates J. J., of G. & Lemon, res. 85 e. Market.
GATES, PRAY & CO., FEED AND SALE STABLE, e. Market square. See card, page 72.
Gates & Lemon, blacksmiths, 14 s. New Jersey.
Gats John J., blacksmith, res. 83 e. Market.
Gattenby Mrs. Emily, res. Water.
Gatz Chas., saloon, res. 13 St. Clair.
Gay Alfred, Supt. Indiana Central Canal, res. 20 n. West.
Gay L., res. 170 w. Market.
Geal Conrad, pump maker, 216 e. Washington.
Gear N., res. 182 s. Illinois.
Gear E. & S. H., grocery, cor. s. New Jersey and Virginia ave.
Geier David, tailor, works 3 e. Washington.
Geiger G. W., salesman, cor. Indiana ave. and Ohio.
Geis Frank, book binder, with J. G., Douglas.
Geise Frank, cabinet turner, res. 68 n. Noble.
Geisel Christ., carpenter, res. 136 n. Davidson.
Geiseb Conrad, blacksmith, res. 88 Fort wayne ave.
Geisel George, blacksmith, res. 94 n. Fort Wayne ave.
Geisel Henry, blacksmith, res. 215 Mass. ave.
Geisendorff C. E., of C. E. G. & Co., res. 170 w. New York.
Geisendorff J. C., of C. E. G. & Co., bds. 60 n. New Jersey.
Geisendorff C. E. & Co., wool dealers and manufacturers of woolen goods, n. side Washington, near river bridge.
Geisendoff Edward, woolen factory, 170 New York.
Geiser J., blacksmith, res. 121 n. Davidson.
Gelzenleichter John, laborer, res. 169 n. Railroad.
Geopper Andrew, butcher, res. 152 w. Michigan.
George A. R., clerk, bds. cor. St. Clair and Michigan road.
George Isaac, res. Eddy.
George James, grocer, 143 w. Washington, res. same.
George Robert, 48 Michigan road.
Gerardy Nicholas, Taylor, res. 92 n. Davidson.
Germain John, works Rolling Mill.
German John, laborer, res. Wyoming, bet. Delaware and High.
German Methodist Episcopal Church, Ohio, bet. New Jersey and East.
GERMAN DRY GOODS STORE, KRAUSE & WITTEN-BERG, PROP'S, 43 and 45 e. Washington.

Gerrett Benjamin, carpenter, cor. Michigan and Minerva.
GERSTNER A. J., MERCHANT TAILOR, 158 c. Washington, res. Pearl, bet. Alabama and New Jersey. See card, page 36.
Gesenger David, tailor, res. 131 n. Maryland.
Gesendaner Wm., clerk, bds. Wemberger's.
Gibbs Mrs. H., (col.) res. 68 Blackford.
Gibbs R., barber, 1 n. Illinois, bds. 145 w. Washington.
Gibson James, marble worker, bds. Mrs. Skelly's boarding House.
Gibson Wm. H., school teacher, 105 North.
Gibson W. S., carpenter, 86 n. Delaware.
GIBSON WM. T., SECY. IND. FIRE INS. CO., AND AGT. CONN. MUTUAL LIFE INS. CO., off. 5 Odd Fellows Hall, res. 60 s. Alabama. See card, p. 110.
Gies L., bar-keeper, bds. 164 c. Ohio.
Giesging Christ., joiner, res. Davidson, bet. Ohio and Market.
Gieger Robert, clerk, bds. 59 c. Ohio.
Gildersleeve Miss E. L., teacher, Indianapolis Female College.
Gillace Thos., works Wiggins & Chandlers.
Gillespie Mrs. Jane, res. 44 n. Delaware.
Gillespie Wm. T., banker, bds. 44 n. Delaware.
Gillet Horace S., instructor, Deaf and Dumb Asylum.
Gillett Mrs. ———, 103 e. Washington, up stairs.
Gillett Rev. S. T., pastor, Wesley Chappel, res. Circle.
Gillet H. S., Deaf and Dumb Asylum, res. 170 n. Penn.
Gillig N., clerk, Union House.
Gillispie Wm. J., clerk, Harrison's Bank, res. 44 n. Delaware.
Gillmore Daniel, brick mason, res. 260 Virginia ave.
Gillmore Wm., soldier, res. 70 n. Spring.
Gimble M., clerk, res. Market, bet. Davidson and Noble.
Gimbel M., cabinet maker, 147 c. Washington, res. 106 n. Davidson.
Gimber Henry, teamster, res. 70 Bluff road.
Gings G., saloon keeper, res. 53 n. New Jersey.
Ginz Henry, saloon keeper, res. 144 c. New York.
Ginz Michael, of G. & Bro., res. 53 n. New Jersey.
Ginz & Bro., Little House Saloon, under Little House.
Girton Frank, hack driver, bds. 149 c. Ohio.
Gis G., bar keeper, bds. Commercial Hotel.
Gisiking Fred., blacksmith, res. 310 Virginia ave.
Glaser Julius, of G. & Bros., res. 15 n. East.

BLAIR & SMITH,

Manufacturers of all kinds of

HARNESS COLLARS AND TRUNKS!

No. 198 West Washington Street,

INDIANAPOLIS, IND.

SAMUEL TAGGART,

MILLWRIGHT!

BOLTING CLOTH, FLOUR PACKERS AND

MILL FURNISHING GENERALLY,

OFFICE---94 SOUTH PENNSYLVANIA ST.,

INDIANAPOLIS, IND.

MILLER & TOMLINSON,

GROCERS:

And Dealers in

PRODUCE, FRUIT, GAME, MEAT, &C.,

No. 212 EAST WASHINGTON STREET,

INDIANAPOLIS, IND.

Cash paid for all kinds of produce. Goods delivered to all parts of the city free of charge.

B. M. SPICER & CO.,

REAL ESTATE AGENTS,

No. 20 1-2 North Illinois Street, (Norwood's Block,)

INDIANAPOLIS, IND.

B. M. SPICER & CO. offer their services for the purchase and sale of Real Estate, Renting Houses, Negotiating Loans, procuring money on Mortgage, Examining Titles, Executing Legal Papers, and all other business appertaining to the Real Estate Business. Having warm and comfortable rooms, they will be open day and evening, and prompt and constant attention given to all business entrusted to them. Business solicited and satisfaction guaranteed.

Glaser & Bros., merchant tailors and clothiers, 2 Bates House.

Glaser J., clothing store, res. 16 n. East.

GLAZIER CHAS., COMMISSION MERCHANT, 16 s. Meridian, res. 100 Virginia ave.

Glaizer Daniel, engineer, Fire Department, No. 3, res. 109 s. New Jersey.

Gleason John, watchman and messenger, Sinking Fund, bds. Maryland.

Glenn's Block, Washington, bet. Meridian and Penn.

GLENN W. & H., PROPR'S NEW YORK STORE, GLENN'S BLOCK, e. Washington, bet. Meridian and Penn. See card, pages 150 and 151.

GLENN WM., W. & H. G., res. 73 n. Meridian.

Glenn Mrs. A., 38 s. Alabama.

Glessing T. B., artist, res. 62 n. Tenn.

Glover G. N. P., plain and ornamental plasterer, 32 n. Penn., res. 98 n. Meridian.

Gochen Wm., carpenter, res. 138 s. East.

Goddard Samuel, res. 18 s. West.

Goddard & Jennings, stone cutters, cor. Market and Tenn.

Godwall T., saddler, res. 90 s. Penn.

Goeke Adolph., grocer, res. 318 Virginia ave.

Goepper Fred., clothing, res. 61 n. Illinois.

GŒPPER F. & CO., MERCHANT NAILORS, 15 e. Washington. See card, page 78.

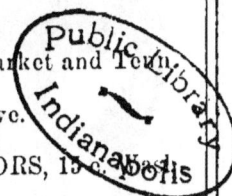

Goetz Chas., bar keeper, 9 n. Penn.

Goff Mrs. E. A., (col.) res. 127 West.

Gogen Mrs. Mary, 26 s. Alabama.

Gohl J. J., carpenter, with M. Gimbel.

Goins Simon, laborer, res. cor. Ohio and West.

Gold Adam, grocer National road, opp. Woolen Factory, res. same.

Gold Samuel N., Prof. Bryant & Spencer's Commercial College, res. w. Washington.

Golding J., blacksmith, works with F. J., Ropp.

Goldman Jacob, peddler, res. 201 s. Delaware.

Goldsbery G. S., book-keeper, bds. 43 n. Penn.

Goldesbery S. S., watch maker, bds. 53 n. Meridian.

Goodell R., engineer, res. 183 e. Vermont.

Goodhart B. F., grocer, 107 e. Washington, res. 70 Ala.

Goodhart J. F., clerk, 107 e. Washington.

Goodman A., tailor, 16 n. Penn., res. 56 e. Market.

Goodwin A. Q., printer, Journal office.

Goodwin Elish., editor Christian Record, Journal building.

Goodwin R. A., photographist, res. 22 Maryland.

WOODLAWN GREEN HOUSE & GARDENS.

I have the largest collection of

NEW AND DESIRABLE GRAPE VINES

Ever offered in the West. The following comprise a portion of my stock:
Anna, Allen's Hybrid, Clare, Canby's Aug., Canada, Canadian Chief,
Catawba, Clinton, Concord, Cuyahoga, Delaware, Dina, Early
Northern Muscakine, Emily, Elsingfiurg, Hartford Prolific,
Herbamont, Logan, Lenoir, Louisa, Lyman, Lincoln,
Norton's Va. Seedling, Ontario, Pauline, Rebecca,
To Kalon, Tayler's Bullitt, Union Village,
York Madeira, and many others.

A FINE COLLECTION OF ROSES

AND DECIDUOUS & EVERGREEN SHRUBS & BEDDING OUT PLANTS,

Unsurpassed for variety and excellence, together with a large and varied
collection of Cammelias, Azalias, and other winter blooming

Parlor & Green House Plants.

I have given special attention to the new and beautiful Foliage Plants'
of which we offer many of the most desirable. Also, a splendid variety
of Bulbs and Tubers.

A DESCRIPTIVE CATALOGUE

And Treatise on the culture of Grapes and other Fruits sent to all who
apply and enclose 15 cents in postage stamps.
All who are interested are respectfully invited to examine my
stock and prices.
I will have an assortment of Grape Vines in Pots on exhibition
at the next State Fair, and an agent to receive orders either for fall or
spring sales.

Wm. H. LOOMIS.

(See Engraving opposite page.)

Gool J., machinist, Washington Foundry.

Goolman Morris & Co., proprietors Western Agricultural Works, s. Tennessee, opp. Rolling Mills.

Goolman W. P., of G., Morris & Co., bds. Mrs. Hipes' boarding house.

Gowell A. W., book-keeper, res. 22 w. New York.

Gowesse Rev. Francis, St. John's Church, res. Georgia, bet. Illinois and Tennessee.

GOOD M. H., DRY GOODS, 5 e. Washington, bds. Bates House. See card, p. 142.

Goodman A., tailor, 18 n. Pennsylvania, res. 56 Market.

Goodman Geo., clerk, res. 9 Market.

Goodman G. K., clerk, res. w. Market, bet. Circle and Illinois.

Goodwin T. A., allotment commission, 7 n. Meridian, res. Washington, east of Deaf and Dumb Asylum.

Gordon J. M., salesman, Hume, Lord & Co.

Gordon J. A., res. 69 Indiana ave.

Gordon Judge Geo. E., res. 92 n. Pennsylvania.

Gorell Willis, clerk, bds. 22. w. New York.

Gorham George L., bricklayer, 179 n. Mississippi.

Gorham Wm. H., res. 173 n. Mississippi.

Gorman D., porter, Mason House.

Gorth Valentine, cooper, res. n. e. cor. Spring and New York.

Goth Peter, of G., Severin & Co., res. 237 n. New Jersey.

Gott Thos., constable, res. 147 s. Tennessee.

Goul Andrew, carpenter, res. 183 e. Market.

Goulden P., fireman, Gas Works.

Gow James, bds. 74 n. Delaware.

Grabhorn Henry, varnisher, res. 81 Fort Wayne ave.

Graham George, gardener, res. Meridian, n. of Third.

Graham John, clerk, New York Store, bds. 20 s. Mississippi.

Graham John, grocer, res. 99 Virginia ave.

Graham Wm. E., carpenter, res. 141 n. Meridian.

Graham Wm. S., meat market, 22 n. Pennsylvania, res. 24 n. Pennsylvania.

Gramling A., res. 16 n. Noble.

Gramling Adam, tailor, res. 79 n. Noble.

Gramling Anthony, res. 116 n. Noble.

Gramling J. A., salesman, res. 79 n. Noble.

Gramling J., of J. & P. G., res. 116 n. Noble.

Gramling P., of J. & P. G., res. 118 n. Noble.

GRAMLING J. & P., MERCHANT TAILORS AND CLOTHING, 41 e. Washington. See card, on front cover.

Gool J., machinist, Washington Foundry.

Goolman Morris & Co., proprietors Western Agricultural Works, s. Tennessee, opp. Rolling Mills.

Goolman W. P., of G., Morris & Co., bds. Mrs. Hipes' boarding house.

Gowell A. W., book-keeper, res. 22 w. New York.

Gowesse Rev. Francis, St. John's Church, res. Georgia, bet. Illinois and Tennessee.

GOOD M. H., DRY GOODS, 5 c. Washington, bds. Bates House. See card, p. 142.

Goodman A., tailor, 18 n. Pennsylvania, res. 56 Market.

Goodman Geo., clerk, res. 9 Market.

Goodman G. K., clerk, res. w. Market, bet. Circle and Illinois.

Goodwin T. A., allotment commission, 7 n. Meridian, res. Washington, east of Deaf and Dumb Asylum.

Gordon J. M., salesman, Hume, Lord & Co.

Gordon J. A., res. 69 Indiana ave.

Gordon Judge Geo. E., res. 92 n. Pennsylvania.

Gorell Willis, clerk, bds. 22. w. New York.

Gorham George L., bricklayer, 179 n. Mississippi.

Gorham Wm. II., res. 173 n. Mississippi.

Gorman D., porter, Mason House.

Gorth Valentine, cooper, res. n. e. cor. Spring and New York.

Goth Peter, of G., Severin & Co., res. 237 n. New Jersey.

Gott Thos., constable, res. 147 s. Tennessee.

Goul Andrew, carpenter, res. 183 c. Market.

Goulden P., fireman, Gas Works.

Gow James, bds. 74 n. Delaware.

Grabhorn Henry, varnisher, res. 81 Fort Wayne ave.

Graham George, gardener, res. Meridian, n. of Third.

Graham John, clerk, New York Store, bds. 20 s. Mississippi.

Graham John, grocer, res. 99 Virginia ave.

Graham Wm. E., carpenter, res. 141 n. Meridian.

Graham Wm. S., meat market, 22 n. Pennsylvania, res. 24 n. Pennsylvania.

Gramling A., res. 16 n. Noble.

Gramling Adam, tailor, res. 79 n. Noble.

Gramling Anthony, res. 116 n. Noble.

Gramling J. A., salesman, res. 79 n. Noble.

Gramling J., of J. & P. G., res. 116 n. Noble.

Gramling P., of J. & P. G., res. 118 n. Noble.

GRAMLING J. & P., MERCHANT TAILORS AND CLOTHING, 41 c. Washington. See card, on front cover.

Graney John, laborer, res. 192 s. Tennessee.
Grang Michael, laborer, res. cor. Meek and Cady.
Granie Thomas, laborer, res. 25 n. Railroad.
Granob Luther, laborer, res. 198 Massachusetts ave.
Grant Thos., Co. II, 7th regiment Indiana volunteers, res.
    cor. McCarty and Tennessee.
Grant Wm., engineer, Terre Haute & Richmond R. R., res.
    149 s. Mississippi.
Grapham A., varnisher, res. 199 s. Pennsylvania.
Grata Louis, cash boy, New York Store, res. 39 n. East.
Grater H., confectioner, res. 39 n. East.
GRAVEN THOMAS, PROP'R CENTRAL HOUSE, 44 s.
    Meridian.
Graves Hailland, carpenter, res. 34 west.
Graves L. W., res. cor. w. North and Meridian.
Gray P. V., moulder, res. 116 e. McCarty.
Gray Jessie, conductor, Indianapolis and Madison R. R.,
    bds. Ray House.
Gray John, policeman, bds. 144 e. North.
Gray Robt., watchman, res. 18 Lord.
Gray Thomas, soldier, res. 57 e. St. Joseph.
Gray Thos., clerk, with Todd & Carmichael, bds 64 e.
    South.
Gray Wm., laborer, res. 44 s. Noble.
Gray William, baker, 64 e. South, res. same.
Gray Wm., machinist, wks. I. & C. Machine Shop.
Graydon A., res. 184 e. Ohio.
Graydon W. M., freight agent, Indiana Central R. R., res.
    cor. Merrill & Alabama.
Grear Joseph, wks. with McCord & Wheatley.
Great Central Railway Engine House, bet. Noble and Ben-
    ton.
GREAT CENTRAL RAILWAY, offices cor. Virginia ave.
    and Delaware.
GREAT WESTERN DISPATCH OFFICE, cor. Virginia
    ave. and Delaware in A. Wallace's Grocery Building,
    T. A. Lewis, agent.
Green Charles W., telegraph operator, General Freight
    Office, Great Central R. W.
Green Geo., tailor, res. 13 Willard.
Green James, assistant quartermaster, res. 93 n. Meridian.
Green John, laborer, res. 320 s. Delaware.
Green Mrs., res. Maple.
Green Miss Mollie, res. 13 s. New Jersey.
Green M., laborer, res. 241 s. Pennsylvania.
Green R., engineer, bds. Ray House.

Greunert Henry, tailor, res. 85 w. South.
Greunert Herman, shoemaker, res. 85 w. South.
Greenfield Robt., miller, res. 229 w. Washington.
Greenlow L., with A. Ball.
Greenwould Albert, res. 129 n. Noble.
Greene A. S., salesman, 18 w. Washington, bds. 93 n. Meridian.
Greer Elisha, grocer, res. cor. s. New Jersey and Virginia ave.
Greer James, cabinet-maker, res. cor. Mississippi and Garden.
Greer W. H., carpenter, res. 11 Ellsworth.
Gregg Dennis, department provost marshal, Blackford's Block, res. 22 w. Michigan.
Gregg J., wagon maker, res. 103 Indiana ave.
Gregory David, fur dealer, cor. Blackford and New York.
Grein Mrs. J., bakery, 214 e. Washington, res. same.
Greiner J., shoemaker, res. 51 s. Illinois.
Grepper A., butcher, 16 Illinois.
Grenard T. L., clerk, bds. Little's Hotel.
Gruenert H., boots and shoes, 51 w. Washington, res. 85 w. South.
Grerock John, wks. Rolling Mill.
Grerock Theodore, wks. Rolling Mill.
Grershapper J., boiler-maker, Washington Foundry.
Grenzard L., painter, res. 134 e. Washington.
Grey Mrs. H., res. 81 South.
Grey John, res. 43 West.
Grey R. P., clerk, res. 242 w. Washington.
Grey Wm., wks. Western Machine Shop.
Gridley F. R., res. 39 California.
GRIDLEY J. E., ATLANTIC SALOON, Palmer House corner, bds. 39 California.
Grieb John, laborer, res. 11 w. Liberty.
Grienewald Henry, cigars, res. 79 n. Davidson.
Grieshaber Sebastian, boiler-maker, res. 231 s. Alabama.
Griesheimer Moritz, clothing, cor. Meridian and Washington.
Griff John, boiler-maker, Western Machine Works.
Griffeth James, laborer, bds. 55 e. St. Joseph.
Griffin A., wks. 12 s. Pennsylvania.
Griffin Dennis, laborer, res. Missouri. bet. South and Merrill.
Griffin James, laborer, res. Water.
Griffin James, messenger, State Offices, res. 300 s. Delaware.
Griffin Jessee, carpenter, res. 116 w. Ohio.
Griffin Michael, drayman, res. 67 Bright.

Griffin Michael, porter, 18 w. Washington.
Griffin Patrick, laborer, res. 316 s. Delaware.
Griffin N. J., clerk, Rolling Mill.
Griffith A. J., messenger, American Express Co.
Griffith G. W., plasterer, res. 155 n. Alabama.
Griffith H., res. 52 Illinois.
Griffith J. R., of Barnitz & G., res. 32 s. Mississippi.
Griffith Samuel, carpenter, res. 263 s. East.
Grinus D. Mc., boarding house, 20 n. Pennsylvania.
Grimm J., blacksmith, res. 106 e. St. Joseph.
Grimm J. C., painter, res. 106 e. St. Joseph.
Grimm V., machinist, wks. at Union Cabinet Factory.
Grimes Wm. H., carpenter, bds. 141 w. Market.
Grinearth Henry, tailor, with F. Goepper & Co.
Grimm Jacob, laborer, res. 106 e. St. Joseph.
Grinsteiner G., undertaker, res. 114 e. Market.
Grischel Charles, tailor, res. 133 n. Noble.
Griswold John N., carpenter, Blake.
Griswould —., cabinet-maker, res. 27 n. East.
Grobhorn H., varnisher, wks. Union Cabinet Factory.
GROSCH JOHN, WHOLESALE ALE DEALER, res. 113
    n. Noble.
Groff R., clerk, res. 12 Lousiana.
Groft Henry, laborer, res. Wyoming, bet. Delaware and
    High.
Groham Samuel, conductor, res. 207 n. Tennessee.
Grooms A. C., book-keeper, Journal off., res. 157 n. Missis-
    sippi.
Grosvenor J. A., superintendent Washington Foundry, res.
    136 s. Mississippi.
Grout J. B., dealer in boots and shoes, 5 w. Washington,
    res. 39 w. Maryland.
Grove Benjamin, lightning-rod agent, res. 71 n. Spring.
Grubbs D. W., of Martindale & G., bds. Bates House.
Grube Jacob, carpenter, res. 26 s. Illinois.
Grunt G., striker blacksmith, Washington Foundry.
Guckler Christ., laborer, res. 73 Fort Wayne ave.
Gudpelt P., clerk, with Spiegel, Thoms & Co.
Guezat Isaac, painter, res. 159 s. Delaware.
Gulinger John, cabinet-maker, res. 146 e. Market.
Gulliver W., barber, cor. Washington and Kentucky ave.,
    res. 63 Kentucky ave.
Gundelfinger Ben., salesman, Glaser & Bros.
Gundelfinger S., clerk, with H. Bamberger.
Gurg Henry, of G. & Bro., res. 53 n. New Jersey.
GUSTIN DR. L., off. cor. Illinois and Louisiana, res. 101 s.
    Tennessee.
10

Gutchnecht John, wks. Union Steam Bakery.
Guth Edward, machinist, res. 32 s. Illinois.
Guthart Fred., clerk, bds. 86 e. Market.
Guthner J. A., laborer, res. 109 Fort Wayne ave.
Guthner John, painter, res. 105 Fort Wayne ave.
GUTHRIDGE C. M., NEWS DEALER, 26 e. Washington,
    bds. 22 w. Maryland. See card, p. 66.
Guthridge J. W., R. R. agent, res. 49 e. Maryland.
Gutig Henry, barber, cor. Washington and Pennsylvania,
    res. 116 e. Market.
Gutman Andina, res. 56 e. Market.
Gutperle Peter, clerk, res. 112 n. Noble.
Gutt John, plasterer, res. 150 n. Liberty.
GYMNASIUM, Meridian, bet. Washington and Maryland.
    See card, p. 96.

H

Habsnary Henry, laborer, res. 113 w. New York.
Hacket William, laborer, res. 22 s. Liberty.
Hackstein C., laborer, res. 50 Union.
Haef August, dyeing establishment, 10 s. Pennsylvania,
    res. same.
Haerle Wm., fancy dry goods store, 36 w. Washington, res.
    same.
Haffermar Luther, shoemaker, bds. 48 Massachusetts ave.
Haffman C. T., clerk, res. 60 w. Ohio.
Hafner A., shoemaker, 103 w. Washington, res. same.
Hagan John, laborer, res. Sharp's Addition, near e. Wash-
    ington.
Hagar E. C., book-keeper, Fletcher's Bank, bds. 21 s. Dela-
    ware.
Hagerst Mrs. C., res. 156 s. Tennessee.
Hagerhorst C. F., grocer, res. California, bet. New York
    Vermont.
Hagerty P., teamster, res. 179 s. Tennessee.
Hagerty Tom, wks. Rolling Mill.
Haggart Wm., blacksmith, Blake.
Hahn C. F., of H. & Rose, res. 41 n. Alabama.
HAHN HENRY, EAST STREET HOUSE, s. East, bet.
    Washington and Georgia.
Hahn L., butcher, 105 w. Washington.
Hahn Philip, musician, res. 143 s. East.
HAHN & ROSE, WHOLESALE DEALERS IN LIQUORS
    AND TOBACCO, 11 s. Meridian. See card, p. 66.
Haines E., clerk, bds. cor. Illinois and Ohio.
Hains J., painter, bds. Pyle House.
Hakelberg Moses, clothing, res. 111 e. New York.
Hakelberg S., clerk, res. 111 e. New York.

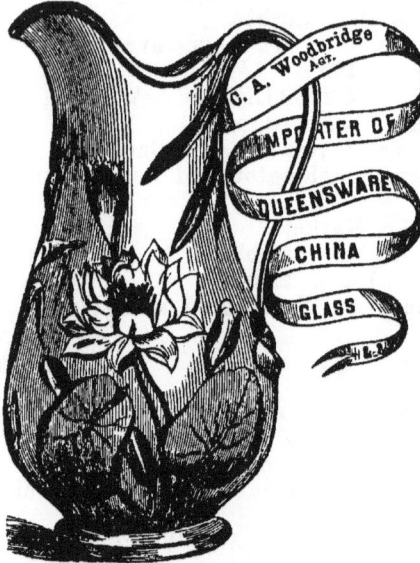

Hale H. J., machinist, Washington Foundry.
Hale John, printer, with Dodd & Co., bds. Woodruff's boarding house.
Haley B., wagon-maker, Bluff road, bet. McCarty and Ray.
Halford Mrs. M. A., res. 114 e. Vermont.
Halia Pat., wks. Bolling Mill, bds. 278 s. Delaware.
Haliham J., res. Elizabeth.
Hallam Thomas, laborer, res. West, bet. Washington and New York.
Hall —., wagon master Army, res. cor. Huron and Noble.
Hall Chas. W., res. 170 n. Illinois.
Hall E. A., merchant tailor, 62½ e. Washington.
Hall Eli, tailor, res. Illinois, bet. First and Second.
Hall H. C., clerk, bds. 32 e. Georgia.
Hall L. A., heater Rolling Mill, res. 164 e. Tennessee.
Hall Nathaniel, sheet iron worker, bds. Cincinnati House.
Hall Reginald H., of Rand & H., res. 47 n. Meridian.
Hall T. Q., clerk, res. 88 n. New Jersey.
Hall Wm., machinist, wks. I. & C. Machine Shop.
Hall W. M., check clerk, Adams Express Co.
Hall & Ross, pump-makers, 81 s. Delaware.
Haller Leon, salesman, 36 w. Washington, bds. Union Hall.
Haller Philip, stone-mason, res. 218 n. Noble.
Halpin M. H., printer, Journal office.
Halsted Dr., 39 s. Meridian.
Halsted A. C., marble-cutter, East.
Halter A., butcher, bds. 91 s. Illinois.
Haly D., wks. Rolling Mill.
Haly L., wks. Rolling Mill.
Haly M., clerk, Post Office.
Haly Pat., wks. Rolling Roll.
Hamburg John, tailor, bds. Union Hall.
Hamburg W., stone carver and engraver, bds. Macy House.
Hamell M., wks. Rolling Mill, bds. with Wm. Johnson.
Hamell Thos., wks. Rolling Mill, bds. cor. Tennessee and Garden.
Hamill Mike, wks. Rolling Mill.
Hamill P., wks. Rolling Mill.
Hamill Tom, wks. Rolling Mill.
Hamilton James, mechanic,
Hamilton J. C., actor, Metropolitan Hall.
Hamilton F. W., department county auditor, res. 189 s. New Jersey.
Hamilton J. W., attorney, off. Court House.
Hamilton N. B., secretary Equitable Fire Insurance Co., off. 16 Talbott & New's Block, res. 73 n. New Jersey.

GLENNS' BLOCK,

INDIANAPOLIS, IND.

See Engraving, opposite page.

This new and elegant block, erected and owned by Wm. Glenn & H. Glenn, is situated on the south side of Washington, between Meridian and Pennsylvania streets, occupying the site of the old Browning Hotel, afterwards called the Wright House. It is three and a half stories high, being 68 feet front on Washington street, and extending back to Pearl street, containing three store rooms and eight offices; the side stores are 17½ feet wide and 132 feet deep. The center store, known as the New York Store, is occupied by the proprietors of the block, W. & H. Glenn, and is 32½ feet in width and 132 feet in depth. This store is the mammoth dry goods establishment of the State. The offices are occupied by the city authorities, namely: His Honor the Mayor, City Treasurer, City Clerk, Civil Engineer, City Attorney, City Marshal and Police, with a chamber for the meetings of the City Council. Store south of entrance on American Alley, is occupied by the Cincinnati Gas Fitting Co. One store, that on the east, is occupied by Merrill & Co., dealers in law books, stationery, &c. The one on the west side is occupied as a shoe store, by Chase & Dawes. The appearance of this block is very attractive, chaste and elegant, without a fault, and is an ornament to our main street. It was re-built at a cost to the Messrs. Glenn of forty-five thousand dollars.

VIEW OF GLENNS' BLOCK!

WASHINGTON STREET,

Between Meridian and Pennsylvania Streets,

INDIANAPOLIS, IND.

Hamilton T. D., proprietor Patterson House, n. Alabama, bet. Ohio and Market.

Hamilton W. H., bookbinder, bds. Pyle House.

Hamilton R., res. 7 Eddy.

HAMLIN C., ATTORNEY, 16 e. Washington, bds. Pyle House. See card, outside back of book.

Hammersmith Jacob, laborer, res. 148 s. New Jersey.

Hammond Upton J., attorney, Johnson's Building, 2d floor, bds. Ohio.

Hance J. D. of H. & Turner, res. 150 n. Mississippi.

HANCE & TURNER, DEALERS IN WATCHES, JEWELRY AND NOTIONS, 9 e. Washington.

Hance David, silversmith, res. n. Mississippi.

Hanchett Mrs. D., Actress, Metropolitan Hall.

Handrahan Pat., laborer, res. 184 s. Tennessee.

Hancison W., clerk, Chas. Mayer, 29 w. Washington.

Hancy J., laborer, wks. with D. Root & Co.

Hancy James, laborer, res. 161 s. Delaware.

Hanft Henry, laborer, res. 51 n. New Jersey.

Hanger L., laborer, res. near Smith's Brewery.

Hanifen Michael, teamster, res. 42 Bates.

Hanigen John, riveter, res. 230 e. Washington.

Hanivan M., laborer, bds. 15 s. Alabama.

Hanley P., currier, wks. with Mooney & Co.

Hanlin Mrs. C., res. 57 Kentucky ave.

Hanna S. C., book-keeper, with Crossland & Pee, bds. Bates House.

Hanna Maj. V. C., res. 35 n. Meridian.

Hannah Samuel, res. 26 n. Meridian.

Hannigan John, boiler-maker, Western Machine Works.

Hannegan S. K., clerk, superintendent Public Instruction, bds. Bates House.

Hanneman J., clerk, bds. 115 w. Maryland.

Hanninger G. F., res. 30 n. Noble.

HANNING JOHN, of J. Pearson & Co., 78 w. Washington.

Hanning John G., of Ramsay & H., res. 130 n. Delaware.

Hannon Ed., wks. Rolling Mill.

HANRAHAN P. G., SALOON, s. Tennessee, res. 184 s. Tennessee.

Hansfurther John S., clerk, 80 w. Washington.

Hanson C., wks. Rolling Mill.

Hanson Peter, wks. Rolling Mill.

Hanway Samuel, mail agent, res. 75 n. New Jersey.

Harbinson A., engineer, Journal office.

Harbison Robt., driver, A. & U. S. Express Co., res. Vermont.

Harbison Mrs. Sarah, res. 70 w. Vermont.

Hardert G. L. K., res. Vermont, bet. Noble and Liberty.

Harderty E. J., engineer, res. 164 s. Alabama.
Hardin Ezra, carpenter, res. 87 c. Market.
Hardin E. C., carpenter, res. 87 c. Market.
Harding A. J., with J. D. Crane.
Harding Thos., carriage trimmer, 60 Kentucky ave.
Hardwick J., blacksmith, wks. with F. J. Rapp.
Hare Marcus, res. Orient, bet. Michigan road and Washington.
Harkness J., of Elder, H. & Bingham, res. 77 n. Pennsylvania.
Harlin G. W., res. 78 n. Tennessee.
Harlin J. W., tinner, res. 78 n. Tennessee.
Harmening Christian, grocer, 205 s. Delaware, res. same.
Harmon L., laborer, wks. Wiggins & Chandler's.
Harmon Pat., wagoner, with C. Glazier.
Harness S., laborer, res. 30 w. McCarty.
Harpman Christ., laborer, res. 139 e. Ohio.
Harpel J., cigar maker, bds. Commercial Hotel.
Harper Henry, cooper, res. 92 Bluff road.
Harper Jefferson, carpenter, res. 132 w. New York.
Harper J. L., book keeper, E. C. Mayhew & Co., res. 117 c. Market.
Harper W. S., printer, res. 92 Bluff road.
Harington Jennis, laborer, res. 260 s. Delaware.
Harrington Pat., laborer, res. 127 w. South.
Harris C. E., carpenter, res. 66 c. North.
Harris H. Clay, student at law, with Barbour & Howland, bds. 68 c. Vermont.
HARRIS J., REPAIRER AND RENOVATING CLOTHING, 38 s. Illinois, res. same. See card, p. 118.
Harris Wm. A., clerk, bds. 147 c. Market.
HARRISON A. & J. C. S., BANKERS, 15 c. Washington.
HARRISON ALFRED, of A. & J. C. S. H., res. 61 n. Meridian.
Harrison Benj., (col.) 70th regiment Indiana volunteers, res. 127 n. Alabama.
HARRISON'S BANK, A. & J. C. S. H., 15 c. Washington.
Harrison John, banker, res. 62 n. Meridian.
HARRISON J. C. S., of A. & J. C. S. H., res. 63 n. Meridian.
Harrison J. H., sutler, 39th Indiana, res. 93 c. Ohio.
Harrison T., blacksmith, res. Illinois, 3 doors s. McCarty.
Harrison T. C., clerk, Headquarters Superintendent Recruiting Service, bds. 45 n. Pennsylvania.
Harrison Tom, wks. Rolling Mill.
Harrison William, printer, 78 Massachusetts ave.
Harsch John, printer, res. 130 c. Washington.
Hart T. J., carpenter, res. 79 Massachusetts ave.
Harter J. A., tinner, res. 20 n. New Jersey.

Hartewig H. W., drayman, res. 123 n. Davidson.
Harting Henry, brewer, res. 35 s. Illinois.
Harting & Bro., brewery, Illinois, near cor. Bluff road.
Hartley John, expressman, res. Ellen.
Hartman Christ., laborer, res. 15 n. Railroad.
Hartman C., porter, Fred. P. Rush.
Hartmann Henry, res. 213 n. New Jersey.
Hartman H., chair maker, 63 n. New Jersey.
Hartmann H., plasterer, res. 108 n. Alabama.
Hartstem M., clerk.
Hartung F., butcher, bds. 91 s. Illinois.
Hartwell E., clerk, Bates House.
Harvey A. C., collector, newspaper, res. 22 s. Meridian.
HARVEY J. S., PREST. IND. FIRE INS. CO., off 5 Odd
    Fellows Hall, res. 54 s. Meridian.
Harwood J. M., cabinet maker, res. 11 Madison ave.
Harkell Geo., carpenter, res. Missouri, near South.
Haskit W. J. & Co., wholesale and retail druggist, 14 w.
    Washington.
Haslinger L., blacksmith, res. c. Washington.
Haslup J., mechanic, res. 221 s. East.
Hason James, sutler, Soldier's Home, res. 147 n. N. Jersey.
Hasselman L. W., of H. & Vinton, res. 38 s. Meridian.
Hasslet E. A., salesman, res. 105 n. Tenn.
Hassleman & Vinton, Prop's Washington Foundry.
Hasson Chas., grocer, res. 117 n. Meridian.
HASTINGS E. L., FOREMAN, Journal office, res. 66 n.
    Pennsylvania.
Hatch Mrs. H., restaurant, 141 w. Washington, res. same.
Hatfield Alfred, soldier, res. 232 n. New Jersey.
Hatfield J. J., machinist, res. 41 w. Walnut.
Hatling Richard, res. 44 s. Meridian.
Hatly Wm., assessor, res, 151 n. Delaware.
Hattendorf Henry, tailor, res. Michigan road, near Cen-
    tral R. R.
Hatten Thos. H., cigar maker, res. New York, bet. Noble
    and Spring.
Hattenbach Nathan, clerk with Dessar, Bro. & Co., bds.
    Pyle House.
Hatterich John, carpenter, res. 72 n. Noble.
Hatterich Geo., varnisher, wooks Union Cabinet Factory.
Hanch E., iron gratings, res. 116 c. Vermont.
HAUCK JOHN, CONFECTIONERY, 12 Louisiana, res.
    same. See card, page 112.
Hanck John, shoemaker, res. 24 St. Mary.
Haug Michael, 60 c. South, res. same.
Haufler John, laborer, res. Second, bet. Meridian and Ill.
Haugh B. F., of H. & Schowe, res. 104 n. Peru.

Haugh C., engineer, res. 116 e. Vermont.
Haugh E., blacksmith, res. 116 e. Vermont.
HAUGH & SCHOWE, MANUFACTURERS IRON RAIL-
ING, 2 n. Delaware. See card, page 154.
Haughey Thos. P., collector, 5th District of Indiana, office,
12 Talbott & News' Block, res. 100 n. Penn.
Hauk T. A., carpenter, res. alley. bet. Alabama and New
Jersey.
Hauley P., fireman, Gas Works.
Haupt Robert, store keeper, res. 7 Chatham.
Hauser A., works Schmidts' Brewery.
Hauser M., bar-keeper, Spencer House Saloon.
Houselman Jacob, laborer, res. 74 Fort Wayne ave.
Hauson J., shoemaker, bds. 103 w. Washington.
Hauson J., works Rolling Mill.
Harvey J., butcher, res. 57 s. New Jersey.
Hawes G. W., of H. & Redfield, bds. Palmer House.
Hawes S., traveling agent, for Asher & Adams, 4 Odd Fel-
lows Hall.
Hawrth H., moulder, Eagle Foundry.
Hawkins E., laborer, bds. 55 e. Ohio.
Hawkins John W., book-keeper, Purdy's Commercial Col-
lege.
HAWKINS MISS. M. A., MILLINER, Yohn's Block. See
card, page 146.
Hawley Miss P., teacher, at Institute for the Blind.
HAWTHORN CHAS. E., IMPORTER CHINA, GLASS
AND QUEENSWARE, 83 e. Washington, res. 98 e.
Maryland. See card, page 104.
Hawthorn Mrs. N. A., res. 103 e. Washington.
Hay Rev. L. G., res. 130 n. Tenn.
Hay W. H., chief clerk, Qr. Dep. U. S. A., bds. 156 e. Ohio.
Hayden Henry J., clerk, Provo Marshal Office, bds. 13 e.
Ohio
Hayden John J., attorney at law, off. Blackfords' Block,
res. 13 e. Ohio.
Hayden N., asst. clerk, Sinking Fund, res. Ohio, bet. Miss-
issippi and Canal.
Hayes David, laborer, res. 55 Huron.
Hayes Mrs. Elizabeth, res. 74 w. Vermont.
Hayns Lewis, traveling agent, Fairbanks' Scales, 74 w.
Washington.
Haynes Philip, confectioner, 40 w. Washington, res. 39 w.
Michigan.
Haynes Wm., cooper, res. w. Market, near California.
Hays A., clothier, 4 Spencer House, bds. same.
Hays A., clothier, res. 24 n. Mississippi.
Hays E. M., of H., Kahn & Co., res. 10 n. Mississippi.

GREAT CENTRAL

RAILWAY LINE!

BETWEEN

INDIANAPOLIS & COLUMBUS

Superior Eastern Route for Passengers and Freight.

2 THROUGH TRAINS DAILY!
WITHOUT CHANGE OF CARS.

CONNECTIONS ARE MADE AS FOLLOWS:

At Columbus with C. C. & C. Central Ohio and Steubenville Railroads for Cleveland, Buffalo, New York, Boston, Steubenville, Pittsburgh, Harrisburgh, Philadelphia, Newark, Zanesville, Wheeling, Baltimore, and Washington City.

At Urbana, for Clyde and Sandusky, and with Atlantic and Great Western Railway, the Great Broad Gauge Route, for New York, Boston and all Eastern Cities.

At Piqua, for Toledo and Detroit.

At Richmond, for Cincinnati, Hamilton, Dayton and Xenia.

☞Passengers and Shippers of Freight, by this line, through its connections at Urbana and Columbus, have the choice of the following Great Eastern Lines:—

Lake Shore Route and Erie and New York Central Roads, Atlantic and Great Western and Erie R. R., Pennsylvania Central, Baltimore and Ohio, an advantage offered by no other route from Indianapolis. Passengers go without change of cars over either the Dayton or Piqua Routes to Columbus.

SLEEPING CARS ON ALL NIGHT TRAINS!
Baggage Checked to all Important Points.

☞Through Tickets for sale at the Union Station, Indianapolis.

☞Call for Tickets, via "Great Central Line."

F. CHANDLER,
Gen'l Ticket Agent.

J. M. LUNT,
Gen'l Sup't.

Hays D. C., salesman, 84 w. Washington.
Hays Isaac C., res. 130 s. Meridian.
Hays James, carpenter, Eagle foundry.
Hays Jas. Mc. D., 1st clerk, Littles Hotel.
Hays L., clerk, with Hays, Kahn & Co., cor. Illinois and Washington.
Hays, Kahn & Co., clothiers, 83 s. Illinois.
HAYS, KAHN & CO., CLOTHING AND FURNISH-ING GOODS, cor. Illinois and Washington. See card, page 116.
Haywood A., carpenter, 129 c. Washington, res. same.
Head-quarters Superintendent Recruiting Service, office, Maryland, bet. Penn. and Delaware.
Healy Annie, wid., dress maker, res. 11 n. Alabama.
Healy B., fireman, works with W. S. Cameron.
Heaton Ely, farmer. res. 270 Indiana ave.
HEBBLE J. W., SALOON AND RESTAURANT, 248 e. Washington, res. 246 e. Washington. See card, p. 62.
Hebner Jacob, cooper, res. 9 Ellsworth.
Henf V., expressman, res. 71 n. Davidson.
Heckman C., flour and feed store, 266 e. Washington, res. same.
Heckman Rev. G. C., res. 134 n. Tenn.
Hedge A., conductor, Central R. R., res. 225 s. Penn.
Hedges Elijah, with Matthew Long, res. circle, one door e. Journal building.
Hedges J. H., cabinet maker, with Matthew Long.
Hedgebeth John, (col.) res. Howard, near First.
Hedrich Peter, machinist, works Union Cabinet Factory.
Heeker Chas., tinner, bds. 97 n. Penn.
Heicenrisch Christ., tailor, res. 50 Huron.
Heider S., piano maker, with G. Traeyser.
Heidelberg C., laborer, res. 109 n. Noble.
HEIDLINGER J. A., WHOLESALE DEALER IN CI-GARS AND TOBACCO, 3 Palmer House and 10 Bates House, res. 278 n. Illinois.
Heim John, clerk, Chas. Mayer.
Hein Chas., res. 154 n. Davidson.
Hein John R., res. cor. Michigan and National road.
Heine H., shoemaker, works with H. Knodle.
Heiner Anthony, night watchman, Indiana Central R. R., res. cor. Noble and Center.
Heiner John, bds. 70 n. East.
Heiner Julius, piano maker, res. 153 e. New York.
Heins Henry, laborer, res. 144 n. Davidson.
Heinninger Michael, machinist, res. 51 e. St. Joseph.
Heininger Richard, res. 51 Huron.
Heirmann J., undertaker, res. 112 e. Market.

Heiser Conrad, carpenter, res. Michigan, bet. Noble and Railroad.

Heiss Levi, grocer, res. cor. Tennessee and New York.

Heitcum Chas., laborer, res. 184 s. Delaware.

Heitkam Charles & Co., furniture dealers, 61 e. Washington.

HEITKAM G. H., MERCHANT TAILOR, 17 n. Illinois, res. 25 n. Liberty. See card, colored leaf.

Heitkam Geo., cabinet maker, res. 25 n. Liberty.

Heitkam John, cabinet maker, works Union Cabinet Factory.

Helet Morris, laborer, res. Keeley's Block, bet. New Jersey and East.

Hell John, laborer, res. 188 Massachusetts ave.

Hellman, Fred., res. Water.

Helm Adam, carpenter, res. 164 n. Liberty, res. cor. Liberty and North.

Helm Henry, res. 155 e. New York.

Helm John, grocer, res. 104 n. Davidson.

Helmstedder John, Tailor, res. 59 Mississippi.

Helwagen C. B., soldier, res. 232 n. New Jersey.

Helwig Chas., of Post, H. & Co., res. 50 n. Alabama.

Helwig Chas., of H. & Schamannxe, res. 50 n. Alabama.

Helwig Peter, works Rolling Mill.

Hemelton Mrs. Jane, res. 44 s. Noble.

Henderson D., salesman, Grover & Baker's sewing machine, 84 w. Washington, res. 52 Bates.

Henderson Joseph, farmer, res. Illinois, n. of Third.

HENDERSON WM., ATTORNEY, off. Ætna building, res. n. Meridian, beyond First. See card, near index.

HENDRICKS, EDMUNDS & CO., WHOLESALE DEALERS IN BOOTS AND SHOES, 40 s. Meridian, Schnull's Block.

Hendricks Isaac C., res. 52 e. Washington.

Hendricks J. C., Capt. 21st Regt. Ind. Vols.

Hendricks Thos. A., of H. & Hoard, bds. Bates House.

HENDRICKS V. K., of H. Edmunds & Co., bds. Mrs. Chapman's.

Hendricks & Hord, attorneys, off. Ætna building.

Henry Barney, laborer, res. cor. Orient and Washington.

Hennessy Daniel, works Gas House, 65 Bright.

HENNING FRED., bds. 152 s. New Jersey.

Henning H. R., of Spicer, H. & Co., res. 152 New Jersey.

Henninger C., of C. H. & Co., res. 87 s. Illinois.

Henninger C. & Co., cigar manufactory, 87 s. Illinois.

Henninger E., of Wilde & H., res. 71 s. Illinois.

Henninger G., of C. H. & Co., bds. Commercial Hotel.

Henninger R., printer, 51 Huron.

Henninger T., printer, bds. Georgia, bet. Meridian & Illinois.

Henry Adam, boarding house, 165 s. Delaware.
Henry Charles, soldier, bds. 61 St. Joseph.
Henry Frank, laborer, res. Tennessee, bet. South and Rolling Mill.
Henry J., carpenter, res. 227 s. Pennsylvania.
Henry John, laborer, res. 61 St. Joseph.
Henry Wm., steward, Soldiers' Home, res. West, bet. Georgia and Maryland.
Henricks Charles, laborer, res. 13 n. Noble.
Henschen Wm., of H. & Hildebrand, carpenters, res. 117 Virginia ave.
Henschen William, carpenter, res. 170 Virginia ave.
Hensley F. M., teamster, res. 233 s. Delaware.
Henson C., res. 76 Bluff road.
Henthorer L. S., assistant clerk, Spencer House.
Herald and Era, M. J. Lee, editor, 111 n. Illinois.
Herall Mrs. C., res. 24 n. Liberty.
Herbert Geo., professor, res. 14 n. Meridian.
HERETH JOHN C., SADDLERY, HARDWARE AND HARNESS MANUFACTURER, 89 e. Washington, res. 62 n. Alabama. See card, p. 34.
Hereth G. L., clerk, Bank of the State, bds. 8 Virginia ave.
Hereth L., clerk, with John Hereth, res. 181 e. Vermont.
Hereth Louis, harness maker, res. 181 e. Vermont.
Hereth Peter, carpenter, res. Vermont, bet. Noble and Spring.
Hereth Philip, harness maker, res. 181 e. Vermont.
Hering Philip, piano trimmer, res. Huron, bet. Noble and Liberty.
Herling B., tailor, res. 141 e. Market.
Herman J., salesman, Rice & Bamberger.
Herman Mrs. S. A., res. cor. First and Mississippi.
Hermann John, cabinet maker, wks. Union Cabinet Factory.
Hermaning Mrs. Christina, res. 13 n. Railroad.
Herniglack H., bar keeper, bds. 25 s. Meridian.
Herrmann Gustave, cabinet maker, wks. Union Cabinet Factory.
Herrmann Jacob, undertaker, 15 s. Delaware, res. 112 n. Market.
Herron F. M., watch maker, res. 92 n. Pennsylvania.
Hervey D. C., 170 e. Washington.
Hervey J. W. M., doctor, res. 123 n. Liberty.
Heshon David, laborer, res. Tennessee, bet. McCarty and South.
Heslink Bernhardt, tailor, res. 141 e. Market.
Hess Mrs., res. 68 e. Merrill.
Hess Frederick, res. 66 n. Ohio.
Hess Mrs. Susannah, res. 191 n. Noble.
11

Hess J. W., of Jones, H. & Davis, res. 17 Indiana ave.

Hetherington B. F., machinist, wks. I. & C. Machine Shop.

Hetherington **C.**, machinist, Washington Foundry.

Hettell J., porter, Mason House.

Hews R. A., bds. 88 Virginia ave.

HEWITT CHAS., ATTORNEY, 30½ w. Washington, 2d floor, bds. New York, near Indiana ave.

Hewitt Wm., harness maker, bds. Jack's boarding house.

HEZEKIAH H. E., SALOON, 13 n. Illinois, res. same.

Hiatt C. C., res. 107 Ohio.

Hibbard D. B., messenger, American Express Co.

HICKMAN & McARTHUR, BATES CITY MILLS, 282 e. Washington.

Hicky John, wks. Rolling Mill.

Hide John, wks. Rolling Mill.

Hider Chas., salesman, James Hess & Davis.

Hieber T. L., salesman, bds. 168 n. Alabama.

Hiecer C., blacksmith, res. Michigan, bet. Noble and Davidson.

Hiegl C., laborer, 137 e. Washington.

Higgins C. B., messenger, American Express Co.

Higgins Joseph B., carpenter, res. 25 Chatham.

Higgins W. B., silver plater, 8 w. Washington, res. 161 New Jersey.

Hight F., actor, Metropolitan Hall, res. 29 n. Liberty.

Hight L., soldier, res. e. Washington.

HILDEBRAND, HENSCHEN & CO., CARPENTERS, shop Walnut, bet. New Jersey and East.

Hild Christ., instrument maker, with Chas. Stoffens & Co.

HILDEBRAND H., of H. & Henschen, carpenters, res. North, bet. New Jersey & East.

Hildebrand J. S., book keeper, res. 7 Madison ave.

Hilgemier Herman, shoemaker, 53 e. South, res. Delaware, bet. McCarty and Merrill.

Hill A., wks. Rolling Mill.

Hill A. C., tailor, res. 18 n. East.

Hill D. F., of Webb & H., bds. 58 w. Vermont.

Hill E. C., traveling agent for Dawes, Evans & McMillin, bds. Spencer House.

Hill James, grocer, 146 w. Washington, res. same.

Hill J. B., clerk, Post Office.

Hill J. F., nursery, res. 38 n. Alabama.

Hill J. W., actor, Metropolitan Hall.

Hill L., clerk, bds. Bates House.

Hill L., wks. Rolling Mill.

Hill Mander, (col.) res. North, near Missouri.

Hill Nelson, laborer, res. 123 e. St. Clair.

Hill R., wks. Rolling Mill, res. Tenn., bet. McCarty & South.

Hill W. B., book keeper, res. 20 n. Mississippi.
Hill W., wks. Rolling Mill.
Hill Wm., wks. Ætna Mills.
Hill W. O., clerk, res. 26 n. Pennsylvania.
HILL & WINGATE, SAW AND PLANING MILLS,
  cor. Georgia and East.
Hillman L. C., M. D., off. 31½ w. Washington, 2d floor.
Hills L., general freight agent, Bellefontaine R. R., res. 49
  Maryland.
Hilt August, laborer, res. 153 n. Davidson.
Hilt C. W., bds. Palmer House.
Hilt F. L., res. 99 n. Maryland.
Hiltebrand J. M., marble cutter, res. 91 Indiana ave.
Hilton W. W., horse dealer, res. 183 Indiana ave.
Himbach Mrs. C., res. 44 s. East.
Hind P., grocery, res. 37 n. East.
Hinde E., of H. & Co., res. 37 n. East.
Hinde E. & Co., grocers, 155 e. Washington.
Hindman Mrs. Sarah, res. 34 Blackford.
Hines C. C., bds. 77 n. Delaware.
Hinesley A. J., of A. J. H. & Co., res. n. Tennessee.
HINESLEY A. J. & CO., SADDLE AND HARNESS MA-
  KERS, 34 w. Washington.
HINESLEY WILLIAM, LIVERY AND SALE STABLE,
  Pearl in rear Palmer House, res. 73 w. New York.
  See card, p. 108.
Hinighar Michael, machinist, res. cor. Delaware and St.
  Joseph.
Hinkle C., spinner, Merritt & Coughlan's Woolen Factory.
Hinkley O. W., clerk, with Asher & Adams, 4 Odd Fellows'
  Hall.
Hinnasy Daniel, wks. Gas Works, res. 65 Bright.
Hinton J., (col.) barber, res. 86 Douglas.
Hinton James, bar keeper, 78 w. Washington.
Hipes Mrs. A. A., res. 188 s. Tennessee.
Hippard Geo., clerk, 18 w. Washington, bds. 50 w. Ver-
  mont.
Hippard Samuel, clerk, res. 50 w. Vermont.
Hirschi F., wks. Schmidt's Brewery.
Hiss Sebastian, laborer, res. 271 n. Illinois.
Hitchew T., tailor, wks. 8 s. Pennsylvania, up stairs.
Hitchcock Alex., trader, res. 119 n. Alabama.
Hitchcock C., soldier, res. 149 e. Ohio.
Hitchens John, blacksmith, res. 157 Massachusetts ave.
Hoah J., carpenter, res. 51 w. McCarty.
Hoard O. B., of Hendricks & H., res. cor. New York and
  California.
Hobbs Mrs. L., res. 232 w. Washington.

Hock George, blacksmith, res. near cor. Noble and Washington.
Hocktter C., wks. Rolling Mill.
Hockmier J. A., wks. Rolling Mill.
Hodges J. A., actor, Metropolitan Hall.
Hodges James, res. 21 Ellsworth.
Hodges Richard, laborer, res. 91 e. St. Mary.
Hodgson Isaac, architect, 8 Yohn's Block, res. Illinois.
Hodgson Isaac, res. 135 n. Meridian.
Hoefgen S. B., attorney, Johnson's Building.
Hoereth John G., carpenter, res. 117 n. East.
Hoerst II., tailor, res. 233 s. Pennsylvania.
Hoffanbaker J., res. 181 s. Tennessee.
Hofferberth Wm., laborer, res. 69 Bright.
Hofmann Casper, blacksmith, res. 224 n. Alabama.
Hofmeier Henry, tailor, res. Liberty, bet. New York and Vermont.
Hofmeister John, grocery, bds. cor. Noble and New York.
HOFMEISTER NICK., GROCERY, res. cor. Noble & New York.
HOFMEISTER N. & J., GROCERS, cor. Noble and New York.
Hoffman Geo., wks. Rolling Mill.
Hoffman H., shoemaker, wks. with L. Wachter.
Hoffman M., blacksmith, Washington Foundry.
Hoffman P., laborer, res. Illinois, 4 doors s. of McCarty.
Hoffman V., laborer, res. 68 s. Noble.
Hoffman T., salesman, Hume, Lord & Co., res. cor. Tennessee and Ohio.
Hoffmier Wm., driver, A. & U. S. Express Co.
Hogan Dan'l, salesman, bds. Oriental House.
Hagon Michael, laborer, res. Sharp's Addition, near e. Washington.
Hogan W., moulder, wks. with D. Root & Co.
Hogan Wm., stove moulder, res. 95 s. Market.
Hogarty M., marbleworker, res. 188 Virginia ave.
Hogle S., carriage maker, res. 180 s. Illinois.
Hogshire A., res. 80 w. Georgia.
Hogshire S. H., of W. R. H. & Co.
HOGSHIRE, W. R. & CO., WHOLESALE AND RETAIL GROCERS, 25 w. Washington.
Hogshire W. R., of W. R. H. & Co., res. 82 n. Pennsylvania.
Hogue O. H., expressman, res. 54 Indiana ave.
HOHL CHRIST, GROCER, 77 e. Washington, res. same.
Hohnan James R., salesman, Jones, Hess & Davis.
Hoit Mrs. Harriet, res. 64 Massachusetts ave.
Holbrook H. C., book keeper, bds. 77 n. Alabama.
Holbrook Thos. E., book keeper, res. 77 n. Alabama.

Holdzkom C. H., whip maker, res. McOuat's Building, Kentucky ave.

Holford E. W., printer, 24 w. Washington, res. 114 e. Vermont.

Holidg W., laborer, res. Michigan, bet. Noble and Liberty.

Hollacher Eusebius, clerk, res. 249 s. Delaware.

Holladay E. G., attorney and notary public, 10 s. Meridian res. 153 n. Illinois.

Holland F. K., clerk, bds. Little's Hotel.

Holland Geo., painter, bds. Dickey's boarding House.

Holland John, carpenter, res. 217 s. Delaware.

Holland John, laborer, res. 177 s. East.

Holland J. W., of J. W. H. & Son, res. 58 n. Penn.

Holland J. W. & Son, wholesale grocers, 72 e. Washington.

Holland T. F., of J. W. Holland & Son, res. 8 e. Michigan.

Holland T., res. 8 e. Michigan.

Holler Philip H., machinist, res. 117 n. Noble.

Holler Wm., cabinet maker, res. 165 n. Noble.

Hallett Thos., res. Liberty, bet. New York and Michigan.

Holliday F. C., minister, res. 117 e. Ohio.

Holliday Wm. A., minister, res. 102 n. Alabama.

Holliday W. J., of W. J. H. & Co , res. 145 n. Penn.

HOLLIDAY W. J. & CO., IRON AND STEEL DEPOT, 34 e. Washington.

Holloway W. R., res. 122 n. Illinois.

Holly T., shoemaker, res. 19 Kentucky ave.

Holly P., shoemaker, 87 w. Washington, res. 19 Kentucky ave.

HOLMAN G. G., PRODUCE AND COMMISSION MERCHANT, 95 e. Washington, res. Ft. Wayne ave.

HOLMES C. L., GROCER, 31 w. Washington, res. 42 Mississippi. See card, page 120.

Holmes James, carpenter, bds. 36 n. Spring.

Holmes J. H., printer, Journal office.

Holmes Jonathan, res. 141 n. Meridian.

Holmes Wm., clerk, res. 59 e. Market.

HOLTON J. L., PROP'R BATES HOUSE, cor. Illinois and Washington.

Holtrof J. C., A. & U. S. Express, bds. Pyle House.

Homan J., cistern builder, res. 17 Virginia ave.

HOME MUTUAL FIRE INS. CO. OF INDIANAPOLS, off. 9 Bates House Block. See card, front cover.

Hook J., res. e. Washington.

Hooker E. M. B., 20th Ind. Regt.

Hooker Henry, agent T. H. & R. R. R., Freight Office, res. 145 e. South.

Hooper W., blacksmith, res. 219 s. Penn.

Hoover Wm. C., miller, Douglas.

Hopkins Chas. G., clerk, with Isaac Davis, 15 n. Pennsylvania, bds. 60 s. Illinois.

Hopkins J. H., book binder, bds. 20 California.

Hopkins J. H., agent, New York Central R. R., res. 60 s. Illinois.

Hoppe G., saloon, res. 81 s. Meridian.

Hopper L. M., carpenter, res. 114 n. Alabama.

Hord Oscar B., attorney, res. cor. California and New York.

Hording Clinton, teamster, res. 29 n. Noble.

Hord H. J., City Grocery, res. 42 Mississippi.

Horm John, machinist, res. 38 s. Illinois.

Hornaday John, carpenter, res. 220 Mass. ave.

Hornaday J. E. of H. & Small, res. 131 n. Alabama.

Horton John, student, bds. 107 s. Alabama.

Hosfeld Louis, clerk, Chas. Mayer, bds. Union Hall.

Hoshour S. K., Prof. of Languages, res. 74 n. East.

Hoslinger L., blacksmith, works Bellefontaine Car Shop.

Hoss David, laborer, res. 359 Virginia ave.

Hoss Nelson, school teacher, 133 West.

Hossfeld Chas., bds. 256 e. Washington.

Hotrict Jasper, machinist, res. 68 n. Noble.

Hotz G., of H. & Co., bds. Commercial Hotel.

Hots G. & Co., clothiers, 69 s. Illinois.

Hough J. R., of Fletcher, Vajen & Co., res. 89 n. N. Jersey.

House Chas., butcher, res. 57 s. New Jersey.

HOUSE OF LORDS SALOON, J. PEARSON & CO. PROP'S, 78 w. Washington. See card, opp. back cover.

Hautzger H., laborer, res. 262 Madison R. R. ave.

Howard A. C., news depot, adjoining Post-office, res. 13 n. Alabama.

Howard Dr. E., of Dr. E. H. & Son, res. 52 s. Illinois.

Howard Dr. E. & Son, cancer physicians, 52 s. Illinois.

Howard Henry, carpenter, res. 194 e. St. Clair.

Howard M., laborer, res. 22 Nelson Alley.

Howard Wm. E., foreman, Government Stable, bds. 136 e. St. Clair.

Howder W., moulder, Washington Foundry.

Howet Mrs. Louisa, res. 79 n. East.

Howland J. A., pressman, with Dood & Co., res. 159 n. East.

Howland J. D., of Barbour & H., res. n. e. cor. Vermont and Tenn.

Hoyt L., blacksmith, with Case & Marsh.

Hoyt W., photographist, bds. cor. Penn. and Market.

Hubacher J., laborer, works with J. Fishback.

Hubard Hannah, res. 3 Elm.

Hubbard Alfred, cooper, res. 30 s. West.

Hubbard Wm., laborer, res. cor. Illinois and Merrill.

Hubbard W. S., of City Bank, res. 9 Circle.

Hudnut Theodore, hominy mill, Pennsylvania, bet. Maryland and South, res. 40 s. Penn.

Hudson C., laborer, with A. Stephens & Son.

Hudson Henry, bar-keeper, res. 51 e. South.

Hues J., railroader, res. 229 s. Penn.

Hues Mrs. E., 229 s. Penn.

Huestis John B., engineer, T. H. & R. R. R., res. 15 Henry.

Huey Milton, artist, res. 84 w. Georgia.

Huey M. S., of Smith & Huey, res. 84 w. Georgia.

Huff B. F., printer, bds. Spencer House.

Huffer John, harnessmaker, with A. J. Hincsley & Co.

Huffer James, of A. J. Hincsley & Co., res. Virginia ave.

Huffer Jas. M., saddler, res. Virginia ave., near 8th ward school house.

Huffman H., tanner, res. 197 e. Washington.

Huffmyer, F., porter, State offices.

Hug Mrs. Christiana, res. 45 n. New Jersey.

Hughes F., works Rolling Mill.

Hughey Wm., res. 88 e. Louisiana.

HUGELE JOHN, SALOON AND SUMMER GARDEN, 128 e. Washington, res. same. See card, page 68.

Hugo Henry, plasterer, res. 249 s. East.

Hughes Joseph, clerk, New York Store, bds. 20 s. Miss.

Hug John, blacksmith, res. 3 n. Noble.

Hugh Mrs. Mina, res. 65 n. Noble.

Hughran McMullan, laborer, 35 Huron.

Hulings J. P., house and sign painter, Market, bet. Pennsylvania and Delaware, res. 3 e. South.

Hull R. L., tallyman, Bellefontaine freight depot, res. 160 s. Alabama.

Hull Wm., teamster, res. cor. Tenn. and Fifth.

Hume E., clerk, with F. L. Mahan, bds. 75 n. Miss.

Hume J. N., salesman, Hume, Lord & Co., bds. 75 n. Miss.

Hume Jas. M., of H. Lord & Co., res. 77 n. Miss.

Hume, Lord & Co., dealers in fancy and staple dry goods, 26 and 28 w. Washington.

Hume Rev. M., res. 75 n. Miss.

Humler Max., confectioner, res. 92 w. New Jersey.

HUMMLER M. B., CONFECTIONER, 21 n. Penn., res. 24 n. Penn. See card, page 88.

Humphrey C. F., watchmaker, with C. G. French, bds. Little's Hotel.

Humphrey James, cooper, 178 w. Washington, res. Douglas, n. of New York.

Humphry John, cooper, 228 Indiana ave.

Humphry S., res. 109 w. Michigan.

Hunn H. H., clerk, res. 63 s. Illinois.

Hunt A., mechanic, res. 180 s. Peru.

HUNT A. L. & CO., AUCTIONEERS AND COMMISSION MERCHANTS, 81 e. Washington. See card, p. 68.

Hunt A. L., A. L. H. & Co., res. cor. East and St. Clair.

HUNT C. C., CIGAR MANUFACTURER, 61 e. Washington, res. same. See card, page 88.

Hunt D. B., clerk, U. S. Mustering office, res. 22 w. New York.

Hunt Mrs. Julia, res. 6 Circle.

Hunt P. G. C., dentist, off. 32 e. Market.

Hunt Silas, pump maker, res. 93 Mass. ave.

Hunt Thos. E., stove manufactory, 14 Miss.

Hunt W. W., clerk, res. cor. East and St. Clair.

Hunt Wm., carpenter, res. 124 e. Michigan.

Hunter M., of M. H. & Co., bds. Bates House.

HUNTER M. & CO., BOOTS AND SHOES, 19 e. Washington.

Hunter Ralph, machinist, res. 72 s. East.

Huntsinger E., off. 23½ n. Miss.

Hurd D. B., boarding house, res. 84 n. Tenn.

Hurd E., res. 163 n. Mississippi.

Hurley F., hackman, res. 81 Bluff road.

Hurrle Ignatz, tailor, res. 23 n. Noble.

Hussey Edmond, teamster, res. 162 Indiana ave.

Husted H. C., tanner and currier, res. 15 McCarty.

Huston C. B., salesman, res. 51 e. Ohio.

Huston Geo., huckster, res. 112 w. Vermont.

Hutchins Mrs. E. C., dress maker, res. 36 n. Illinois.

Hutchins H. H., book-keeper, res. 148 Virginia ave,

HUTCHINSON C. P., PRINTER, firm H. H. Dood & Co. res. 45 n. Penn.

Hutchison Wm., machinist, res. Massachusetts ave., bet. St. Clair and railroad crossing.

HYDE A. R., PROP'R LITTLE'S HOTEL. See card, page 58.

Hyde & Bogle, livery and sale stable, Washington, bet. N. Jersey and East.

Hyeland James, brick mason, res. cor. Fifth and Illinois.

Hyeland Michael, brick mason, res. Illinois, n. of Third.

Hyer Frank, brakesman, res. 35 s. Liberty.

I

Idler Clinton, foreman, T. H. & R. R. R. Machine Shop, res. 113 w. South.

Igale Isaiah, hats and gents' furnishing goods, 50 s. Illinois, bds. Pyle House.

Igo Patrick, laborer, Eagle Foundry.

Igoe Martin, quartermaster, res. Loukabee, bet. East and Liberty.

Igon J. W., boarding stable, res. 22 w. Maryland.
Ihndrisz John, carpenter, res. 68 c. St. Joseph.
Ihroll Isaac, res. 133 n. Illinois.
ILG GEO., PROPRIETOR UNION HOUSE, cor. South
and Illinois. See card, p. 54.
Iliff Joseph, laborer, res. 46 n. Liberty.
ILIFF JOSEPH, GROCER, 250 c. Washington, res. same.
See card, p. 112.
Iliff Richard W., res. 37 n. Alabama.
INDEPENDENT DETECTIVE POLICE, off. cor. Illinois
and Louisiana.
INDIANA FIRE INSURANCE CO., off. 5 Odd Fellows'
Hall. See card, p. 110.
Indiana Free Press, 36 c. Washington.
Indiana School Journal, monthly, 37 c. Washington, up
stairs.
Indiana State Sentinel, daily and weekly, Elder, Harkness
& Bingham, proprietors, Sentinel Building, cor. Meri-
dian and Pearl.
INDIANA U. S. ARSENAL, Market, bet. Tennessee and
Mississippi.
Indiana Volksblatt, Julius Boetticher, editor, 130 c. Wash-
ington.
Indianapolis Baptist Female Institute, Rev. C. W. Howes,
principal, cor. Pennsylvania and North.
Indianapolis Branch Banking Co., Calvin Fletcher, presi-
dent, T. H. Sharpe, cashier, s. w. cor. Washington and
Pennsylvania.
Indianapolis Chamber of Commerce, T. B. Elliott, president,
J. Barnard, secretary, rooms Exchange Building, n.
Illinois.
Indiana Fire Insurance Co., —— Gibson, secretary, gen-
eral off. Odd Fellows' Hall. See card, p. 110.
INDIANAPOLIS McLEAN FEMALE COLLEGE, REV.
CHARLES STURDEVANT, PRESIDENT, cor. Meri-
dian and New York.
Indianapolis Gas Light and Coke Co., Samuel Van Laning-
ham, secretary, off. Ray's Building.
INDIANAPOLIS GAS WORKS, Pennsylvania, bet. South
and Pogus Run.
INDIANAPOLIS GAZETTE, DAILY AND WEEKLY,
JOHNSON H. JORDAN, EDITOR AND PROPRIE-
TOR, 14 and 16 s. Meridian.
Indianapolis Gymnasium Club, rooms 32 s. Meridian.
Indianapolis Journal, daily and weekly, off. Journal Build-
ing, cor. Meridian and Circle.
INDIANAPOLIS JOURNAL CO., J. M. TILFORD, PRE-
SIDENT, Journal Building, cor. Meridian and Circle.

INDIANAPOLIS ROLLING MILL CO., J. M. LORD, PRESIDENT, JOHN THOMAS, MANAGER, off. 8 Blake's Block.

Indianapolis Rolling Mill, s. Tennessee, s. of R. R.

INDIANAPOLIS & CHICAGO AIR LINE, via Kokomo and C. & C. air line, off. Peru & Indianapolis R. R. office.

INDIANAPOLIS & CINCINNATI RAILROAD, offices cor. Delaware and Louisiana.

INDIANAPOLIS AND CINCINNATI FREIGHT DEPOT, s. Delaware, bet. Maryland and South.

INDIANAPOLIS & PERU R. R., freight office, cor. New Jersey and Union track, general ticket office, cor. Washington and Delaware, D. Macy, superintendent, V. T. Malott, ticket agent.

Indicutte J. W., (col.) whitewasher, res. 86 Douglas.

Ingham J., stone cutter, bds. Mechanics' Boarding House.

Ingles Alexander, wks. Indiana Central R. R. Machine Shop.

Inwall Benj., bar-keeper, Atlantic Saloon.

Ireland W. H., carpenter, cor. Vermont and Ellsworth.

Irick William H., brick mason, res. 156 n. New Jersey.

Irish G., bar-keeper, bds. Palmer House.

Irons Harry, messenger, with Union Telegraph, bds. 119 w. Maryland.

Irons Mrs. C., res. 119 Maryland.

Irwin Sam'l N., salesman, E. H. Mayo & Co., bds. 159 Virginia ave.

Isaac M., clerk, 10 w. Washington.

Isaacs Isaac, watchman, Bates House.

Isgrigg James, of I. & Brackin, res. cor. California and Maryland.

Isgrigg & Brackin, lumber yard, Market, bet. Mississippi and Canal.

Ish Frank, laborer, res. 16 Georgia.

Iske Wm., carpenter, res. 109 e. Ohio.

Ittenbach F., of Smith, I. & Co., res. Pennsylvania, bet. Merrill and McCarty.

Ittenbach G., of Smith, I. & Co., res. Pennsylvania, bet. Merrill & McCarty.

Ittenbach Gerard, marble yard, res. 180 s. Delaware.

Ivens & Co., cloak and millinery store, 1 s. Meridian.

J

Jacob Chas., works Rolling Mill.

Jacobs Richard, box maker, with Burton & Shilling, bds Pyle House.

Jacobs V., marble business, res. 58 e. Maryland.

Jackson A. A., blacksmith, with Case & Marsh.

Jackson H., blacksmith, with Case & Marsh.

Jackson John T., law student, with Hendricks & Hord, bds. 68 Vermont.

Jack M. W., boarding house, 44 n. Penn.

Jackson Thos. B., clerk with Williams & Van Camp.

Jackson Wm., slate roofer, res. 26 n. Liberty.

Jackson W. N., Gen. Ticket Agt., Secy. and Treas. Union R. R. Co., bds. Dr. Gatlins.

Jaeger John, butcher, res. 39 n. Spring.

Jaeger Wm., drayman, res. 166 n. Noble.

James Seth, res. 24 c. Huron.

James G. E., engineer, res. 174 c. Washington.

James O. H., Asst. Buckeye Saloon, res. $18\frac{1}{2}$ n. New Jersey.

James S. C., marble worker, res. 24 Huron.

James W. W., of W. W. J. & Co., res. n. Illinois.

James W. W. & Co., marble dealers, 58 s. Meridian.

Jameson Rev. L. H., Christian Church, res. 97 w. South.

Jameson P. H., physician, of J. & Funkhouser, res. 51 n. Alabama.

Jameson & Funkhouser, physicians, 5 s. Meridian.

Jamison F., fireman, Mason House.

Jaquess J. H., butcher, Missouri, bet. Market and Ohio.

Jarvis Thos., moulder, works Wiggins & Chandlers.

Jasper A., (col.) wood sawyer, res. cor. Second and Mo.

Jasper Fred., grocer, cor. Delaware and McCarty, res. same.

Jasper H., laborer, res. Wyoming, bet. Delaware and High.

Jaycox Orlin R., grocer, res. cor. Illinois and South.

Jaycox & Fitzhugh, wholesale grocers, also manufacturers of tobacco, opp. Union Depot.

Jefferson House, cor. South and Penn.

JEFFERSONVILLE R. R. OFFICE, at Madison Depot.

Jefferson Robert, carpenter, res. 37 Missouri.

Jeffry Mrs. S., res. Market, near cor. California.

Jenison A. F., watch maker, res. 9 w. Ohio.

Jenison G. M., of W. H. Talbott & Co., res. 9 w. Ohio.

Jenison Mrs. H., res. 9. w. Ohio.

Jenkins Avanesy, paper hanger, res. 32 e. Ohio.

Jenkins A. W. & J., grocers, cor. North and Penn.

Jenkins George, carpenter, res. 215 Mass. ave.

Jenkins G. W., laborer, res. 184 n. Delaware.

Jenkins J., of A. W. & J. J., res. 126 e. Market.

Jenkins John, grocer, res. 126 c. Market.

Jenkins W. S., feed stable, 31 s. Penn.

Jenning Geo., conductor, I. & M. R. R.

Jenings G., railroader, res. 108 e. McCarty.

Jennings Pat., teacher, res. 133 n. Davidson.

Jennings W. T., res. First, bet. Illinois and Meridian.

Jewell Miss E. M., teacher, Indianapolis Female College.

Jodchimi Augustus, candle factory, res. 93 w. Maryland.

Johumrsson Clans., shoemaker, res. 32 n. Spring.
John C., res. 199 e. Washington.
Johnson Aaron, grocer, Mississippi, near First.
Johnson Andrew, brakesman, bds. Ray House.
Johnson A. T., carpenter, res. 38 Michigan road.
Johnson A. W., carpenter, res. 57 w. South.
Johnson Capt. B. F., of 4th Indiana Battery, res. 171 s.
     Mississippi.
Johnson Benj., hack driver, res. 280 Indiana ave.
Johnson Chas., works Rolling Mill.
Johnson C. R., bar-keeper, bds. 246 e. Washington.
Johnson Christ., works Rolling Mill.
Johnson D., brick maker, res. 9 Eddy.
Johnson Daniel, with McCord & Wheatly.
Johnson D. T. A., res. 56 s. Illinois.
Johnson Mrs. Elizabeth, res. Clinton, bet. Ohio and East.
Johnson E. C., res. Meridian, bet. Merrill and McCarty.
Johnson G., (col.) laborer, bds. 34 e. Maryland.
Johnson Geo., blacksmith, res. 74 e. Louisiana.
Johnson Geo., clerk, res. 240 s. Alabama.
Johnson Geo. H., salesman, bds. 121 e. Ohio.
Johnson Geo H., res. cor. Third and Illinois.
Johnson Isaac, carpenter, bds. bet. Delaware and Penn.
Johnson Isaac E., carpenter, bds. North.
Johnson J. A., bds. 57 w. South.
Johnson I. E., real estate broker, res. 58 n. Michigan.
Johnson James, harness maker, 78 Bluff road, res. 90 Bluff
     road.
Johnson James E., gardner, res. 76 Elm.
Johnson James, carpenter, res. 38 Michigan road.
Johnson Jesse, salesman, 17 w. Washingion, bds. Pyle
     House.
Johnson John, physician, cor. Washington and Alabama,
     res. same.
Johnson John, works Rolling Mill.
Johnson John, cutter, with Owen McGinnis, res. 39 Wal-
     nut.
Johnson John B., inspector, Subsistance Depot, res. 101 w.
     Maryland.
Johnson I. E., real estate broker, 4 Blakes Block, res. cor.
     Ohio and Miss.
Johnson J. S., carpenter, res. Meridian, bet. Merrill and
     McCarty.
Johnson J. W., carpenter, works Washington Foundry.
Johnson M. A., res. I. & C. R. R., bet. Alabama and New
     Jersey.
Johnson Melville, brick mason, res. 110 Miss.
JOHNSON M. L., PUBLISHER, res. Illinois, near cor. First.

Johnson Philip, carpenter, res. 155 n. East.
Johnson Robert, hack driver, res. North.
Johnson U. S., police, res. cor. St. Clair and James.
Johnson W., moulder, works with D. Root & Co.
Johnson Wm., grocer, cor. Garden and Tenn., res. same.
Johnson Wm., res. 43 West.
Johnson Wm., farmer, res. 160 Blake.
Johnson Wm., hackman, res. 110 Blake.
Johnson W. H. H., bds. Meridian, bet. Merrill and Mc-
Carty.
Johnson W. J., of Munson & J., res. 86 e. Vermont.
Johnson W. S., moulder, res. 262 s. Delaware.
Johnson W. W., printer, Journel office.
Johnson Samuel, (Pindy,) printer, works Dodd & Co., bds.
Ohio, bet. Pennsylvania and Meridian.
Johnston Mrs. Fidelia, seamstress, res. 184 n. East.
Johnston John F., dentist, off. and res. 11 w. Maryland.
Johnston J. H., clerk, res. 17 Mass. ave.
Johnston Mrs. Mary, res. 219 n. New Jersey.
Johnston O. N., res. 172 e. South.
Johnston Samuel A., book-keeper, Munson & Johnston, bds.
86 e. Vermont.
Johnston T. D., clerk, New York Store, res. 17 Mass. ave.
Johnston Wm. J., Munson & Johnston, res. 86 e. Vermont.
Johnston W. W., printer, res. 112 e. Vermont.
Johnston W. W., of Murphy, Kennedy & Co., res. 161 n.
Pennsylvania.
Jolley Joseph, blacksmith, res. 1 cor. Huron and Noble.
Jolly G., watchman, I. & C. R. R., res. 11 Lord.
Jolly John, labore., res. 11 Lord.
Jolly Wm. E., painter. res. 76 s. East.
Jolly Wm., works I. & C. machine shop.
Jones A., Treasurer of Ind. Rolling Mill Co., off. 8 Blakes
Block.
Jones Aquilla, sr., of J. Vinnedge & Co., res. 79 n. Penn.
Jones Aquilla, jr., of J., Vinnedge & Co., res. 79 n. Penn-
sylvania.
Jones Barton D., of Delzell & J., res. 66 n. Delaware.
Jones C., blacksmith, bds. Macy House.
Jones Caper, tailor, res. 137 e. South.
Jones Charles, (col.) barber, bds. William Wallace's.
Jones E., res. 79 n. Pennsylvania.
Jones E., (col.) laborer, res. 49 w. Georgia.
Jones E. C., salesman, 17 w. Washington, bds. Oriental
House.
Jones Fleming J., broom maker, res. cor. n. Illinois and
Tinker.
Jones George, farmer, res. n. Illinois, near Third.

JONES, HESS & DAVIS, DEALERS IN DRY GOODS,
3 Odd Fellows' Hall, e. Washington. See card, p. facing front cover.
Jones Jessee, res. 106 n. Illinois.
Jones John, wks. Rolling Mill.
Jones J., (col.) laborer, wks. with W. F. Jenkins.
Jones Col. J. G., assistant superintendent recruiting service, bds. Oriental House.
Jones J. L., res. 135 n. Alabama.
Jones J. M., harness maker, res. near cor. New Jersey and Massachusetts ave.
Jones John P., clerk, Superior Court, 27 w. Washington.
Jones J. W., yard master, T. H. & R. R. R., res. 75 w. South.
Jones J. W., with Jones, Vinnedge Co., res. 79 n. Pennsylvania.
Jones L., res. cor. McCarty and Illinois.
Jones Lewis H., harness maker, bds. n. w. cor. Illinois and McCarty.
Jones Luther, farmer, res. w. Indianapolis.
Jones Mrs. M. A., res. 154 w. Vermont.
Jones M. C., salesman, Jones, Hess & Davis.
Jones N. W., moulder, Washington Foundry.
Jones Robert, stair builder, res. 169 n. Noble.
Jones Spicer, sutler, 47th regiment, res. cor. Illinois and Walnut.
JONES, VINNEDGE & CO., WHOLESALE AND RETAIL BOOTS AND SHOES, 17 w. Washington.
Jones W., (col.) barber, bds. Macy House.
Jones W. B., switchman, res. 157 s. Alabama.
Jones W. H., of Coburn & J., res. 169 n. Illinois.
Jones W. M., clerk, Mason House.
Jones W. T., carpenter, res. 9 Fletcher's ave.
Jones W. W., of J., Hess & Davis, res. 114 n. Pennsylvania.
Jordan E. G., res. 104 n. Tennessee.
Jordan J. H., editor and proprietor Indianapolis Daily Gazette, res. Pennsylvania.
JORDAN JOHN, GROCER, 144 w. Washington, res. 108 n. Mississippi.
Jordan S. J., agent Daily Journal, res. 157 Mississippi.
Jordan T., of J. & Spotts, bds. Palmer House.
Jordan Thos., bds. 188 s. Tennessee.
Jordan Wm., barber, res. 99 n. Meridian.
Jordan & Spotts, commission merchants, cor. Pennsylvania and Union R. R. track.
Jorger John & Bro., meat shop, 200 e. Washington.
Jose Albert, frame maker, bds. Union Hall.
Jose N., furniture store, 4 s. Pennsylvania.
Joseph G. W., clerk, Post Office.

Joseph J. G., salesman, 2 Palmer House, bds. Oriental House.

Joseph R. C., Court House, res. California, bet. New York and Vermont.

Journal Building, cor. Circle and Meridian.

Joyce E., laborer, res. 245 s. Pennsylvania.

Judd Fred., carder, Merritt & Coughlan's Woolen Factory, res. w. Market.

Judge Tom, wks. Rolling Mill.

Judge James, laborer, res. Wyoming, bet. Delaware and High.

Judge Jos., wks. Rolling Mill.

JUDSON CHAS. E., GROCER, res. 97 n. Illinois.

Judson Henry, clerk, bds. Palmer House.

Julius R., tinner, res. 256 s. Delaware.

Justus L. L., carpenter, res. 108 e. McCarty.

Juse Joseph, government teamster, res. 176 Mass. ave.

K

KABIS LEOPOBD, DEALER IN FRUITS, CONFEC-TIONERY AND VEGETABLES, Illinois, front of meat market, Bates House Block, bds. 149 s. Tennessee.

Kady D. L., boots and shoes, 20 e. Washington, res. 112 n. New Jersey.

Kahl Criff, res. cor. Massachusetts ave. and East.

Kahler James, wks. Wiggins & Chandler's.

Kahle S. F., master cabinet shop, Deaf and Dumb Asylum.

Kahle S. F., clerk, R. R. office, res. cor. Vermont and East.

Kahl S. V., clerk, res. cor. Vermont and East.

Kahn A., clothier, 2 Palmer House.

Kahn J., clothier, res. 16 s. Mississippi.

Kahn L., clothier, 35 e. Washington, bds. 16 Mississippi.

Kahn Moris, of Hays, K. & Co., res. Mississippi.

Kahoa Michael, res. 52 e. South.

Kain Robert, moulder, Eagle Foundry.

Kalb Henry, gas lighter, res. 98 e. St. Joseph.

Kalb Philip, laborer, res. 65 e. St. Mary.

Kamb Christ., laborer, res. 130 n. Davidson.

Kamm G., laborer, with Spiegel, Thoms & Co.

Kammel Eli, preacher, res. 14 Michigan road.

Kane Dennis, blacksmith, res. 88 Benton.

Kane D., blacksmith, Washington Foundry.

Kappes J. H., of Seidensticker & K., res. North, bet. Alabama and Delaware.

Kares Joseph, carpenter, res. 58 n. Davidson.

Karle C., boot and shoe store, 73 e. Washington, res. 72 s. Delaware.

Karle J. J., shoemaker, res. 33 South.

Karnell J., laborer, Washington Foundry.
Karnetz John, wks. 16 w. Washington.
Karney John, gas fitter, res. 131 s. Alabama.
Karnitz John, shoemaker, with Jones, Vinnedge & Co.
Karntz J., shoemaker, res. 137 e. Washington.
Kasberg P., moulder, Washington Foundry.
Kase John B., engineer, res. 75 n. Noble.
Kasting F. L., of Brinkmeyer & Co., res. 82 n. East.
Katzman C., clerk, bds. Spencer House.
Katzenstein Julius, of K. & Wachtel, res. cor. Meridian and
    Georgia.
Katzenstein & Wachtel, merchant tailors, 3 Bates House.
Kaufman Aaron, tobacco agent, res. 143 n. Pennsylvania.
Kaufman G. A., collar maker, 66 s. Delaware.
Kaufmann Morris, butcher, res. 117 n. East.
Kaufman S., wholesale liquor and tobacco store, 209 e.
    Washington.
Kautman C. J., salesman, with Jones, Hess & Davis.
Kawn Mrs. H. A., res. 144 e. North.
Kay Joseph, wagon maker, 205 w. Washington, res. 114 w.
    Ohio.
Kearney John, foreman Gas Works.
Keating J. J., bar-keeper, 71 s. Pennsylvania.
Keatinge Joseph, saloon, res. 69 s. Pennsylvania.
Keckest Gottfreed, res. 143 e. Market.
Keean J., engineer, Journal office.
Keehn H. W., of Tarlton & K., res. n. Mississippi.
Keeley Oliver, brick mason, res. 157 e. Ohio.
Keeley W. H., grocer, res. 163 e. Ohio.
Keeley Daniel, brick mason, res. 105 n. Noble.
Keelmeier Henry, laborer, I. & M. R. R. Freight Depot.
Keely Henry S., printer, with Dodd & Co., res. cor. Ohio
    and Liberty.
Keely Isaac I., physician and surgeon, res. 62 e. Michigan.
Keely John, bricklayer, res. 48 n. East.
Keely Joseph, carpenter, res. 147 e. Ohio.
Keely William, sr., res. 62 e. Michigan.
Keely Wm. H., grocer, res. 163 e. Ohio.
Keen Mrs. Kelay, res. 43 n. Tennessee.
Keen Hiram, grocery, res. 72 n. Mississippi.
Keen J., (col.) engineer, Journal off., bds. 151 n. Alabama.
Keenan Mrs. Margaret, res. 61 s. Noble.
Keesee Wm. N., grocer, cor. Blake and North, res. same.
Keffer Jacob, machinist, res. 155 s. Miss.
Kehler Frank, hack driver, res. 74 n. Noble.
Kehler Jerre, res. 127 e. New York.
Kehler Wm., white washer, res. 44 n. Spring.
Kehing Barnhardt, res. 157 n. Liberty.

Kehrer Mrs. Louisa, res. 90 e. St. Joseph.
Kehs John, engineer, res. n. Noble.
Keifer A., of K. & Rush, res. 138 e. McCarty.
Keiser Dr. ——, off. 133 Virginia ave.
Keiser Kate, res. 50 Mass. ave.
Keiser J., machinist, works Washington Foundry.
Keifer & Rush, commission merchants, 74 s. Meridian.
Keker Sophia, (wid.) res. 168 n. New Jersey.
Kelcher James, shoemaker, res. 9 s. New Jersey.
Kelleher David, peddler, res. Illinois, n. of Third.
Keller D., stone cutter, res. 82 e. Vermont.
Keller F., editor, Indiana Free Press, 272 n. New Jersey.
Keller Z. P., machinist, res. Meek.
Kellog Newton, res. cor. West and Market.
Kelley James, works Rolling Mill, res. 168 s. Tenn.
Kelley Mrs. J., res. 168 s. Tennessee.
Kelley J. E., clerk, res. 11 n. Meridian.
Kelley John, works Rolling Mill, bds. 168 s. Tennessee.
Kelly Cornelius, painter, res. 55 e. Maryland.
Kelly J., laborer, bds. 32 s. Illinois.
Kelly J., fireman, Gas Works.
Kelly James, peddler, res. 66 Bluff Road.
Kelly J. B., works Rolling Mill.
Kelly John, works Gas Co., res, Illinois, below McCarty.
Kelly L., currier, res. 11 McCarty.
Kelly W., porter, Little's Hotel.
Kelso ——, res. 173 s. Mississippi.
Kemker C., grocer, cor. McCarty and Meridian, res. same.
Kemmer James, shoemaker, with J. B. Grout.
Kemper J. M., street commissioner, res. 122 s. New Jersey.
Kenady James, laborer, res. 21 Benton.
Kencel George, hook and ladder wagon, res. 15 s. New
    Jersey.
Kendle J. A., porter, A. & U. S. Express.
Kendrick A., (col.) bds. Pyle House.
Kendrick Edward, laborer, works D. Root & Co.
Kendrick O. H., justice peace, 1 old post office building, res.
    128 Davidson.
Kendrick W. H., doctor, res. 35 n. East.
Kenedy Thomas, laborer, 113 e. South.
Kennington J., drayman, Gas Works.
Kennington, R., of M. Simpson & Co., res. 45 e. Georgia.
Kennedy Dan., blacksmith, works Western Machine Works.
Kennedy M., bar-keeper, Empire Saloon.
Kennedy Pat., works Rolling Mill.
Kennedy R. F., of Murphy, K. & Co., bds. cor. Ohio and
    Illinois.
    12

Kenney Thomas, tailor, shop and res. 34 s. West.
Kennerthy Wm. J., clerk, general freight office Great Central R. R., bds. 64 Mass. ave.
Kentmann Matthias, well digger, res. 182 Mass. ave.
Kentzel Joseph, printer, res. 111 n. Illinois.
Kenny Wm., carpenter, res. Meek, near Benton.
Keople Henry, works Rolling Mill, res. 153 s. Mississippi.
Kepp & Schriver, family grocery, cor. Mass. ave. and Alabama.
Kepple M., clerk, res. 151 s. Tennessee.
Kepple Joshua, works Rolling Mill, res. 67 Louisiana.
Kepple H., works Rolling Mill.
Kepple J., works Rolling Mill.
Kepple Joshua, works Rolling Mill.
Kepple Martin, clerk, res. 51 s. Tennessee.
Kern Jacob, salesman, Hume, Lord & Co.
Kern Joseph, works Schmidt's Brewery.
Kerper Chas., res. cor. Ohio and Indiana ave.
Kerper D., currier, res. cor. Illinois and Michigan.
Kerper W., currier, bds. Mechanic's House.
Kerron D., laborer, res. Michigan road, near Orient.
Kesner T., tailor, res. 29 Union.
Kesseler H. G., bar-keeper, bds. 25 s. Meridian.
Kettenbach & Rentch, grocers, 207 Mass. ave.
Ketcham Miss J., res. 19 Talbott & News Block.
Ketcham J. L., attorney at law, res. 97 e. Merrill.
Kettenbach H., of K. & Rentch, res. 207 Mass. ave.
Kettenbach H., grocer, res. 214 n. Noble.
Kevill Robt. L., tin and sheet iron, res. 64 e. Louisiana.
Keyser John, carpenter, res. 132 e. North.
Keckard Margaret, dress maker, res. 131 e. New York.
Kid Peter, engineer, bds. Ray House.
Kieler Frank, hardware, res. 74 n. Noble.
Kiefer Augustus, of K. & Rush, res. 138 e. McCarty.
Kiefer J., salesman, bds. Bates House.
Kieser A., shoemaker, works with Wachter.
Kiger H. F., attorney, res. 268 n. Illinois.
Kiger Rev. John, res. 268 n. Illinois.
Kightley J. W., with Miller & Moore, bds. Bates House.
Kilshner Fred., laborer, res. 29 Union.
Kindle C., locksmith and bell hanger, 17 Kentucky ave.
King Andrew, laborer, res. 85 e. St. Mary.
King Cornelius, lumber dealer, cor. St. Clair and Alabama.
King Cris., carpenter, res. 93 e. McCarty.
King David, carpenter, res. 218 Indiana ave.
King Francis, res. 72 n. Tenn.
King Geo., carpenter, res. Elizabeth.
King L., hack driver, bds. 150 n. Delaware.

King Jacob, of Springer, Barrows & K., bds. Mrs. Bricket's, w. Market.
King James, shoemaker, res. 141 n. Mississippi.
King I., laborer, res. 108 e. McCarty.
King James, clerk, bds. 141 n. Miss.
King John H., blacksmith, res. 107 Ohio.
King J. W., wool dyer, res. 175 e. Ohio.
King Peter, moulder, works with Root & Co.
King W., book-binder, Fall Creek road.
King W. A., book-keeper, bds. Little's Hotel.
King W. H., book-keeper, with Wiggins & Chandler, res. 258 w. Washington.
Kingham Joseph, broom manufacturer, res. 185 Mass. ave.
Kingman Nelson, book-keeper, res. 59 e. New York.
Kingsbury F. H., Union Line Office, bds. 22 w. Maryland.
Kingsbury J. E., watch maker, res. 181 Mass. ave.
Kinnman Augustus, stone cutter, res. 37 Orsborn.
Kinney Walter, laborer, res. 220 w. Washington.
Kirby J. S., telegraph operator, Bellefontaine Line, bds. 37 e. Georgia.
Kirby N., engineer, res. 25 e. Georgia.
Kirby Mrs. Susan, res. Meek.
Kiritzer Henry, laborer, res. Wyoming, bet. Delaware and High.
Kirk D. A., turner, res. 101 Meek.
Kirk Jas., laborer, works Hill & Wingate.
Kirk N. H., milliner store, res. 39 n. Penn.
Kirk Thos., laborer, works Hill & Wingate.
Kirkwood ——, boiler maker, works I. & C. R. R. machine shop.
Kirkwood Geo., boiler maker, res. Bates, e. of Cady.
Kirkwood John, laborer, res. 108 e. South.
Kirlin James, merchant, res. cor. Illinois and First.
Kirlin & Staton, dry goods, 27 n. Illinois.
Kirzenclamner Mrs. Annie, res. 191 n. Noble.
Kiser Fred., barber, bds. 147 s. Miss.
Kissell J. W., saloon, 11 n. Illinois, res. same.
KISTNER ADAM, PROP'R CALIFORNIA HOUSE, 136 s. Illinois See card, page 90.
Kistner H., shoemaker, res. 89 w. Market.
Kistner J. G., boot and shoe store, 51 s. Illinois, res. same.
KITCHEN JNO. M., M. D., off. s. w. cor. Washington and Meridian, res. 67 n. Penn.
Kirterbark Peter, shoemaker, bds. 176 e. Washington.
Kittemeier Frank, laborer, res. 198 Mass. ave.
Klaiber J. S., confectionery, 115 e. Washsngton, res. same.
Klaner H., marble polisher, res. 188 e. Washington.
Klansner J., watch maker, 141 w. Washington, res. same.

Klem A., laborer, res. 96 e. Louisiana.
Klein Dr. E., res. 100 e. New York.
Klin Nicholas, shoemaker, res. 181 n. Railroad.
Kline W. H., blacksmith, res. Spring, bet. Noble and R. R.
Kline Andrew, carpenter, res. 96 e. Louisiana.
Kline Geo., machinist, with Sinker & Co.
Kline L., res. Missouri, near cor. Merrill.
Kling Jacob, carpenter, res. 100 Bates.
Klinscach H., cigar maker, 73 s. Illinois.
Klingensmith Christ., drayman, res. 120 e. Market.
Klingensmith Israel, broker, bds. 79 w. Maryland.
Klingensmith J., of H. & Bro., 79 w. Maryland.
KLINGENSMITH & BRO., BROKERS, 6 Blakes building.
KLOTZ EMIL, NEW YORK BAZAAR, 37 e. Washington.
    See card, page 46.
Klotz Frank, baker, res. 148 s. New Jersey.
Klumpp D. F., grocer, cor. Washington and Blake.
Klusmann Louis, soldier, res. 63 e. St. Mary.
Kluts John, carpenter, res. Illinois, near cor. McCarty.
Knanb Adam, baker, res. 189 Mass. ave.
Knapton James, stone cutter, res. 32 e. Georgia.
Knapton Thos. J., salesman, New York Bazaar.
Knaus H., res. e. Washington.
Knauss Wm. J., miller, 220 e. Washington, 2d floor.
Knefler Chas., with Span & Smith.
Kneip J., carpenter, res. Liberty, bet. North and Michigan.
Knight E., boarding house, 19 w. Georgia.
Knight John, of Cottrell & K., res. 72 e. Lousiana.
Knight J. N., house and sign painter, 10 s. Meridian.
Knippenberg J., clerk, 29 w. Washington, bds. 62 e. North.
KNODLE A., BOOT AND SHOE STORE, 32 e. Washington, res. 8 Indiana ave.
Knodle G., clerk, bds. 8 Indiana ave.
Knoff Michael, boiler maker, works, I. & C. R. R. shop.
Knos C., bar-keeper, res. 173 e. Washington.
KNOTTS NIM K., SIGN AND ORNAMENTAL PAINT-
    ER, shop 16½ e. Washington, 3d floor, res. 96 e. Market.
    See card, p. 40.
Knott Charles, wks. Indiana Central Machine Shop, bds.
    163 e. Ohio.
Knotts N. K., painter, res. 96 e. Market.
Knowlton G. F., clerk, bds. Oriental House.
KNOX JOHN L. & CO., GROCERS, 181 w. Washington.
Koch Geo., lithographer, res. 97 Fort Wayne ave.
Koch Henry, brick mason, bds. 20 Chatham.
Koch H. H., grocer, cor. South and Noble, res. same.
Koch William, res. 47 s. East.

Koehne Charles, of K. & Co., res. 164 n. Delaware.

Koelresh M., wks. 16 n. Illinois.

Koeniger Geo., grocery and saloon, Meridian, bet. Marion and McCarty.

Kohl Joseph, bricklayer, res. 69 e. St. Mary.

Kohler John, hack driver, res. 134 n. Noble.

Kohley Calvin, school teacher, res. 3 n. Liberty.

Kohne Charles C., publisher Free Press, res. 162 n. Delaware.

KOHN JOSEPH, CLOTHIER AND FURNISHING GOODS, 80 w. Washington. See card, p. 80.

Kohun E., tailor, bds. Commercial Hotel.

Koho Thomas, laborer, res. 133 e. New York.

Kohring Chas., grocer, res. 317 Virginia ave.

Kolb Mrs., res. 71 s. Illinois.

Kolb Louis, job turner, Georgia, bet. Pennsylvania and Meridian.

Koleman Henry, res. 73 s. Illinois, 2d floor.

Koller E. H., grocer, 165 e. Washington, res. same.

Kolthoff Henry, laborer, res. Michigan road, near Central R. R.

Kolk John, laborer, res. 20 Chatham.

Kolp L., turner, res. 5 e. South.

Koothe W., watchman, Washington Foundry.

Korn K., cabinet maker, res. 172 e. Michigan.

Korn M., courier, res. 171 n. New Jersey.

Korpeter William, tailor, res. 161 n. Alabama.

Kose J., locksmith, wks. with J. Reinhart.

Kostley Christ., laborer, res. 155 n. Noble.

Kothe Wm., grocer, res. 67 n. Davidson.

Kotthmin W., varnisher, with Spiegel, Thoms & Co.

Kottmeier W., of Thonssen & Lahey, bds. Bates House.

Kraas Wm., bakery, 58 w. Meridian, res. same.

Krag W. A., clerk, with A. & H. Schnull, res. 63 e. Washington.

Kraglo Jacob, carpenter, res. 40 e. St. Clair.

Kramer Henry, butcher, res. 71 e. St. Mary.

Kramer W., carpenter, Washington Foundry.

Kranhs Jacob, carpet merchant, res. 58 n. East.

Kraus Charles, grocer, res. 202 Massachusetts ave.

Krause Philip, laborer, res. 66 St. Mary.

Krause R., tailor, 107 e. Ohio.

Krause Wm., of K. & Wittenberg, res. 75 n. Alabama.

Krause William, dry goods store, res. 41 Alabama.

KRAUSE & WITTENBERG, PROPRIETORS GERMAN DRY GOODS STORE, 43 and 45 e. Washington.

Krauss Jack, bar-keeper, 14 s. Pennsylvania.

Krauss G., of J. & G. K., bds. 58 n. East.

Krauss J., of J. & G. K., res. 58 n. East.
KRAUSS J. & G., CARPETS, WALL PAPER AND
  PIANOS, cor. Washington and Delaware. See card,
  p. 26.
Krauth E. W., clerk, 14 w. Washington, res. 65 n. Tennes-
  see.
Kray Wm., stone cutter, res. 92 e. Market.
Kreahan Henry, res. 47 e. Georgia.
Kregelo Charles, clerk, bds. cor. South and Delaware.
Kregelo David, lumber yard, res. 132 n. West.
Kretsch Peter, cigar store, 93 s. Illinois, res. same.
Krider R. G., salesman, E. H. Mayo & Co.
Krieger H., tailor, res. 103 e. Washington.
Kropf Gustave, of Frese & K., bds. Union Hall.
Krohm August, school teacher, res. 188 e. Ohio.
Krohm Christ., res. 188 e. Ohio.
Krug G., musician, res. 13 w. Ohio.
Kruger Joseph, brick maker, res. 115 e. Market.
Krupp John, harness maker, bds. 255 s. Pennsylvania.
Krupp P., saddler, res. 255 Pennsylvania.
Kubush Alexander, res. 131 n. Liberty.
Kuerter Frank, blacksmith, res. 45 Union.
KUESTER C. E., MINISTER GERMAN PRESBYTER-
  IAN CHURCH, s. of Little's Hotel.
Kugelman Wm., cigar maker, res. 133 n. Mississippi.
Kuhlmann E. H., res. 187 w. Washington.
Kuhn Chas., meat market, cor. Missouri and Michigan, res.
  same.
Kuhn Ph. J., wagon maker, res. 106 Fort Wayne ave.
Kuhn Wm., bakery, res. 64 n. East.
Kulb H., lamp lighter, res. 98 St. Joseph.
Kumann Augusta, grocer, res. 275 Virginia ave.
Kunkal A., cigar maker, bds. Union Hall.
Kunkal B., cigar maker, 30 s. Union.
Kunkel C., miller, res. 36 Union.
Kunkel Henry, clerk, res. cor. Georgia and Liberty.
Kunkel J. A., harness maker, bds. 30 Union.
Kunkelman Rev. John A., pastor English Lutheran Church,
  res. 156 n. Pennsylvania.
Kunlin George, laborer, res. 34 Orsbrook.
Kunz G., clerk, bds. Little's Hotel.
Kurse C., carpenter, res. 9 McCarty
Kurts Hilpat, blacksmith, res. 290 Indiana ave.
Kuster W., cigar roller, res. s. New Jersey.

L

Laaz J., works Union Depot, res. cor. McCarty and Bluff Road.

Labarr L., moulder, works with D. Root & Co.

Lack R., clerk, Harrison's Bank.

Lacy Joseph, orderly sergeant, bds. 27 s. Delaware.

Ladies' Home, 176 and 178 s. Illinois.

Lafayette W., pressman, with Dodd & Co., res. 50 n. Indiana ave.

Laffery M., blacksmith, works Western Machine Works.

Laing David, carpenter, res. 35 w. New York.

Laird John P., carpenter, res. 38 s. Noble.

Laird Robert, res. Illinois, bet. First and Second.

Laird W. H., clerk, Washington Foundry.

Lahman Frederick, grocer, res. 88 corporation line.

Lake John, butcher, res. 241 s. Delaware.

Lally Thomas, tailor, res. 143 w. South.

Lamb D., machinist, works I. & C. R. R. Machine Shop.

Lamb L., works Rolling Mill.

Lamb P., res. 15 Willard.

Lamb Yancy, laborer, res. 146 w. Market.

Lamber James, of Ray & L., Ray House.

Lame John, conductor Jeffersonville R. R., bds. 129 w. Maryland.

Lampe Henry, porter, Little's Hotel.

Lampheir ———, painter, 11 s. Illinois.

Lamott C., tinner, res. cor. East and Massachusetts ave.

Lamott Joseph, tinner, res. 138 Massachusetts ave.

Lancaster H. H., salesman, bds. Mississippi, 3 doors s. Vermont.

Landauer N. J., salesman, 3 e. Washington, bds. Macy House.

Landauer S., clerk, with M. Dernham.

Lander Thomas, works Rolling Mill.

Landfier E. painter, res. First, near Mississippi.

Landis M. M., general freight agent, T. H. & R. R. R. Co.

Landormi Mrs. D., res. 139 e. North.

Lane Samuel, laborer, res. Liberty, bet. New York and Vermont.

Lane Uria, works lumber yard, res. 170 n. New Jersey.

Lang J. K., res. w. Maryland.

LANG LOUIS, SALOON, AND RESTAURANT, 13 e. Washington. See card, opp. title.

Langbein J., groceries and notions, 160 e. Washington, res. same.

Langenberg H. H., grocer, 194 w. Washington, res. same.

Langsdale J. W. S., res. 26 e. Market.

Langsenkamp William, copper smith, res. 130 s. Delaware.
Landers Mrs. Catherine, res. 104 Virginia ave.
Landis J., of L. & Mills, bds. Macy House.
Landis M. M., general freight agent, T. H. & R. R. R., 86 w. Washington.
Landis & Mills, sale stable, 8 e. Maryland.
Landig P., painter, western agricultural works.
Laner C., saloon, 162 e. Washington, res. same.
Lanpheimer A., bar-keeper, 106 e. Washington.
Lanpheimer Gustave, bar-keeper, res. 207 n. Alabama.
Lanphere James, painter, cor. Meridian and Washington, res. First, bet. Mississippi and Tennessee.
Lantry George, laborer, res. 99 Indiana ave.
Large Michael, laborer, 252 Indiana ave.
Larned Miss S. J., teacher at Institute for the Blind.
Lasee Thomas, works Indiana Central Railway Machine Shop.
Latham Charles, clerk, A. & U. S. Express Co.
Latham Henry, railroader, res. e. Washington, out of corporation.
Latham W. H., instructor, Deaf and Dumb Assylum.
Latham W., teacher, res. e. Washington.
Laton Frank, candy maker, bds. Macy House.
Latta W. R., restaurant, opp. Union Depot, res. same.
Laty H., works Rolling Mill.
Laughrey J., fireman, bds. Ray House.
Laun John, laborer, res. 59 Orsbrook.
Laurie William, clerk, New York Store, bds. 14 e. Ohio.
Law John, machinist, res. 229 s. Delaware.
Law Thomas D., carpenter, res. 233 Indiana ave.
Lawler W., engineer, Bates House.
Lawler Wm., laborer, res. 184 e. South.
Lawless Michael, grocer, 85 s. Noble, res. same.
Lawlin C. A., clerk, Jeffersonville R. R. Freight Depot, bds. Oriental House.
LAWRENCE A. V., GROCER, 133 e. Washington. res. same.
Lawrence Thomas, book-keeper, res. West, bet. South and Merrill.
Lawyer P. C., of L. & Hall, bds. Little's Hotel.
LAWYER & HALL, PROPRIETORS PERU ELEVATORS, s. New Jersey, near Peru Freight Depot. See card, page 74.
Layon Mike works Rolling Mill.
Layton T. M., book-keeper, with A. Lintz, bds. 73 w. New York.
Leach J., carpenter, res. 78 Bluff Road.
Leathers Geo. C., clerk, A. & U. S. Express Co., res. 80 s. East.

Leathers W. W., of L. & Carter, res. 139 n. New Jersey.
LEATHERS & CARTER, ATTORNEYS AND CLAIM
    AGENTS, 3 Odd Fellows' Hall. See card, outside
    cover.
Leary P. C., attorney, 39½ w. Washington.
Lecheane C., shoemaker, works with A. Knodle.
Lechene Charley, shoemaker, res. 160 Madison R. R.
Leek Robert M., salesman, German Dry Good Store.
Leddy Thomas, boiler maker, res. 205 Hudson.
Ledlie John, clerk, Palmer House.
Ledrich Louis, clerk, 22 w. Washington.
Ledwich W. P., Treasurer Sinissippi Insurance Co., bds. 21
    s. Delaware.
Ledwith T., carpenter, res. 211 s. Alabama.
Lee B. J., salesman, M. H. Good, res. 55 South.
Lee E. S., doctor, res, 11 Indiana ave.
Lee E. T., Hackman, res. 22 n. New Jersey.
LEE H. H., DRUGGIST AND DEALER IN TEAS, 12
    and 14 n. Illinois, res. 125 n. Illinois. See card, pages
    122 and 123.
Lee M. G., editor Herald and Era, res. 111 n. Illinois.
Lee John W., salesman, res. 59 w. New York.
Lee Wm. E., saloon, res. 161 w. Vermont.
Leffler James, res. cor. New Jersey and Wabash ave.
Lehr Andrew, blacksmith, res. Keely's Block, bet. New Jer-
    sey and East.
Lehr F. A., carpenter, res. 98 n. East.
Lehr Henry, carpenter, res. 165 e. New York.
Lehr Philip, carpenter, res. 80 n. Davidson.
Lehrritter C., of L. & Co., e. Wabash.
Lehrritter & Co., saloon, 14 e. Washington.
Leibhart James, dyer at Merritt & Coughlen's Wollen
    Factory.
Leinningee Mike., barber, res. 102 e. Vermont.
Leiprich Louis, res. 172 w. North.
Leiseman Wm., laborer, res. 174 n. Noble.
Lemman Jennie, dress maker, res. 34 e. Ohio.
Lemme W., blacksmith, Bluff Road, bet. McCarty and Ray.
Lemmon Ed., of Gates & L., res. 86 e. Market.
Lennest F., res. 18½ s. Illinois.
Lennest Mrs. S. E., stamping for embroidering, 18½ s. Illinois.
LENOX ED., TAILOR, 15 s. Illinois, res. same. See card,
    page 82.
Lentz Christ., laborer, res. 115 Fort Wayne ave.
Lentz Gotlew, porter, C. E. Hawthorn.
Lentz Theo. J., lithographer, res. cor. Meridian and Wash-
    ington, 3d floor.
Lentz Wm., clerk, res. 83 n. Davidson.

Lentz William, packer, C. E. Hawthorn.
Leon A., boot and shoe maker, 3 Illinois, under Bates House, res. 53 New Jersey.
Leonard M., laborer, bds. 55 c. Ohio.
Leonard Mrs. Abgial, res. 116 n. Illinois.
Leoeders Mrs. A. M., embroidering and machine sewing, 16 s. Illinois, res. same.
Leppert Nichols, blacksmith, res. 14 Lord.
Levi H., peddler, res. cor. Tennessee and McCarty.
Levitt Wm., carpenter, res. 190 n. Illinois.
Levy Mrs. Mary F., res. 74 w. Vermont.
Lesh A. B., of L. & A. B. L., bds. 48 n. California.
Lesh L., of L. & A. B. L., res. 48 n. California.
Lesh L. & A. B., produce and commission merchants, 29 s. Meridian.
Letty John, laborer, res. Wyoming, bet. Delaware and High.
Leutch Wesley, wagon maker, res. 128 c. St. Clair.
Levien S., sutler army, res. 22 s. Mississippi,
Lewis Hiram L., teamster, res. 283 s. East.
Lewis Jordan, teller, National Bank, bds. Clay's, Sinking Fund Building.
Lewis Wm., painter, bds. bet. Illinois and Meridian.
Lewis Wm., wks. Rolling Mill.
LEWIS T. A., AGENT GREAT WESTERN DISPATCH, res. 57 n. Meridian.
Lewitt Miss Susan, salesman, 84 w. Washington.
Lewitt W. H., wks. 84 w. Washington.
Lex Mrs. Elizabeth, res. 178 c. Vermont.
Lex Jacob L., printer, bds. 178 c. Vermont.
Lex Louis, pressman, printing office, bds. 178 e. Vermont.
Linohan John, res. 42 s. Illinois.
Licking B., book binder, with J. G. Douglass.
Lieber Herman, frame dealer, res. 160 n. Delaware.
LIEBER H., PICTURE FRAMES AND MOULDINGS, 13 n. Pennsylvania, res. 223 n. Delaware. See card, opp. title.
Lieber Peter, of Gagg & Co., res. 26 s. Pennsylvania.
Lietz T., colorist, res. Stirngtown.
Lightford James, wks. Western Machine Works.
Likert Mrs. E., res. 125 s. Delaware.
Likert Peter, wks. Rolling Mill.
Linck Mrs. E. D., res. 112 s. East.
Linck J. C., proprietor Capital Garden, cor. Tennessee and Kentucky ave.
Lindemann F., clerk, 101 c. Washington.
LINDENBOWER WM. H., REAL ESTATE BROKER, 30½ w. Washington, res. 200 n. Mississippi.
Linder John, laborer, res. 271 s. East.

Lindley Calvin, clerk, bds. 58 w. Vermont.
Lindley H. J., book-keeper, McKerman & Pierce, res. 26 w. Maryland.
Lindsey Henry, grocer, res. 10 w. Georgia.
Lindsay P., of P. L. & Co., res. 12 w. Georgia.
Lindsay P. & Co., grocers, 39 s. Illinois.
Line I., of Peyton & L., res. 65 s. Illinois.
Lingenfelter W. H., boarding house, 19 Circle.
Lingenfelder A., carpenter, res. 148 n. Davidson.
Lingenfelter Archibald, watchman, res. 172 Tennessee.
Linn A., clerk, Post Office.
Linn Mrs. J., res. 8 s. Pennsylvania.
Linn Miss Mary L., teacher, Indianapolis Female College.
Linter John, wks. Schmidt's Brewery.
Linthicum J., laborer, wks. with W. Hinesley.
Lintner C. H., grocer, res. 205 Indiana ave.
Lintner Daniel, res. Blake.
LINTNER J. & C., DRY GOODS AND GROCERIES, cor. North and Dunlop.
LINTZ ANTHONY, BOOT AND SHOE MANUFACTU-RER AND DEALER, 39 w. Washington, res. 17 s. Mississippi. See card, p. 120.
Lintz Gottlieb, clerk, res. 103 n. Railroad.
Lintz John K., with A. Lintz, bds. 17 s. Mississippi.
Lipkin Charles, shoemaker, res. 64 n. Noble.
Lipinsky M., clerk, bds. Spencer House.
Lipinsky Isaac, clothing and military goods, 24 Louisiana, bds. Spencer House.
Lipp Henry, tailor, res. 178 Ohio.
LIPPERD H. T., DRY GOODS AND GROCERIES, res. 138 n. East.
Lippus W., stone cutter, res. 174 n. East.
Lippert Henry, laborer, res. 97 n. Railroad.
Lippman J., clerk, 6 Bates House.
Lippus Wm., stone cutter, res. 174 n. East.
Littenden Moses, egg packer, res. 143 n. New Jersey.
Little Mary E., res. 130 n. Alabama.
Little W. F., clerk, bds. 130 n. Alabama.
LITTLE'S HOTEL, A. R. HYDE, PROPRIETOR, cor. Washington and New Jersey.
Little Milton E., with Osgood & Smith.
Little O. H. P., machinist, res. cor. Meek and Benton.
Little Wilber, clerk, with H. M. Scowell.
Little W. T., brass founder, res. Grear, bet. McCarty and Virginia ave.
LIVERPOOL AND LONDON FIRE AND LIFE INSUR-ANCE CO., SPANN & SMITH, AGENTS, cor. Washington and Pennsylvania.

Lock Chas., with Louis Lang.

Lockport W., portrait painter, bds. cor. Pennsylvania and Market.

Locke Erie, agent depot, 40 California.

Locke Josiah, publisher Daily Journal, res. 163 n. Pennsylvania.

Locks Phillips, cooper, res. 136 n. Mississippi.

Lockwood C. F., teacher, bds. 176 n. Delaware.

Lockwood Henry, cooper, res. Market, bet. California and West.

Lockwood Nelson, cooper, res. California, near Washington.

Lockwood W. W., clerk, Head-quarters Supt. Recruiting Service, bds. Macy House.

Loehman Chas., res. 315 Virginia ave.

Logan B., grocer, 129 w. South.

Logan Pat., laborer, res. 187 s. New Jersey.

Logan T. J., carpenter, Sinker, bet. Alabama and N. Jersey.

Lohrman Paul, harness maker, res. 11 St. Clair.

Lolton Wm., works Rolling Mill.

Lomeine Louis, laborer, res. 160 n. Noble.

Lonegan Morris, works Western Machine Works.

Lonergan John, grocer, res. 171 s. Noble.

Long D. D., painter, res. 9 Mass. ave.

Long E. C., grainer, res. 129 n. Penn.

Long E. F., salesman, bds. Macy House.

Long Fred., clerk, 22 w. Washington.

Long Joseph, shoemaker, res. 147 n. Pennsylvania.

Long J. T., notary public, 8 w. Washington, bds. Little's Hotel.

Long Matthew, undertaker, Circle, first door e. Journal building, bds. Macy House.

Longsdorf H., laborer, res. 17 Virginia ave.

Longsdorff W., carpenter, res. 79 Mass. ave.

Lonnay Wm., laborer, res. 35 Huron.

Looker Mrs. Fidelia, res. 140 Mississippi.

LOOMIS WM. H., WOODLAWN NURSERY, SECY. STATE BOARD OF AGRICULTURE, s. w. cor. Washington and Meridian, GREEN HOUSE AND GARDEN, 189 Virginia ave, res. 137 Virginia ave. See cards, pages 138 and 139.

Lord E. N., of Hume L. & Co., res. 12 w. North.

Lord F. B., of Cox, L. & Peck, bds. 43 s. Meridian.

Lord J. M., Pres't Indianapolis Rolling Mill, off. 8 Blakes Block, res. cor. North and Penn.

Losey John, cooper, res. 189 Virginia ave.

Loucks C. R., clerk, 5 n. Penn., bds 179 e. Market.

Loucks Christ., carpenter, res. 161 Mass. ave.

Loucks James, carpenter, res. 194 n. New Jersey.

Louck M., finisher, Eagle Foundry.
Loucks W. W., police, res. 123 w. Alabama.
Louden Andrew, carpenter, res. 57 n. Illinois.
Louir John, soldier, res. 186 n. Noble.
Louis Andrew, blacksmith, res. 33 n. Noble.
Love Miss J., actress, Metropolitan Hall.
Love John, res. 49 n. Tenn.
Love W., carpenter, res. 148 e. North.
Love Samuel, watchman, I. & C. R. R. Depot, res. 101 s. East.
LOVE WM., REAL ESTATE AGENT, 1 Talbott & New's Block, up stairs. See card, page 78.
Loveland E. P., Astt. Paymaster, 9 Bates House, up stairs.
Low Mrs. M., res. 227 w. Washington.
Lowden James, res. 46 Indiana ave.
Lowe C. G., carpenter, res. 148 e. North.
Lowe George, carriage shop, 99 e. Washington, res. 113 n. Penn.
LOWE WM. A., ATTORNEY, off. 16½ e. Washington, room 3, bds. Palmer House.
Lower J., laborer, res. 41 Union.
Lowery John, miller, res. w. Washington.
Lowes John, carpenter, res. 152 n. Delaware.
Lowry W. M., druggist, 53 Mass. ave., res. same.
Lowmon N., blacksmith, res. 58 e. St. Clair.
Lowman Nancy, res. 58 e. St. Clair.
Lowman Wm., blacksmith, works 8 n. East.
Lowrey John, miller, res. 247 w. Washington.
Lowrey G. E., orderly, 13th Regt. Indiana Vol., 53 Massachusetts ave.
Loyd Allen, of T. A. L. & Co., res. e. end of Market.
Loyd Thomas A., of T. A. L. & Co., res. e. end Market.
LOYD THOS. A. & CO., DEALERS IN HARDWARE, &c., 12 w. Washington. See card, page 82.
Lucky George, clerk, res. 185 n. East.
Lucus Harmon, (col.) barber, res. 54 Blackford.
Lucus James, (col.) white washer, res. 149 n. Alabama.
Ludington M. E., res. 14 n. New Jersey.
Ludlum J. E., foreman, Bellefontaine car shop, res. 230 n. Illinois.
Ludlow Jason C., carpenter, res. 89 e. Market.
Ludlow Silas, traveling agent, res. 147 n. Delaware.
Ludwig H., piano maker, res. cor. Noble and Ohio.
Lueders Mrs. Louisa, teacher, Indianapolis Female College.
Luken G. H., barber, bds. 54 Blackford.
Lukens R. L., of L. & Brackebush, res. 214 Virginia ave.
Lukens & Brackebush, agricultural implements, 81 and 83 w. Washington.

Lundey J. C., gunsmith, bds. 97 Mass. ave.
Lundy J. C., gunsmith, s. Penn., res. 79 Mass. ave.
Lupton G., dentist, 32 s. Meridian.
Lupton Geo., dentist, res. 78 e. Pratt.
Lupton Wm. C., paymaster, res. 134 n. West.
Luther A., painter, bds. Dickey's boarding house.
Luther Dr. Robert, res. cor. Vermont and Mass. ave.
Lutz Geo., shoemaker, res. 297 Virginia ave.
Lynch J., res. Missouri.
Lynch J. J., of L. & Keane, res. 100 n. East.
Lynch P., engineer, with Sinker & Co.
Lynch & Keane, dry goods, 33 w. Washington.
Lynn Adam, teamster, res. 143 e. South.
Lynn W. C., clerk, Indiana Central R. R. Depot, bds. Macy
    House.
Lyons Adolph., shoemaker, res. 53 n. New Jersey.
Lyons Daniel, works Rolling Mill.
Lyons John, works Rolling Mill.
Lyons J. W., trader, bds. Ray House.
Lyons Pat., laborer, res. Wyoming, bet. Delaware and
    High.
Lyons Wm., railroader, res. 161 s. Delaware.

M

McAndrews Walter, works Conklin & Redmond.
McArthur J. B., of M. & Heckman, res. 158 n. West.
McBaker Thos., Pearl Saloon, cor. alley and Pearl, res. 68
    e. Michigan.
McBhesmy G. G., clerk, Post-office.
McBride John, works Rolling Mill.
McBride Michael, res. 142 n. Liberty.
McCabe M., machinist, works I. & C. R. R. machine shop.
McCab Matthew, machinist, res. 5 Forest ave.
McCaffery James, laborer, res. West, bet. Georgia and
    Maryland.
McCaffery John, laborer, res. 157 w. Maryland.
McCallian John, machinist, res. 8 e. Huron.
McCann Dr. S. D., res. 29 n. East.
McCurron Geo., tailor, res. 164 n. Delaware.
McCarthy S., res. 9 s. Mississippi.
McCarty Mrs. Margaret, res. 60 n. Penn.
McCarty J., works Rolling Mill.
McCarty Nicholas, off. s. w. cor. Meridian and Washington.
McCarty Simon, res. 9 Mississippi.
McCarty Theo., works Rolling Mill.
McCarty T., laborer, res. Wyoming, bet. High and Dela-
    ware
McCarty Wm., moulder, Eagle Foundry.

McChesney Edwin, clerk, Post-office.
McChesney J. B., Treas. Ind. Central R. R., res. 132 n. Ill.
McCinley James, res. 148 e. New York.
McClain Moses, drayman, res. near Orient.
McClay Cyrus, clerk, 22 w. Washington.
McCloskey B., real estate and U. S. claim agent, 8 w. Washington, bds. Spencer House.
McCloud Mrs. M., res. 93 s. Tennessee.
McClure Maj. Daniel, res. 42 s. Meridian.
McClure Mrs. ———, res. s. Tenn., near cor. McCarty.
McClure Theophilus, printer, res. 140 w. Market.
McConnol Miss M., dress maker, Ætna building.
McCool Wm., morticer, res. 273 s. Delaware.
McCord B. R., of M. & Wheatley, res. 1½ miles from city, Shelbyville road.
McCORD & WHEATLEY, DEALERS IN LUMBER, LATH AND SHINGLES, 119 s. Delaware. See cards, pages 68 and 134.
McCord L. W., student, bds. Little's Hotel.
McCorkle J., works 74 w. Washington.
McCormick Chas., moulder, res. 252 s. Delaware.
McCormick Jas., works with McCord & Wheatley.
McCormick J., carpenter, res. 204 n. Mississippi.
McCormick J. L., carpenter, res. cor. Tenn. and Fifth.
McCormick L., tailor, res. n. Liberty.
McCoy Mrs. Elizabeth, res. 73 s. Noble.
McCoy Jas., minister, res. 46 s. Penn
McCoy Robert, of McCoy & Orr, bds. Palmer House.
McCoy W., railroader, res. 20 Madison ave.
McCOY & ORR, PHOTOGRAPH GALLERY, 33 w. Washington. See card, p. 106.
McCready Frank, clerk, bds. 42 Alabama.
McCready Jas., book-keeper, Branch Bank State of Indiana, res. cor. Ohio and Vermont.
McCrery Joseph, res. 72 n. East.
McCune Capt. Willis, U. S. Army, res. 181 e. Ohio.
McCulley Charles B., plasterer, res. North, bet. Massachusetts ave. and New Jersey.
McCullough Rt., wks. Rolling Mill.
McCullough W. J., clerk, Head-quarters Superintendent Recruiting Service.
McCullough William, res. Michigan, bet. New Jersey and East.
McCune Thomas, clerk, res. cor. Cady and Georgia.
McCurdy G. W., of A. L. H. & Co., bds. cor. East and St. Clair.
McCutchen H. C., res. 93 e. Ohio.
McCutcheon George, switchman, Bellefontaine R. R.

McCutcheon John, T. H. & R. R. R. freight office, res. 51 n. Meridian.

McCutcheon Wm., clerk, New York Store, bds. cor. Tennessee and Market.

McDavit John, bar-keeper, res. 199 s. Delaware.

McDeerlott James, boiler maker, Western Machine Works.

McDermond J. W., clerk, res. St. Joseph, bet. Pennsylvania and Meridian.

McDermott James, res. 81 w. Maryland.

McDermott Joseph, stove mounter, res. 101 s. Alabama.

McDevitt John, Exchange Billiard Rooms.

McDonald C., machinist, res. 89 e. Washington.

McDonald David, of McD. & Porter, res. n. e. cor. Pennsylvania and Vermont.

McDonald Pat., wks. Rolling Mill, res. 10 Willard.

McDonald Joseph E., of McD. & Roache, res. 93 n. Pennsylvania.

McDONALD & PORTER, ATTORNEYS, Yohn's Block, over Branch Bank.

McDonald & Roache, attorneys, Ætna Building.

McDonough Carpenter, res. 59 e. Vermont.

McDougal Wm., res. 225 w. Washington.

McDougal W. R., attorney, Yohn's Block, 2d floor.

McElwer John, carpenter, res. 154 n. Mississippi.

McEntyre L. D., wks. Rolling Mill.

McEwen A., carpenter, Eagle Foundry.

McEwen D., wks. Rolling Mill.

McFadden Dr. Samuel, res. 91 s. New Jersey.

McFarland Charlotte Laura W., res. 14 e. St. Clair.

McFarlane J., clerk, res. 97 n. Meridian.

McFarlan James M., clerk, New York Store, res. 20 s. Mississippi.

McFarlan W., baker, with Q. Thomson.

McGan C. B., moulder, Eagle Foundry.

McGee Edward, machinist, res. 131 s. Alabama.

McGee R., physician, cor. Alabama and Washington, res. 183 e. New York.

McGee Jacob, engineer, I. & M. R. R.

McGee William, engineer, bds. Ray House.

McGee Wm. S., printer, Journal office.

McGehee J. F., grocery, res. 131 n. East.

McGlenley James, tinner, res. 127 n. Mississippi.

McGibson Josiah, carpenter, res. 210 n. New Jersey.

McGiffin Samuel, master mechanic work department of Institution for the Blind, cor. Walnut and Pennsylvania.

McGill Wm. A., clerk, New York Store, res. 20 s. Mississippi.

McGinnis John, grocer, 230 e. Washington, res. same.

McGINNIS OWEN, MERCHANT TAILOR AND MANU-
FACTURER OF READY-MADE CLOTHING, 39 e.
Washington, res. 26 Virginia ave. See card, p. 90.
McGlenn Michael, expressman, res. cor. Douglas and North.
McGlew Thomas, clerk, 89 n. Illinois.
McGragh P., school teacher, bds. 51 Mississippi.
McGrath John C., tailor, 8 s. Pennsylvania, bds. Pyle House.
McGuire James E., clerk at Metzger & Striblin, Odd Fel-
lows' Hall.
McHenry P., laborer, res. 182 s. Delaware.
McHenry A.. brakesman, res. Tennessee, bet South and
Rolling Mill.
McIntire James, auctioneer, res. 22 California.
McIver J. C., of Baker & M., res. 15 Ohio.
McKain James, carpenter, res. 101 w. South.
McKelvey J. S, carpenter, res. 53 s. Pennsylvania.
McKenna John, machinist, res. 69 s. New Jersey.
McKenna W. B., machinist, res. 69 s. New Jersey.
McKeon B., railroader, res. 225 s. Pennsylvania.
McKernan J. H., of McK. & Pierce, res. 10 Circle.
McKernan D. S., of Walker & McK., res. 10 Circle.
McKernan & Pierce, dealers in real estate, 39½ w. Wash.
McKernan & Pierce, lumber yard, Maryland, bet. Meridian
and Pennsylvania.
McKisley John, res. 41 w. Georgia.
McKinley Alexander, expressman, res. 100 Ft. Wayne ave.
McKinley Hugh, carriage painter, res. 100 Ft. Wayne ave.
McKinnie Henry, clerk, Post Office.
McKinny John, machinist, res. 69 s. New Jersey.
McKinney Mrs. Eliza, res. 72 n. Illinois.
McKinney Wm., machinist, res. 69 s. New Jersey.
McKowen James N., printer, works Sentinel Office.
McLane Albert, printer, res. 8 w. North.
McLain Mrs. Mary & A. E., res. 142 n. Illinois.
McLaughlin J. A., gunsmith, res. 232 s. Alabama.
McLaughlin Thomas, soldier, res, 285 s. East.
McLaughlin W. B., book-keeper, M. Hunter & Co.
McLennan D., marble cutter, bds. Ohio House.
McLene J., jeweler, under Bates House.
McLene Wm., clerk, New York Store. bds. 14 e. Ohio.
McLene J. & Co., Central Paper Mill, w. Washington, on
River Bank.
McManmon Bryan, 39th regiment Ind. Vol., res. Tennessee,
near McCarty.
McMan P., works Exchange Livery Stable.
McMerry ———, res. 112 n. Missouri.
McMillin J. T., of Dawes, Evans & M., bds Macy House.
13

McMillin M., finisher, Eagle Foundry.
McMillin Samuel, of McM. & Redford, res. 38 e. Vermont.
McMillin Thomas, brakesman, bds. 38 e. Vermont.
McMILLIN & REDFORD, REAL ESTATE BROKERS,
   19 w. Washington, See card, page 90.
McMurphey H., clerk, bds. Pyle House.
McMurray Robert, res. 101 w. New York.
McNab P., of Brown & McN., res. 210 n. New Jersey.
McNally Terance, laborer, res. Elm, near Noble.
McNamara Michael, railroader, res. 95 s. Alabama.
McNeely E., barrel factory, res. 136 n. Illinois.
McNeely J., carpenter, res. 151 n. Mississippi.
McNeil George H., carpenter, res. 176 n. East.
McNutt Orrin, conductor in yard, I. & M. R. R.
McOmber J. H., clerk, Bates House.
McOuat A. W., stove store, res. 15 e. Laukabee.
McOuat Mrs. J., res. 65 n. East.
McOuat R. L. & A. W., stove and tinware store, 69 w. Wash-
   ington.
McPowell James, barber, with W. A. Franklin.
McQuade P., watchman, Spencer House.
McShane O., res. 111 w. Michigan.
McSweany Dennis, res. cor. Orient and Washington.
McVea David, blacksmith, 203 w. Washington.
McVeter A. W., tailor, res. bet. Market and Ohio.
McVickers Achor, res. s. New Jersey, bet. Market and Ohio.
McVicker A. W., with K. & W., 3 Bates House, res. New
   Jersey, bet. Market and Ohio.
McWiggin P., hostler, bds. Knights.
McWilliams A., (col.) blacksmith, 130 Indiana ave.
McWilliams Mrs. C., (col.) res. 127 w. Washington.
McWilliams J., clerk, res. 16 St. Clair.
McWorkman H., clerk. Post Office.
McWorkman ———, res. 38 n. East.
Maas Jacob, boarding house, 115 w. Maryland.
Maas Louis, cigar maker, with G. F. Myers & Co.
Mabb Mrs. M., res. 9 Bates House, up stairs.
Macadam D. H., military clerk, bds. cor. Vermont and Illi-
   nois.
Macarthur John B., miller, res. 158 n. West.
Macarthy Mrs. M., res. 184 e. Market.
Macarthy Mrs. S., res. 70 n. Davidson.
Machette R. M., carpenter and builder, res. 95 e. St. Joseph.
MacIntire Thomas, superintendent Deaf and Dumb Assy-
   lum.
MacIntire John, Paper Mill, res. West, bet. Washington and
   Maryland.
Mack John, works Rolling Mill.

Mackey John, harness maker, res. 149 Virginia ave.

Macy House W. H. Campbell, proprietor, cor. Illinois and Market.

Macy David, President Peru & Indianapolis R. R., office cor. Washington and Delaware, up stairs, res. 78 n. Delaware.

Madison Edwin, res. e. Washington, near Corporation Line.

Magan C., moulder, res. 225 s. Pennsylvania.

Magu E., boiler maker, res. 131 s. Alabama.

Magon Philip, machinist, res. 141 n. Davidson.

Magratch Daniel, laborer, res. 19 Georgia.

Maguire C., carriage maker, cor. Kentucky ave. and Georgia, bds. Palmer House.

Maguire D., of M., Jones & Co., res. Ohio, bet. Pennsylvania and Delaware.

Maguire, Jones & Co., wholesale grocers, 7 & 8 Bates House building.

Mahan F. L., cigar stand, Bates House.

Mahan F. M. N., works Bates House, res. 217 n. Illinois.

Mahan W. H., book-keeper, res. 12 n. Georgia.

Mahannan G., gas fitter, Alabama, bet. Maryland and Virginia ave.

MAHORNEY J. T., ORNAMENTAL HAIR WORK, WIGS, &c., 20 n. Illinois. See card, page 78.

Mahoning Pat., res. 210 s. Delaware.

Maker Geo., painter, bds. 9 Mass. ave.

Maier F., carpenter, Washington Foundry.

Maier J., carpenter, Washington Foundry.

Maier Nicholas, shoemaker, 116 Virginia ave., res. near Madison engine shop.

Major Stephen, attorney, Johnson's building, res. National Road.

Maker Geo., painter, works Spurgin & Long.

Maker Thos., soldier, res. 124 e. Washington.

Malghan Thos., works Rolling Mill.

Malone Abner, carpenter, res. 107 Virginia ave.

Malone Pat., laborer, res. Wyoming, bet. Delaware and High.

Maloney John, 1st. Lieut. 35th Regt. Ind. Vols., res. 169 s. Mississippi.

Malott V. T., Treas., Secy. and Gen. Ticket Agent, P. & I. R. R., off. cor. Washington and Delaware, res. 78 n. Delaware.

Malton ——, machinist, works. I. & C. R. R. shop.

Mangrum C. W., photographist, bds. cor. Meridian and South.

Manheimer David, clothier, res. 30 n. Miss.

Manheimer D., clothier, 55 w. Washington.

MANHEIMER H., AGT. FOR RINDSKOFF, BROS. & CO., AND AUB, FRENKEL & CO., 77 w. Washington.
Mankedick W., core maker, Eagle Foundry.
Manlove Wm. R., of Perrin & M., bds. 130 n. New Jersey.
Mann D. O., teacher, res. 66 n. East.
Mann Mrs. Margaret, res. Tennessee, n. of Third.
Mann A. G., carpenter, res. 78 n. Davidson.
Mann A. J., of M. & Rubush, res. 80 e. Davidson.
Mann J. B., grocer, res. 95 s. East.
Mann John, teamster, res. 163 n. Noble.
Mann Theodore, wks. with McCord & Wheatley.
Mann & Rubush, carpenters, shop 219 w. Washington.
Mann, Seibert & Co., grocery, cor. East and Virginia ave.
Mannfield Geo., of Goepper & Co., res. 146 n. East.
Mannfield Julius, tailor, res. 15 Chatham.
Manning Wm., wks. Post, Helwig & Co.'s Planing Mill.
Manny C., carpenter, res. 137 n. Railroad.
Mansheld T., blacksmith, res. 99 W. Maryland.
Mansur Frank, pork packer, res. 8 e. Vermont.
Mansur I., res. cor. Vermont and Meridian.
Mansur J., res. 8 e. Vermont.
Mansur Josiah, of Pettibone, M. & Co., res. cor. Vermont and Meridan.
Mansur Wm., res. 9 e. Ohio.
Many Carmiel, carpenter, res. 91 n. Railroad.
Many Gerard, teacher, French Indianapolis Female College.
Many John, moulder, wks. with D. Root & Co.
Many John B., carpenter, res. n. Noble.
Marbach Henry, bar keeper, 121 s. Pennsylvania.
Marchant Isaac, clerk, res. cor. California and Market.
Marcy Theo., cooper, wks. 178 w. Washington.
Marion County Agricultural and Horticultural Society Rooms, s. w. cor. Washington and Meridian.
Mark Martin, engineer, res. 26 n. Noble.
Mark Martin, engineer, wks. Union Cabinet Factory.
Marks M. H., clothier, 81 s. Illinois.
Markham T., blacksmith, Pennsylvania, bet. Pearl and Maryland, res. 26 Massachusetts ave.
Marmon Hugo, saloon, 136 w. Washington, res. same.
Maron I., wks. Rolling Mill.
Marowky John, laborer, res. 201 e. Ohio.
MAROT J. R., SECOND HAND FURNITURE, 177 e. Washington, res. same.
Marota Daniel, laborer, res. 174 s. Delaware.
Marquis J O., laborer, res. 113 e. McCarty.
Marrarty Daniel, res. Ann, bet. Mississippi and Tennessee.
Marreson D. A., res. 51 e. Vermont.
Mars E. J., printer, bds. Circle.

Marsh Louis, tailor, res. 149 e. Market.
Marsee Joseph, of M. & Son, res. 147 e. South.
Marsee J. L., of M. & Son, bds. 147 e. South.
MARSEE J. & SON, SAW AND PLANING MILLS, rear
 Little's Hotel. See card, p. 34.
Marsh D. M., agent Osgood & Smith, res. 237 s. Alabama.
Marsh Harmon, M. D., occulist, Blackford's Block, res. 114
 n. Meridian.
Marsh H. B., of Case & M., res. 12 w. New York.
Marsh Lewis, tailor, res. 149 e. Market.
Marshall Rev. Chas., pastor Presbyterian Church, res. cor.
 Tennessee and St. Charles.
Marshall C. M., clerk, res. 12 s. Illinois.
Marshall Levi, carpenter, res. 77 s. New Jersey.
Marshall Mrs., dress maker, 12 s. Illinois.
Marshall Benjamin, laborer, res. 8 Chatham.
Marshell Edward, government teamster, res. 128 e. St. Clair.
Marshell J. W., government teamster, res. 91 e. St. Joseph.
Martin C. M., of M. & Co., bds. 10 e. Michigan.
Martin C. M. & Co., government claim and real estate agents,
 3 e. Washington.
Martin Dennis, salesman, bds. Bates House.
Martin G. W., varnisher, res. cor. Meridian and Market.
Martin J., ostler, wks. with H. Delzell.
Martin Jersey, grocery keeper, res. 199 n. New Jersey.
Martin John, brick mason, res. Orient, bet. Michigan road
 and Washington.
Martin John, brick mason, res. Tennessee, bet. South and
 Merrill.
Martin J. L., grocer, 95 Washington, res. same.
MARTIN LUTHER R., of Wiley & M., res. 6 e. Michigan.
Martin P., tailor, wks. 18 n. Pennsylvania.
Martin Robert, moulder, res. 103 s. New Jersey.
Martin Robert, moulder, Western Machine Works.
Martin Wm., tailor, res. 237 Indiana avenue.
Martin William, saloon keeper, res. 96 Mississippi.
Martindale E. B., of M. & Grubbs, res. n. Meridian, n. of
 Third.
Martindale Mrs. J. A., res. 130 w. Georgia.
Martindale W., clerk, bds. Little's Hotel.
MARTINDALE & GRUBBS, ATTORNEYS AND IN-
 SURANCE AGENTS, 4 New & Talbott's Block.
Martz H. H., miller, res. 99 n. Noble.
Martz Mrs. Laurie, res. 3 Massachusetts ave.
Maskill Denny, laborer, res. Illinois, n. of Third.
Mason B., messenger, American Express Co.
Mason House, B. Mason, proprietor, Louisiana, opp. Union
 Depot.

Mason H., cook, res. 67 Douglas.
Mason J., tobacconist, bds. 96 e. Louisiana.
MASON M., EATING SALOON, cor. Illinois and Louisiana, res. 107 North. See card, p. 72.
Mason T. A., clerk, Mason House.
Mason W. P., carpenter, wks. with D. Root & Co.
MASONIC HALL, cor. Washington and Tennessee.
Mass Andrew, engineer, res. 128 Georgia.
Mather John, engineer, res. 93 Bates.
Matthews Cyrus, carpenter, res. 229 s. East.
Matthews Fred., engineer, bds. Ray House.
Matthews J. W., clerk, New York Store, res. 14 e. Ohio.
Matthews Mrs. Martha, res. 137 n. Noble.
Matthis J. T., salesman, bds. Beck's boarding house.
Mathewey John, saloon and res., Tennessee, bet. Merrill and South.
Matlock J. M., clerk, U. S. Account Department, res. 81 e. South.
Matlock W. W., clerk, U. S. Account Department, res. 13 School.
Matthe C., blacksmith, res. 124 e. Market.
Matthes C., saloon, 7 s. Delaware, res. Washington, bet. Delaware and Pennsylvania.
Matthe Mrs. Margaret, dress maker, res. 124 e. Market.
Matthe Wm., of Fred. P. Rush, res. 256 n. Tennessee.
Mattler S., of M. & Weaner, 164 e. Ohio.
Mattler & Weaner, U. S. Saloon, 3 and 5 s. Delaware.
Matty G., drayman, res. rear 169 s. Alabama.
MAULDIN, ADAMS & CO., BOOT AND SHOE STORE, 53 w. Washington.
Mauldin & Adams, clothiers, West, bet. Georgia and Maryland.
Maurice John, shoemaker, with A. Lintz.
Mawer Chas., Yankee notions, res. 175 n. Illinois.
Mayfield George W., res. 176 n. Tennessee.
Maxwell S. C., book-keeper, 11 e. Pearl, res. 117 n. Meridian.
Maxwell Col. S. D., res. 156 e. Ohio.
Maxwell Wm. D., salesman, New York Bazaar.
May Andrew, cooper, res. 81 s. East.
May John, drayman, res. 119 e. McCarty.
May B. & Co., clothiers, 24 Louisiana.
May Edwin, loan, off. 18½ n. Illinois, res. 75 n. Pennsylvania.
May M., clerk, 6 Bates House.
May R. R., res. 116 w. New York.
MAYER CHAS., DEALER IN FANCY GOODS, TOYS, &c., 29 w. Washington. See card, p. 98.
Mayer Christopher, laborer.

Mayer Joseph, harness maker, bds. Pyle House.
Mayer J. F., umbrella maker, 65 e. Washington, res. 63 n. St. Joseph.
Mayhew E. C., of E. C. M. & Co., res. 39 w. Maryland.
MAYHEW E. C. & CO., WHOLESALE BOOTS AND SHOES, 8 Roberts' Block, opp. Union Depot. See card, p. 64.
Mayhew J. N., clerk, with L. W. Moses, bds. Macy House.
Mayhew Oscar, res. 20 Circle.
Mayhew P. L., traveling agent, E. C. Mayhew & Co.
Mayo E. H., of E. H. M. & Co., bds. cor. Massachusetts ave. and New Jersey.
Mayo E. H. & Co., boots and shoes, Glenn's Block.
MAYOR'S OFFICE, Glenn's Block, John Cavin, Mayor.
Mears Geo. W., M. D., s. w. cor. Meridian and Washington, res. 47 n. Meridian.
Meanshardt P., res. e. Washington.
Means Caleb, salesman, Owen McGinnis, bds. 26 Virginia ave.
Means W. C., tobacco manufacturer, 261 e. Washington.
Mecum Dennis, laborer, res. Elm, near Noble.
Meek Alonzo, R. R engineer, res. 171 e. South.
Megger R., melter, Eagle Foundry.
Mei Christ., clerk, res. 125 n. Liberty.
Meier C. F., carpenter, res. 125 n. Liberty.
Meierhoff Henry, laborer, res. 158 s. Alabama.
Meikel Mrs. C. M., res. 65 n. Mississippi.
Meikel C. P., printer, res. 108 n. Mississippi.
Meikel Jacob, teamster, res. 60 n. Delaware.
Meikel J. P., saloon, 137 w. Maryland, res. same.
MELDRUM R. C., AGENT, UNION OR STAR LINE, fast freight off. 14 s. Meridian, res. 69 w. New York.
Mellally E., laborer, Washington Foundry.
Mellen A. P., clerk, New York Store, bds. 14 e. Ohio.
Mellender Rev. J. W., res. 173 s. New Jersey.
Melander W., painter, bds. Dickey's boarding house.
Melville R. B., tailor, 2 Bates House, res. 70 n. Tennessee.
Mendel Moses, clerk, 19 w. Washington.
Mendenhall N. M., agent, W. H., Turner, 84 w. Washington.
Mengis F., manufacturer cigars, 125 e. Washington.
Merchants' Dispatch, W. F. Clark, agent, cor. Virginia ave. and Alabama.
Mercus A., carpenter, res. 59 w. Georgia.
Meredith Albert, marble cutter, bds. 121 e. Ohio.
Meredith Edward, saw maker, res. 22 Henry.
Meredith Sam'l C., mail agent, res. 52 Blackford.
Meredith Capt. W. M., Co. E, 70th Indiana regiment, res. 132 n. New Jersey.

Meredith Samuel, res. 155 Massachusetts ave.
Merriam E. D., clerk, res. 141 n. Illinois.
Merrick W., laborer, wks. with W. Hinesley.
Merrrill C. J., clerk, res. 250 e. Washington.
MERRILL JOHN F., M. D., ECLECTIC PHYSICIAN, 156 w. Washington, res. 134 w. New York. See card, p. 144.
Merrill Maj. Samuel, of Merrill & Co., res. 207 s. Alabama.
Merrill & Co., publishers and booksellers. Glenn's Block.
Merritt ——, of Davies & M., 26 and 28 w. Washington.
Merritt Geo., of M. & Coughlan, res. 102 n. West.
Merritt J. J., artist, res. 126 w. New York.
MERRITT & COUGHLIN, WOOLEN MANUFACTUR-ERS AND WOOL DEALERS, w. end Washington, on bank of river.
Merriman J. M., of Drake & M., Fletcher's ave.
Merz Mrs., midwife, res. 9 s. Alabama.
Meskill W., book binder, with Wm. Sheets.
METROPOLITAN FIRE INSURANCE CO., SPANN & SMITH, AGENTS, cor. Washington and Pennsylvana.
METROPOLITAN HALL, BUTSCH & CO., PROPRIE-TORS, 84 w. Washington. See card, p. 52.
METROPOLITAN LITERARY INSTITUTE, meets Fri-day evenings at 6, A. Wright's off. Temperance Hall.
METROPOLITAN PHOTOGRAPH GALLERY, College Hall Building. See card, p. 76.
Metz John, of F. Robinius & Co., res. 61 n. West.
Metzger A., real estate agent, res. 139 n. Pennsylvania.
Metzger Alexander, of M. & Striblen, res. 139 n. Pennsyl-vania.
Metzger E., stove store, res. 41 n. East.
Metzger E. J., of Voegtle & M., res. s. e. cor. East and Ohio.
Metzler John E., bar keeper, Louis Lang's Saloon.
Metzger & Striblen, real estate rgents, 6 Odd Fellows' Hall, up stairs.
MEYER C. J., FURNITURE STORE, 171 e. Washington, res. same. See card, p. 60.
Meyer Frank, driver, Cincinnati Bakery.
Myers Fred., carpenter, bds. 78 e. North.
MEYER GEO. F., WHOLESALE & RETAIL DEALER IN CIGARS AND TOBACCO. ALSO, COUNTY TREASURER, 35 w. Washington, res. 56 Vermont. See card, p. 56.
Myer J. C., carpenter, res. 181 Indiana ave.
Myers L., drayman, res. 49 n. Davidson.
Myer M., umberella maker, 11 s. Alabama, res. same.
Myer Nick., shoemaker, res. 267 s. Delaware.
Myer P., res. 266 s. Delaware.

Mez Frederick, clerk, with Munson & Johnson.
Mialled Felix, carpenter, res 242 e. Washington.
Michael Mrs. E., res. 246 Madison R. R. ave.
Michaels J., teamster, res. 59 Union.
Michelsen Geo., salesman, New York Bazaar.
Micheles Henry, cabinet maker, res. 78 s. Benton.
Michael H., carpenter, works Union Cabinet Factory.
Mick J. F., res. 154 n. Delaware.
Mick W. E., res. 72 n. Alabama.
Mick W. S., commission merchant, res. 72 n. Alabama.
Middles David, grocer, 200 w. Washington.
Meger J., umberella maker, res. 63 e. St. Joseph.
Migga John, laborer, res. Wyoming, bet. Delaware and
    High.
Miety Christ., bar keeper, res. 165 e. New York.
Millard Elisha, laborer, res. cor. Orient and Michigan Road.
Mile Chas., works Rolling Mill.
Miles James, carpenter, res. 158 n. Delaware.
Military Hall, n. side Washington, bet. Pennsylvania and
    Meridian.
Millan Wm., works Rolling Mill.
Miller Adam, artist, bds. 59 Maslachusetts ave.
Miller A , drayman, res. 162 s. Tennessee.
Miller Mrs. Amanda, 280 Indiana ave.
Miller August, school teacher, res. Fletcher's ave., near
    Noble.
MILLER A. R., METROPOLITAN PHOTOGRAPH
    GALLERY, 43½ e. Washington, bds. 59 Massachusetts
    ave. See card, page 76.
Miller Andrew, carpenter, res. 107 e. Vermont.
Miller Bryant, painter, res. Meek, near Cady.
Miller C., carpenter, res. 125 n. Davidson.
Miller C., laborer, res. 11 Virginia ave.
Miller Cris., silversmith, res. cor. South and East.
Miller Edward, commissary, res. 135 e. Ohio.
Miller F., cook, bds. 14 e. Washington.
Miller Frank, shoemaker, res. 150 w. Washington.
Miller Fred., cigar maker, bds. Nagal House.
Miller G., moulder, Washington Foundry.
Miller Geo., blacksmith, with Case & Marsh.
Miller G. W., M. D., off. 152 s. Illinois, res. 158 n. Illinois.
Miller H., carpenter, res. 121 n. Davidson.
Miller Henry, laborer, res. 118 n. Missouri.
Miller Henry, grocer, res. 142 n. Noble.
Miller Henry, stair builder, res. 154 n. East.
Miller Isaac, French boot maker, with A. Lintz.
Miller Jacob, clerk, 10 Bates House, bds. 58 w. La.
    14

Miller J., tailor, res. 131 e. Washington.
Miller J., school teacher, res. 49 n. New Jersey.
Miller J., clerk, Head-quarters Supt. Recruiting Service, res. 39 Indiana ave.
Miller J., shoemaker, res. 27 n. East.
Miller J. R., res. 29 Indiana ave.
Miller J. V., carpenter, res. 12 Indiana ave.
Miller John, res. 144 s. Illinois.
Miller John, works Schmidt's Brewery.
Miller John, cooper, works 178 w. Washington.
Miller John, carpenter, res. 196 n. East.
Miller J. V. R., minister, res. 35 n. Penn.
Miller Joseph, shoemaker, res. 27 n. East.
Miller Joseph, res. 155 w. Vermont.
Miller L., blacksmith, bds. cor. Davidson and Ohio.
Miller Leonhardt, tailor, res. 175 e. Pratt.
Miller Mrs. L., res. 58 n. Noble.
Miller Mrs. Mary, res. Maryland, bet. West and R. R
Miller Mrs. M. M., res. 268 e. Washington, 2d floor.
Miller R. A., jeweler, 51 s. Illinois, res. same.
Miller T., tailor, res. 137 e. Washington.
Miller T. P., of M. & Tomlinson, res. 212 e. Washington.
Miller V., laborer, works with Mooney & Co.
Miller Wm., driver Hoes Fire Department No. 3.
Miller W., laborer, res. near colored church.
Miller Wm., laborer, res. 110 w. Georgia.
Miller Wm., res. Missouri, bet. Merrill and South.
Miller Wm., Fire Department, bds. 109 s. Alabama.
Miller Wm., Asst. Gen. Ticket Agent, Secy. and Treasurer Union R. R. Co., cor. Indiana ave. and Ohio.
Miller & Moore, manufacturers and dealers in agricultural implements, 76 w. Washington.
MILLER & TOMLINSON, GROCERS, 212 e. Washington. See card, page 136.
Millet Wm., Mechanic's Boarding House, 52 s. Delaware.
Millikan Eli, res. 86 n. Alabama.
Milliken John, coppersmith, res. Davidson, bet. Market and Ohio.
Mills David, livery stable, res. bet. Delaware and Penn.
Mills James, chief clerk Gen Freight Agent, off. Great Central Railway, bds. 116 s. New Jersey.
Mills L., of Landis & M., res. 134 Mass. ave.
Millschaup R. B., clerk, New York Store, bds. Patterson House.
Milner J., attorney at law, 86 e. Washington.
Milton H. T., carpenter, 254 Indiana ave.
Miney John, laborer, res. Maple.
Minic H., res. 259 s. Pennsylvania.

Miniger Christ., repairer, W. U. Telegraph, res. Illinois, s. of California House.

Mink B. H., iron dealer, res. 45 e. Georgia.

Mitchell ——, (col.) barber, bds. Macy House.

Mitchel Jacob, book-keeper, Glaser & Bros., res. 170 n. Penn.

Mitchell Robert, res. Michigan road, near Washington.

Mitchell L., (col.) barber, bds. Macy House.

Mitchell W. M., carriage maker, res. 138 e. St. Clair.

Mittay J. C., bar-keeper, 107 Washington, res. 159 e. New York.

Mitty Wm., bar-keeper, 7 n. Illinois.

Mix G., clerk, bds. 48 e. Market.

Mix Samuel N., clerk, bds. 132 e. Market.

Mock M., tailor, res. 45 n. Noble.

Mode M., shoemaker, res. 73 e. Washington.

Moesch T. H., confectioner, 76 e. Washington.

Moffit John, res. 155 w. Michigan.

Moffit John, printer, 24 w. Washington, res. New Jersey, below South.

Moffit Oliver J., printer, 24 w. Washington, res. N. Jersey, below South.

Moffitt R. L., machinist, works, Wiggins & Chandler's.

Moffitt Mrs. Sarah, res. 148 s. New Jersey.

Moffitt Wm., clerk, Browning & Slown.

Mollon M. A., salesman, Bee Hive Store, res. 42 w. Maryland.

Molloy James, clerk, New York Store, bds. cor. Tennessee, and Market.

Molloy Roger, clerk, with R. Simpson.

Molone P., works Rolling Mill.

Nolony James, carpenter, res. 87 Mass. ave.

Moloney John, railroader, res. 31 Henry.

Moloney Thos., works Western Machine Works.

Malpas Henry, agent, res. 279 s. Delaware.

Molton R. L., clerk, with Wiley & Martin.

Mon D., works Rolling Mill.

Monenger Daniel, res. 231 n. Tennessee.

Monohan P. H., works Rolling Mill.

Monohan Mrs. C., res. Tennessee, near Rolling Mill.

Monohan J., works Rolling Mill.

Monroe Jas., carpenter, res. 142 e. McCarty.

Montgomery Andrew, shoemaker, res. 112 n. Meridian.

Moneck Martin, tailor, res. 45 n. Noble.

Monninger Conrad, saloon, 164 w. Washington res. same.

Montgomery Mrs. ——, (wid.) res. 154 s. Illinois.

Montgomery Mrs. A., res. 59 Louisiana.

Morminger Jacob, mail agent, res. 60 n. Davidson.

Montague Mrs. Martha, res. 59 s. New Jersey.

Mooney J. E., of M. & Co., bds. 21 s. Delaware.
MOONEY & CO., DEALERS IN LEATHER, HIDES AND OILS, 75 s. Meridian.
Moore Benj., brick mason, res. 18 w. Ohio.
Moore C. G., collector, bds. 100 n. Penn.
Moore Chas. W., of Merrill & Co., res. 83 cor. Merrill and Alabama.
Moore Mrs. D., res. 9 e. Washington.
Moore Geo. W., res. 34 e. Louisiana.
Moore Mrs. H. A., teacher at Institute for the Blind.
Moore H., bds. 90 n. Alabama.
Moore Dr. H. H., res. 164 e. Ohio.
Moore H. A., clerk, bds. 118 n. Penn.
Moore J., laborer, res. 22 s. Alabama.
Moore J. A., book-keeper, Indianapolis Branch Banking Co.
Moore J. L., clerk, Qr. Dep. U. S. A., bds. 155 n. N. Jersey.
Moore Nicholas, works Rolling Mill.
Moore R., tailor, res. 39 West.
Moore Thos., laborer, res. 144 e. Walnut.
MOORHEAD ROBERT I., PROP'R EXCHANGE LIVERY STABLE, 25 n. Illinois. See card, page 104.
Moormann J. J., shoemaker, res. 134 e. Ohio.
Moorss Chas., book store, 83 e. Merrill.
Moorman D., laborer, res. 236 s. Delaware.
Mooran John, laborer, res. 42 s. Liberty.
Moran Pat., laborer, res. 192 s. East.
Morarty D., fireman, Gas Works.
Morce A. C., engineer, res. 90 n. Alabama.
Morehouse W. L., agent, Cincinnati Newspapers, 8 n. Penn., res. 69 n. Delaware.
Morell Gen., off. Blackford's building.
Morgan D., res. Missouri, bet. Smith and Merrill.
Morgan D., res. 5 Willard.
Morgan Daniel, carpenter, res. 169 n. Mississippi.
Morgan Daniel, engineer, I. & M. R. R.
Morgan Daniel, railroader, res. 104 e. McCarty.
Morgan S. W., of Stewart & M., res. 117 s. Alabama.
Morgan John, laborer, res. 173 s. Delaware.
Morgan John, switchman, Bellefontaine R. R.
Morgan Mrs. P., res. 21 McCarty.
Morgan S. C., produce dealer, 95 e. Washington.
Morgan S. W., druggist, res. 117 s. Alabama.
MORGAN T. W., FEED AND GROCERY STORE, 250 e. Washington, res. same.
Morgan W., engineer, works with Root & Co.
Morgan Wm., engineer, res. 59 Kentucky ave.
Morganveck Valentine, grocer, res. 9 Catharine.
Moriarty D., works Rolling Mill.

Moriarty L., works Rolling Mill.
Moriarty Morris, res. 208 s. Delaware.
Moritz, Brother & Co., clothiers, 19 w. Washington.
Moritz Brother, & Co., merchant tailors and clothiers, 3 c.
　　Washington.
Moritz S., of M. Bro. & Co., bds. Louis Lang's.
Morley Albert H., engineer, res. c. Washington.
Morley B. T., moulder, works with D. Root & Co.
Morley Burton, res. 57 s. New Jersey.
Morley Thos., laborer, res. 159 w. Maryland.
Morrell W. S., Librarian, Young Mens' Association, s. w.
　　cor. Meridian and Washington, res. Blackford's Block.
Morrey Isreal, of Morrey & Co., res. 27 n. Illinois.
MORREY & CO., TRUNK MANUFACTURERS, 27 n. c.
　　cor. Illinois and Maryland. See card, p. 84.
Morris Mrs. A. W., res. 53 s. Meridian.
Morris E. J., book binder, with Dodd & Co., 16½ c. Wash.
Morris G. B., (col.) cook, Palmer House.
Morris Geo., artist, res. 33 n. Alabama.
Morris H., expressman, res. 248 Indiana ave.
Morris J. C., photographer, bds. Palmer House.
Morris John D., agent, Cincinnati Depot, res. 50 s. Meridian.
Morris J. D., freight agent, I. & C. R. R., res. 160 n. Penn.
Morris M. res. 19 Union.
Morris Sanford, grocer, res. New Jersey, bet. St. Clair and
　　Pratt.
MORRIS S. V., GROCER, 16 and 18 e. Market, res. Madi-
　　son ave. and corporation line. See card, page 114.
Morris Thos. C , clerk, Bellefontaine R. R. Office.
Morris Thos., shoemaker, res. 18 Benton.
Morris W. B., clerk, res. 179 Huron.
Morrison Chas., clerk, Bellefontaine R. R. Office.
Morrison Jacob, with Wetmore, res. 109 Virginia ave.
Morrison Jas. B., Dept. Secy. State, res. 70 n. Illinois.
Morrison James, attorney at law, 24½ c. Washington, res.
　　cor. St. Marys' and Gravel road.
Morrison Mrs. A. F., res. 32 n. Penn.
Morrison Squire, res. cor. California and Maryland.
Morrison Wm., teamster, res. 243 n. New Jersey.
Morrison Wm., clerk, res. 69 n. Alabama.
Morrison W. H., of Alford, Talbott & Co., res. Circle.
Morrison W., book binder, bds. 40 s. Illinois.
Morrity Pat., laborer, res. 11 e. Bates.
Morrow Thos., res. Market, bet. California and West.
Morton John, machinist, bds. Mechanic's Boarding House.
Morton John, works Rolling Mill.
Morton Lyman, photograph gallery, cor. Washington and
　　Illinois, res. 152 n. Mississippi.

MORTON HON. O. P., GOVERNOR OF THE STATE, res. cor. Market and n. Illinois.
Morton M. J., book binder, with Dodd & Co., res. cor. Maryland and Illinois.
Morton T. R., res. 91 Virginia ave.
Mosbaugh John H., salesman, 4 Bates House, bds. E. Snyders.
Mosel Henry, laborer, res. 27 Nelson alley.
Moses Noah, printer, bds. 20 s. Mississippi.
Moses L. W., optician, 50 e. Washington, bds. Macy House.
Mosher Theodore, engineer, res. 171 e. South.
Mosler S., clothing, res. 24 n. Penn.
Moss Louis, foreman, Rolling Mill, res. Mississippi, near Garden.
Mossler A. I., fancy store, 75 e. Washington.
Mossler L. I., clothier, West, bet. Georgia and Maryland.
MOSSLER L. I., WHOLESALE AND RETAIL CLOTHING, HATS, CAPS, &c., 10 w. Washinton, res. 121 w. Washington. See card, front of book.
Mossler S., book-keeper, 10 w. Washington, res. 24 Penn.
Mothershead Mrs. E., res. 22 n. Meridian.
Mottery F., works Union Steam Bakery, res. Illinois.
Mount A. S., of Mooney & Co., res. 50 s. Illinois.
Mount H., carpenter, res. 46 Benton.
Mounts H. M., conductor, Madison R. R., bds. 129 w. Maryland.
Mower John, tailor, res. Elizabeth.
Moygan D., works Rolling Mill.
Moyler Pat., laborer, Gas Works.
Moymhan A., fireman Gas Works.
Mosar G., butcher, works with Roos & Brother.
Mucho Wm., cigar manufactory, 3 Virginia ave., res. 158 s. Alabama.
MUELLER C. G., SALOON, cor. East and Washington, res. same.
Mueller John, dealer in liquors, cigars, &c., 256 e. Washington, res. same.
Muir James, tea merchant, res. 33 w. Market.
Muirson Alx., 69 w. Alabama.
Mulancy D. J., clerk, res. 53 s. Miss.
Mulchay Mrs. Margaret, res. 25 Benton.
Muldram Thos., works Rolling Mill.
Mull Jacob, carriage maker, res. 35 w. New York.
Mull J. H., carriage maker, cor. Kentucky ave. and Georgia, res. 35 New York.
Mullan Wm., res. 143 e. South.
Mullally Edward, laborer, res. 2 e. Huron.
Mullarkey J. H., salesman, bds. Little's Hotel.

Mulleney Mrs. Mary, res. 53 s. Miss.
Muller L. P., res. 136 e. South.
Mullin Henry, clerk, bds. 152 n. Pennsylvania.
Mulliker J., coppersmith, wks. I. & C. Machine Shop.
MUMFORD J. C., PROPRIETOR J. C. MUMFORD'S
    BUSINESS COLLEGE, 3d floor, Sentinel Building,
    bds. Macy House.
Munderhill Thos., wks. Rolling Mill.
Munger F., porter, wks. with Pomeroy, Fry & Co.
Munhall C., salesman, 17 w. Washington.
Munhall H., clerk, with J. H. Baldwin.
Munsell E., wagon maker, res. Peru, bet. Davidson and
    Railroad.
Munsell Newton, fireman, Bellefontaine Car Shop.
Munson C. H., of M. & Johnson, res. 120 n. Alabama.
Munson David, of M. & Johnson, res. 88 e. Market.
Munson Louis, bds. 120 n. Alabama.
MUNSON W. L., GROCER, 21 n. Alabama.
Munson & Johnson, stove manufactory, 66 e. Washington.
Murdock Mrs. A. E., res. 42 n. Spring.
Murdock J., moulder, wks. with D. Root & Co.
Murphey Henry, laborer, res. 176 s. Alabama.
Murphey J. K., clerk, bds. Spencer House.
Murphey J. Y., policeman, res. 193 e. St. Clair.
Murphey Daniel, res. 64 Bright.
Murphy James, boot fitter, with A. Lintz.
Murphy J. W., of M., Kennedy & Co., res. 33 e. Ohio.
Murphy James, res. Elizabeth.
Murphy John W., dry goods, res. 33 e. Ohio.
Murphy J., fireman, Gas Works.
Murphy John, res. Missouri Place.
Murphy John, wks. Rolling Mill.
Murphy, Kennedy & Co., wholesale dry goods, 42 and 44 e.
    Washington.
Murphy M., head waiter, Little's Hotel.
Murphy Milton, clerk, res. alley, bet. Washington and Mar-
    ket.
Murphy Peter, wks. Rolling Mill.
Murphy T. A.. clerk, A. & U. S. Express Co., bds. Macy
    House.
Murphy Tobias M., cooper, res. 43 e. Georgia.
Murphy Timothy, laborer, res. 129 Blake.
Murphy Wm. H., carpenter and joiner, res. 176 n. East.
Murray John, clerk, New York Store, bds. 20 s. Mississippi.
Murry M., laborer, bds. 149 e. Ohio.
Mussman D., clerk, bds. cor. Virginia ave. and East.
Muth P. J., bar-keeper, Louis Lang's Saloon.
Myer Christ., shoemaker, bds. 176 e. Washington.

Myer C., brass moulder, res. cor. East and Louisiana.
Myer Jacob, res. 89 Market.
Myer J. G., laborer, res. 177 n. Noble.
Myer Moses, dealer in clothing, 4 w. Washington, res. 16 Ohio.
Myer Moses, of Fox & M., res. 116 Ohio.
Myer S., salesman, 2 Palmer House, bds Hotel De La Maas.
Myer Wm., blacksmith, res. 25 Harrison.
Myer Wm., bar-keeper, Crystal Palace Saloon.
Myers Christopher, brass foundry, res. 50 s. East.
Myers F., carpenter, res. Bickner, bet. Delaware and High.
Myers G., printer, res. 154 n. New Jersey.
Myers J., res. 24 Louisiana.
Myers J., carpenter, res. 181 s. Tennessee.
Myers John, tinner, res. 111 e. McCarty.
Myers J. A., tinner, res. 111 e. McCarty.
Myers J. G., laborer, res. 177 n. Noble.
Myers Jake, finisher, wks. with D. Root & Co.
MYERS J. D., COMMISSION MERCHANT AND WHOLESALE AND RETAIL DEALER IN CHOICE FAMILY FLOUR, FEED, &c., 8 and 12 s. Pennsylvania, bds. Palmer House. See card, p. 80.
Myers L. F., confectioner, res. 154 n. New Jersey.
Myers L., drayman, Washington Foundry.
Myers Myer, book-keeper, 9 Bates House, bds. Macy House.
Myers Philip, shoemaker, res. 108 n. Noble.
Myers Peter, laborer, Eagle Foundry.
Myers W., apprentice, Washington Foundry.
Myers Xavery, stove mounter, Eagle Foundry.
Myrich John, cooper, wks. 178 w. Washington.
Myrt John, carpenter, res. 17 Willard.

N

Nagle Daniel, laborer, res. 23 Harrison.
Nahan Wm., shoemaker, with Jones, Vinnedge & Co.
Nakel Augustus, driver at Western Engine House, res. 50 w. Maryland.
Nall Jonathan, produce dealer, res. 108 e. Market.
Naltner A., real estate sale agent, for Seidensticker and Kappes, res. 93 s. Meridian.
Nann Wm., laborer, res. 162 e. Michigan.
Nash Thomas, machinist, bds. East Street House.
Nather E., real estate agent, res. 93 s. Meridian.
National Hotel, David Bender, proprietor, 217 w. Washington.
Neab C., copper smith, bds. Pyle House.
Neall J. R., dealer in produce, 180 e. Washington, res. 110 e. Market.

Neff J. D., carriage maker, res. 12 e. Walnut.
Neffle F., butcher, bds. 91 s. Illinois.
Neffle Fred., res. 105 s. West.
Negley S. B., clerk, bds. 113 w. Washington.
Neiger Fred., wagon maker, res. 159 e. St. Clair.
Neighbors Chas., expressman, res. 23 Henry.
Neighbors R., drayman, res. 33 Union.
Neil E., of W. F., Winkle & Co., res 134 e. Washington.
Neimann Christ., carpenter, res. 122 n. Davidson.
Neiman John S., proprietor Ohio House, Market, bet. Illinois and Tennessee.
Neiman Joseph, res. 207 Indiana ave.
Nell James, laborer, res. 46 Bates.
Nell J. B., book keeper, New York Bazaar, res. 33 n. Noble.
Nelson Henry, sheriff supreme court, res. 73 n. Mississippi.
Nelson H. L., of W. H. Talbott & Co., res. cor. South and Alabama.
Nelson John, machinist, works I. & C. Machine Shop.
Nelson John, machinist, res. 25 Orsbrook.
Nelson Sandy, plasterer, res. 78 n. Missouri.
Nelson Thomas, builder, bds. 17 Mass. ave.
Nelson T. A., salesman, bds. 17 Mass. ave.
Nemyer Wm., res. 64 s. Noble.
Nersthimer G., tinner, bds. 199 e. Washington.
Netser F., blacksmith, res. 45 Union.
Netzel J., butcher, res. Bluff Road.
Neugent J. M., clerk, bds. 54 n. East.
Neugens J. J., salesman, Hume, Lord & Co., bds. Pyle House.
New John C., res. 102 n. Pennsylvania.
Newbery J., harness maker, bds. Bicking House.
Newbery Mrs. S , res. 110 n. Pennsylvania.
Newby Mrs. C., res. 114 w. Georgia.
Newcomb H. C., of N. & Tarkington, res. 58 n. Alabama.
Newcomb R. H., clerk, res. 144 e. New York.
NEWCOMB & TARKINGTON ATTORNEYS AT LAW, 24½ e. Washington.
Newcomer Dr. F. S., assistant post surgeon, cor. Virginia ave. and Maryland.
NEW YORK LIFE INSURANCE CO., W. J. Wynn, general agent, s. w. cor. Washington and Meridian.
NEWMAN JOHN S., PRESIDENT GREAT CENTRAL RAILWAY, res. 97 n. Pennsylvania.
Newman P., laborer, res. 95 Missouri.
New York Bazaar, Emil Klotz, proprietor, 37 e. Wash.
NEW YORK STORE, W. & H. GLENN PROPRIETORS, GLENNS' BLOCK, e. Washington. See card, pages 150 and 151.

Ney D. M., boiler maker, works I. & C. R. R. Machine Shop.
Niccum J. G., blacksmith, Illinois, s. Union Depot.
Nichols A. D., clerk, res. 151 Virginia ave.
Nichols A. II., painter, bds. 25 Chattham.
Nichols J. M., teller, Branch Bank State of Indiana, res. 80
    n. Meridian.
Nichols T. M , dentist, 24 s. Meridian.
Nichols William, clerk, res. 37 c. St. Clair.
Nichols Wm., (col.) res. 100 Douglas.
Nicholson D., stone cutter, res. 38 s. Pennsylvania.
Nicholson Geo., teamster, res. 147 n. Tennessee.
Nicholson J. C., painter, res. 147 n. Tennessee.
Nicholson Wm. T., laborer, res. 13 Lord.
Nickum John R., of N. & Parrott, res. 66 n. East.
NICKUM & PARROTT, PROP'S. UNION STEAM BA-
    KERY, 11 n. Pennsylvania.
Nicolai F., laborer, Washington Foundry.
Nicolai G., res. 89 w. Washington.
Niculai Charles, harness maker, 268 c. Washington, res.
    same.
Niebergall J., carpenter, res. Winson, bet. Michigan and
    North.
Neiman Chas., blacksmith, bds. 215 Mass. ave.
Nies Louis, carpenter, res. 190 n. East.
Nigar Jacob, laborer, res. 103 c. Washington, up stairs.
Night J. F., agent for patent rights, bds. 88 n. Alabama.
Niowanger S. T., clerk and notary public, with C. Hamlin,
    res. cor. Mass. ave. and Alabama.
Nixon Rev. J. H., res. Michigan, bet. Pennsylvania and
    Delaware.
Nixon Robert, clerk, with Haskit & Co., bds. Oriental
    House.
Nixon Robert M., clerk, 14 w. Washington.
Noakes Mrs. W., res. 33 s. Liberty.
Noble W. P., Noble Farm, res. c. Market.
Noble Wm., general ticket agent, I. & C. R. R., res. s. end
    Delaware.
Nobin G. D., farmer, res. 176 n. East.
Nodle Mrs. Margaret, res. 200 Mass. ave.
Noe M., of S. Behymer & N., res. 38 s. Liberty.
Noe Mrs. Martha, res. 73 s. New Jersey.
Noel S. V. B., commission merchant, res. 160 s. New Jersey.
Nolan Michael, clerk, New York Store, bds. cor. Tennessee
    and Market.
Nolding Chas., laborer, res. 65 c. St. Joseph.
Nolcin S. C., cabinet maker, res. 172 c. Washington up stairs.
Nollan Thomas, hackman, res. 95 s. Tennessee.
Nooe Daniel, blacksmith, res. 75 s. New Jersey.

Nopper Christ., with Louis Lang.
Northway A. M., plasterer, res. 94 n. New Jersey.
Northway John, plasterer, res. 146 e. North.
Norwood F., res. 26 n. Illinois.
Norwood Mrs., 72 w. Maryland.
Norwood George, res. 95 n. Illinois.
Nowland J. H. B., res. 177 e. South.
Null Mrs. Sarah, res. 104 w. Vermont.
Null Thos. E., book binder, bds. 108 w. Vermont.
Nutman Fred., cooper, res. West, near South.
Nuttmeyer Christ., car builder, res. 151 e. Ohio.
Nutts Jacob, baker, res. 60 e. Maryland.
Nye M., tailor, res. cor. South and Tennessee.

O

O'Brian Timothy, bill poster, Great Central Railway Line,
    bds. Spencer House.
O'Brien Mrs., res. 157 s. Tennessee.
O'Brien Jerry, tinner, res. Wyoming, bet. Delaware and
    High.
O'Bryen John, laborer, res. 176 s. Alabama.
O'Brien L., res. w. Washington, near Woolen Factory.
O'Brien M., carpenter, bds. cor. Biddle and Vinton.
O'Brien Thos., laborer, res Maple.
O'Bryan Thos., laborer, res. Keely's Block, bet. New Jersey
    and East.
O'Connel D., laborer, 232 Madison R. R. ave.
O'Connel J., fireman, Gas Works.
O'Connel J., saloon, 210 w. Washington, res. same.
O'CONNOR JOSEPH, AGENT SAND'S CELEBRATED
    CREAM AND STOCK ALE, 30 s. Illinois. See card,
    in front of book.
O'Connor J., clerk, res. 202 s. Pennsylvania.
O'Coner James, laborer, res. 24 Lord.
O'Conners Michael, res. 37 s. Noble.
ODD FELLOWS' HALL, cor. Pennsylvania and Washing-
    ton.
O'Donald Mrs., res. 153 s. Tennessee.
O'Driscoll John, stereotyper, with Dodd & Co., res. cor.
    Market and Tennessee.
Oehler A., jeweler, 1 s. Delaware.
Oehler R., watchmaker, 23 s. Illinois.
O'Faut W., harness maker, with A. J. Henisley & Co.
Off Christ., of O. Off & Co., bds. 137 n. Davidson.
Off Christ. & Brother, saw mill, n. Davidson.
Off Gottlieb, of O. & Off, bds. 32 n. Railroad.
Off Jacob, laborer, bds. 32 n. Railroad.
Offutt C. G., clerk, bds. Meek, bet. Noble and Liberty.

Offutt Thomas, clerk, res. Meek, bet. Liberty and Noble.
Offutt T. H., salesman, res. 12 Meek.
Oglesby J. H., steam boating, res. 91 n. Tennessee.
O'Hare Mat., tailor, res. 127 w. South.
Ohaver Jackson, carpenter, res. 109 Blake.
O'Haver John, laborer, res. Ann, near Rolling Mill.
Ohear J., wks. Rolling Mill.
Ohear J. O., wks. Rolling Mill.
O'Horro A., laborer, res. West, bet. South and Merrill.
Ohr A. D., assistant general ticket agent, secretary and
    treasurer, Union R. W. Co., res. 240 n. Illinois.
Ohr Henry, collecting clerk, Adams Express Co.
OHR JOHN H., AGENT ADAMS EXPRESS CO., 12 e.
    Washington, res. 91 e. Ohio.
Okey Edward, wks. lumber yard, res. 167 n. New Jersey.
Okey James D., carpenter, res. 82 n. Alabama.
Okey Joseph, carpenter, res. 144 n. East.
Okey Philip A., carpenter, res. 228 n. New Jersey.
Oldham Wm., grocer, res. 155 Alabama.
Oleary J., City Saloon, 53 s. Illinois, res. 155 s. Illinois.
Olin C. C., general agent Equitable Fire Insurance Co., 16
    Talbott & New's Block, res. 61 w. New York.
Olin E. D., res. 61 w. New York.
Olsen Peter, wks. Rolling Mill.
O'Mara Richard, wks. Palmer House, res. 111 Blake.
O'Neal J., bds. Wm. Johnson.
O'Neall M., tailor, res. 143 s. Tennessee.
Onealy Patrick, laborer, res. 14 Georgia.
Onsill John, laborer, res. 79 e. Narket.
Orbison W. O., salesman, E. H. Mayo & Co.
Oreilly M., shoemaker, wks. with A. Knodle.
O'Reiley Tim, laborer, res. Tennessee, bet. Merrill and South.
Oriental House, Illinois, bet. Maryland and Georgia.
Orileg J., shoemaker, wks. A. Knodle.
Orlopp R., of O. & Taylor, bds. Little's Hotel.
ORLOPP & TAYLOR, LIVERY AND SALE STABLES,
    22 and 24 s. Pennsylvania. See card, p. 56.
Ormond Jas., wks. Rolling Mill.
ORMSLEY G., FOREMAN U. S. COMMISSARY DE-
    PARTMENT.
Ornduff D. H., money receiving clerk, Adams Express Co.,
    res. 28 Indiana ave.
Orr Geo., of McCoy & O., bds. Palmer House.
Orsborn Elizabeth, res. 99 Indiana ave.
Orth Geo., teamster, res. West, near South.
Oswald Christ., varnisher, wks. Union Cabinet Factory.
Osborn Wm., carpenter, wks. Wiggins & Chandler's, bds.
    258 w. Washington.

Osborn J. C., harness maker, bds. Bicking House.
Osgood C. J., clerk, 12 w. Washington.
Osgood John B., painter, res. 80 e. Market.
Osgood J. R., of O. & Smith, res. 52 s. Meridian.
OSGOOD & SMITH, HUB, SPOKE AND LAST FAC-
    TORY, Illinois, 1 square s. of Union Depot.
Osleameier Fred., res. e. Washington, near Corporation line.
Ossenforth Fred., drayman, Maguire, Jones & Co.
Ostertag Charles, cooper, bds. Davidson.
Osterman J., clerk, with Fred. P. Rush.
Ostermeier Christ., drayman, res. 137 e. Ohio.
Ostermeyer Anthony, switchman, Bellefontaine R. R., res.
    Meek.
Ostermeyer F. & Co., dry goods and groceries, 258 e. Wash-
    ington.
Ostermeyer F., of O. & Co., res. National road.
Ostermeyer Henry, res. Meek, near Liberty.
Ostermeyer Louis, laborer, res. 145 n. Liberty.
Oswald Gottfried, painter, res. 165 n. Railroad.
Ott Chas., wks. Rolling Mill.
Ott M., wks. Rolling Mill.
Otten D., saloon, res. same.
Otto Charles, doctor, res. 5 n. Noble.
Otto Wm., carpenter, res. 155 e. Ohio.
Ottoe P., laborer, res. 77 Bluff road.
Otts M., laborer, res. 269 s. East.
Oval Joseph, miller, res. California, near Washington.
Overfill I., laborer, res. 326 s. Delaware.
Overhall T., (col.) wks. with W. F. Jenkins.
Overstrus James M., laborer, res. 5 e. New York.
Outland Edward, (col.) barber, res. 57 w. Georgia.
Owens John, plasterer, res. Market, bet. California and West.
Owings N., res. 87 e. South.
Oyler Wm., department marshall, res. alley, bet. Alabama
    and New Jersey.

P

Padlon James C., blacksmith, res. 100 s. Noble.
Paff Wm., carpenter, bds. 279 s. East.
Paffman Jacob, painter, res. 340 Virginia ave.
Page Louis, bar-keeper, Atlantic Saloon.
Paige Miss L. B., matron, Deaf and Dumb Asylum.
Paine Daniel, printer, res. 82 n. Tennessee.
PAINE DANIEL L., EDITOR, JOURNAL.
Palmer Daniel, carpenter, res. 11 Huron.
Palmer E. L., book binder and dealer in blank books, pa-
    per, &c., 34 s. Illinois, res. 40 s. Illinois.
Palmer G. W., clerk, Oriental House.

Palmer House, Bussey & Davis, Prop's, cor. Washington
and Illinois.
Palmer James, (col.) barber, res. 143 n. Tenn.
Palmer Capt. J. J., res. 149 n. Pennsylvania.
PALMER T. G., DEPT. AUDITOR OF STATE, res. 90 n.
Illinois.
Pander M., horse buyer, res. 60 n. East.
Pander Wm., laborer, res. 129 e. North.
Park T., res. cor. Washington and Tenn.
Parker C. C., clerk, with D. Titcomb, cor. Maryland and
Virginia ave.
Parker E. F., clerk, U. S. Commissary Department, res.
121 w. Maryland.
Parker E., tailor, 69 s. Pennsylvania.
Parker Edward, clerk, res. 121 w. Maryland.
Parker Geo., moulder, res. 9 Henry.
Parker Mills, harness maker, bds. cor. Market & Circle.
Parker R. R., dealer in shirts and mens' furnishing goods,
30 w. Washington, res. 14 s. Mississippi.
Parker Wilson, brick mason, res. 103 s. Tenn.
Parkhill H. H., salesman, bds. Pyle House.
Parkman C. B., Secy. Rolling Mill Co., 8 Blakes Block, res.
30 s. Tennessee.
Parks H. J., carpenter, res. 76 s. Benton.
Parks H. J., (col.) cook, Little's Hotel.
Parks P. S., res. 42 s. Meridian.
Parsley A., teamster, res. n. Mississippi.
Parmelee E. L., telegraph operator, bds. California.
Parmelee Geo., telegraph operator, bds. California, bet. N.
York and Vermont.
Parmelee Mrs. H., res. California, bet. Vermont and New
York.
Parmelee W. H., agent, L. & I. R. R., res. 71 w. New York.
Parr W. P., physician, of Duzan & P., bds. s. Delaware.
Parrott H., bakery and confectionery, res. 141 n. Delaware.
Parrott Horace, Union Steam Bakery, 11 n. Penn., res. 141
n. Delaware.
Parrott Thos., cooper, res. 192 w. Maryland.
Parry R., blacksmith, res. Henry, bet. Canal and Miss.
Parsons John J., of H. H. Dodd & Co., res. 94 n. West.
Parvin J., currier, res. cor. Illinois and Ohio.
Parvin Theophelus, M. D., res. 75 n. Alabama.
Pasanir John, carpenter, res. 136 n. Davidson.
Pascoes James, barber, Market, res. 126 Cady.
Patrie John, boarding house and saloon, 222 e. Whshington.
Patterson S. D., clerk, I. & C. R. R, res. Michigan road,
near Washington.
Patterson Mrs. E., res. cor. Missouri and Georgia.

Patterson J. P., wholesale grocer, res. 85 n. New Jersey.
Patterson John, carpenter, res. 30 s. Illinois.
Patterson K. D., (wid.) res. 104 Massachusetts ave.
Patterson M., feed stable, 34 e. Maryland.
Patterson Mill, Washington, near river bridge.
Patterson R. R., livery stable, res. 260 n. Tenn.
Patterson Samuel, miller, res. Wilson.
Patterson W. A., clerk, with J. F. Wingate.
Patterson Wm. A., clerk, res. 114 n. Alabama.
Pattison A. E., book-keeper, Murphy, Kennedy & Co.
Pattison C. B., salesman, with Crossland & Pee, res. 228 n. Illinois.
PATTISON E. W., OF P. & CO., res. n. end Illinois.
Pattison Isaac, res. 40 n. East.
PATTISON J. D., OF P. & CO., res. cor. St. Clair and Ill.
Pattison Joseph, merchant, res. 228 n. Ills.
Pattison Joseph D., of P. & Co., res. cor. Illinois and St. Clair.
PATTISON W. A., OF P. & CO., bds. Mrs. Morrison's.
PATTISON & CO., PORK PACKERS, 1 Talbott & News' Block, up stairs.
Pattison & Co., pork house, bank of river, near railroad.
Paul H., policeman, res. 62 e. South.
Paule Henry, carpenter, res. 88 n. Davidson.
Paule John, baker, 107 n. Noble.
Paynter J. P., hackman, res. cor. Second and Tennessee.
Payton Wm., (col.) leather currier, res. 139 n. West.
Paxton Mrs. E., res. 3 Circle.
Peabody C. P., laborer, works with J. Peabody.
PEABODY JOHN, LIVERY AND FEED STABLE, 18 e. Maryland. See card, p. 52.
Peacock Wm. H., machinist, res. e. Washington, near Corporation Line.
Pearce S. J., printer, with Dodd & Co., bds. 163 e. Ohio.
Pearson John, J. P. & Co., 78 w. Washington, res. same.
Pearson Joseph, stone cutter, res. 127 n. Mississippi.
PEARSON J. & CO., PROP'RS. HOUSE OF LORDS SALOON, 78 w. Washington. See card, opp. back cover.
Pearson Mrs. Mary, res. 120 e. Michigan.
Pearsall P. R., music teacher, res. 26 s. Tennessee.
Peaslee W. A., photographer, 16½ e. Washington, bds. Bates House.
Peck E. J., president T. H. & R. R. R., res. w. Maryland.
Peck James, carpenter, res. 176 n. East.
Peck T. S., of Cox, Lord & P., res. Meridian, bet. South and McCarty.
Peden J., bar keeper, Washington Hall.
Pedicord Mrs. L., res. 179 e. Market.

Pedlo R., moulder, Eagle Foundry.
Pedrick E., dress maker, 19 w. Washington, 3d floor.
Pee G. W., of Crossland & P., bds. Macy House.
Pee I. E., entry clerk, with Crossland & Pee.
Peelle Wm. A., president Equitable Fire Insurance Co., 16 Talbott & New's Block.
Pegan Mrs. J. R., dress maker, res. 52 n. East.
Pence Adam, baker, res. 186 s. Delaware.
Pelkington James, soldier, res. 19 n. East.
Pellett Wm. A., conductor, res. 35 s. Noble.
Peltier Leon, marble worker and cutter, res. 55 n. Orsbrook.
Pendergast J. G., wks. Byrkit & Reans, bds. Mrs. Deming.
PENN GEO. W., BOOK-KEEPER, Sinker & Co., bds. 120 n. Delaware.
Pennoyer Miss M. A., actress, Metropolitan.
Pense Augustus, book binder, with Dodd & Co., bds. Kentucky ave.
Pentecost George F., proprietor Oriental House.
PENTECOST G. F., PROPRIETOR ORIENTAL HOUSE, Illinois, bet. Maryland and Georgia. See card, p. 126.
Pentecost M. B., dealer in fruit cans, 188 e. Washington.
Pentecost M. B., of P. & Rersener, cor. North and Alabama.
Pentecost S. F., clerk, bds. cor. North and Alabama.
PENTECOST & REISENER, CANED FRUITS, 188 e. Washington. See card, p. 86.
Percell Sarah, (col.) washing, res. n. Missouri.
Perdue M. W., carpenter, res. 184 n. Noble.
Perigo S. W., res. 28 Willard.
PERINE P. R., COAL AND LIME YARD, 12 w. Maryland, res. 121 n. Alabama. See card, p. 78.
Perkins Ambrose, laborer, res. 42 Bates.
Perkins James, wks. Western Machine Works.
Perkins Sam'l E., judge supreme court, res. 152 w. New York.
Perkinson Pat., blacksmith, wks. Sinker & Co.
Peoples Nancy, (wid.) res. 123 n. Alabama.
Pero Chas. R., messenger, American Express Co.
Perren George K., lawyer, res. 35 e. Michigan.
Perrin Geo. K., of P. & Manlove, res. 35 e. Michigan.
Perrin & Manlove, attorneys and U. S. claim agents, 45 e. Washington, College Hall Building.
PERRINE C. O., PUBLISHER, Odd Fellows' Hall.
Perrott Samuel, grocer, 191 Indiana ave., res. same.
Perry J. C., clerk, res. 175 n. New Jersey.
Perry Mrs. M. A., res. cor. Ohio and Meridian.
Perry Matthew, moulder, res. Grier.
Perry M., moulder, Western Machine Works.
Perry N., barber, cor. Washington and Kentucky ave.

Perry John C., grocery keeper, res. 175 n. New Jersey.
Peterson J. D., carpenter, res. 94 n. New Jersey.
Peterson Peter, wks. Rolling Mill.
Pettibone Asa, of P., Mansur & Co., bankers, res. cor. New York and Pennsylvania.
Pettiford John, res. cor. Georgia and Missouri.
Petty Julius, farmer, 266 Indiana ave.
Peyton E. B., of P. & Line, res. 188 e. Washington.
Peyton & Line, restaurants, 65 s. Illinois.
Pfaendler N., varnisher, res. Maryland, bet. West and Canal.
Pfafflen P., bar-keeper, res. w. Market, near Canal.
Pfafflin Theodore, grocer, res. 15 w. North.
Pfeiffer J. G., laborer, res. 86 e. St. Joseph.
Pfleger Jacob, tailor, res. 64 n. Davidson.
Pfleger L., laborer, res. 6 Madison ave.
Pfleger R., locksmith, res. cor. Delaware and Market.
Pfliger George, soldier, res. 26 n. Delaware.
Pfliger Ludwig, expressman, bds. 26 n. Delaware.
Pfliger Reimund, locksmith, bds. 26 n. Delaware.
Phalen M., currier, wks. with Yandes & Co.
Phelan Wm., boiler maker, res. 288 Virginia ave.
Phelan Patrick, res. 288 Virginia ave.
Phelps A. E., harness maker, res. 51 e. Market.
Phelps N. Allen E., saddler, res. 51 e. Market.
Phelps Simon B., engineer, res. 102 Louisiana.
Phelps Wm., clerk, I. & M. R. R. Freight Depot, bds. Ray House.
Phillips Chas., wks. Western Machine Works.
Phillips H. M., blacksmith, res. w. New York.
Phillips Jacob, carpenter, res. 76 s. Noble.
Phipps E. R., silversmith, with W. H. Craft.
Phipps John M., res. 120 s. Noble.
Phipps I. N., real estate agent, 36 e. Washington.
Phipps L. M., assessor, res. 175 n. Alabama.
Picken John, book-keeper, bds. 8 Virginia ave.
Pickerill G. W., doctor, res. 36 e. Pratt.
Pickering Lieut. Col. C. H., U. S. (col.) troops, res. 52 e. Market.
Pickering E. H., res. 52 e. Market.
Piel Wm., grocer, res. Washington, near Orient.
Piel W. F., of P. & Co., res. National road.
Piel Wm. F. & Co., dry goods and groceries, 240 e. Washington.
Pierce N. A., res. 122 n. Illinois.
Pierce W. S., of McKernan & P., res. 92 n. West.
Pierce Wm., gardener, Deaf and Dumb Asylum.
Pierce Wm., wks. with McCord & Wheatley.

15

Pierson John, brick mason, res. 4 Liberty.
Pierson L. W., res. 112 n. Alabama.
Pig John, laborer, res. 40 e. Louisiana.
Pilkenton James, doctor, res. 19 n. East.
Pillbean George, 11th Indiana cavalry, res. s. Missouri.
Pitts Frank, farming, res. n. Illinois, near Tinker.
Pitts George, res. 78 cor. Vermont and Mississippi.
Pitzer J. B., res. 48 n. Tennessee.
Plane T. S., brick moulder, res. 183 e. Market.
Planks Henry W. K., railroader, res. 37 Orsbrook.
Plant G., res. 193 o. Washington.
Plasinck C., cabinet maker, 206 n. Alabama.
Plumb Dexter, painter, res. 59 e. Market.
Plumb D. S., painter, bds. 61 e. Market.
Plumb H. H., salesman, res. 61 e. Market.
Plumb H. H., clerk, res. 59 e. Market.
Plumb H. H., salesman, Fancy Bazaar, bds. 61 e. Market.
Plummer Mrs. A., res. 82 e. Market.
Plummer Hiram, porter, New York Bazaar.
Pohler Christopher, drayman, res. 312 Virginia ave.
Pohler Lewis, grocer, res. 142 e. Market.
Pohler William, laborer, res. 314 Virginia ave.
Poirier Henry, moulder, wks. with D. Root & Co.
Poirier Henry, moulder, res. 170 s. Tennessee.
Poirier John, wks. Western Machine Works.
Poler Henry, laborer, wks. I. & M. R. R. Freight Depot.
Pomeroy, Fry & Co., wholesale hardware and iron, 24 s.
    Meridian.
Pomeroy J. A., of P., Fry & Co., bds. Bates House.
Pool A. J., engineer, Central R. R., res. 24 n. New Jersey.
Poole J. E., book-keeper, bds. 21 s. Delaware.
Pope Abner, res. North, bet. Illinois and Tennessee.
Pope Christian, res. 33 Harrison.
Pope Henry, machinist, res. 117 West.
Pope Wm. A., res. cor. First and Mississippi.
Poppenseaker G., laborer, res. 108 s. Noble.
Porter Albert G., of McDonald & P., res. 109 cor. Michigan
    and Delaware.
Porter H., teamster, res. 47 w. McCarty.
Porter N. F., saloon, 49 e. South.
Porter N. F., Vinegar Factory, 49 e. South, res. 152 w.
    Georgia.
Porter O. T., clerk, with Tousey & Byram.
Porter Nathaniel, liquors, res. 152 w. Georgia.
Porter T. R., tailor, res. 86 e. Michigan.
Porter Wm. W., (col.) barber, 218 e. Wash., bds. 76 Benton.

Post Chas., wks. Planing Mill, res. 164 w. New York.
POST, HELWIG & CO., PLANING MILL AND LUM-
BER YARD, cor. New York and Canal.
Post Office, A. H. Conner, postmaster, cor. Pennsylvania
and Market.
POTTAGE BENJ., DEALER IN HARDWARE, IRON,
CUTLERY AND CARRIAGE TRIMMINGS, 76 w.
Washington, res. 91 Market.
Potter John L., boarding house, res. 12 n. East.
Potts Mrs. Mary A., res. North, bet. Illinois and Tennessee.
Powalky P., machinist, wks. Western Machine Works.
Powell J., wks. Rolling Mill.
Powell Thos., wks. Rolling Mill.
Power Jacob, policeman, res. 31 n. East.
Powers Martin, watchman, res. 62 Indiana ave.
Powers M. B., watchman.
Powers P., laborer, res. 209 s. Pennsylvania.
Powers Pat., boiler maker, Western Machine Works.
Powers S., wks. Rolling Mill.
Powers Thos., wks. Rolling Mill.
Powers Thomas, laborer, res. Nelson alley.
Poyntz John C., clerk, New York Store, res. 14 e. Ohio.
Prange Chas., of Ostermeyer & Co., res. 258 e. Washington,
2d floor.
Pratt H. M., cook, Mason House.
Pratt W. B., agent, P. & I. R. R., res. 43 e. Pratt.
Pray Wm., res. 168 Tennessee.
Pray W., of Gates, P. & Co., res. 130 Massachusetts ave.
Presley J. T., railroader, res. 75 s. East.
Presse Henry, shoemaker, res. 345 Virginia ave.
Pressel Wm., carpenter, res. 70 e. Louisiana.
Preston Eliott, railroader, res. 239 s. Alabama.
Prett Wm. B., book-keeper, R. R. depot, res. 43 e. Pratt.
Price Mrs. E. J., teacher, Institute for the Blind.
Price Mrs. Margaret, res. 140 e. Market.
Price Jas., wks. Rolling Mill.
Price John, shoemaker, res. 71 n. East.
Prince J. T., clerk, 35 n. Noble.
Prindle Merwin, superintendent Union Railway Co., bds.
Coens.
Prinz John D., clerk, res. 35 n. Noble.
Prossen Henry, shoemaker, E. H. Mayo & Co.
Prudhomme Thos. W., clerk, New York Store, bds. 20 s.
Mississippi.
Prunk D. H., doctor, res. 21 w. Michigan.
Ptrapp Michael, teamster, res. 192 n. Noble.

Pugh James, res. California, near cor. Maryland.
Pugh Wm., res. West, near cor. Maryland.
Purcell Geo. W., salesman, with Jones, Hess & Davis.
Purcell Wm., weaver, Merritt & Coughlin's Woolen Factory.
Puckey Mrs. Elizabeth, res. Illinois, n. of Third.
Purdy Wm., Commercial College, Ætna Building, bds. Palmer House.
Purnell John, cabinet maker, res. 121 n. New Jersey.
Purnell M., clerk, bds. 70 s. Tennessee.
Pursell A. E., dentist, res. 32 n. Meridian.
Pursell ——, carpenter, res. 78 s. Pennsylvania.
Pursel J., shoemaker, res. 78 s. Pennsylvania.
Pursel P., turner, res. 32 e. Georgia.
Pursel Peter M., tinner, res. 32 e. Georgia.
Purviance J. H., clerk, A. & U. S. Express Co., bds. Pyle House.
Pyle John, proprietor Pyle House, cor. Maryland and Illinois.
Pyle J. H., clerk, bds. Palmer House.
Pyle House, cor. Illinois and Maryland.
Pynter Joseph, carpenter, res. 108 e. South.

Q

Quartermaster's U. S. Clothing Depot, cor. Meridian and Louisiana.
Querlin Jas., wks. Rolling Mill.
Quigly James F., carpenter, res. 36 n. Illinois.
Quigley P., shoemaker, res. 1 Eddy.
QUIMBY MRS. H. N., MILLINERY, 20 s. Illinois, res. same. See card, p. 112.
Quin J., ostler, res. 28 n. Pennsylvania.
Quinn J., laborer, res. 28 s. Pennsylvania.
Quinn Wm., wks. City Hotel, res. 161 s. Tennessee.
Quiser Julius, express wagon driver, res. 277 Virginia ave.

R

Raback Henry, laborer, res. 30 Michigan road.
Raber A., drayman, res. cor. North and Union.
Rabbe H. G., clerk, bds. 136 e. South.
Race R. T., salesman, Bee Hive, bds. Macy House.
Raferd A. F., carpenter, res. bet. Walnut and St. Clair.
Raible C., carpenter, res. e. Washington.
Raible John, tailor, res. 173 s. Delaware.
Raible Louis, cabinet maker, res. 97 w. Washington.
Rain T., street grader, res. 15 s. Alabama.
Rainman Reneholt, res. 131 e. Market.

Raisener A., drayman, res. 15 McCarty.
Raisener Wm., grocer, res. Michigan road, near Washington.
Ramis Victor, gardener, res. s. Noble, near Virginia avo.
Ramsaier Christ., gardener, res. 74 e. St. Joseph.
Ramsay J. F., dealer in furniture, 21 s. Illinois, res. 21 n. Maryland.
Ramsay & Hanning, plumbers and gas fitters, Pearl, bet. Neridian and Pennsylvania.
Ramsey Barten, hostler, res. cor. New York and Blake.
Ramsey Lizzie, (col.) res. 147 n. Alabama.
Ramsey T., of Drum & R., res. 121 e. Washington.
Ramsey Waldron, res. 130 n. Delaware.
Ramsey Wm., engineer, bds. Ray House.
Ramsey W. L., of R. & Hanning, res. 130 n. Delaware.
Rand Fred., of R. & Hall, res. 162 n. Illinois.
Rand & Hall, attorneys at law, 24½ e. Washington.
Randall Geo., carpenter, res. n. Illinois, near Tinker.
Randall J. H., printer, 20 n. Penn.
Randall N. A., printer, res. 18 Talbott & News' Block.
Randall W. H., machinist, works I. & C. R. R. machine shop.
Rankins Albert, plasterer, res. 208 n. New Jersey.
Ram Kate, (col.) res. 121 Indiana avo.
Ranols John, res. cor. Ohio and Tenn.
Rapp F. J., farmers' tools, 154 e. Washington, res. 92 e. Market.
Rasche Theodore, butcher, res. 315 Virginia avo.
Rachig Chas. M., tobacconist, 11 e. Washington, res. 111 e. Vermont.
Rasener F. W., of Piel & Co., res. Michigan road.
Rasener W., laborer, res. 37 Union.
Rasman C., saloon, 119 e. Washington, res. same.
Rass Valentine, cabinet maker, works Uunion Cabinet Factory.
Rathbone Geo. W., Prest. Bank of the State, cor. Kentucky ave. and Illinois.
Rathrock Valentine, res. 55 n. Meridian.
Ratti F. A., pressman, with Dodd & Co., res. 92 St. Joseph.
Ratti Joseph, printer, with Dodd & Co., res. 92 St. Joseph.
Ran John, teamster, res. 157 n. Liberty.
Ranschen W. H., works Rolling Mill, res. Tennessee, bet. South and McCarty.
Ranser G., baker, 86 s. Illinois, res. same.
Rankins Geo., stair builder, bds. 154 n. Noble.
Raver Wm., drayman, res. 242 Madison R. R. avo.
Ravert Wm., res. 153 e. Market.
Ray Andrew, carpenter, res. 82 s. East.

Make single and double Lock-Stitch.

Ray Chas. A., judge, res. 80 n. Illinois.
Ray David, res. 133 n. Pennsylvania.
Ray J. M., cashier, State Bank, res. 19 n. Meridian.
Ray J., carpenter, res. 53 Madison ave.
Ray Dr. J. N., res. 117 n. Alabama.
RAY & PHIPPS, ATTORNEYS AT LAW, 36 e. Washington.
Ray John W., attorney at law, 36 e. Washington.
Ray M. M., attorney, 11 Talbott and News' Block, res. 148 n. Pennsylvania.
RAY HOUSE, cor. Delaware and South, Ray & Lambert, proprietors.
RAY & LAMBERT, PROP'S RAY HOUSE, cor. South and Delaware.
Raymond C. H., res. 82 n. Delaware.
Raymond Henry, book-keeper, res. 241 s. Alabama.
RAYMOND SAMUEL, BLACKSMITH, 6 e. Maryland, res. 4 n. Delaware.   See card, page 72.
Rea John H., clerk, res. 56 Meridian.
Reack Geo. L., painter, res. Illinois, bet. First and Second.
Reading A. D., plasterer, res. 13 e. Lankbeo.
Reading T., carriage trimmer, bds. with S. Beck.
Reagan Edward, boiler maker, res. 168 s. Tenn.
Reame Eugene, clerk, bds. Little's Hotel.
Reanme John A., clerk, 30 w. Washington, bds. Palmer House.
Reasnor Wm., tallyman, Beilefontaine Freight Depot, res. 37 Union.
Reben G., stone cutter, res. 190 s. Delaware.
Rebentisch C., shoemaker, with J. G. Krestuer.
Rech G., clerk, with Adam Bretz.
Recker Fred., book-keeper, res. 152 s. New Jersey.
Recker Godfrey, clerk, 13 n. Penn., res. 152 s. New Jersey.
Rector Benj., cooper, res. 70 s. Noble.
Rector Benj., cooper, res. 18 Lord.
Redfield Alexander, clerk, with Hawes & Redfield.
Redfield D. A., with G. W. Hawes, res. 43 w. Michigan.
Redford J. E., real estate, res. 7 Market.
Redick J. W., res. 158 w. Vermont.
Redman Mrs., (wid.) res. 212 w. Washington.
Redman Mrs. Harriet, res. 56 Orsbrook.
Redman Dennis, marshal, Union Depot, res. 125 w. South.
Redman Mrs. N. J., res. w. Washington, near Woolen Factory.
Redman John, res. 212 w. Washington.
Redman J., stove mounter, works with D. Root & Co.

Redman James, res. 212 w. Washington.

Redman Thos., wholesale liquors, res. Illinois, 2d door from
South.

Redmond Samuel, clerk, 76 w. Washington, bds. 134 w.
Washington.

Redmond T., of Conklin & R., res. cor. South and Illinois.

Redstone A. E., of R., Bros. & Co., res. 20 n. Meridian.

REDSTONE, BROS. & CO., MACHINE SHOP, s. Delaware, opp. Cincinnati depot. See card, page 140.

Redstone J. H., of R. Bros. & Co., res. 20 n. Meridian.

Reed Capt. B. F., res. 149 n. East.

Reed E., clerk, with W. R. Hogshire & Co.

Reed Geo. D. M., machinist, res. 46 s. Noble.

Reed Jacob, cooper, res. 164 n. Tenn.

Reed Rev. J. C., res. 107 n. Tenn.

Reed John, salesman, with M. Derhham.

Reed Mrs. J., res. 54 n. East.

Reed S. A., 25 n. Alabama.

Reeder E. C., res. Michigan road, near Washington.

Reese Chas., grainer, res. 104 n. Noble.

REES H., M. D., res. 102 n. East.

REESE H. & CO., WHOLESALE AND RETAIL GRO-
CERS, 91 and 93 w. Washington and 204 Noble. See
card, p. 76.

Reeser Dr. Alfred, res. 99 s. New Jersey.

Reeves C. C., driver Adams Express Co.

Reeves F., clerk, with K. & W., 3 Bates House.

REEVES J. S., PUBLISHER, cor. Washington and Meridian, bds. Palmer House.

Reeves J. S., sole proprietor of Dr. James Halls Diarrhea
Pills, cor. Washington and Meridian, bds. Palmer
House.

Reevis Mrs. Sarah, res. 57 s. New Jersey.

Reeves Thos., boiler maker, Western Machine Works, res.
cor. Illinois and South.

Reffart Wm., res. 153 e. Market.

Redman Wm., laborer, works I. & C. R. R. machine shop.

Regar E., boiler maker, res. 168 s. Tenn.

Regemeir Henry, miller, res. 59 e. St. Joseph.

Reeger Wm., cabinet maker, works Union Cabinet Factory.

Rihl C. H., brick mason, 38 California.

Rehling C., boots and shoes, 176 e. Washington, res. same.

Rehning Wm., shoemaker, 177 s. Delaware, res. 579 s. Delaware.

Reible David, laborer, res. cor. Missouri and Maryland.

Reible Jacob, meat market, Virginia ave.

Reich G. S., carpenter, cor. Liberty and Lankebee.
Reichardt John, carpenter, res. 241 n. New Jersey.
Reichwein P., bar-keeper, bds. 14 e. Washington.
Reick August, grocer, cor. Georgia and Liberty, res. same.
Reiken Heinrich, cigar maker, res. 93 Fort Wayne ave.
Reid Earl, salesman, 17 w. Washington, bds. Oriental
    House.
Reid Mrs. Julia, res. 153 Virginia ave.
Reife George, carriage trimmer, res. 231 s. East.
Reiger J., laborer, res. 72 Bluff road.
Reiley Michael, shoemaker, res. Tennessee, near McCarty.
Reinman Reinhart, saloon keeper, res. 131 e. Market.
Reimcashneider H., grocery keeper, res. 47 n. New Jersey.
Reinacher Jacob, laborer, res. 158 n. New Jersey.
Reiner J., laborer, Eagle Foundry.
Reinhart Jos., locksmith and bell hanger, 49 s. Illinois,
    res. same.
Reinhardt Ludwig, shoemaker, res. 48 Mass. ave.
Reinman R., saloon, 186 e. Washington.
Reising Louis, gas fitter, bds. Pyle House.
Reiseness Mrs. L., res. 160 s. Tennessee.
Reisen F., bds. 13 w. McCarty.
Reisner F. S., farmer, res. e. of Indianapolis.
Reissner A., currier, works with Yandes & Co.
Reitz F. A., jr., salesman, res. 157 n. Penn.
Reitz F. A., of R. & Rollweg.
REITZ & BALLWEG, COMMERCIAL HOTEL, cor. Illi-
    nois and Georgia.   See card, page 62.
Reitzel C., machinist, Washington Foundry.
Renn Mike, works Rolling Mill.
Renierd John B., stone mason, res. 151 e. New York.
Renner C., blacksmith, Bluff road, bet. McCarty and Ray.
Renehan James, saloon, res. 123 w. Maryland.
Repp L. P., of R. & Schriver, res. cor. Alabama and Massa-
    chusetts ave.
Reinacher Jacob, clerk, Post-office.
Rennahan Joseph, res. 240 Indiana ave.
Rengdamin ——, works I. & C. R. R. machine shop.
Rentch Herman, clerk, res. 195 n. Noble.
Rentsch E., grocer, 126 s. Illlnois, res. same.
Reschic Chas., cigar dealer, 11 e. Vermont.
Resener Charles, blacksmith, bds. 215 Mass. ave.
Resnir Henry, shoemaker, res. 311 Virginia ave.
Retzinger Fred., res. 124 e. Ohio.
Revels Dr. W. R., res. 119 West.
Revel Wm. W., engineer, res. 27 e. Georgia.

Reyer G., harness maker, 343 Virginia ave.
Reymond Samuel, blacksmith, res. 46 n. Delaware.
Reynolds C. H., of R. & Coffin, res. 89 n. Noble.
Reynolds Frank, res. 107 w. South.
Reynolds John, of Sulgrove, R. & Co., res. 75 w. New York.
Reynolds L. S., patent right agent, res 16 Lankabee.
Reynolds Mrs. Mary, res. 123 n. New Jersey.
Reynolds N. W., painter, res. 89 n. Noble.
Reyuolds Thos., Miller, res. 89 n. Noble.
Reynolds Wm., checkman, T. H. & R. R. R.
Reynolds S. G., res. 62 Missouri.
REYNOLDS & COFFIN, CIGAR DEALERS, cor. New
    York and Noble.
Rexford E. M., job tin shop and stencil cutting, 4 Pearl,
    res. 133 n. Meridian.
Rahr Fred., stone mason, 10 Lord.
Rhoads M., res. 133 Blake.
Rhoads Chas. W., watchman, res. 129 w. New York.
Rhoads W. H., orderly sergeant, bds. 27 s. Delaware.
Rhoads Mrs. E., col., res. 136 w. Georgia.
Rhodius G., Enterprise Saloon, 27 s. Meridian, res. same.
Rice Gustave, clerk, 6 Bates House.
Rice Solomon, of R. & Bamberger, 6 Bates House.
Rice W., shoemaker, works with A. Wands.
RICE & BAMBERGER, CLOTHIERS, 6 Bates House,
    and 9 w. Washington. See card, page 44.
Richards Mrs. R., res. 110 n. Missouri.
Richards Fred., printer, Journal office.
Richards F. A., laborer, res. 22 Michigan road.
Richards James, moulder, works Wiggins & Chandler.
Richards Richard, res. 110 n. Missouri.
Richardson B. F., cooper, res. 135 s. Alabama.
Richardson D. F., clerk of special Premium Rolls, Pro.
    Mar. Office.
Richardson J. J., horse dealer, Exchange Stable.
Richardson J. W., teamster, res. 114 Maple.
Richardson Warren, Bartlett & R., res. 149 s. Tenn.
Richey John, res. 74 n. Missouri.
Richmann C., wagon maker, 204 e. Washington.
Richmann H., harness maker, works with John Andra
    & Co.
Richmire Henry, res. 55 St. Joseph.
Richmond John, laborer, res. 272 s. Delaware.
Richmond J. S., works American Express Co., res. 54 s.
    Noble.
Richter August, stone mason, res. Virginia ave.

RICHTER FRED., GROCER, 115 s. Tenn., res. same.
RICHTER FRED., PAINTER, res. 125 n. Railroad.
Richter Florence, saloon, 1 e. Pearl.
Richters Henry, grocer res. Illinois, bet. Second and Third.
Richter J., shoemaker, 161 e. Washington, res. same.
Rickar Godfrite, res. 141 e. Market.
RICKARDS THOMAS, CARPENTER, 81 s. Delaware, res.
    138 e. Market. See card, p. 70.
Rickards W. C., carpenter, 138 e. Market.
Ricker R. E., Supt., T. H. & R. R. R.
RICKETTS DILLARD, PRES'T. JEFFERSONVILLE
    R. R., res. Jeffersonville.
Ricketts W. H., book binder, with Dodd & Co., res. Geor-
    gia, bet. Illinois and Meridian.
Rickter Henry, saw mill, res. 175 s. Mississippi.
Rieck C., tailor, bds. cor. South and Illinois.
Riedeman Henry, res. 15 St. Clair.
Riegger Arnold, pattern maker, Eagle Foundry, res. 66 In-
    diana ave.
Riemenschneider H., shoemaker, res. 47 n. New Jersey.
Riesmer Herman, laborer, res. 127 n. Liberty.
Riggs & Davis, meat market, 6 s. Meridian.
Right Henry, teacher, res. 221 s. Pennsylvania.
Riley B. F., clerk, County Treasurer's Office, bds. w. end
    North.
Riley E., fireman, Gas Works.
Riley E., laborer, res. 198 s. Delaware.
Riley James, brick maker, Missouri.
Riley Martin W., clerk and solicitor, with C. Hamlin.
Riley Thomas, steward, Palmer House.
Riley Wm. H., acting and stage manager, Metropolittn Hall,
    bds. Little's Hotel.
Riner Joseph, laborer. res. 258 s. Delaware.
Rinehart F., carpenter, res. 59 Madison ave.
Rinehart Samuel, works R. R., res. 45 e. Louisiana.
Ring David, harness maker, bds. with A. J. Hinesley.
Ring Michael, laborer, res. Ann, bet. Mississippi and Ten-
    nessee.
Ringer Mrs. Mary, res. 121 n. East.
Ringer Quincy, laborer, res. 108 St. Joseph.
Rinkle D., barber, 62 e. South.
Ripley L., carpenter, res. 77 w. Washington.
Rise Oliver, pump maker, res. 11 Railroad.
Risner Albert, res. North, near Blackford.
RISTINE JOSEPH, AUDITOR STATE, 7 and 9 Kentucky
    ave., res. 74 n. West.

Ritchey Mrs. Marilla, res. 191 s. New Jersey.
Ritschweine John, laborer, res. cor. Vermont and Davidson.
Rittenhouse G. L., grocer, 88 e. Washington, res. 111 East.
Ritter Peter, of R. & Seybold, bds. Mississippi.
Ritzinger Frank, clerk, Fletcher's bank, res. 124 e. Ohio.
Ritzinger J. B., teller, Fletcher's bank, res. 124 e. Ohio.
Roach John, laborer, res. 210 n. Noble.
Roache A. L., of McDonald & R., res. n. Pennsylvania, bet.
  Tinker and St. Joseph.
Roach J. W., engineer. with Case & Marsh.
Roake Thos., steward, Spencer House, res. 60 Louisiana.
Roback Eli T., book binder, with Dodd & Co., res. 7 w.
  Walnut.
Roback Mrs. Sarah, res. 7 w. Walnut.
Roberts D., saddler shop, res. 32 n. East.
Roberts James, laborer, res. 184 n. Delaware.
Roberts J. W., machinist, res. 63 s. New Jersey.
Roberts Samuel, res. 233 Indiana ave.
Roberts T. L., Sup't. Eagle Foundry.
Roberts Thomas, machinist, res. 261 Virginia ave.
Roberson James E., merchant, res. 45 w. Vermont.
Robertson A. M., clerk, bds. Macy House.
Robertson J., of R. & East, res. Vermont, bet. Illinois and
  Tennessee.
ROBERTSON & EAST, DRY GOODS, 10 e. Washington.
  See card, page 118.
Robinius F., of F. R. & Co., res. 61 n. West.
Robinius F. & Co., boot and shoe makers, 150 w. Wash-
  ington.
Robertson A. J., adjutant, res. 149 n. Delaware.
Robinson A., prop'r. Gem saloon, 14½ n. Pennsylvania, bds.
  Jack's boarding house.
Robinson A. C., grocer, cor. North and Illinois, res. n. Ten-
  nessee.
Robinson C. B., Asst Supt. P. & I. R. R., res. 249 s. Ala.
Robinson Mrs. Charlotte, res. 87½ n. Pennsylvania.
Robinson Chas., carpenter, res. Tennessee, bet. First and
  Second.
Robinson G., painter, res. 19 s. Alabama.
Robinson Geo. C., law student. with Wm. Henderson.
Robinson H. E., clerk, bds. 8 e. Michigan.
Robinson J. W., plasterer, 225 s. Alabama.
Robinson R. W., stair builder, res. 68 n. Missouri.
Robinson M. B., farming, res. 93 e. Market.
ROBINSON W. J. H., SHERIFF MARION COUNTY
  res. cor. Market and Alabama.

Rockey H. F., clerk, 7 s. Meridian, bds. 61 n. New Jersey.
Rockey H. S., lamp store, 7 s. Meridian res. 61 n. New Jersey.
Rockey J. L., clerk, 7 Meridian, bds. 61 n. New Jersey.
Rockey M., lamp store, res. 61 n. New Jersey.
Rockwell J. S., clerk, Palmer House.
Rockwood W. O., Treasurer I. & C. R. R., res. 30 s. Tennessee.
Rode Anthony, laborer, res. 148 n. Noble.
Rodges R. H., doctor, res. 169 n. Noble.
Rodgers M., brakesman, I. & M. R. R.
Roderus A., barber, bds. 62 e. South.
Rodewald Henry, grocer, 283 s. Delaware, res. same.
Roe H., manager Rolling Mill, res. Meridian, bet. Merrill and McCarty.
Roesch Chas., tinner, bds. cor. East and Ohio.
Roeth John, tailor, bds. 16 Georgia.
Rofert Charles, laborer, res. 79 e. Merrill.
Rofet Henry, res. 193 n. Illlnois.
Rogers John, shoemaker, bds. opp. post office.
Rogers J. W., brick maker, res. Michigan Road, near c. Washington.
Rogers Herbert, cabinet maker, res. 144 e. Market.
Rohl J., with J. A. Heidlinger.
Romerill J. H., clerk, G. F. Meyers, bds. 148 n. East.
Rolff & Winter, dry goods and groceries, 160 Indiana ave.
Rolfing Christ., laborer, res. 150 n. Noble.
Roll Joseph, res. 145 n. New Jersey.
ROLL W. H., CARPETS, WALL PAPER AND WINDOW SHADES, 16 s. Illinois, res. 71 w. Maryland.
Rolston Chas., upholster, bds. Bates House.
Roney B., laborer, res. Ann, near Rolling Mill.
Rooker G. S. D., painter, California, bet. Michigan and North.
Rooker J. S., painter, res. 106 Indiana ave.
Rooker Samuel, painter, res. 160 n. West.
Rooney B., works Rolling Mill.
Roop John, spinner, Merritt & Coughlen's Woolen Factory.
Roos Immanuel, of R. & Bro., res. 91 s. Illinois.
ROOS & BROTHER, DEALERS IN FRESH AND SALT MEATS, 89 s. Illinois. See card, p. 62.
Root Delos, stove dealer, res. 33 n. Meridian.
ROOT D. & CO., STOVES AND TINWARE MANUFACTURERS, 66 e. Washington.
Root J. B., of D. Root & Co., res. 18 s. Mississippi.
Root Miss M. F., dress making, 9 Bates House, up stairs.
Roperts Catherine, res cor. Delaware and Market.

Ropkoy F., groceries, cor. McCarty and Madison R. R. ave.

Rorark T., steward, Spencer House.

Rose Frank, engineer, res. cor. Bates and Benton.

Rose Thomas, messenger, Am. Express Co.

Rose W. C., of Hahn & R., bds. 41 n. Alabama.

Rosebrock Fred., grocer, res. 328 Virginia ave.

Rosebrock Geo., grocer, res. 198 Mass. ave.

ROSEBROCK H. H., GROCERIES AND FEED, cor. Virginia ave. and East, res. same.

Rosenbaum C., porter, bds., cor. Meridian and Ohio.

Rosenberg S., of R. & Co., res. 125 n. Noble.

Rosenberg & Co., saloon, 75 e. Washington.

Rosener W. F., laborer, res. 177 e. Ohio.

Rosengarten Louis, musician, res. 163 n. Railroad.

Rosenthal A., wholesale dealer in liquors, 38 Louisiana, res. cor. Michigan and Illinois.

ROSENTHAL HENRY, OF HAYS, KAHN & CO., res. 16 n. Mississippi.

ROSENTHAL H. & CO., CLOTHIERS, cor. Illinois and Washington. See card, p. 116.

Rosenthal S., liquors, res. cor. South and Illinois.

Rosenthal S. L., clerk, res. cor. Illinois and Michigan.

Roser F., tailor, works 9 Bates House.

Roshan Wm., works Rolling Mill.

Ross A. D., carpenter, bds. Vermont, bet. Noble and Liberty.

Ross H. B., book binder, with Dodd & Co., bds. Bates House.

Ross J., cooper, res. 192 Maryland.

Ross James, painter, res. 207 n. Tennessee.

ROSS J. H., COAL OFFICE, 11 Pearl, res. 174 n. Tennessee. See card, p. 116.

Ross J. T., carpenter, res. Vermont bet. Noble and Liberty.

Ross N. M., res. 56 s. Meridian.

Ross Robert, laborer, res. cor. Second and Mississippi.

Rosswingel Geo., clerk, res. 123 n. East.

Rost E., cabinet maker, res. 52 s. New Jersey.

Roswinkel Geo., clerk, 10 Bates House, res. 123 n. East.

Roszel M. D., painter, res. 23 Union.

Roth Conrad, works Sheffield Saw Works, bds. Union House.

Roth Matthew, apprentice, bds. 85 Indiana ave.

Roth S., works Schmidt's brewery.

Rothchilds H., notions, 5 Spencer House Block.

Rou S., salesman, 21 w. Washington.

Rouoan M., marble polisher and rubber, Tennessee.

Rouen M., marble worker, res. 89 s. Tennessee.
Rouhette Arthur, clerk, res. 244 e. Washington.
Rouse H. J., laborer, 23 Indiana ave.
Rouse Harry, runner, Little's Hotel.
Routier John, carpenter, res. 65 Elm.
Routur Peter, carpenter, res. 312 Virginia ave.
Rowselb H., machinist, bds. 179 e. Market.
Rowe Aston, engineer, res. 27 n. Spring.
Rowe H., foreman, Rolling Mill.
Rowe Samuel, salesman, res. 192 n. Mississippi.
Rowe Wm., clerk, Post Office.
Rozier Aaron, res. Blackford, bet. Vermont and New York.
Ruble W. R., of Cravin & R., bds. W. H. Stringer.
Rubsch, Geo., tinner, bds. East Street House.
Rubush Fletcher, carpenter, res. 59 n. Noble.
Rubush Jacob, brick mason, res. cor. New York and East.
Rubush Wm., brick mason, res. 15 e. Georgia.
Rubush W. G., carpenter, bds. 59 n. Noble.
Rude G. D. M., machinist, works I. & C. machine shop.
Ruf John, meat market, 208 w. Washington, res. same.
Ruffel Jacob, butcher, res. 320 Virginia ave.
Rugg Samuel L., Sup't Public Instruction, off. old post office
    building, res. same.
Rumel J. A., carpenter, res. s. Tennessee, near city limits.
Rumell J. W., works Rolling Mill.
Rumerill C. E., plasterer, res. 148 n. East.
RUNNION WM., PHOTOGRPH GALLERY, 32½ e. Wash.,
    bds. cor. Market and Pennsylvania. See card, p. 116.
Ruoff Charles, salesman, 32 w. Washington, res. 192 n. Illi-
    nois.
Rupley M. H., printer, Journal Office.
Rupp, W. F., merchant tailor, 105 e. Washington, res. same.
Ruschhaupt A., cashier German Dry Good Store.
Ruschhaupt F., of R. & Balls, res. 110 n. Delaware.
Ruschhaupt & Balls, liquors, 82 e. Washington.
Ruschhaupt W., of Brinkman & R., res. 67 n. New Jersey.
Rush Charles, tinner, res. 134 e. Ohio.
Rush E. P., grain dealer, res. 35 n. New Jersey.
Rush F. P., produce and commission merchant, 81 and 83
    w. Washington, res. 35 n. New Jersey.
Rushhaupt Gustave, saloon keeper, res. 168 e. Michigan.
Rushhaupt Wm., livery stable, res. 67 n. New Jersey.
Russe C., stone mason, res. e. Washington, near Bates.
Russel D., moulder, res. 72 s. Delaware.
Russell David, moulder, Western Machine Works.
Russell Geo. B., conductor, res. 23 Henry.

Russell J. S., department city marshal, res. 284 s. Delaware.
Russell Jas., clerk, Post Office, res. cor. Merrill and Meridian.
Russell J. N., clerk, Post Office.
Russell John, carpenter, res. 122 s. Noble.
Russell L. M., engineer, res. 99 Meek.
Ryan Mrs. Ellen, res. 51 Mississippi.
Ryan J., fireman, Gas Works.
Ryan J., laborer, wks. with D. Root & Co.
Ryan James, fireman, Palmer House.
Ryan James, blacksmith, bds. 232 w. Washington.
Ryan John, laborer, res. 198 s. Delaware.
RYAN JOHN B., HOUSE AND SIGN PAINTER, basement of 10 n. Meridian. See card, p. 134.
Ryan J. B., of C. A. Elliott & Co., res. 100 n. Mississippi.
Ryan John A., brick mason, res. 136 e. St. Clair.
Ryan John, wks. Rolling Mill.
Ryan John B., painter, 8 n. Meridian, res. 277 s. East.
Ryan John, machinist, wks. I. & C. Machine Shop.
Ryan John, carpenter, res. 205 n. Noble.
Ryan Michael, laborer, res. 172 n. Noble.
Ryan P., shoemaker, with A. Lintz.
Ryan Pat., wks. Rolling Mill.
Ryan Patrick, shoemaker, res. 162 Indiana ave.
Ryan N., laborer, res. 43 West.
Ryan Wm., porter, M. H. Good.
RYDER P. S., PHOTOGRAPHIST, Talbott & New's Block, res. 22 Maryland. See card, p. 18.

S

Saam Bernardt, engineer, res. Davidson, bet. Ohio and Market.
Sackser Karl, tanner, res. 79 Fort Wayne ave.
Saehcinger L., cabinet maker, res. 81 n. Davidson.
Sage Chas., of T. Stout & Co., res. 231 w. Washington.
Sage John, laborer, res. 25 Henry.
Sahur Ludwig, grocery keeper, res. 88 Fort Wayne ave.
Sain H. A. N., clerk, Great Western Dispatch Office, bds. Pennsylvania, bet. Maryland and Louisiana.
St. John J., wagoner, res. 99 Bluff road.
St. John's Institute, conducted by Sisters of Providence, cor. Tennessee and Georgia.
St. John's Church, Rev. A. Bessonus, Georgia, bet. Illinois and Tennessee.
St. Mary's Seminary, Geo. Herbert, principal, cor. Meridian and Ohio.
St. Paul Lutheran, cor. East and Georgia, school in rear.

Salter W. H., clerk, Sentinel off.
Sample S. C., carpenter, res. 192 e. St. Clair.
Sanbourn E., dyer, res. 225 w. Washington.
Sanburn J. B., painter, res. Meridian, bet. First and Second.
Sanders Mrs. E., res. 188 e. Washington.
Sanders Fred., laborer, res. 116 s. Noble.
Sanders S. C., carpenter, 83 n. New Jersey.
Sanderson W., tallyman, Bellefontaine Freight Depot, bds.
　　Little's Hotel.
Sandefur S. H., laborer.
Santo E., Verandah Saloon, 36 Louisiana, res. same.
SAPP W. D., CHIEF CLERK, Spencer House.
Sanborn Geo., machinist, Western Machine Works.
Sargent A. W., carpenter, res. 160 n. Pennsylvania.
Sargeant E. A., fireman, Bellefontaine R. R., carpenter shop,
　　res. 19 n. East.
Sargent Ezra D., res. 19 n. East.
Sargent F. L., blaksmith, res. 88 s. East.
Saunders W. L., clerk, Central House, 44 s. Meridian.
Sauer John, wks. Rolling Mill.
Sawyer C. D., photographist, bds. cor. Meridian and Mary-
　　land.
Sawyer J., wholesale grocer, res. 23 s. Delaware.
Sawyer J. S., of S. & Starrett, res. 23 s. Delaware.
SAWYER & STARRETT, WHOLESALE GROCERS, 13
　　s. Meridian.
Sayers A., laborer, res. 207 s. Pennsylvania.
Sayers Thomas, laborer, res. Meek, near Bates.
Sayert T., wks. Rolling Mill.
Sayler Horatio, blacksmith, res. Michigan road, near Wash-
　　ington.
Saylor Jackson, wks. Rolling Mill, res. Mississippi, bet.
　　South and Henry.
Saylor Wm., wks. Rolling Mill.
Saylor Wm., bds. with J. Saylor.
Saxe C., currier, with J. R. Sharpe.
Saxton Dick, res. Madison R. R., opp. Depot.
Scaulin Anne, (wid.) seamster, res. 82 c. Vermont.
Schacko Chas., machinist, wks. Western Machine Works.
Schad G., wagon maker, res. 52 n. Davidson.
Schad George, baker, res. 32 n. Spring.
Schafer C., saloon, res. Georgia, bet. West and Missouri.
Schaffner Chas. J., laborer, res. 219 n. Noble.
Schaler Henry, striker, res. 139 s. Alabama.
Schaler J., laborer, works with A. Stephenson & Son.
Scharp Jacob, shoemaker, res. 77 n. East.
Schaaf Abel, laborer, res. 40 n. Noble.
Schaub Geo., bar-keeper, 6 w. Washington.

Schaub Geo., shoemaker, res. 125 Noble.
Schaub H., saloon, 6 w. Washington.
Schaub Henry, saloon keeper, res. 121 n. Noble.
Schaub Henry, saloon keeper, res. 135 n. Noble.
Schaub John, painter, res. 215 n. Alabama.
Schaub Peter, express driver, bds. 53 n. Noble.
Schaw G. D., res. 77 n. Noble.
Schay Daniel, laborer, res. 23 Nelson alley.
Schay John, laborer, res. 199 c. Ohio.
Scherer J., plow maker, works F. Kopp.
Scheier John, laborer, res. 213 n. Noble.
Scheigert F., works Commercial Hotel, res. 174 s. Illinois.
Schildmeier C., apprentice, Washington Foundry.
Schellschmidt Adolph., res. 110 e. Ohio.
Schering Mrs. Mary, res. 81 n. Davidson.
Schildmeier Fred., tailor, res. Davidson, bet. Ohio and Market.
Schilling H., cabinet maker, works with C. J. Meyer.
Schilling Nicholas, clerk, Post-office, res. 158 n. Liberty.
Schildmeier & Rogge, merchant tailors, 144 e. Wash.
Schillinger Geo., laborer, res. 89 n. Spring.
Schemburg Wm., shoemaker, 11 s. New Jersey, res. 66 Davidson.
Schmdler R., clerk, res. 148 e. Washington.
Schiply Fred., carpenter, res. 224 n. Alabama.
Schlater W. H., military secretary, res. bet. Market and Ohio.
Schlear Christ., saloon keeper, res. 76 Ft. Wayne ave.
Schliebitz F. W., jeweler with Geo. Feller, 107 e. Washington.
Schleimlein Frank, Prop'r Franklin House, 46 s. Meridian.
Schlver C., saloon, res. Ft. Wayne ave.
Schlver M. A., works Rolling Mill.
Schlotzhaner Adam, cabinet maker, works Union Cabinet Factory.
Schlotzhaner V., cabinet maker, works Union Cabinet Factory.
Schmalkottz John, laborer, res. 32 n. Noble.
Schmalzieth Chas., res. 241 n. Illinois.
Schmuck Chas., shoemaker, res. 124 n. Miss.
SCHMIDT C. F., BREWERY, cor. High and Wyoming. See card, page 40.
Schmidt L., turner, res. 215 s. Delaware.
Schmidt R., of S. & Co., res. 24 s. Alabama.
SCHMIDT R. & CO., WHOLESALE LIQUOR DEALERS, Washington, bet. Delaware and Alabama.
Schmidt George, laborer, res. 95 n. Railroad.
16

Schmitt J., cigar maker, res, 13 w. McCarty.
Schmitt L., laborer, res. 13 McCarty.
Schmit Wm., butcher, res. 161 Mass. ave.
Schmuck P., foreman, Free Press.
Schneider A., harness maker, bds. 343 Virginia ave.
Schneider Adam, laborer, res. 45 e. Maryland.
Schneider John, moulder, res. 190 s. Alabama.
Schnull A., of A. & H. S., res. Alabama, bet. Market and Ohio.
Schnull A. & H., wholesale grocers, cor. Meridian and Maryland.
Schnull H., of A. & H. S., res. Alabama bet. Market and Ohio.
Schoemaker G., shoemaker, res. n. Miss., near Second.
Schoettle Christ., bar keeper, 136 w. Washington.
SCHOLTZ LOUIS, MERCHANT TAILOR, 19 n. Penn. See card, page 92.
Schonacker H., res. 95 n. Tenn.
Schopp G., shoemaker, res. 27 s. Union.
SCHOPPENHORST WM., DEALER IN PRODUCE, GROCERIES, FEED, &c., 101 e. Washington, res. same. See card, page 58.
Schoht Gottlieb, carriage maker, res. 52 n. Davidson.
Schott Joseph, grocer, 177 e. Washington, res. same.
Schover Jacob, laborer, res. 212 s. Alabama.
Schowe Fred., laborer, res. 291 Virginia ave.
Schowe F., of Haugh & S., s. e. city limits.
Schowe Fred., blacksmith, res. Water.
Schowmeier Wm., watchman, Terre Haut Depot, res. 187 n. Noble.
Schrader Chas., machinist, res. 75 e. Merrill.
Schrader Christ., salesman, 16 w. Washington, bds. 66 n. Mississippi.
Schrader Rudolph, laborer, res. 148 e. Market.
Schrader Anthony, miller, works Capital Mills.
Schrader August, cabinet maker, res. 23 n. Liberty.
Schrader Fred., cooper, res. 192 n. Noble.
Schreck Mrs. Mary, res. 143 n. Noble.
Schriner W., tanner, res. 78 Madison Railroad ave.
Schriner Henry, of S. & Repp, bds. cor. Alabama and Massachusetts ave.
Schroder Anthony, miller, res. 144 n. Liberty.
Schroder August, tailor, res. 23 n. Liberty.
Schroder C., carpenter, Washington Foundry.
Schroder Fred., cooper, res. 192 n. Noble.
Schroeder J. C., tobacconist, res. 144 e. Washington.

Schroeder Rudolph, Machinist, res. 148 e. Market.
Schroy J., of Brothers & S., bds. Palmer House.
Schroy W. J., with Brothers & Schroy, bds. Palmer House.
Schrumm A., tailor, bds. 107 e. Washington.
Schuer John, res. Washington, near Orient.
Schuho Leonhard, watch maker, res. 64 n. Davidson.
Schuler F., cabinet maker, res. 56 e. Market.
Schulmeier L. C., druggist, res. 59 St. Mary.
Schulmeier W. F., laborer, res. 55 e. Marion.
Schulmyer L., clerk, 59 St. Marys.
Schumburg Wm., shoemaker, res. w. Davidson, bet. Ohio
  and Market.
Schussler Conrad, laborer, res. 152 n. New Jersey.
Schuster Joseph, tailor, res. Railroad, bet. Market and
  Ohio.
Schwammle John, baker, 186 s. Delaware, res. same.
Schwammeier Christ., drayman, res. 164 e. Michigan.
Schwan G., works Schmidt's Brewery.
Schwartz F. W., laborer, res. 129 n. Railroad.
Schwartz August, porter, Germam Dry Goods Store.
Schweinhart A., tinner, res. 68 n. St. Mary.
Schweinhart Edward, shoemaker, works with J. K. Sharpe.
Schwicho Chas., grocer, Bluff road, bet. Ray and McCarty,
  res. 87 Union.
Schwoneyer Henry, cooper, res. 180 n. Noble.
Schmidt C. F., Brewery res. 131 e. McCarty.
Scofield E., engineer, T. H. & R. R. R., 12 Henry.
Scott Adam, marble dealer, res. 46 n. East.
Scott A. A., res. 8 2 n. Davidson.
Scott Amos, laborer, res. 85 n. Davidson.
Scott Geo. W., soldier, res. 100 e. Market.
Scott John, clerk, New York Store, res. 118 n. Miss.
Scott John, clerk, res. 118 Mississippi.
Scott John N., Capt. 79th Ind. Vols., A. A. A. Gen., off.
  Blackford's Block.
Scott S., clerk, Bellefontaine Railroad Office.
Scott Samuel T., Bellefontaine Railroad Office, res. 37 e.
  Georgia.
Scott Walter K., res. 78 w. New York.
SCOTT & NICHOLSON, STONE AND MARBLE YARD,
  Kentucky ave., near Terre Haute R. R.
Scott Wm., carpenter, res. Maple.
Scrolte H., laborer, res. 123 e. McCarty.
Scrwegel D., horse collar maker, 201 s. Penn.
Scudder Caleb, boarding house, 46 cor. Market and n.
  Tennessee.

Scudder M. R., constable, res. 131 Mass. ave.
Scudder Wm., carpenter, res. 51 New York.
Seafart A., butcher, res. 241 s. Delaware.
Seaman E., clerk, with Wm. Sheets.
Sebert G. W., grocer, res. 95 s. East.
Secrest Chas., brick mason, res. 205 s. Alabama.
Serger A., salesman, 3 e. Washington, bds. Bates House.
Sergan Hugh, laborer, res. Michigan road, near Orient·
Seeler Henry, laborer, res. 174 n. Liberty.
Seibert S. M., blacksmith, 152 c. Washington, res. 3 n.
    Liberty.
Seichrest H. A., candy maker, res. Huron, bet. Libery
    and Noble.
Seidensticker A., of S. & Kappes, res. 21 n. Noble.
Seidensticker & Kappes, real estate and law office, 1 Judah's
    Block.
Suter J. A., clerk, German Dry Goods Store, res. 104 Mass-
    achusetts ave.
Seitz Fred., saloon, 73 s. Illinois, res. same.
Seitrist John, laborer, res. 299 Virginia ave.
Seebert W., clerk, res. 91 s. East.
Seebert Samuel, blacksmith, res. 3 n. Liberty.
Seidenstucker F., works 126 s. Illinois.
Sergins King, (col.) res. 143 n. Tennessee.
Selder J. B., carpenter, res. 101 w. South.
Self Berry, clerk, Isaac Davis', 15 n. Penn.
Selking W., City Bakery, 201 e. Washington, res. same.
Sell Mrs. B., dress maker, 97 w. Washington, res. same.
Sellers W. B., telegraph operator, bds. Patterson House.
Semmons & Co., jewelers, 23 s. Illinois.
Senger P., tailor, 115 Virginia ave., res. 148 s. N. Jersey.
Senour John, clerk, 5 w. Washington.
Senour J. F., druggist, 5 Bates House, res. 205 n. Illinois.
Server Mrs. C., res. 110 n. Pennsylvania.
Severin Henry, of S., Goth & Co., res. 247 n. New Jersey.
Severn, Goth, Bushman & Co., wholesale and retail gro-
    cers, 247 n. New Jersey.
Sewer L., saw maker, res. Wyoming, bet. Delaware and
    High.
Seybold A., res. 121 e. Ohio.
Seybold J. H., marble dealer, res. 161 n. Liberty.
SEYBOLD & RITTER, MARBLE SHOP, Market, bet.
    Penn. and Delaware, opp. Post-office.
Shackelford A. S., agent, Little Miami R. R., bds. Bates
    House.
Shackleton Joseph, pattern maker, res. 31 s. Liberty.

Shade R. W., clerk, New York Store, res. 127 w. N. York.
Shae M., hostler, bds. Knight's.
Shafer M., horse collar maker, with Mooney & Co.
S..aghnessy J., harness maker, res. 61 Madison ave.
Shaker C., laborer, res. 230 s. Alabama.
Shanaberger D. H., cashier, Adams Express Co., 12 e. Washington.
Shannon John, bar-keeper, 212 w. Washington.
Share Geo. K., of G. K. S. & Co., bds. Patterson House.
SHARE GEO. K. & CO., DEALERS IN SADDLERY, HARDWARE AND CARRIAGE TRIMMINGS, 72 w. Washington. See card, back of title.
Shariff Nathan, salesman, with Feibelman & Rauh.
Sharp Abraham, res. 140 n. Penn.
Sharp Geo., cigar maker, with G. F. Meyer & Co.
Sharp J., shoemaker, res. 77 n. East.
SHARPE A. W., TOBACCONIST, 12 n. Penn., res. 151 n. East. See card, page 100.
Sharpe E., clerk, Fletcher and Sharpe's Bank, cor. Penn. and Washington.
Sharpe John S., book-keeper, res. cor. Laukabee and Noble.
Sharp J. K., boots and shoes, 90 e. Washington.
Sharpe L. L., actor, Metropolitan Hall, bds. Little's Hotel.
Sharpe T. H., banker, res. 95 n. Penn.
Sharpless Pennell, book-keeper, res. 102 n. Meridian.
Shaule G., shoemaker, res. 125 n. Noble.
Shaughnassy T., laborer, res. 63 Madison ave.
Shaughreng J., works Rolling Mill.
Shaughnessy James, harness maker, res. 61 Madison ave.
Shaughreng Thomas, works Rolling Mill.
Shaw B. C., of Drew & S., res. Ft. Wayne ave., bet. Delaware and Penn.
Shaw C. B., carriage maker, res. bet. Delaware and Fort Wayne ave.
Shaw H. G., carriage maker, res. 40 Spring.
Shaw Vinton, plasterer, res. North, bet. Noble and Liberty.
Shaw Rev. Wm., bds. 121 n. Alabama.
Shawver Alex., carpenter, res. 19 Chatham.
Shawber Christ. J., saddler, res. s. w. cor. Rosette and Grove.
Shea Mrs. H., res. 25 n. Railroad.
Shea J., res. Missouri.
Shea J., laborer, works with W. Hinesley.
Shea J., laborer, res. 14 s. East.
Shea J., works Rolling Mill.
Shea J. R., clerk, res. 26 Michigan road.

Shea Mary, res. 110 s. East.
Shea Michael, laborer, res. 26 Michigan road.
Shea T. R., laborer, with Fred. P. Rush.
Shearer Mrs. Mary, res. cor. New York and Vermont.
Sheahean Daniel, laborer, res. West, near South.
Sheerley Fred., saddler, res. 11 St. Clair.
Shoesler Eli, miller, works Bates City Mills.
Sheets Wm., paper Mill, Market, bet. West and Mississippi.
Sheets Wm., book store, res. 51 n. Penn.
Sheets Wm., paper manufacturer, 79 w. Waghington, res.
    51 n. Pennsylvania.
Sheively Albert, bds. 20 n. Meridian.
Shellenberger John, pattern maker, res. 142 n. N. Jersey.
Shelt M., with Feibelman & Rank.
Shelt W., salesman, bds. Bates House.
Sheneberyer David, clerk, Adams Express Office, bds. 91 e.
    Ohio.
Shepard Thos. L., carpenter, res. 107 Blake.
Sherburne Wm., engineer, T. H. & R. R. R., res. cor. South
    and Mississippi.
Sherkaet Fred., porter, Commercial Hotel.
Sherman ——, works Madison Depot, res. 80 Bluff road.
Sherman G., of Post, Helwig & Co., res. cor. New York and
    Meridian.
Sherman Gustavus, res. 29 n. Meridian.
Sherman Paul, harness maker, res. 44 Indiana ave.
Sherman S. B., paper maker, at Wm. Sheets', bds. cor.
    West and Market.
Sherwood W. O., of Fitchey & S., bds. Mrs. Bricketts.
Shear F., laborer, res. 91 Bluff road.
Sheideler J. L., Fire Department, res. cor. South and New
    Jersey.
Shilling John, cabinet maker, res. cor. Meek and Noble.
Shilling C., blacksmith, res. cor. Noble and Spring.
Shilling Richard L., of Burton & S., res. 46 w. Maryland.
Shilling Robert W., trunk maker, bds. 5 n. Noble.
Shine John, laborer, res. 110 s. Noble.
Shipley Madison O., laborer, bds. 188 e. Washington.
Shipley Wm., carpenter, res. West, between Merrill and
    South.
Shipp S. M., clerk, I. & C. Freight R. R. Depot, bds. Pyle
    House.
Shire P., cigar roller, bds. Pearidge House.
Shirling N., clerk, Post-office.
Shipley D. B., contractor, res. 38 w. Washington.
Shoecraft A., (col.) barber, bds. 127 n. East.

Shoecraft Silas, (col.) barber, 8 and 9 New & Talbott's Block, res. 127 n. East.
Shoecraft S., (col.) barber, res. 127 n. East.
Shoemaker Mrs. M., res. 15 Maryland.
Sholes John, laborer, res. 23 Georgia.
Sholes Lyman, baggage master, Union Depot, res. 86 s. East.
Sholtcaner V., cabinet maker, res. 75 n. Davidson.
Sholtz Lewis, merchant tailor, res. 18 n. East.
Shoniker G. A., clerk, res. 95 n. Tennessee.
Shook John, carpenter, works Hill & Wingate.
Short C. B., bricklayer, res. 159 n. New Jersey.
Shortridge A. F., collector, res. 118 n. Illinois.
Shrader C., laborer, res. 92 e. McCarty.
Shroof V., carpenter, res. cor. Market and Davidson.
Shubert Geo., laborer, res. 10 Michigan road.
Shuldz John, moulder, wks. with D. Root & Co.
Shy G., blacksmith, with Case & Marsh.
Sibb Charles, machinist, res. 43 n. New Jersey.
Sibert C., blacksmith, res. 75 e. Market.
Sibert David, blacksmith, res. 75 e. Market.
Sibert H., blacksmith, 43 Virginia ave., res. 91 s. East.
Siebert ———, blacksmith, res. 87 s. East.
Siebert Hiram, blacksmith, res. 91 s. East.
Siedle Engelbert, watchmaker, res. 103 n. Noble.
Sieder Karemehr, cooper, res. 27 n. Noble.
Siefert A. & Co., meat shop, cor. Delaware and Washington.
SIEGRIST REV. S., PASTOR ST. MARY'S CHURCH, res. 59 e. Maryland, next to church.
Siersdorfer Louis, boot and shoe maker, 3 n. Meridian, res. 152 s. New Jersey.
Sievert Fred., laborer, res. 29 n. Noble.
Simmelink Wm., carpenter, res. 157 e. Ohio.
Simms C., (col.) ostler, wks. with Landis & Mills.
Simmons Henry, grocer, res. 36 Indiana ave.
Simon Christ., laborer, res. 151 n. Noble.
Simon F., bds. with Geo. Koeniger.
Simon Fedell, drayman, wks. Union Cabinet Factory.
Simon Jacob, carver, res. 59 n. Mississippi.
Simon J. P., currier, wks. with Mooney & Co.
Simon P., courier, res. Maple.
Simon & Reese, grocers, 104 n. Noble.
SIMMONS BENJ., JR., CLOTHING AND FURNISHING GOODS, 14 e. Washington.
Simpson ———, actor, Metropolitan.
Simpson Chas., barkeeper, 13 n. Illinois, bds. same.

Simpson F. F., of Danforth & S., res. 117 n. Pennsylvania.
Simpson Francis, grocery keeper, res. 117 n. Pennsylvania.
Simpson Fred., grocer, res. 104 n. Noble.
Simpson M., of M. S. & Co., res. 82 s. Delaware.
Simpson James B., carpenter, res. cor. Spring and Ohio.
Simpson Mrs. L., boarding house, res. 27 Indiana ave.
Simpson Mat., grocer, res. 199 s. Delaware.
SIMPSON M. & CO., GROCERS, cor. South and Delaware.
    See card, p. 72.
Simpson N., grocer, 167 s. Delaware, res. same.
Simpson R., grocery, 58 e. South.
Simpson Wm., barkeeper, 15 n. Illinois, bds. Macy House.
Sims F., wks. Western Agricultural Works.
SINDLINGER JOHN M., HOUSE AND SIGN PAINTER,
    shop 81 e. Washington, res. 341 Virginia ave. See
    card, p. 82.
Sinex Wm., plow maker, res. Blackford, bet. Vermont and
    New York.
Singleton Calvin L., carpenter, res. 33 n. New Jersey.
Singer Manufacturing Co., Sewing Machine, 48 e. Wash-
    ington.
Sinix C., blacksmith, with Case & Marsh.
Sinix J., blacksmith, with Case & Marsh.
Sinix Wm., blacksmith with Case & Marsh.
Sinker E. T., foundry, res. 101 Virginia ave.
SINKER & CO., WESTERN MACHINE WORKS, one
    square e. Union Depot. See card, p. 98.
Sinking Fund Office, corner Virginia ave. and Pennsyl-
    vania.
Sinney P., laborer, res. 13 Union.
SINNISSIPPI INSURANCE CO., J. R. BERRY, SECRE-
    TARY, 79½ e. Washington. See card, p. 88.
Sipp C., machinist, Washington Foundry.
Sipp Hendricks, tailor, res. 178 e. Ohio.
Sippel Henry, barkeeper, bds. 27 s. Meridian.
Sires Frederick, laborer, res. 95 Bates.
Sisco H., wks. with Osgood & Smith.
Sittinhaim B., clerk, 2 Bates House.
Skelly Mrs. T., res. 55 e. Meridian.
Skillen J., of J. S. & Co., res cor. West and Market.
Skillen James, miller, res. 24 n. West.
SKILLEN J. & BRO., ÆTNA MILLS, w. Washington,
    bet. West and Blake. See card, p. 68.
Skillen R. G., of J. S. & Co., res. w. Washington, near Ætna
    Mills.
Skinner Wm. H., engineer, res. 55 s. Noble.

Skinner Wm., engineer, wks. Indiana Central R. R. Machine Shop.
Slatter Chas., carpenter, res. 199 Indiana ave.
Slatter James O., carpenter, res. 50 Bates.
Slavin Hugh, drayman, res. 157 s. Tennessee.
Sloan ———, Express off., res. cor. Pratt and Tennessee.
Sloan Geo. W., of Browning & S., res. 22 w. Washington.
Sloan J., of S. & Burk, res. 61 s. Tennessee.
Sloan E. W., res. 69 w. New York.
Sloan John, furniture, res. 83 s. Tennessee.
Sloan & Burke, manufacturers and dealers in furniture, 57 w. Washington.
Small Mrs. Elizabeth, res. Michigan road, near Washington.
Small G., minister, res. 40 n. Delaware.
Small L., clerk, Quartermaster Department U. S. A., res. 40 n. Delaware.
Small & Harmaday, carpenters, shop e. North.
Smelser James W., doctor, res. 141 Virginia ave.
Smelser Dr. J. W., druggist, 172 e. Washington, res. 151 n. East.
Smelser Dr. J., res. 151 n. East.
Smeth Charles, clerk, bds. cor. Delaware and McCarty.
Smidt Christ., marble yard, res. 180 s. Delaware.
Smidt Geo., varnisher, res. 186 s. Delaware.
Smidt Fred., blacksmith, res. Water.
Smidt J., tailor, bds., National Saloon.
Smidt P., shoemaker, res. 125 n. Noble.
SMITH ———, res. 24 s. Alabama.
Smith Mrs. A., res. 11 n. Meridian.
Smith A., blacksmith, with Case & Marsh.
Smith Andrew, engineer, res. 25 Bates.
Smith Andrew, conductor, P. & I. R. R., bds. Palmer House.
Smith Miss Annie, teacher, res. 36 e. Ohio.
Smith B. K., clerk, Repps & Co., bds. 113 Massachusetts ave.
Smith C., of S., Ittenbach & Co., res. 180 Delaware.
Smith C. H., carpenter, res. 65 n. New Jersey.
Smith C. W., general freight agent, Great Central Railway Line, bds. 67 n. Pennsylvania.
Smith C., actor, Metropolitan Hall, bds. Little's Hotel.
Smith C. E., moulder, wks. Wiggins & Chandler's, bds. 258 w. Washington.
Smith Capt. J. J., res. 122 n. Illinois.
Smith E. H., bread peddler, 11 n. Pennsylvania, res. 80 e. Vermont.
Smith Mrs. Elizabeth, res. 158 New York.

Smith Mrs. Ellen, res. 107 s. Alabama.
Smith E. H., wks. Union Steam Bakery.
Smith F. E., clerk, bds. 21 n. Michigan.
Smith Francis, res. s. e. cor. Washington and Mississippi.
Smith Fred., grocery, res. 126 n. Mississippi.
Smith George, printer, res. 12 n. New Jersey.
Smith G. W. B., printer, res. 12 n. New Jersey.
Smith F., printer, res. 12 n. New Jersey.
Smith Henry, farmer, res. 196 n. Illinois.
Smith Hugh H., shoemaker, res. cor. Alabama and Market.
Smith, Ittenbach & Co., stone yard, cor. Pennsylvania and Merrill.
Smith J., book binder, bds. James, bet. St. Clair and Indiana ave.
Smith J., machinist, I. & C. R. R. Machine Shop.
Smith J., fruit stand, opp. Union Depot, res. same.
Smith J., clothes cleaner.
Smith J. S., coach painter, res. 123 Massachusetts ave.
Smith Mrs. Jane, res. 70 s. Noble.
Smith Jacob, of S. & Huey, res. 46 s. East.
Smith Jacob, stone cutter, res. 30 Henry.
Smith Jason, farmer, res. Lord, near Benton.
Smith James F., carpenter, res. 87 n. Davidson.
Smith James, brick maker, res. 10 s. West.
Smith James, laborer, res. 139 n. Liberty.
Smith J. C., printer, Journal office.
Smith J. G., blacksmith, 36 Kentucky ave., res. 84 n. New Jersey.
Smith J. D., veternary surgeon, bds. Dell's.
Smith J. H. C., book binder, res 191 w. Washington.
Smith J. R., res. 116 s. New Jersey.
Smith J. S., painter, 123 Massachusetts ave.
Smith John, stone cutter, res. 12 Willard.
Smith John C., conductor, I. & C. R. R., res. 161 Virginia ave.
Smith John, res. Washington, near Orient.
Smith John, painter, res. Spring, bet. New York and Vermont.
Smith John, wks. Rolling Mill.
Smith Joseph, machinist, res. 38 Elm.
Smith Jos., wks. Rolling Mill.
Smith Josiah, trunk maker, res. 153 w. Vermont.
Smith L., res. 215 s. Delaware.
Smith Mrs. M. C., boarding house, 44 s. Pennsylvania.
Smith Mary A., res. bet. Alabama and Delaware.
Smith Robt. L., trunk maker, res. 153 w. Vermont.
Smith Sophia, dress maker, res. 86 e. Pratt.

Smith S. F., of Osgood & S., res. 10 s. Meridian.
Smith S. F., peg and last factory, res. 10 Madison ave.
Smith Stephen, bill poster, off. 16 e. Washington, res. 102 n. Mississippi.
Smith T., (col.) boot black.
Smith Tom, wks. Rolling Mill.
Smith Thomas, shoemaker, 70 n. Mississippi.
Smith T. M., salesman, Bee Hive Store, bds. 140 n. Illinois.
Smith Wm., photographist, res. 102 n. Mississippi.
Smith Wm., res. Missouri, bet. South and Merrill.
Smith W., clerk, Adams Express Co.
Smith W. C., messenger, American Express Co.
Smith W. H., clerk, with J. Fishback.
Smith Wm. G., coal dealer, res. 78 n. East.
Smith Wm., res. 37 Delaware.
Smith Wm., wagon maker, 14 s. New Jersey, res. 50 s. East.
Smith W. S., oyster dealer, Exchange Saloon, res. 169 Vermont.
Smith Wm. S., Exchange Resturant, 169 w. Vermont.
Smith & Huey, photographers, 35½ e. Washington.
Smither Henry C., clerk, res. 49 and 51 Indiana ave.
Smither John, laborer, res. 51 Indiana ave.
Smither J. W., mail agent, I. & C. R. R., res. 97 Virginia ave.
Smither Theo., money delivering clerk, Adams Express Co.
SMITHMYER J. L., ARCHITECT AND U. S. PATENT AGENT, AND AGENT FOR TERRA COTTA WORKS, off. 14 e. Market. See card, p. 60.
Smitt Clay, laborer, res. Noble, bet. New York and Ohio.
Smock George, clerk, res. 51 s. New Jersey.
Smock M., shoemaker, res. 126 e. Washington.
Smock Mrs. Nancy, res. 17 Huron.
Smock Peter, clerk, res. 183 n. East.
SMOCK WILLIAM C., DEPUTY CLERK, CIRCUIT COURT MARION CO., res. 15 e. Ohio.
Snapp Chas. P., jeweler, res. 71 w. Vermont.
Sneible John, laborer, res. Tennessee, bet. St. Charles and Pratt.
Snell S. R., physician, 79½ e. Washington.
Sneider Conrad, carpenter, res. 133 n. Liberty.
Sneider P., laborer, res. 62 Bluff road.
Snull Henry, res. Alabama, bet. Market and Ohio.
Snyder C., laborer, res. Wyoming, bet. High and Delaware.
Snyder Charles, clerk, with H. M. Socwell.
Snyder D. E., cashier Branch Bank State of Indiana, res. 119 n. Meridian.
Snyder Edward, res. 32 Elizabeth.

Snyder Henry, wks. Cincinnati Bakery.
Snyder Henry, wks. Western Agricultural Works.
Snyder J. A., stove blacker, with D. Root & Co.
Snyder Thomas, machinist, bds. 15 w. Ohio.
Soar J., brick mason, res. 15 e. Georgia.
Socwell H. M., grocer, 190 e. Washington, res. 18 n. Dela-
    ware.
Socwell J. C., clerk, bds. 18 n. Delaware.
Sogemier August, clerk, cor. McCarty and Meridian.
SOLDIERS' HOME, CAPT. S. A. CRAIG IN CHARGE,
    West, bet. Georgia and Maryland.
Solomon Bros., notions, Spencer House square.
Solomon J. & M., notions, 53 s. Illinois.
Solomon J. & M., notions, 88 s. Illinois.
Solomon S. H., clerk, 10 w. Washington.
Sonderegger F., watchman, res. 69 Madison ave.
Sonnefield Wm., teamster, res. cor. Noble and Meek.
Southard J. P., banker, res. cor. 68 Vermont and Alabama.
Southard Macy, clerk at Treasurer's Office P. & I. R. R.,
    bds. 68 e. Vermont.
Southard M. R., clerk, res. 40 w. St. Clair.
Sowder Calvin, woodhauler, res. 92 e. Market.
Sowtop J., laborer, res. 45 s. Illinois.
Spaeth C., butcher, res. cor. Missouri and Michigan.
Spann Henry, carriage maker, res. 40 n. Spring.
Spann J. R., produce dealer, 93 e. Washington, res 30 e.
    Ohio.
SPANN JOHN S., OF S. & SMITH, res. 74 n. Penn.
SPANN & SMITH, REAL ESTATE, INSURANCE AG'TS
    AND LOAN BROKERS, n. w. cor. Pennsylvania and
    Washington. See card, inside front cover.
Sparks C. H., clerk, 3 n. Illinois.
Spath B., porter, with S. Siegrist.
Speaker Mrs. H., seamstress, res. 37 n. Noble.
Speakes J. E., clerk, res. 71 n. Delaware.
Speake J. W., captain, res. 71 n. Delaware.
Speake E. L., clerk, 14 w. Washington.
Speckman H., cigar store, 57 s. Illinois.
Spelsey Eli, miller, works Bates City Mills.
Spehn Andrew, bds. Walks' boarding house.
Speigel John, tailor, res. 93 Massachusetts ave.
Spencer C. F., salesman Bee Hive, bds. 140 n. Illinois.
Spencer C. N., clerk, bds. 132 e. Market.
Spencer Dr., res. 106 n. Noble.
SPENCER HOUSE, J. W. CANAN PROP'R, n. w. cor.
    Union Depot. See card p. 120.

Spencer James, (col.) saloon, res. 135 n. Tennessee.

Spencer James, (col.) restaurant, basement Blackford's Building.

SPENCER MILTON, WHOLESALE AND RETAIL GROCER, 202 e. Washington, res. 132 e. Market. See card, page 118.

Spencer P. R., jr., of Bryant & S., Commercial College, 30 w. Washington.

Spencer Stephen, wholesale and retail hat store, 32 w. Washington, res. 194 n. Illinois.

Spitznagel L., barber, bds. 116 e. Market.

Spicer B. M., of S., Henning & Co., res. 161 n. Mississippi.

SPICER B. M. & CO., REAL ESTATE AGENTS, 20½ n. Illinois. See card, p. 136.

Spicer H. C., res. 163 n. Mississippi.

Spicer, Henning & Co., prop'rs Dr. Frink's family medicines, Norwood's Block, 18 and 20 n. Illinois.

Spicer J. Y., res. 163 n. Mississippi.

Spiegel A., of S., Thoms & Co., cor. Vermont and Liberty.

Spiegel C., of S., Thoms & Co., res. 136 n. East.

Spiegel Christ., furniture dealer, 136 n. East.

SPIEGEL, THOMS & CO., MANUFACTURERS AND WHOLESALE DEALERS IN FURNITURE, 73 w. Washington. See card, p. 96.

Spier Fred., grocery keeper, res. e. Washington.

Spigel Augustus, furniture dealer, res. 121 n. Liberty.

Spulain Timothy, res. 183 e. Market.

Splann James, laborer, res. 57 s. West.

Spotts W., (of Jordan & S.,) res. cor. Noble and Fletcher's avenue.

SPOUSEL C., GROCER, 277 s. Delaware, res. same.

Spousel Henry, clerk with C. Spousel.

Spradee ——, clerk at the Armory, res. 102 w. Vermont.

Sprague W. B., superintendent U. S. Quartermaster's Clothing Depot.

Spran Mrs. L., res. 173 n. Noble.

Spratt Martha, res. bet. Alabama and Delaware.

Spray J., hostler, works with J. Peabody.

Spray J., laborer, res. 67 s. Pennsylvania.

Spressel Mrs. E., res. 267 s. Delaware.

Spring Adam, stone cutter, res. 151 e. Ohio.

Springer David, carpenter, res. 5 Chatham.

Springer M. B., of S., Barrows & King, res. 109 e. Georgia.

Springsteen A., builder, res. 110 e. Market.

Springsteen Jeff., painter, res. 35 N. Spring.

SPRINGER, BARROWS & KING, FOUNDERS AND
MACHINISTS, cor. Kentucky ave. and Mississippi.
See card, p. 74.
Sproul W., bds. 42 W. Maryland.
Spurgin J. M., of S. & Long, res. 92 n. East.
Spurgin Joseph, painter, res. 92 n. East.
SPURGIN & LONG, HOUSE, SIGN AND ORNAMEN-
TAL PAINTERS, 6 s. Meridian. See card, page 46.
Staats Geo. D., painter, Odd Fellows' Hall, 6 e. Michigan.
Stabler Mike, teamster, res. 45 Spring.
Stacey H., superintendent Gas Works, res. at works.
Stacey M. D., watch maker C. G. French, res. 112 e. Michi-
gan.
Stacy Milton, finisher at Merritt & Coughlen's woolen fac-
tory, res. n. West.
Stacy W., grocer, 153 e. Washington.
Stafford M., student, bds. 107 s. Alabama.
STAGG CHARLES W., ATTORNEY AND NOTARY
PUBLIC, 4 Yohn's Block, res. 76 w. New York. See
card, page 76.
Stagg John, meat shop, cor. New Jersey and Virginia ave-
nue.
Stagg J. R., butcher, res. Virginia ave.
Stahlhuth Chas., carpenter, res. First, bet. Illinois and Me-
ridian.
Stainruck E., baker, res. cor. McCarty and Illinois.
Staker Franklin, moulder, res. 276 s. Delaware.
Stalding Charles, laborer, res. 19 n. Railroad.
Stallut Fred., carpenter, res. 99 n. Railroad.
Stalting Frederick, grocery store, 163 cor. North and West.
Stanlidge H. G., soldier, res. Vermont, bet. Noble and Lib-
erty.
Stans Gustave, machinist, works I. & C. shop.
Stanton J., moulder, works with D. Root & Co.
STAPP JAMES H., REAL ESTATE AND COLLECTING
AGENT, 9 Bates House, up stairs, res. —— w. St.
Clair.
Stark Christiana, dress maker, bds. 57 e. Pratt.
Stark G., of Cabinet Makers Union, res. 81 Fort Wayne
ave.
Stark Herman, boots and shoes, 185 e. Washington, res.
same.
Stark Sophia, dress maker, bds. 56 e. Pratt.
Starling Mrs. S. S., teacher Indianapolis Female College.
Starling Samuel, grocer, 3 n. Illinois, res. 151 n. Pennsyl-
vania.

Starr Jason, carpenter, works Western Machine Works.
Starr John, carpenter, res. cor. Merrill and Illinois.
Starrett James, of Sawyer & S., res. 200 n. Illinois.
State Mrs. P., res. 190 c. Washington, third floor.
State Sentinel Office, 11 and 13 s. Meridian.
Statton J. A., of Rislin & S., bds. cor. Illinois.
Statsman H., blacksmith, with Case & Marsh.
Staub Joseph, of S. & Tapking, 110 n. Noble.
Staub & Tapking, clothiers, 2 Odd Fellows' Hall.
Stebbins John, boiler maker, res. 141 s. Alabama.
Stechman S., shoemaker, res. 75 n. Mississippi.
Stechman L., upholstering, 140 c. Washington, res. same.
Stechmager Perceval, clerk, res. 171 s. New Jersey.
Stechmann Dr. E. P., res. 40 Massachusetts ave.
Steele Thos. J., printer, Journal office, bds. 165 n. Liberty.
Steele W. H., carpenter, res. 165 n. Liberty.
Steelsmith Simon, bds. 43 n. New Jersey.
Steeley Wallace, barkeeper, 11 n. Illinois, bds. same.
Steffens Charles W., of Chas. S. & Co., res. 169 Alabama.
Steffens E. F., of Chas. Steffens & Co., res. 31 Blake.
Steffens Ferdinand, res. Black.
STEFFENS CHAS. & CO., MATHEMATICAL, OPTICAL
   AND PHILOSOPHICAL INSTRUMENTS, s. w. cor.
   Meridian and Washington, second floor. See card, p.
   42.
Stegall J., blacksmith, with Case & Marsh.
Steidle John, laborer, res. cor. Massachusetts ave. and Wood.
Steierberg Charles, carpenter, res. 203 s. Delaware.
Stein Frederick, justice peace, res. Market, bet. Noble and
   Davidson.
Stein H., ditcher, 54 c. South.
Stein Joseph, shoemaker, res. 266 s. Delaware.
Steiner Jacob, laborer, res. 158 n. East.
Steinmann John, tailor, res. 41 n. Spring.
Steinruck E., works Union Steam Bakery.
Steinwinter Andrew, laborer, res. 68 c. St. Joseph.
Steinway Wm., soldier, res. 189 n. New Jersey.
Stelter William, billiard saloon, res. 159 s. Alabama.
Stelzer Jacob, laborer, res. 64 e. St. Joseph.
Stelzel John, barber, res. 13 North.
Steneberger W. A., carpenter, bds. 91 c. Ohio.
Stephens A. D., printer, with Dodd & Co., res. 78 s. East.
Stephens A., of A. S. & Son, bds. 156 c. Ohio.
STEPHENS A. & SON, WHOLESALE DEALERS IN
   TEAS, COFFEES, SPICES, &c., 191 and 193 c. Wash-
   ington.

Took first premium at Iowa State Fair, 1863.

Stephens Henry, soldier, res. 82 n. Alabama.
Stephens S. R., of A. S. & Son, bds. 156 e. Ohio.
STERN ISRAEL, SALOON AND BOARDING HOUSE,
   14 s. Pennsylvania.
Stern Rev. M. G. J., German Reformed Church, res. 15 n.
   Alabama.
Stevens A. G., student, bds. 43 n. Pennsylvania·
Stevens C. H., bill poster, res. 182 s. Pennsylvania.
Stevens Isaac, laborer, res. Howard, near First.
Stevens L., brick maker, res. 256 Madison R. R. ave.
Stevens Mrs. Marinda, res. 78 s. East.
Stevens Thaddeus M., physician and surgeon, off. Harrison's
   Block, res. cor. Illinois and First.
Steward A., (col.) cook, Palmer House.
Steward Adam, (col.) res. 37 n. Tennessee.
Steward Jacob, pump maker, res. 334 s. Delaware.
Stewart A. J., messenger, American Express Co.
Stewart Albert, wks. Rolling Mill.
Stewart Andrew, farmer, res. Elizabeth.
Stewart Mrs. Anna, res. 51 n. Meridian.
Stewart C. G., of Bowen, S. & Co., res. 8 Virginia ave.
Stewart Daniel, drugs, res. 163 n. Illinois.
Stewart D. W., apprentice, Bellefontaine Car Shop.
Stewart James, policeman, res. 230 Indiana ave.
Stewart John A., brakeman, res. 221 n. Tennessee.
Stewart Miss Louisa V., teacher, Indianapolis Female Col-
   lege.
Stewart M., wks. Rolling Mill.
Stewart N. N., painter, res. 86 n. Alabama.
Stewart R. R., mailing clerk, Journal off., res. 12 w. Geor-
   gia.
Stewart Mrs. S. W., res. 87 n. Illinois.
Stewart Thos., barber, wks. cor. Meridian and Washington.
Stewart W., machinist, wks. I. & C. R. R. Machine Shop.
Stewart W. H., machinist, wks. I. & C. R. R. Machine Shop.
Stewart & Morgan, druggists, 40 w. Washington.
Stich Flaribert, carpenter, res. 181 s. New Jersey.
Stiedel George, file maker, res. 55 n. Noble.
Stiegmann C., dry goods and groceries, Madison ave., bet.
   Merrill and McCarty.
Stien A., butcher, 21 Kentucky ave.
Stienmann J., tailor, res. 41 n. Spring.
Stiles John, carpenter, res. 124 n. East.
Stilinger David, railroader, res. 71 e. Merrill.
Stillenger David, yard master, I. & M. R. R. Freight Depot.
Stilwell J. D. B., book-keeper, bds. Little's Hotel.
Stilz Daniel, laborer, res. 224 n. New Jersey.
Stilz J., clerk, with Egner & Wocher, 85 e. Washington.

STILZ J. GEORGE, SEED AND AGRICULTURAL IM-
PLEMENTS, 74 e. Washington, res. s. e. City Limits.
Stine J., watchman, Eagle Foundry.
Stineunts John, laborer, res. 59 Orsbrook.
Stinger Mrs. Mary, res. 14 w. North.
Stinhilber M., res. 16 s. Alabama.
Stion Ferdinand, barber, bds 175 s. New Jersey.
Stiver George M., carpenter, res. Meek, near Benton.
STOCKINGER J., MARBLE YARD, 173 e. Washington,
res. same. See card, p. 54.
Stofer John, R. R. switcher, Union Track.
Stoilte Henry, laborer, res. Wyoming, bet. Delaware and
High.
Stokeley B., finisher, Eagle Foundry.
Stokes R. M., wks. Byrkit & Beam's, bds. Mrs. Deming.
Stokes William, baker, wks. Cincinnati Bakery.
Stolding Christ., laborer, res. 115 e. New York.
Stollberg Augustus, tailor, res. e. Washington.
Stone W. C., of Hendricks, Edmunds & Co., bds. e. Market.
Stoneman W. H., clerk, bds. S. Beck.
Storher E. F., clerk, res. 113 e. Market.
Stout B. G., grocery, res, 84 n. Mississippi.
Stout Benj. S., res. 84 n. Mississippi.
Stout C., res. 93 w. South.
Stout D. L., bds. 84 n. Mississippi.
Stout F., of F. S. & Co., res. 142 w. Washington.
Stout F. & Co., grocers, 142 w. Washington.
Stout J. B., printer, res. 93 w. South.
Stout John R., of O. B. S. & Bro., bds. 84 n. Mississippi.
Stout O. B., of O. B. S. & Bro., res. 84 e. Market.
Stout O. B. & Bro., grocers, 42 w. Washington.
Stout Remson, wks. Rolling Mill, res. 93 w. South.
Stout R. C., of O. B. S. & Bro., res. 117 w. Maryland.
Stowell M. A., of Willard & S., 4 Bates House.
Strachan G. C., clerk, bds. West, bet. Maryland and South.
Strachm Geo., clerk, 49 s. West.
Straubenmueller ——, baker, res. 86 s. Illinois.
Strang G. L., shoemaker, 161 e. Georgia.
Strange Wm., res. 108 e. Vermont.
Strange W. R., deputy county auditor, res. 108 e. Vermont.
Strasner Fred., tailor, res. 207 n. Alabama.
Strattan C. W., carriage painter, res. 12 e. Walnut.
Stratton E. H., clerk, Head-quarters Superintendent Re-
cruiting Service, bds. 51 and 52 Indiana ave.
Straus Isaac, salesman, Glasers & Bros.
Straus Samuel, res 170 n. Pennsylvania.
Strauss Sol., salesman, 19 w. Washington.
17

Street E. S., clerk, U. S. Mustering Office, res. cor. Market and Tennessee.

Streif David, tanner, res. cor. Benson and Washington.

STREIGHT COL. A. D., PUBLISHER, Yohn's Block, 3d floor.

Strengmier Fred., porter, East House, s. Delaware.

Stretcher Mrs. E., res. 245 n. Tennessee.

Stretcher Howard, res. 245 n. Tennessee.

Stretmann W. B., clerk, bds. Circle.

Stretton C., painter, bds. 12 e. Walnut.

Striblen C. C. A., of Metzger & S., res. 115 e. Ohio.

Strickland D. ll., foreman, Wm. Sheet's Paper Mill, bds. David Bender's.

STRICKLAND T. C., CITY HOTEL, 77 s. Illinois. See card, p. 60.

Stringmeyer Frank, clerk, res. 344.

Stripp Peter W., railroader, res. 11 e. Georgia.

Strubenger George, laborer, res. 169 n. Illinois.

Struchmann F., laborer, 57 Union.

Stuard Thomas P., minister, res. 110 n. Davidson.

Stuart John, hack driver, res. 139 n. Noble.

Stuck John, laborer, res. 287 Virginia ave.

Stuck J. W., brick mason, res. 191 s. New Jersey.

Stuck Robert, laborer, res. 287 Virginia ave.

Stuckey Charles, cooper, res. 27 n. Spring.

Stuckmeyer Henry, carpenter, res. 299 Virginia ave.

Stuckmeyer J. H., carpenter, res. 338 Virginia ave.

Studle Andrew, shoemaker, 185 e. Washington, res. same.

Sturdevant Rev. Chas., president Indianapolis Female College, res. cor. Meridian and New York.

Stump George, brick mason, res. Noble, bet. Ohio and New York.

Stump H., carriage maker, 74 e. St, Joseph.

Stump Henry, laborer, res. 148 n. East.

Stump Henry, switchman, Bellefontaine R. R.

Stump Hugh, carriage maker, res. 74 e. St. Joseph.

Stumph John B., city assessor, off. Talbott & New's Block, res. Cady, bet. Washington and Market.

Stumpf J., blacksmith, with George Lowe.

Stundon Thos., way freight man, Bellefontaine R. R.

Sturm George, brick mason, res. 142 e. Ohio.

Suart J., laborer, res. 35 w. McCarty.

Sudbrock Frank, laborer, res. 120 n. Davidson.

Suddith G. A., teamster, McCord & Wheatley.

Sudmier W., porter, Union Depot, res. 54 Union.

Suhar Louis, wks. Sheffield Saw Works, res. 26 Wyoming.

Suhre Fred., shoemaker, wks. 177 s. Delaware.
Suhs Gottfred, shoemaker, res. 178 e. Ohio.
SULGROVE BERRY R., EDITOR INDIANAPOLIS
JOURNAL, res. 87 w. South.
Sulgrove H. J., clerk, 20 w. Washington, bds. 59 w. Mary-
land.
Sulgrove James, of S., Reynolds & Co., res. 59 w. Maryland.
Sulgrove James W., of S., Reynolds & Co., res. 115 n.
Alabama.
Sulgrove J. W., of S., Reynolds & Co., res. 115 n. Alabama.
Sulgrove John, harness maker, res. 59 Maryland.
Sulgrove Milton, foreman, 20 w. Washington, res. cor. Illi-
nois and Ohio.
Sulgrove, Reynolds & Co., wholesale and retail dealers in
Saddles, hardware, &c., 20 w. Washington.
Sulgrove W., laborer, res. 39 w. McCarty.
Sullivan D., laborer, wks. with W. Hinesley.
Sullivan Dennis, plasterer, res. 186 Massachusetts ave.
Sullivan Dan., laborer, res. 15 s. East.
Sullivan D. W., shoemaker, wks. with James Davis.
Sullivan Geo. T., agent T. H. & R. R. R. Freight Office, res.
155 Massachusetts ave.
Sullivan James, wks. Ætna Mills, bds. with R. G. Skillen.
Sullivan J. B., livery stable, 10 e. Pearl, res. 40 e. Pratt.
Sullivan Jas., wks. Rolling Mill.
Sullivan James, res. Missouri, near Canal.
Sullivan John, laborer, res. 5 e. Bates.
Sullivan John, laborer, 218 Indiana ave.
Sullivan T., plasterer, res. 51 w. McCarty.
Sullivan Thomas, bar-keeper, Crystal Palace Saloon.
Sullivan Wm., magistrate, off. College Hall Building, res.
107 n. Meridian.
Sullivan Wm., carpenter, res. 247 n. Tennessee.
Sullivan W. H., book-keeper, 74 w. Washington, bds. cor.
California and Vermont.
Suss Chas., tailor, res. 270 Delaware.
Suter J. A., salesman, res. 104 Massachusetts ave.
Sutherd George A., teamster, res. 124 n. Davidson.
Sutherland James, soldier, res. Grier.
Sutherland L., carpenter, Washington Foundry.
Sutman Samuel, carpenter, res. 60 n. Noble.
Sutorp H., wks. Rolling Mill.
Sutorp J., wks. Rolling Mill.
Sutton J., teamster, res. cor. Washington and Tennessee.
Sutton S. L., engineer, res. 99 Meek.
Sutton S. M., plasterer, res. 62 Massachusetts ave.

Swain Mrs., res. 20 s. Mississippi.
Swain E. J., conductor, P. & I. R. R., bds. Palmer House.
Swain Loring R., cash boy, New York Store, res. 20 s. Mississippi.
Swaninger J., shoemaker, with A. Lintz.
Swartz J., baker, res. 137 e. Washington.
Swartz Jacob, wks. Union Steam Bakery.
Swartzeim F. C., stove agent, res. 25 n. Liberty.
Swecer Chas., wks. Rolling Mill.
Sweeney J., cigar maker, res. cor. Washington and Kentucky ave, up stairs.
Sweeney Thos., afraid of being drafted, refused to give information.
Sweenhart William, cutter, res. 165 n. Alabama.
Sweetland F. A., secretary Farmers' and Merchants' Insurance Co., Blackford's Building.
Sweetser G. M., clerk, Post Office.
Sweetser J. N., attorney, Johnson's Building.
Swick Henry, tailor, bds. 54 n. Noble.
Swift H. J., salesman, Hume, Lord & Co.
Swift Mrs. M., res. 52 n. Liberty.
Swinehardt Jason, res. 131 n. East.
Swinesback Wm., butcher, 243 s. Delaware, res. same.
Swomier C., drayman, res. 87 Bluff road.
Sym James, machinist, res. 222 s. Alabama.
Symmes James, machinist, res. 222 s. Alabama.
Symons H. W., carpenter, 38 e. St. Clair.
Syrup Henry, grocery keeper, res. 141 Massachusetts ave.

T

Tabel Chas., cabinet maker, works Union Cabinet Factory.
Taggart S., mill-wright, 24 s. Penn., res. 66 n. Miss.
Taggart Samuel, mill-wright, res. 64 n. Mississippi.
TAGGART SAMUEL, MILL-WRIGHT, office, 94 s. Pennsylvania, res. 64 n. Mississippi. See card, p. 136.
Tailor Israel, book-keeper, res. 57 Mass. ave.
Talbott C. H., book-keeper, J. M. Talbott & Co.
Talbott J. M., of J. M. T. & Co., res. 66 n. Tennessee.
Talbott J. M. & Co., wholesale dealers in hats, 26 s. Meridian.
Talbott R. L., grocer, res. 64 e North.
Talbott W. H., Prest. Sinking Fund, res. cor. Meridian and Ohio.
Talbott W. H. & Co., jewelers, 24 e. Washington.
Tanganney Dennis, clerk, res. 95 s. Alabama.
Tanner James, carriage driver, res. Elizabeth.

Tapking F., of Staub & S., res. 174 n. Delaware.
Tapking John, cabinet maker, works Union Cabinet Factory.
Tarkington J. S., of Newcomer & T., res. 35 e. Ohio.
Tarkington W., book-keeper, bds. 163 n. Illinois.
Tarlton John, of Droper & T., res. 66 n. Delaware.
Tarlton J. A., of T. & Keehn, res. 152 n. Penn.
TARLTON & KEEHN, WHOLESALE AND RETAIL
 GROCERS, 8 and 10 s. Meridian.
Tarr Martin, bowling saloon, Georgia, near cor. Illinois.
Tarr M. M., bowling alley, res. 147 Virginia ave.
Tate James, driver, Adams Express Co.
Tate James, waiter, Palmer House.
Tayer Carler, works I. & C., R. R. machine shop.
Taylor D. M., book-keeper, Branch Bank State Indiana,
 bds. Bates House.
Taylor D. W., works Western Agricultural Works.
Taylor E., clerk, res. 196 n. New Jersey.
Taylor Isaac, carpenter, bds. Ray House.
Taylor Israel, book-keeper, with B. Coffin & Co., res. 157
 Massachusetts ave.
Taylor J., laborer, res. Maple.
Taylor Miss Julia A., matron, Deaf and Dumb Asylum.
Taylor Miss Mary C., res. 144 n. Mississippi.
Taylor N. B., attorney, 4 Brown's building, cor. Penn. and
 Washington, res. 109 n. Alabama.
Taylor Oliver, col., res. 120 w. Georgia.
Taylor R. A., brakesman, res. 175 Mass. ave.
Taylor Robert R., carpenter, res. Market, near California.
Taylor S. O, of Orlopp & S., bds. Little's Hotel.
Taylor T. W., painter, res. 131 n. Mississippi.
Taylor Wm., bds. Bates House.
Taylor Wm. H., foreman, res. 121 e. Market.
Taylor W. H., tinner, 206 cor. Washington and East, res.
 121 e. Market.
Teal Dr. N., 5 2d floor, Blakes Block, res. one square n. corporation Illinois.
Telley Chas., engineer, res. 38 s. Noble.
Templer Jas., carpenter, res. Bickner, bet. Delaware and
 High.
Teneyck John, shoemaker, res. 86 Indiana ave.
Tennis J. M., salesman, Bee Hive Store, bds. Palmer House.
Tepking Fred., tailor and clothier, res. 174 n. Delaware.
Tepking John, furniture, res. 65 n. New Jersey.
Teppa Chas., laborer, res. 13.
Terrell W. H. H., res. Louis Block, Ohio.

Terre Haute & Richmond R. R. Freight Office, Louisiana, bet. Tennessee and Mississippi.
Terre Haute & Richmond R. R. Engine House, Louisiana near West.
Tess J., cabinet maker, res. 238 Madison R. R. ave.
Tetar H. L., grocer, res. 160 e. Ohio.
Teufel Jacob, foreman, at A. Lintz, bds. 25 s. Meridian.
Thalman Isaac, book-keeper, res. 244 w. Washington.
THALMAN ISAAC, TREAS. HOME MUTUAL FIRE INS. CO., office, 9 Bates House Block.
Thalman John, baker, 39 n. Alabama, res. same.
Thamsy L. P., works Rolling Mill.
Thau O., res. 117 n. Liberty.
Thatcher Amos, laborer, res. 13 e. Georgia.
Thatcher James, pump maker, res. McCarty, bet. East and Greer.
Thatcher Louis, works cor. Kentucky ave. and Miss., bds. 13 e. Georgia.
Thayer Daniel, grocer, res. 145 e. Market.
Thayer Geo., salesman, Bee Hive Store, 145 e. Market.
Thayer John, marble cutter, res. 128 n. Alabama.
Thayer Lucus, salesman, Hume, Lord & Co.
Thayer Oel, of T. & Bro., res. 119 cor. Liberty and Vermont.
Thayer S., of Wilmot & T., res. Market, bet. New Jersey and East.
Thayer ——, of T. & Bro., res. 147 e. Market.
Thayer & Bro., grocers, 220 e. Washington.
Theodore Thos., brick mason, res. 125 n. East.
Theophilus M., printer, 140 w. Market.
Thenis P., porter, with Dawes, Evans & McMillin.
The Witness, E. W. Clark, editor, Journal building.
Thicke R. P., cash boy, New York Store.
Thicke John H., machinist, res. Michigan Road, near Washington.
Thinke J. H., machinist, works I. & C. machine shop.
Thirner G., laborer, res. Michigan Road, near Central R. R.
THISTLETHWAITE J. P., AGENT, bds. Palmer House.
Thomas A., clerk, with W. R. Hogshier.
Thomas Mrs., millinery goods, 46 w. Washington.
Thomas B., dyer, res. w. Washington, near tole gate.
Thomas Chas., clerk, with C. L. Holmes, res. 69 n. Noble.
Thomas F., bar-keeper, bds. 85 e. Washington.
Thomas Geo., laborer, res. 61 n. Noble.
Thomas Henry, res. Illinois, near Third.
Thomas John, Prop'r Rolling Mill, res. Meridian, bet. Merrill and McCarty.

Thomas Lewis L., carpenter, res. 23 Indiana ave.
Thomas Mrs. M., res. 257 s. Delaware.
Thomas R., works Rolling Mill.
Thomas R. Z., works Rolling Mill, res. Meridian, bet. Merrill and McCarty.
Thomas Wm., clerk, New York Store, bds. 20 s. Miss.
Thompson ———, machinist, res. Tennessee, bet. South and Merrill.
Thompson Archibald, machinist, res. 66 e. Louisiana.
Thompson Mrs. Annie, res. 63 n. Alabama.
Thompson D. J., policeman, res. 124 n. Noble.
Thompson E., carpenter, 133 w. New York.
Thompson E., moulder, works with D. Root & Co.
Thompson Geo., works Rolling Mill.
Thompson I., works Rolling Mill.
Thompson J., laborer, res. 61 Madison ave.
Thompson John, blacksmith, res. 339 Virginia ave.
Thompson Joseph, moulder, res. Greer.
Thompson John, works Rolling Mill.
Thompson J. C., conductor, P. & I. R. R., bds. Bates House·
Thompson W., finisher, Eagle Foundry.
Thompson Wm., book store, res. 65 n. Alabama.
Thompson Dr. W. C., res. 58 Illinois.
Thompson W. J., marble cutter, 30 Orsbrook.
Thompson Wm. J., stone cutter, res. 43 Orsbrook.
Thompson Wm., tobacconist, 5 n. Penn., res. 65 n. Alabama,
Thompson W. A. C., res. 79 e. Washington.
Thompson Mrs. & Son, news and stationery, 7 n. Penn.
Thompson & Kregelo, dry goods and groceries, cor. South and Delaware.
Thoms F., of Spiegel, T. & Co., res. East, bet. Market and Ohio.
Thomson Quintin, bakery, 4 s. Meridian, res. same.
Thorington L., res. Laukabee, bet. East and Liberty.
Thorn F., col., cook, Mason House.
Thorn J. R., of Apple & T., bds. Little's Hotel.
Thornberry Wm., res. 233 n. Illinois.
Thornly Jasper, engineer, res. Fletcher's ave.
Thorpe J. D., res. 39 e. Market.
Thorpe K., artist, res. 69 Fort Wayne ave.
Thorpe Thomas, artist, bds. 69 Fort Wayne ave.
Thoussen E. B., of T. & Lahey, bds. Palmer House.
Thoussen & Lahey, wholesale dealers in furnishing goods.
Thurston Mrs., res. 172 e. Washington, up stairs.
Thurston B., clerk, res. 159 n. Penn.
Thurston Mrs. C., res. Ramsey's Block.

Thurston W. B., of Pomeroy, Fry & Co., res. 159 n. Pennsylvania.

Tickert Jacob, carpenter, res. 128 n. West.

Ticknor Geo. P., printer, Journal Office, res. 127 Massachusetts ave.

Tierney M., blacksmith, with Case and Marsh.

Tietz W., cigar maker, res. 133 e. Washington.

Tilford Mrs. A. L., res. 192 n. Miss.

TILFORD J. M., PRES'T JOURNAL CO., res. 67 n. Meridian.

Tindall Henry, res. 116 n. Tennessee.

Tino Christ., shoemaker, bds. Davidson.

Titcomb D., produce dealer, cor. Maryland and Virginia ave., res. 48 e. Market.

Titman Alex., res. cor. South and Tenn.

Tizolel Mrs. C., Jefferson House, cor. South and Penn.

Tobeen T., laborer, Washington Foundry.

Toben Thos., boiler maker, res. Ann, bet. Tenn. and Miss.

Toburn Thos., laborer, res. cor. McCarty and Tenn.

Todd Chas. N., of T. & Carmichael, res. 132 n. Tenn.

Todd John M., grocer, res. 150 n. East.

Todd Mrs. Catharine, res. 39 w. Vermont.

Tood R. N., physician, 10 Virginia ave.

Todd Samuel, res. 186 n. Illinois.

TODD & CARMICHAEL, WHOLESALE AND RETAIL BOOKSELLERS AND STATIONERS, 2 n. Penn. See card, page 64.

Tollmann Isaac, baker, res. 180 e. Ohio.

Tomlinson C. C., of Miller & T., res. 220 e. Washington, 2d floor.

Tomlinson J. D., carpenter, res. 55 e. St. Joseph.

Tomlinson J. M., of T. & Cox, res. cor. Meridian and St. Clair.

Tomlinson S., student, bds. 117 n. Delaware.

Tomson F. B., works Western Agricultural Works.

Tomlinson & Cox, druggists, 18 e. Washington.

Toohey Michael A., book-keeper, 18 w. Washington, bds. Pyle House.

Tool M., blacksmith, Washington Foundry.

Tool Martin, laborer, 177 s. East.

Topp T., shoemaker, bds. Culps boarding house.

Totton Stewart, clerk, New York Store, res. 14 e. Ohio.

Touhy John, res. in rear of Soldiers' Home.

Townley G. E., clerk, with Fred. P. Rush.

Tousey Geo., Prest. Branch Bank State Indiana, res. 80 n. Meridian.

Tousey Oliver, of T. & Byram, res. 37 Meridian, bet. Ohio and New York.
TOUSEY & BYRAM, DRY GOODS, 70 e. Washington.
Tout C. F., brick layer, res. 215 n. Alabama.
Tout Isaac W., brick mason, res. cor. Illinois and Second.
Tout Wilkinson, brick mason, res. n. Meridian, n. of First.
Tout Wm., artist, res. Illinois, bet. First and Second.
Tout Z. F., agent, J. W. Copeland, cor. Washington and Meridian.
Townley Thomas, res. 42 s. Penn.
Townsend J. M., auditor, Bellefontaine R. R., bds. 49 w. Maryland,
TRAEYSER G., PIANO MANUFACTURER, Alabama, bet. Pearl and Washington, res. Alabama, bet. Pearl and Maryland. See card, page 28.
Traeyser P., piano maker, with G. Traeyser.
Trask Geo. K., laborer, res. 125 w. New York.
Traub Chas., furniture repairer, res. cor. Plum & Cherry.
Traub Conrad, laborer, res. 117 Fort Wayne ave.
Traub D., wood sawyer, res. 51 s. Illinois.
Traub Israel, painter, res. 214 n. Alabama.
Traub Jacob, baker, res. 230 n. New Jersey.
Traub Magdalena, res. 123 n. East.
Traver C. H., salesman, Bee Hive Store, bds. 15 s. Miss.
Traver Geo. M., clerk, res. 15 s. Mississippi.
Trego C. D., clerk, Head-quarter Supt. Recruiting Service, bds 27 s. Delaware.
Trevarn John, (col.) laborer, res. n. Miss.
Trester John, hackman, res. 146 Blake.
Triter John, brick mason, res. 205 n. New Jersey.
Troner John, works Union Depot, res. 26 Henry.
Troup John, laborer, res. 8 New York.
Trowbridge Joseph F., carpenter, res. 309 Virginia ave.
Trueblood James, res. 139 n. Delaware.
Trueblood & Co., real estate agents, room No. 1, 26 w. Washington.
Trueblood & Street, wholesale book and map agents, room No. 1, 26 w. Washington.
TRUKSESS JOHN, BLACKSMITH, 60 Kentucky ave., res. 62 Kentucky ave.
Tuckenbroke C., blacksmith, res. bet. Delaware and Alabama.
Tucker J., agent Maguire, Jones & Co., res. cor. Vermont and Tennessee.
Tucker Joshua, res. 50 w. Vermont.
Tucker W. S., salesman, 3 Bates House, bds. Palmer House.

Tucker Martin, laborer, res. 134 e. New York.
Turley Dr., cor. Washington and Alabama.
TURNER A., BARBER, 15½ w. Washington, res. 67 Georgia.
Turner A. H., of Hance & T., res. 167 e. Ohio.
Turner Andrew, jewelry dealer, res. 167 e. Ohio.
Turner B., res. 80 Douglas.
Turner, Bronson & Coburn, saloon, 15 n. Illinois.
Turner C., clerk U. S. Acct. Dept., bds. 21 s. Delaware.
Turner G. W., saloon, 15 n. Illinois.
Turner James, township trustee, res. 121 s. Alabama.
Turner M. C., book-keeper, 84 w. Washington, res. 300 n. Tennessee.
Turner Theodore, student, res. 121 s. Albama.
Turner Wm., brick mason, res. 104 n. New Jersey.
TURNER WM. H., GENERAL COMMISSION MERCHANT AND DEALER IN AGRICULTURAL IMPLEMENTS, &c., 84 w. Washington, res. 270 n. Illinois. See card, p. 125.
Tuttle L. B., canvassing agent, bds. cor. Market and Circle.
Tuttle Orrin, drive fire engine, engine house No. 3.
Tutewiler C. W., of T. & Bros., res. 64 Mass. ave.
TUTEWILER BROS., STOVES AND TIN WARE, 182 e. Washington. See card, p. 64.
Tutewiler Henry, plasterer, res. 65 Mass. ave.
Tutewiler H. W., of T. & Bros., res. 65 Mass. ave.
Tutewiler J. W., of T. & Bros., res. 65 Mass. ave.
Tweey Harmon, blacksmith, res. 271 Virginia ave.
Twohy H., works Rolling Mill.
Twombly Richard, res. 26 w. New York.
Twohy J., works Rolling Mill.
Tyer Madison, apprentice machinist, res. East, bet. Louisiania and Georgia.
Tylee J., cook, Spencer House.
Tyler A. P., clerk Qr. Dep. U. S. A., res. 8 Virginia ave.
Tyler L. H., Bee Hive dry goods store, 2 w. Washington, res. same.
Tyner H. R., clerk Post Office.
Tyre Geo. W., conductor, res. 89 s. East.

U

Uhl Peter, cigar maker, res. St. Clair, bet. Meridian and Illinois.
Ulhoof G., tinner, res. 238 Madison R. R. ave.
Umversall J. A., policeman, res. 65 e. Merrill.
Underwood Benj., bds. 129 w. Ohio.

Underwood II., (col.) barber, bds. J. G. Britton's.
UNDERWOOD J. II., GENERAL AGENT HOME MU-
TUAL FIRE INSURANCE CO., res. 44 Pratt. See
card, outside front cover.
Unger N., res. c. Washington.
Union Steam Bakery, 11 n. Pennsylvnia.
UNITED STATES EXPRESS CO., J. BUTTERFIELD,
AGENT, cor. Meridian and Washington.
Union Cabinet Factory, on Hosbrook.
Union Depot, Louisiana, from Illinois to Meridian.
UNION HOUSE, GEO. ILG, PROP'R, cor. South and
Illinois. See card, p. 54.
UNION TRANSPORTATION AND INS. CO.'S FAST
FREIGHT LINE, R. C. MELDRUM, AGENT, 14 s.
Meridian.
Unversaw J. N., city marshal, res. 227 s. Alabama.
Unversaw L., of L. U. & Co., res. 147 s. Alabama.
Unversaw L. & Co., livery and sale stable, 11 and 13 w.
Pearl.
Upfold George, Bishop, res. 51 n. Tennessee.
Upham Alfred, res. 113 n. Meridian.
Uphost Henry, laborer, Eagle Foundry.
Uphouse Henry, shoe maker, res. 188 s. Delaware.
Urban Michael, laborer, res. 101 n. Noble.

V

Vagt Fred., clerk, 194 w. Washington.
Vail Sydney J., Instructor Deaf and Dumb Asylum.
Vajen J. H., hardware merchant, 21 w. Washington, res.
Meridian.
Valentine William, baker, works Cincinnati Bakery.
Vanantwerp George W., blacksmith, 8 n. East, res. 22 n.
Liberty.
Vanbergen Wm., carpenter, res. 45 w. Michigan.
VANBLARICUM J. M., WAGON AND BLACKSMITH
SHOP, cor. Pennsylvania and Georgia, res. 177 w.
Washington.
Van Brocklin B. F., res. 133 w. Vermont.
Vanc Thomas P., clerk, res. 94 n. East.
Van Camp G. C., fruit dealer, res. 122 w. Ohio.
Vance Samuel C., res. cor. Cady and Washington.
Vance T. P., clerk, 3 n. Pennsylvania, res. 94 n. East.
Vandegrift Benj., printer, res. 98 n. Mississippi.
Vandegrift B. C., clerk, Post Office, res. 33 Kentucky ave.
Vandegrift Henry, notary public, office 16½ c. Washington,
res. 33 Kentucky ave.

Van Houten C. W., grocery, res. 134 n. Alabama.
VAN HOUTEN & GRAHAM, GROCERS, 34 cor. Market and Illinois.
VANLANNINGHAM L., SECRETARY GAS CO., res. cor. Delaware and South.
Vanlanningham Mrs. Elizabeth, res. 128 n. New Jersey.
Vannantwert George, blacksmith, res. 22 n. Liberty.
Vanneble Welles, laborer, res. 123 e. St. Clair.
Van Nida Philip, watchman government stable, res. 197 n. Noble.
Vantile Abram, works Indiana Central R. R. Machine Shop.
Vajent ——, res. Meridian, bet. Ohio and New York.
Vajin J. H., of Fletcher, V. & Co., res. — n. Meridian.
Vater Thomas, brick mason, res. 43 w. Walnut.
Vater S., Western Union Telegraph, res. 41 w. Walnut.
Vaughn Jacob, carpenter, res. Mississippi, bet. First and Second.
Vawter M., machinist, res. 18 Union.
Veach Joseph, wagon master, res. 28 e. St. Clair.
Veck Joseph, laborer, res. West, near South.
Vequsney Gustave, laborer, res. 95 Fort Wayne ave.
Veist Wm., laborer, res. 26 s. Alabama.
Veeb C. G., lawyer, res. Market, bet. Noble and Davis.
Vest D., laborer, works with D. Root & Co.
Vert Daniel, foundryman, res. 97 Massachusetts ave.
Vick Aby, res. 138 Ohio.
Vickers Wm. B., druggist, Odd Fellows' Hall, res. 69 n. Alabama.
Victor Catherine, (wid.) res. 89 n. Alabama.
Victor Louis, grocer, res. 160 e. Ohio.
Vieweeg A., tailor, res. 101 e. Washington, up stairs.
Vierenkel Joseph, baker, res. Nelson alley.
Vilson A. A., printer, res. 134 e. Market.
Vinan Ann, res. 6 Chatham.
Vincent Felix A., comedian.
Vincent G. D., carpenter, res. Delaware, bet. St. Joseph and St. Marys.
Vincent J., salesman, with A. Stephens & Son.
Vincent W. H., carpenter, res. 91 n. Davidson.
Vinnedge J. A., of Maguire, Jones & V., res. s. Tennessee.
Vinnedge J. D., of Jones, Vinnedge & Co., res. 85 n. Ala.
Vinton A. E., of Hasselman & V., res. Meridian, bet. Ohio and New York.
Violland E. L., clerk Major D. McClure, res. Tennessee, with Mrs. Stretcher.
Viscus Thomas, brickmason, res. e. Chatham.

VŒGTLE & METZGER, WHOLESALE AND RETAIL
DEALERS IN STOVES, HOLLOW AND TIN
WARE, 83 c. Washington. See card, page 38.
Vœgele Henry, works Schmidt's Brewery.
Vœgtle Jacob, of V. & Metzger, res. 125 c. Market.
Vogle W., clerk, cor. Maryland and West.
Vogt Barney, musician, leader of City Band, res. 63 n. New
Jersey.
Vogtel Jacob, tinner, res. 125 c. Market.
Voight Louis, Western House, cor. Louisiana and Illinois.
Voight H. W., of W. J. Holliday & Co., 113 Michigan.
VOLLMER JOHN PH., HEAD CLERK MERRILL &
CO.'S BOOK STORE, bds. Bates House.
Vollmer Philip, distiller, res. 159 c. St. Clair.
Volmer Charles, liquor merchant, res. 141 n. Noble.
Vondersaar Wendell, blacksmith. bds. 94 Fort Wayne ave.
VONNEGUT CLEMENS, HARDWARE AND CUTLE-
RY, 142 c. Washington, res. same.
Vordermark R., chair maker, res. 89 c. Meridian.
Vowress J. W., plasterer, res. Fort Wayne ave.
Vrooman J., moulder, res. 186 s. Pennsylvania.

W

Wachter Moses, of Katzenstein & W., res. cor. Georgia and
Meridian.
Wachter L., shoe shop, s. Illinois.
Wachtstetter J., saloon, 25 s. Meridian.
Wachtstetter J. M., Nebraska Saloon, 12 Louisiana.
Waddel John, res. 11 c. North.
Waddell John, salesman, German Dry Goods Store.
Wagner ——, wks. Rolling Mill, res. 7 willard.
Wagner A., hackman, res. 61 Kentucky ave.
Wagner Henry, miller, bds. Michigan, bet. New Jersey and
East.
Wait V. B, carpenter, res. 127 w. New York.
Wainwright S., tinner, 11 s. Illinois, res. cor. Meridian and
New York.
Wakdel Moses, clothing, res. Georgia, near cor. Meridian.
Walcott F. H., City Bank, res. 67 Pennsylvania.
Walden E., soldier 1st (col.) regiment Indiana volunteers,
res. n. Mississippi.
Walder W., shoemaker, bds. Walk's Boarding House.
Waldo A., wks. Byrkit & Bean's, bds. Coen's Boarding
House.
Waldo G. W., tinner, wks. with D. Root & Co.
Waldo Mrs. M. T., res. 63 Louisiana.

Took first Premium at Alabama State Fair, 1863.

Walk Anthony, shoemaker, res. 150 e. Market.
Walk C., butcher, bds. 91 s. Illinois.
Walk Julius, jeweler, res. Bluff road, bet. McCarty and Ray.
Walk Julius, watch maker, res. s. Illinois.
Walk Louis, boarding house, 14 w. Georgia.
Walker A., teamster, res. 229 s. Alabama.
Walker Henry, laborer, res. 315 Elm.
Walker I. D., of W. & McKernan, bds. Bates House.
Walker J. S., res. 115 n. Illinois.
Walker T. P., clerk, Quartermaster's Department U. S. A.,
    bds. Bates House.
Walker Thomas R., salesman, bds. Macy House.
WALKER & McKERNAN, REAL ESTATE AND U. S.
    CLAIM AGENTS, 8 w. washington. See card, out-
    side front cover.
Wall G., bar-keeper, res. 73 s. Illinois.
Wall James, res. 114 w. Georgia.
Wall Thomas, laborer, res. e. Louisiana.
Walla John, blacksmith, 166 s. Delaware.
WALLACE ANDREW, WHOLESALE GROCER, cor.
    Delaware and Virginia ave., res. 34 n. Delaware. See
    card, p. 20.
Wallace B. T., deputy clerk, Marion Circuit Court, bds.
    Macy House.
Wallace George, clerk, res. 25 Alabama.
Wallace Mrs. Gov. G. G., res. 139 n. New Jersey.
Wallace G. E., book-keeper, res. 35 n. Alabama.
Wallace J., student, bds. 64 Massachusetts ave.
Wallace James, carpenter, res. 165 n. East.
Wallace Samuel, brick mason, bds. 165 n. East.
WALLACE W. B., CITY INTELLIGENCE AND GEN-
    ERAL INFORMATION OFFICE, 63 e. washington,
    res. 221 n. New Jersey. See card, p. 32.
Wallace Wm. J., res. 161 e. Market.
WALLACE WILLIAM, CLERK, MARION CIRCUIT
    COURT, res. 121 n. Delaware.
Wallace W. P., clerk, res. 34 n. Delaware.
Wallace W. W., marble shop, 92 s. Illinois, res. 94 s. Illinois.
Wallace Wm., county clerk, res. 121 n. Delaware.
Wallace Wm., laborer, wks. I. & C. R. R. Machine Shop.
Wallace Wm. John, commission department, res 161 e.
    Market.
Walle Mat., blacksmith, wks. Gates & Lemon.
Walley John, blacksmith, res. 29 s. Liberty.
Waller B., shoemaker, cor. Indiana ave. and Missouri, res.
    same.

Walley Mat., blacksmith, res. Meek, near Liberty.
Walleck Jno. F., division superientendent western Union Telegraph Co., bds. n. w. cor. Michigan and Pennsylvania.
Walls Henry, res. 9 e. North.
Walls John, apprentice, Journal off.
Wallsman F., saloon, res. 14 s. Illinois.
Walpole Mrs. Esther, res. 156 n. Illinois.
WALPOLE R. L., ATTORNEY, off. 16½ e. washington, room 2, up stairs, res. 87 n. Meridian.
Walsh Thomas, boiler maker, res. 216 s. Alabama.
Walsh T., boiler maker, washington foundry.
Walton E. H., family grocery, res. Delaware and New York.
Walton W., wks. Rolling Mill, res. Tennessee, bet. South and Merrill.
Waltze W., jeweler, 64 e. washington, res. same.
Wands A., shoemaker, 39 s. Meridian, res. 131 n. Pennsylvania.
Wands John, shoemaker, res. cor. Grier and McCarty.
Wandely H., clerk, res. 73 n. Davidson.
Wander Philip, res. 58 Orsbrook.
Wanton W. R., book-keeper, res. 64 e. North.
Wants A. J., shoemaker, res. 131 n. Pennsylvania.
Ward John, butcher, res. Tennessee, n. of Third.
Ward L. D., messenger, American Express Co.
Ward Mrs. Lucinda, res. 262 Indiana ave.
Ward Robert, clerk, res. 208 n. New Jersey.
Ward Wm., machinist, res. 50 Bates.
Ward Wm., machinist, wks. I. & C. R. R. Machine Shop.
Ware Chas. S., M. D., s. w. cor. Meridian and washington, res. 97 n. Tennessee.
Ware T. S., M. D., s. w. cor. Washington and Meridian, res. 87 n. Pennsylvania.
Warner Col. A. J., post commander, off. 191 w. washington.
Warner C., bar-keeper, res. 68 n. Mississippi.
Warren C. F., clerk, bds. Macy House.
Warner C. G., printer, res. 209 n. Alabama.
Warner Chas., liquor dealer, res. 68 n. Mississippi.
Warner Lewis S., mill wright, bds. 64 n. Mississippi.
Warner T. D., printer, res. 58 e. Michigan.
Warner Thos., pressman, Journal off.
Warren G. S., clerk, bds. Macy House.
Warren John, wks. Rolling Mill.
Warren Stephen, wks. Rolling Mill.
Warrick Henry, wks. Rolling Mill.

Took first premium at California State Fair, 1863.

Washinan S., tailor, 103 e. washington, up stairs.
Washington Allen, res. 51 n. East.
Washington Foundry, e. end Union Depot.
Washington S., (col.) laborer, wks. with M. Patterson.
Washington Max., machinist, wks. Sinker & Co.
Wason A. W., veterany surgeon, 297 Virginia ave., res. 116 s. Mississippi.
Waters John, res. 16 w. Michigan.
Watkins G., bar-keeper, res. 53 s. Illinois.
Watkins J. M., carpenter, res. First, near Mississippi.
Watson James, tailor, res. 15 s. Illinois.
Watson J. M., machinist, works I. & C. machine shop.
Watson J. S., printer, res. 129 w. Maryland.
Watson Morris, res. 19 w. washington.
Watson R., machinist, works I. & C. R. R. machine shop.
Watson Samuel, clerk, Fletcher's Bank, res. 73 w. Maryland.
Watson Samuel W., book-keeper Harrison's Bank, res. 73 w. Maryland.
Watson Wm., tinner, bds. 121 n. East.
Watson W. P., ticket agent Little Miami R. R., res. 138 n. Illinois.
Watson W. T., stove moulder, works with D. Root & Co.
Watts W., marble cutter, res. 65 n. Pennsylvania.
Way Truman, R. R. Master, Peru road, res. 115 e. McCarty.
Way Wm., works Rolling Mill.
Wayne C. B., foreman Rolling Mill.
Wehtestetter G., saloon, res. 20 Madison ave.
Weagand S., clerk, res. 12 s. Alabama.
Weakley J. A., tinner, res. 97 w. New York.
Weakley J. A., clerk, res. 97 w. New York.
Weakley J. F., tinner, works with Munson & Johnson.
Weakley P., works Rolling Mill.
Weaner Mrs. Elizabeth, res. 188 s. East.
Weaner J., of Mattler & W., res. 188 s. East.
Weaver E. A., harness maker, res. 172 s. Alabama.
Weaver Wm. W., of W. & Williams, res. 147 n. Illinois.
Weaver Wm., res. 159 w. Maryland.
Weaver William, tailor, res. 173 e. washington.
Weaver & Williams, undertakers, 9 Bates House Block.
Webb Alfred, res. 107 Indiana ave.
Webb A. L., of W. & Hill, 107 Indiana ave.
Webb Mrs. M., res. 69 s. Pennsylvania.
WEBB & HILL, FLOUR, FEED AND AGRICULTURAL IMPLEMENTS, under Masonic Hall, 85 w. washington. See card, p. 42.
Webber J. B., bookbinder, with J. G. Douglass, res. 128 w. New York.

Weber Fred., laborer, res. 173 n. Railroad.
Weber John, blacksmith, res. 94 Fort wayne ave.
Weber William, blacksmith, res. 36 n. Liberty.
Webster G. C., of Daggett & Co., res. cor. Meridian and Pennsylvania.
Webster J. H., fireman, res. 43 Massachusetts ave.
Weeks William H., grocer, 31 s. Meridian, bds. Alvord's Block.
Weger H., laborer, res. s. New Jersey.
Wehling C., wagonmaker, res. Pearl.
WEHLING CHARLES, WAGONMAKER, 166 s. Delaware, res. Alley, near J. J. Gates' blacksmith shop.
Wehle L., shoe shop, 179 o. washington, res. same.
Wehn C., currier, works with Yandes & Co.
Weibel Edward, barber, 181 n. Illinois.
Weible Ed., barber, 188 n. Illinois.
Weigle Gottlieb, soldier, res. 65 n. Noble.
Weile George, carpenter, res. 119 n. Noble.
Weinberger H., clerk, res. 60 s. Meridian.
Weinberger J. C., bakery and confectionery, 10 Louisiana, res. 15 w. Georgia.
WEINBURGER JOHN C., BAKER AND CONFECTION‌ER, 10 Louisiana.
WEINBERGER & MULLER, NEWS AND FANCY GOODS DEALERS, Union Depot. See card, page 70.
Weir D. H., bds 88 Virginia ave.
Weir W., Marble shop, 13 Virginia ave., bds. cor. Penn. and Maryland.
Weinch M. D., engineer, res. 215 s. Penn.
Weise A., apprentice, washington foundry.
Weis John, brick mason, res. n. Delaware.
Weiss John, saloon, res. cor. Bates and washington.
Weismeir J., works Rolling Mill.
Weise P., shoemaker, 61 Madison ave.
Weitmann Peter, cabinet maker, res. 161 n. Railroad.
Weitmeier Fred., laborer, res. 199 n. Alabama.
Welch A., laborer, res. 157 s. Tennessee.
Welch John, laborer, res. 312 s. Delaware.
Welch John, conductor, Jeffersonville R. R.
Welch Mrs. L., res. 6 willard.
Welch Mat, works Rolling Mill.
Welch M., hostler, works with J. Peabody.
Welch W., laborer, res. 71 Madison ave.
Welch & Reighen, saloon, under Palmer House.
Welden Wm., (col.) white washer, res. 151 west.
Wells A., porter, Adams Express Co.

18

WELLS GRAHAM A., DENTIST, office, over Harrison's Bank, res. 57 n. Pennsylvania.

Wells Jas., laborer, res. 136 e. washington.

Wells J., laborer, with Stephens & Son.

Wells J. T., clerk, bds. Little's Hotel.

Wells Dr. M., dentist, bds. 68 e. Vermont.

Wells M., dentist, 4 Yohn's Block, res. 7 e. North.

Wells O., teamster, res. 103 Georgia.

Wendt G., wagon maker, Railroad.

Wenger Frank, clerk, bds. 20 n. Noble.

Wenger G. M., saloon keeper, res. 20 n. Noble.

Wenmer Jacob, market-master, res. 48 n. Liberty.

Wentworth James, works Post & Helwig's Planing Mill.

Wentz W. W., conductor, I. & C. R. R., res. 103 s. Alabama.

Werbe C. G., attorney, s. w. cor. Meridian and washington.

Werbe L. F., grocer, 185 w. washington, res. same.

Werden & Co., book store, 26 e. washington.

Werend A., blacksmith, works with Haugh & Schowe.

Werkler Adolph, carpenter, res. Liberty, bet. Laukabee and New York.

Werland Chas., checkman, I. & M. R. R. Depot.

Werner G., laborer, res. cor. Madison Railroad ave. and McCarty.

Wert F., tinner, res. 63 n. Alabama.

WERT JOS., BOOT AND SHOE DEALER, 6 s. Penn., res. 63 n. Alabama.

Wesieman Wm., laborer, res. Meek, near Benton.

Wesling Conrad, drayman, res. Michigan, bet. Noble and Railroad.

Wesmir John, laborer, res. 25 Nelson alley.

West, Dudly & Co., dealers in boots and shoes, 17 e washington.

West C. M., clerk, bds. w. Clay.

West C. W., of W., Dudly & Co., res. 119 n. Penn.

West Geo. E., res. Lowe's Block, Ohio.

West Geo. H., clerk, res. 49 w. Michigan.

West G. W., of W., Dudley & Co., 119 n. Penn.

West J., res. 118 n. Pennsylvania.

Westcott E. R., carpenter, bds. Little's Hotel.

Western Machine Works, Sinker & Co., one square e. Union Depot.

Western Scale and Agricultural Works, Coolman, Morris & Co., s. Tennessee, opp. Rolling Mill.

Western Union Telegraph Office, n. w. cor. washington and Meridian.

Westover J. M., moulder, works with D. Root &. Co., res. 64 e. Merrill.

Westwood John, gas engineer, res. 95 Virginia ave.

Westwood John, foreman, Western Machine Works.

Wetmore John, engineer, Capital Mills.

Wetmore K., laborer, res. 340 s. Delaware.

Wetmore S. F. & Co., printers, 37 c. washington, bds. cor. Circle and Market.

Wetzell E., bar-keeper, Washington Hall.

Wetzel F., tinner, 224 s. Mississippi.

Whatts Wm., stone cutter, res. 65 n. Penn.

Wheeler E., cook, res. 143 e. New York.

Wheathers Michael, laborer, res. 137 e. New Jersey.

Wheatley W. M., of McCord & W., res. 108 e. Ohio.

Wheden Wm., conductor, I. & M. R. R., bds. Ray House.

Wheeler Jos., col., cook, Little's Hotel.

Wheeler Prof. J. H., teacher, vocal music, Indianapolis Female College.

Wheeler W. R., painter, bds. Central House.

Wheeler & Wilson Sewing Machine, C. C. Claflin, agent, Journal building, cor. Meridian and Circle.

Whight Richard, laborer, res. Michigan Road, near Central Railroad.

While G., miller, res. 68 s. East.

Whilliam Chas., carpenter, res. 9 Liberty.

Whipple Chas. W., machinist, res. 44 e. Louisiana.

Whitcomb J. G., agent, Jeffersonville R. R., res. 50 e. Market.

Whitcomb Wm., works I. & C. R. R. machine shop.

Whitafft Henry, cabinet maker, res. 22 s. East.

Whitard A. W., railroader, bds. Ray House.

White Chas., farmer, res. n. Illinois, near Tinker.

White F. G., actor, Metropolitan Hall.

WHITE G., GROCER, 101 w. washington.

White Henry, works with Osgood & Smith.

White Hannah L., res. 51 n. Liberty.

White H. W., tailor, res. 120 n. East.

White J., works Rolling Mill.

White J., machinist, bds. Ray House.

White Jacob, laborer, res. 36 n. Illinois.

White Joseph, drover, res. cor. Huron & School.

White Oren D., orderly sergeant, bds. 29 Indiana ave.

White Mrs. S., res. 135 c. McCarty.

White Mrs. Sarah, res. 67 n. Mississippi.

White W. H., carpenter, res. 233 s. East.

Whitehead N. H., carriage maker, 122 n. Miss.

Has taken the Premium at every Fair where exhibited.

Whitehead Thos., miller, res. w. washington, near river bridge.

Whitehead T. J., carpenter, res. Alabama, bet. Merrill and South.

Whitehead Thos., works, Byrkit & Beam's.

Whitehouse Wm., carpenter, res. 213 Indiana ave.

Whiteman T. B., clerk, bds. 152 n. Penn.

Whiteside J., laborer, bds. 146 w. Meridian.

Whiting John, switchman, res. 42 e. Louisiana.

Whiting Miss M. H., teacher, Indianapolis Female College.

Whitley Hiram, laborer, at Ray House.

Whitley Wm. M., lumber, res. 108 e. Ohio.

Whitman Rev. Milton, bds. 12 e. Walnut.

Whitman John, engineer, Indiana Central R. R. Machine Shop.

Whitney Charles C., telegrapher, res. 42 e. New York.

Whitney Edward, bar-keeper, 13 n. Illinois, bds. same.

WHITNEY T. D., QUARTERMASTER, 9TH CAVALRY, res. 64 w. St. Clair.

Whitsett J. B., enginner, res. 16 n. New Jersey.

Whitsit Mrs. Margaret, res. 246 Virginia ave.

Whitsit P. B., res. 244 Virginia ave.

Whittemore J. B., engraver, res. 53 n. Davidson.

Whitted John, brakeman, Indianapolis and Madison R. R., bds. Ray House.

Wick ———, res. Meek.

Wick F. H., carpenter, res. 17 Meek.

Wick George, attorney, res. cor. New York and Indiana ave.

Wickert John, salesman, 21 w. washington.

Widner G. O., messenger, U. S. Express Co.

Widner W. H., messenger, U. S. Express Co.

Wiedenhorn Rosa, (wid.) hair braider, res. 46 e. Market.

Wiegand Anton, res. cor. Missouri and South.

Wiegand L., porter, res. 12 s. Alabama.

Wiegand & Co., florists, cor. Kentucky ave. and Missouri.

WIERT JOHN, TURNER, 94 Fort wayne ave., res. 97 Fort wayne ave. See card, p. 86.

Wiese Charles, carpenter, res. 145 e. Ohio.

Wilcox W. B., cabinet maker, res. 169 s. Delaware.

Wilde J., of W. & Henninger, res. 71 s. Illinois.

Wilde & Henninger, mouldings and fancy goods, 71 s. Illinois.

Wiggins C. P., of W. & Chandler, res. 258 w. washington.

Wiggins D., laborer, bds. Ohio House.

WIGGINS & CHANDLER, FOUNDERS AND MACHINISTS, 262 w. washington.

Wigmore J. S., watchmaker, with C. A. Ferguson, bds. Palmer House.

Wigmis Henry, laborer, 164 w. New York.

Wiles T., stoneware, 16 s. New Jersey, res. 32 n. Liberty.

Wiles Thomas, clerk, res. 32 n. Liberty.

Wiley D., doctor, off. 30 e. Market, res. 32 e. Market.

Wiley W. H., student, University, bds. 38 e. St. Clair.

WILEY WM. Y., OF W. & MARTIN, res. 32 n. Meridian.

WILEY & MARTIN, REAL ESTATE BROKERS AND MILITARY CLAIM AGENTS, 10 e. washington, up stairs. See card, inside back cover.

WILGUS G. D., GROCER, cor. Tennessee and New York, res. n. Illinois.

Wilgus J., engineer, res. 65 South.

Wilham Christ., laborer, res. 165 s. Alabama.

Wilhoff G., currier, 138 Madison ave.

Wilkens John, res. 34 e. Market.

Wilkes T. A., artist, res. 99 n. Meridian.

Wilkeson Dan., grocery, res. cor. North and Massachusetts ave.

Wilkeson W. H., res. 31 n. Delaware.

Wilkin Henry, shoemaker, res. 37 n. Noble.

Wilkins Peter, U. S. detective, res. 173 n. New Jersey.

Will John F., laborer, res. 46 n. Noble.

Willard A. B., dealer in satinet, jeans, warps, machine cards, &c., 4 Bates House, res. 66 e. New York.

Willard A. G., of W. & Stowell, res. 92 Massachusetts ave.

Willard William, instructor, Deaf and Dumb Asylum.

WILLARD & STOWELL, DEALERS IN MUSIC AND MUSICAL INSTRUMENTS, 4 Bates House. See card, near front cover.

Willetts J. S., agent Freedmen's Aid Commission, 8 n. Pennsylvania.

Willetts Wm. P., bds. 118 n. Meridian.

Willitt Franklin, (col.) res. 119 Indiana ave.

Willets J. S., agent, res. 118 n. Meridian.

Willetts W. P., agent, Security Life Insurance Co., 8 n. Pennsylvania.

Williams August, res. 127 w. Vermont.

Williams B. A., of Buell & W., bds. Bates House.

Williams S. Charles, laborer, res. 9 n. Liberty.

Williams Chas. C., grocer, 3 n. Illinois, opp. Bates House.

Williams Chas., of Weaver & W., res. Michigan.

Williams Chas., undertaker, res. 20 w. Michigan.

Williams D., wks. Rolling Mill, res. Tennessee, near McCarty.

Williams D. G., of Werden & Co., res. 16 w. St. Clair.
Williams David, boiler maker, western machine works.
Williams David, laborer, res. 136 n. Mississippi.
Williams D. N., wks. Rolling Mill.
Williams George, teamster, res. 123 e. St. Clair.
Williams H., painter, res. 216 Virginia ave.
Williams J., res. Missouri.
Williams J., wks. Rolling Mill.
Williams J. C., (col.) barber, res. 93 s. Tennessee.
Williams Jacob T., book binder, 46 California.
Williams J. M., harness maker, wks. with John Andra & Co.
Williams John, res. 97 Missouri.
Williams John, baggage master, Jeffersonville R. R., bds. Ray House.
Williams J. T., book binder, 46 n. California.
Williams H. E., res. 48 e. New York.
Williams M., wks. Rolling Mills.
Williams Martin, of W. & Van Camp, res. cor. St. Charles and Missouri.
Williams O., with Voegtle & Metzger.
Williams Owen, grocer, 134 w. washington, res. 134 n. Illinois.
Williams R. R., wks. Rolling Mill.
Williams R., engineer, res. 13 Union.
Williams Thomas H., res. 53 Huron.
Williams Wm., blacksmith, res. 114 Georgia.
Williams W. D., salesman, Hume, Lord & Co.
Williams Wm., clerk, bds. 59 e. Ohio.
Williams Wm., police, res. 50 Indiana ave.
Williams Wm., tailor, res. 50 Indiana ave.
Williams W. B., clerk, Bellefontaine R. R. office, bds. 59 e. Ohio.
Williams & Van Camp, canned fruit dealers, Ohio, w. of Canal.
Williamson L., engineer, res. 34 n. Ellsworth.
Williamson M. D., lumber dealer, res. 114 n. East.
Williard A. B., book-keeper, res. cor. New York and Alabama.
Willis Geo., messenger, American Express Co.
Wilmot Mrs. C., res. McCarty, bet. Tennesse and Illinois.
Wilmot & Thayer, hats, caps and furs, 8 w. washington.
Wilmington E. M., deputy county auditor, res. 113 n. New Jersey.
Wilson A., printer, res. 134 e. Market.
Wilson A. J., marble works, 10 n. Delaware.

Wilson B. A., photographer, cor. Meridian, near Union Depot.

Wilson A. J., stone cutter, res. 65 n. Pennsylvania.

Wilson C., clerk, res. 174 s. Mississippi.

Wilson Chas. G., painter, res. 174 s. Mississippi.

Wilson C. H., actor, Metropolitan Hall, res. 31 n. Liberty.

Wilson G. S., clerk, 72 w. washington, bds. 46 s. Pennsylvania.

Wilson Henry, laborer, Ray House.

Wilson J. B., hardware, 59 w. washington, res. 266 n. Illinois.

Wilson Junius, painter, res. 58 Indiana ave.

Wilson John, baker, with Q. Thomson.

Wilson John, laborer, res. 128 w. Georgia.

Wilson John T., plasterer, res. 167 e. Ohio.

Wilson Joseph, merchant, res. 266 n. Illinois.

Wilson J. S., attorney, res. n. w. cor. Pennsylvania and Market.

Wilson J. S., builder, res. 26 n. East.

Wilson L. B., res. 63 Maryland.

Wilson O. M., attorney, res. e. side Tennessee, bet. Georgia and Maryland.

Wilson P., res. 29 n. Davidson.

Wilson Mrs. S. A., res. 45 e. Louisiana.

Wilson S. V., plasterer, res. 250 Madison R. R. ave.

Wilson T., laborer, wks. with William Hinesley.

Wilson T. K., clerk, res. 266 n. Illinois.

Wilson T. S., res. 114 s. New Jersey.

Wilson Wm., watchman, Madison Depot, res. 288 s. Delaware.

Wilson Wm., grocery, 56 South, res. same.

Wilson Wm., book-keeper, res. Georgia, bet. Illinois and Meridian.

Wilson Wm., watchman, I. & M. R. R. Freight Depot.

Wilson Wm., minister, res. 92 n. Alabama.

Wiley Wm., real estate agent, res. 53 e. New York.

Wineberger John, bakery, res. 15 w. Georgia.

Wingate J. F., grocer, 27 w. washington.

Wingate E. H., grocer, res. 100 n. Illionis.

Wingate W. L., of Hill & W., res. 91 Virginia ave.

Wingler Adolph, gardener, res. bet. New York and Liberty.

Wink Mrs., midwife, 115 e. washington, up stairs.

Winkel Berthy, dress maker, bds. 70 e. St. Joseph.

Winkel Fred., feed store, res. 70 e. St. Joseph.

Winkle W. F., of W. F. W. & Co., res. 70 e. St. Joseph.

WINKLE W. F. & CO., FLOUR AND FEED, 157 e. washington. See card, p. 58.
Winter A., laborer, res. 95 St. Mary.
Winter J. N., tailor, wks. 3 e. washington, res. 89 Massachusetts ave.
Winterstine E., messenger, American Express Co.
Wirth J. R., clerk, with J. George Stilz.
Wirtz Jacob, horse farrier, res. 212 w. washington.
Wisbey Ephraim, cooper, res. 200 w. Maryland.
Wise Benjamin, laborer, res. 143 n. New Jersey.
Wise R. G., wks. western machine shop.
Wise Wm., agent, res. 94 n. Illinois.
Wiseman Mrs. B. A., res. 83 n. Pennsylvania.
Wiseman Simon, teamster, res. 245 w. washington.
Wishmeyer H., shoemaker, with C. Aldag.
Wishmier A., laborer, res. 148 e. Ohio.
Wishmeier C. F., miller, res. 173 n. Davidson.
Witham J. L., wks. Rolling Mill.
Witley Mrs. Lucy, res. 73 n. Spring.
Witman H. N., carpenter, res. 127 s. Illinois.
Witman M. O., carpenter, bds. 127 s. Illinois.
Witridge Wm., painter, res. 181 n. New Jersey.
WITT B. F., ATTORNEY AND CLAIM AGENT, s. w. cor. Meridian and washington, 2d floor.
Wittenberg Chas., of Krause & W., res. 111 e. Ohio.
Wittlinger Jacob, grocer, cor. Georgia and Noble.
Wocher F., of Egner & W., bds. Emmeniger's.
Woerner P. F., clerk, bds. 78 w. washington.
Woeser Fred., teamster, bds. n. Delaware.
Woilk C. A., confectioner, res. Michigan, bet. Noble and Liberty.
Wolf A., bar-keeper, bds. Jefferson House.
Wolf Mrs. C., Cincinnati House, 124 s. Delaware.
Wolf G. W., clerk, bds. 124 s. Delaware.
Wolf M., clerk, res. 71 w. washington.
Wolff Henry, clerk, 4 w. washington.
Wolff R., gunsmith, 17 Kentucky ave., res. 125 s. Alabama.
Wolford Albert, mattress maker, s. Delaware.
Wolfram Christian, tinner. res. cor. Vermont and New Jersey.
Wolfeaston R., bar-keeper.
Wolfrom E., clerk, Indianapolis Branch Banking Co.
Wolfrom G., pressman, Journal office.
Wollam Lieut. H. M., 9th cavalry Indiana volunteers, res. 165 n. Liberty.
Wollam R. D., carpenter, res. 165 n. Liberty.
Wolff S., cigar maker, bds. Chicago House.
Wolleber G., marble cutter.

Woltz Mrs., res. 163 s. Tennessee.
WOOD A. D., HOUSE BUILDING AND HOUSE FUR-
NISHING HARDWARE, MECHANICS' AND FAR-
MERS' TOOLS, &c., 64 c. washington, res. 79 cor. Ver-
mont and Delaware.
Wood Alexander, res. 127 n. Illinois.
Wood Browning, clerk, 22 w. washington.
Wood P. A., cattle merchant, res. e. washington, near Orient.
Wood Jacob, wks. Rolling Mill.
Wood James, wks. Wiggins & Chandler's.
Wood John A., livery stable, res. 53 n. Pennsylvania.
Wood John F., clerk, Post Office, res. 36 n. East.
Wood John J., carpenter, res. Bates, near Cady.
Wood J. L., cooper, 270 Indiana ave.
Wood L., res. 99 n. New Jersey.
Wood Nick, wks. Rolling Mill.
Wood W., saddler, bds. 256 Madison R. R. ave.
Wood Wm. C., horse dealer, res. 140 n. Pennsylvania.
Wood & Foudray, livery stable, 10 n. Pennsylvania.
WOODBRIDGE C. A., QUEENSWARE, CHINA AND
GLASSWARE, 16 w. washington, res. 87 n. Tennessee.
See card, p. 148.
Woodbridge John, clerk, 16 w. washington, bds. 87 n. Ten-
nessee.
Woodin A. M., printer, with Dodd & Co., bds. Oriental
House.
Woodman G., laborer, wks. with D. Root & Co.
Woodruff Mrs. Addie, res. 4 s. New Jersey.
Woodruff J. C., boarding house, 47 w. Georgia.
Woods L. D., res. Norwood, bet. Illinois and Tennessee.
Woods N. M., clerk, 5 Bates House, bds. Macy House.
Woodward E. F., of Faught & W., 132 n. Alabama.
Woolen W. I., of Sloan & Burk, bds. Palmer House.
Woolen Wm. W., attorney, res. 124 n. Delaware.
Woolen Mrs. Thos., (wid.) seamster, res. 33 n. Alabama.
Woolfe Isaac, clerk, bds. Little's Hotel.
Woolf M., clerk, res. 65 w. New York.
Woolfrom Adolph, tinner, res. 101 n. New Jersey.
Woollen Mrs. Keziah, res. 33 n. Alabama.
Woollen Milton, constable, res. 149 cor. West and Michigan.
Woollen Milton, messenger, telegraph office, n. c. cor. West
and Michigan.
Woollen Wm. M., groceries, res. 82 w. Vermont.
Wollen W. W., attorney, office, College Hall building.
Wopner Henry, laborer, res. 29 Harrison.
Worland S. B., clerk, with W. Worland.
Worland W., groceries and feed, cor. Delaware and Virginia
avenue, res. same.

Worman Wm., salesman, with Crossland & Pee, res. Fort Wayne ave.

Warth Alex., Secy. I. & C. R. R., res. 246 s. Alabama.

Wren E., wagon maker, res. 51 s. New Jersey.

Wriedt W. H., saloon, 91 e. washington, res. same.

Wright A. L., deputy county treasurer, res. 92 n. Alabama.

Wright B. C., clerk, Post-office.

Wright Chas., boarding house, 14 e. Ohio.

Wright Chas. A., real estate agent and broker, 30½ e. washington, bds. Bates House.

Wright Frank, brewery, res. 71 Indiana ave.

Wright E. J., clerk, bds. 76 n. Illinois.

Wright F., laborer, res. e. Davidson.

WRIGHT FRANK, BREWERY, office, 20 s. Meridian, res. 71 Indiana ave.

Wright G., res. 28 Huron.

Wright Isaac, pump maker, res. 126 s. Noble.

Wright Jacob T., county auditor, res. 117 n. Delaware.

Wren John, carpenter, res. 192 s. Delaware.

Wright John C., res. 39 n. Meridian.

Wright J. J., res. 192 w. Maryland.

Wright Miss M. E., dress maker, 8 e. washington, 4th floor.

WRIGHT M. H., M. D., res. cor. Ohio and Meridian.

Wright R. M., shoemaker, res. Orient, bet. Michigan Road and washington.

Wright R., house painting, res. 19 s. Miss.

Wright R. M., foreman, shoe shop, Deaf and Dumb Asylum.

Wright Thos., clerk, New York Store, res. 14 e. Ohio.

Wright Wm., railroader, res. 173 n. Alabama.

Wright Wm. M., cashier and book-keeper, Jones, Hess & Davis.

Wright & Bro., pump shop, Maryland, bet. Virginia ave. and Alabama.

Wrihe Henry, laborer, res. 25 Harrison.

Wyatt Thos., plasterer, res. 55 Benton.

Wyland E., bar-keer, bds. 67 s. Illinois.

Wylan C., switchman, res. 20 Union.

Wyland C., laborer, res. 32 Union.

Wyland W. C., clerk, cor. McCarty and Meridian.

WYNN W. J., GEN. AGT. N. Y. LIFE INS. CO., office, s. w. cor. washington and Meridian, res. 41 w. walnut.

Wysong C., brick mason, res. cor. Illinois and Merrill.

Wysong Madison, brick mason, res. 58 Bluff Road.

Y

Yabroth Peter, engineer, res. cor. Market and Cady.

Yabrongh Francis, carpenter, res. 271 s. Delaware.

Yoeger C., grocer, 215 e. washington, res. same.
Yoeger Chas., brewery, res. 93 e. St. Joseph.
Yancy Samuel, laborer, res. 146 e. Market.
Yandes D., sr., res. 64 n. Penn.
Yandes D., jr., of Y. & Co., res. 83 e. New York.
Yandes G. B., of Y. & Co., res. 64 n. Penn.
Yandes Simon, attorney, office, Johnson's building, second floor.
Yandes & Co., wholesale leather store, 38 e. washington.
Yarbrough P. T., engineer, res. cor. Meek and Cady.
Yeaman Mrs. E., res. 27 s. Delaware.
Yelling P., tailor, res. 31 Virginia ave.
Yeoman Richard, printer, res. 118 n. East.
Yewell S., clerk, res. 195 s. Penn.
Yohms Fred., cabinet maker, res. 30 n. East.
Yohn James C., pay-master in army, res. 74 n. Delaware.
Yordell David, porter, Little's Hotel.
York Henry, carpenter, with Wm. Wise.
Youart Dr. J. M., res. 18 n. Delaware.
Yougerman Geo., laborer, res. 56 s. East.
Young Christ., with Louis Lang.
Young Christ, pattern maker, res. 7 Ellsworth.
Young G. D., machinist, res. 68 s. New Jersey.
Young Henry H., book binder, res. 20 California.
YOUNG HENRY H., LOCAL EDITOR, Journal, res. 120 n. East.
YOUNG LOUIS, BARBER, 32 w. washington.
YOUNG MENS' LIBRARY ASSOCIATION, W. S. MOR-RELL, LIBRARIAN, s. w. cor. Meridian and washington.
Young Wm., carpenter, res. 85 Indiana ave.
Youngerman C., res. 14 n. Delaware.
Youngerman G., saloon, cor. washington and Delaware, res. 56 s. East.
Youngerman J., bar-keeper, G. Youngerman.

Z

Ziegler Alex., carpenter, res. 67 n. Noble.
Zigler Wm., res. 31 n. Meridian.
Zimmer F., of Z. & Co., res. 138 e. washington.
Zimmer & Co., saloon, 138 e. washington.
Zimmerman C., slate and gravel roofer, office, 130 e. Market, res. cor. Market and Liberty.
Zimmerman T., works with McCord & Wheatly.
Zimmerman Geo., drayman, res. 129 n. Liberty.
Zink Henry, barber, res. 125 s. Illinois.
Zorger Geo., clerk, U. S. Mustering Office, bds. Tyler's, Virginia ave.

Zorger Martin, clerk, U. S. Mustering Office, bds. Macy House.
Zschech Fred., carpenter, res. 215 s. Delaware.
Zschech G., carpenter, washington foundry.
Zumbush T., jeweler, washington, bet. Delaware and Penn., res. s. Delaware.
Zweifer H. J., clerk, Exchange Saloon.
Zwier Christ., grocer, res. c. washington.

BUSINESS MIRROR.

Containing the Name and Location of principal Business
Men in the City, under the particular Trade or
Profession in which they are engaged.

Agent American Bible Society.

4 Talbott and News' Block.

Agricultural Implements.

Goolman, Morris & Co., Tenn., opp. Rolling Mill.
Lukins & Brackebush, 81 and 83 w. Washington.
Miller & Moore, 76 w. Washington.
Rapp S. J., 154 e. Wash.
Stilz J. George, 74 e. Washington.
TURNER WM. H., 84 w Washington. See card, p. 125.
WEBB & HILL, 85 w. Washington. See card, p. 42.

Ale Dealer.

GROSCH JOHN, 113 n. Noble.

Architects.

BOHLEN D. A., 3d story, Ætna Building.
Curzon Joseph, Journal Building.
Hodison Isaac, 3 Yohn's Block.
SMITHMYER J. L., 14 e. Market. See card, p. 60.

Attorneys at Law.

BARBOUR & HOWLAND, 4½ w. Washington.
Beal John A., 15½ e. Washington.
BOWLES THOS. H., 3 Talbott & News' Block.
Brown P. A., Blackford's Building.
Bufkin J. C., College Hall.
Caven & Sulgrove, 15½ e. Washington.
COLERICK JOHN, 16½ e. Washington.
Colcey S. A., 10 s. Meridian.
Culon Chas., 97 e. Washington.
DAVIS E A., 3 Talbott & News' Block. See card, p. 84.

Duncan R. B., 3 Brown's Block.
Dye J. T., 6 News' Block.
Elliott B. K., 24½ e. Washington.
Fishback W. P., 62½ e. Washington.
Hamilton J. W., off. Court House.
HAMLIN C., 16 e. Washington. See card, outside back of book.
Hammond Upton J., Johnson's Building, 2d floor.
Hayden John J., Blackford's Block.
HENDERSON WM., Ætna Building.
Hendricks & Hord, off. Ætna Building.
HEWITT CHAS., 30½ w. Washington.
Hoefgen S. B., Johnson's Building.
Holladay E. G., 10 s. Meridian.
Leary P. C., 39½ w. Washington.
LEATHERS & CARTER, 3 Odd Fellows Hall. See card, outside cover.
LOWE WM. A., 16½ e. Washington.
McDONALD & PORTER, Yohn's Block.
McDonald & Roache, Ætna Building.
McDougal W. R., Yohn's Block.
Major S., Johuson's Building.
MARTINDALE & GRUBBS, News & Talbo.t's Block.
Milner J., 86 e. Washington.
Morrrison James 24½ e. Washington.
NEWCOMB & TARKINGTON, 24½ e. Washington.
Rand & Hall, 24½ e. Washington.
Ray M. M., Talbott's & News' Block.
Ray & Phipps, 36 e. Washington.
STAGG CHAS. W., 4 Yohn's Block. See card, p. 76.
Sweetser J. N., Johnson's Building.
Taylor N. B., Brown's Building.

WALPOLE R. L., 16¼ e. Washington.

Werbe C. G., cor. Meridian and Washington.

WITT B. F., cor. Meridian and Washington.

Wollen W. W., College Hall.

Yandes Simon, Johnson's Building, 2d floor.

Auction and Com. Merchants.

HUNT A. L. & CO., 81 e. Washington. See card, p. 68.

Bakers and Confectioners.

Ball A., 132 s. Iillinois.

Bollmann Fred., Washington, bet. Delaware and Alabama.

Brown J. W., 150 n. New Jersey.

Bussert John. 54 Bluff Road.

CUNNINGHAM F. P., cor. Illinois and Market. See card, p. 48.

Gray Wm., 64 e. South.

Grein Mrs. J., 214 e. Washington.

Kraas Wm., 58 w. Meridian.

NICKUM & PAROTT, 11 n. Penn.

Selking W., 201 e. Washington.

Thomson Quintin, 4 s. Meridian.

WEINBERGER J. C., 10 Louisiana.

Banks.

Bank of State, cor. Illinois and Ky. ave.

BRANCH OF THE BANK OF THE STATE, cor. Washington and Meridian.

CITY BANK, PETTIBONE, MANSUR & CO., 3 w. Washington.

FIRST NATIONAL BANK OF INDIANAPOLIS, 3 n. Penn., under Odd Fellows Hall. See card, p. 146.

FLETCHER'S BANK, 30 e. Washington.

FLETCHER, VAJEN & CO.'S BANK, 6 n. Meridian.

HARRISON A. & J. C. S., 15 e. Washington.

Indianapolis Branch Banking Co., cor. Washington and Penn.

Barbers.

Britton J. G., 145 w. Washington.

CURRY J. H., cor. Washington and Fenn.

Elff Frank, 81 e. Washington.

Fisher Benedict, cor. Illinois and Louisiana.

Frankenstein G., Mason House.

FRANKLIN W. H., sr., cor. Washington and Meridian. See card, p. 102.

TURNER A., 15½ w. Washington.

Blacksmiths.

Allaire A., Clinton, bet. New Jersey and East.

Affantranger S. J., 111 North.

Botenmiler L., cor. Kentucky ave. and Georgia.

Flertz C., 99 Bluff Road.

Forshee G. W., Tenn., bet. Washington and Kentucky ave.

Gates & Lemon, 14 s. New Jersey.

McVea David, 203 w. Washington.

Markham T., Pennsylvania, bet. Pearl and Maryland.

RAYMOND SAMUEL, 6 e. Maryland. See card, p. 72.

Seibert S. M., 152 e. Washington.

Vonblaricum J. M., cor. Pearl and Georgia.

Walla Jonn, 166 s. Delaware.

Boarding Houses.

Adams A, 53 Indiana ave.

Barnes W., 72 s. Illinois.

Bright Mrs. Eliza, 45 n. Penn.

Coen J., 107 s. Tenn.

Crage Wm., 116 n. Missouri.

Dummeyer C., Illinois, s. of Depot.

Ender A. M., 83 s. Meridian.

Fry Miss R. N., 122 n. Illinois.

Grimus D. M., 20 n. Penn.

Graven T., 44 s. Meridian.

Jack M. W., 44 n. Penn.

Henry Adam, 165 s. Delaware.

Hurd D. B., 84 n. Tenn.

Knight E., 19 w. Georgia.

Lingenfelter W. H., 19 Circle.

Maas Jacob 115 w. Maryland.

Macy House, cor. Illinois and Market.

Millet Wm., 52 s. Delaware.

Ohio House, Market, bet. Illinois and Tenn.

Potter John L., 12 n. East.

Pyle House, cor. Maryland and Illinois.

Schleinlein Frank, 46 s. Meridian.

Scudder A., 46 Market.

Simpson Mrs. L., 27 Indiana ave.

Smith Mrs. M. C., 44 s. Penn.

Walk Louis, 14 W. Georgia.

Wolf Mrs. C., 124 s. Delaware.

Woodruff J. C., 47 w. Georgia.

Booksellers and Stationers.

Asher & Adams, 4 Odd Fellows Hall.
BOWEN, STEWART & CO., 18 w. Washington. See card, p. 66.
Braden Wm., 24 w. Washington.
Merrill & Co., Glenn's Block.
Thompson Mrs. & Son, 7 n. Pennsylvania.
TODD & CARMICHAEL, 2 n. Pennsylvania. See card, p. 64.
Trueblood & Street, 26 w. Washington.
Werden & Co., 26 e. Washington.

Book & Job Printing Offices.

Cameron W. S., 8 e. Pearl.
DODD H. H. & Co., 16½ e. Washington.

Book Binders.

Dodd H. H. & Co., 16½ e. Washington.
Douglas James G., Journal Building.
Palmer E. L., 34 s. Illinois.

Builder.

Beeber Geo. P., 25 Meek.

Boots and Shoes.

Aldag C., 137 e. Washington.
Aldag L., 36 n. Liberty.
Apple G. W. & Co., 85 e. Washington.
Bannworth B., Washington, bet. East and Liberty.
BRUNDAGE E. C., 19 e. Washington.
Busch C., 138 w. Washington.
CHASE & CADY, 20 e. Washington.
Dury & Cox, 63 e. Washington.
Friedgon C., 126 e. Washington.
Grout J. B., 5 w. Washington.
Gruenert H., 51 w. Washington.
HUNTER M. & CO., 19 e. Washington.
JONES, VINNEDGE & CO., 17 w. Washington.
Karle C., 73 e. Washington.
Kistner J. G., 51 s. Illinois.
KNODLE A., 32 e. Washington.
Leon A., 3 Illinois.
LINTZ ANTHONY, 39 w. Washington. See card, p. 120.
Maier N., 116 Virginia ave.
MAULDIN, ADAMS & CO., 53 w. Washington.

19

Mayo E. H. & Co., Glenn's Block.
Robinius F. & Co., 150 w. Washington.
Schemburg Wm., 11 s. New Jersey.
Sharpe J. K., 90 e. Washington.
Sierdorfer Louis, 3 n. Meridian.
Stark Herman, 185 e. Washington.
Wands A., 39 s. Meridian.
Wehle L., 179 e. Washington.
WERT JOSEPH, 6 s. Pennsylvania.
West, Dudley & Co., 17 e. Washington.

Boots and Shoes, Wholesale.

DAWES, EVANS & McMILLIN, 75 w. Washington. See card, p. 38.
HENDRICKS, EDMUNDS & CO., 40 s. Meridian.
MAYHEW E. C. & CO., 8 Roberts' Block. See card, p. 64.

Brass Foundries.

DAVIS J. W. & CO., 96 s. Delaware. See card, p. 106.
Garrett Joseph, near Union Depot.

Breweries.

Busher H., 14 s. Alabama.
CITY BREWERY, 26, 27 and 28 w. Washington.
Gagg & Co., City Brewery, 27 and 28 e. Pennsylvania.
Harting & Bro., Illinois, near Bluff road.
SCHMIDT C. F., cor. High and Wyoming. See card, p. 40.
WRIGHT FRANK, off. 20 s. Meridian.

Brokers.

KLINGENSMITH & BRO., 6 Blake's Building.

Butchers.

BORST F. & CO., 16 n. Illinois. See card, p. 114.
Davis S., 59 e. Washington.
Graham Wm. S. 22 n. Pennsylvania.
Grepper A., 16 Illinois.
Jaquess J. H., Missouri, bet. Market and Ohio.
Jorger John & Bro., 200 e. Washington.
Kaufmann Morris, 117 n. East.
Kuhn Chas., cor. Missouri and Michigan.
Riggs & Davis, 6 s. Meridian.

ROOS & BRO., 89 s. Illinois. See
card, p. 62.
Siefast A. & Co., cor. Delaware and
Washington.
Stagg John R., cor. New Jersey and
Virginia ave.

Cabinet Makers.

Berands J., 4 s. Pennsylvania.
Dohn Philip, 21 s. Meridian.
Gimble M., 147 e. Washington.

Canned Fruits.

PENTECOST & REISENER, 188 e.
Washington. See card, p. 86.
Williams & Van Camp, Ohio, w. of
Canal.

Carpenters and Builders.

Colestock Hiram, 150 n. Illinois.
Ebert John, 32 Kentucky ave.
EMERSON R. B., 141 w. Market.
Fernley John, 18 Circle.
FITCHEY & SHERWOOD, Market,
bet. Mississippi and Canal.
Fowler & Mount, 21 s. East.
Haywood A., 129 e. Washington.
HILDERBRAND, HENSCHEN &
CO., Walnut, bet. New Jersey and
East.
Mann & Rubush, 219 w. Washing-
ton.
RICKARDS THOS., 81 s. Delaware.
See card, p. 70.
Small & Harmaday, e. North.

Carriage Manufactueers.

DREW & SHAW, e. Market Square.
See card, p. 60.
Lowe George, 99 e. Washington.
Maguire C., cor. Kentucky ave. and
Georgia.
Mull J. H., cor. Kentucky ave. and
Georgia.

**Carriage Hardware and
Trimmings.**

SHARE GEORGE K., 72 w. Washington. See card, back of title.

**China, Glass and Queens-
ware.**

HAWTHORN CHAS. E., 83 e. Washington. See card, p. 104.
McCrury Joseph, 84 e. Washington.
WOODBRIDGE C. A., 16 w. Washington. See card, p. 148.

Cloaks and Mantillas.

Burrows & Edwards, 22 s. Illinois.
Ivens & Co., 1 s. Meridian.

Clock Store.

Daumont H. & Co., 17 n. Pennsylvania.

Cigars and Tobacco.

HEIDLINGER J. A., 3 Palmer
House and 10 Bates House.
Henninger C. & Co., 87 s. Illinois.
HUNT C. C., 61 e. Washington.
See card, p. 88.
Kratsch Peter, 93 s. Illinois.
Means W C., 261 e. Washington.
Mengis F., 125 e. Washington.
MEYER GEO. F., 35 w. Washing-
ton. See card, p. 56.
Mucho Wm., 3 Virginia ave.
Rachig Charles M., 11 e. Washing-
ton.
Reynolds & Coffin, cor. New York
and Noble.
SHARPE A. W., 12 n. Pennsylva-
nia. See card, p. 100.
Thompson Wm., 5 n. Pennsylvania.

Clothiers.
See, also, Merchant Tailors.

BEHRISCH B., Spencer House
Block. See card, p. 80.
Criqui M., 84 e. Washington.
DERNHAM M., cor. Meridian and
Washington. See card, p. 80.
Engrees H., 182 e. Washington.
FEIBELMAN & RAUH, Palmer
House corner. See card, p. 132.
Fox & Myer, 38 w. Washington.
Hots G. & Co., 69 s. Illinois.
Hays A., 4 Spencer House.
HAYS, KAHN & CO., 83 s. Illinois,
and cor. Illinois and Washington.
See card, p. 116.
Kahn A., 2 Palmer House.
Katzenstein & Wachtel, 3 Bates
House.
KOHN JOSEPH, 80 w. Washington.
See card, p. 80.
Lipinsky Isaac, 24 Louisiana.
Manheimer D., 55 w. Washington.
Marks M. H., 81 s. Illinois.
Mauldin & Adams, West, bet. Geor-
gia and Maryland.
May B. & Co., 24 Louisiana.
Moritz, Bro. & Co., 19 w. Washing-
ton.
MOSSLER L. I., 10 w. Washington.
See card, front of book.
Myer Moses, 4 w. Washington.
RICE & BAMBERGER, 6 Bates
House, and 9 w. Washington. See
card, p. 44.

ROSENTHAL H. & CO., cor. Illinois and Washington. See card, p. 116.
SIMMONS B., jr., 14 e. Washington.
Staub & Tapking, 2 Odd Fellows Hall.

Clothing, Wholesale.

DESSAR BRO. & CO., Schnull's Building, cor. Meridion & Maryland. See card, p. 94.

Coal, Lime &c.

BUTSCH VALENTINE, e. South opp. Union Depot. See card, p. 54.
PERINE C. R., 12 w. Washington. See card, p. 78.
ROSS J. II., 11 Pearl. See card, p. 116.

Coffee and Spice Mill.

STEPHENS A. & SON, 191 and 193 e. Washington.

College.

Indianapolis McLean Female College, Rev. Chas. Sturdevant, President, cor. Meridian and New York.

Commission Merchants.

DUNN J. T., 12 s. Penn.
GLAZIER CHAS., 16 s. Meridian.
Jordon & Spotts, cor. Penn. and Union R. R.
Keifer & Rush, 74 s. Meridian.
HOLMAN G. G., 95 e. Washington.
MYERS J. D., 8 and 12 s. Pennsylvania. See card, p. 80.
TURNER WM. H., 84 w. Washington. See card, p. 125.

Commercial and Business Colleges.

BRYANT & SPENCER, 30 w. Washington. See card, inside front cover.
MUMFORD J. C., Sentinel Building.
Purdy Wm., Ætna Building.

Candies, Fruits, &c.

Daggett & Co., 22 s. Meridian.
Ganter C., 181 e. Washington.
HAUCK JOHN, 12 Louisiana. See card, p. 112.
Haynes Philip, 40 w. Washington.

HUMMLER M. B., 21 n. Pennsylvania. See card, p. 88.
Cloiber S. C., 115 e. Washington.
Moesch T. H., 76 e. Washington.

Coppersmiths and Gas Fitter.

Cottrell & Knight, 94 s. Delaware.

Coopers.

Boor Philip, 134 Indiana ave.
Corey & Dills, near Soldier's Home.
Humphrey James, 178 w. Washington.

Dentists.

Burgess C. C., Odd Fellows Hall.
FRINK & WELLS, 4 Yohn's Block. See card, p. 132.
Hunt P. G. C., 32 e. Market.
Johnston John F., 11 w. Washington.
Lupton G., 32 s. Meridian.
Nichols T. M., 24 s. Meridian.
Wells G. A., over Harrison's Bank.

Dress Makers.

Biden Mrs. E. E. 139 e. Wash.
Champane Mrs. C., 79 e. Washington.
Daniels Mrs. C. F., 60 n. Delaware.
Hutchins Mrs. E. C., 36 n. Illinois.
Lemman Jennie, 34 e. Ohio.
McConnol Miss M., Ætna Building.
Marshall Mrs., 12 s. Illinois.
Pedrick E., 19 w. Washington.
Root Miss M. F., 9 Bates House.
Sell Mrs. B., 97 w. Washington.
Wright Miss M. E., 8 e. Washington.

Dry Goods.

Bee Hive Store, H. L. Tyler, 2 w. Washington.
Callinan D. J., 28 e. Washington.
GERMAN DRY GOODS STORE, 43 and 45 e. Washington.
GLENN W. & H., PROPR'S NEW YORK STORE. See card, p. 150 and 151.
GOOD M. H., 5 e. Washington. See card, p. 142.
Haerle Wm., 36 w. Washington.
Hume, Lord & Co., 26 and 28 w. Washington.
JONES, HESS & DAVIS, 3 Odd Fellows Hall. See card, facing front cover.
Kirlin & Staton, 27 n. Illinois.
KRAUSE & WITTENBERG, PROPRIETORS GERMAN DRY GOODS STORE, 43 and 45 e. Washington.

Lintner J. & C., cor. North and Dunlop.
LIPPERD H. T., 138 n. East.
Lynch & Keane, 33 w. Washington.
NEW YORK STORE, W. & H. GLENN, PROPR'S, GLENNS' BLOCK.
Ostermyer F. & Co., 258 e. Wash.
Piel Wm. F. & Co., 240 e. Wash.
ROBERTSON & EAST, 10 e. Wash. See card, p. 118.
Rolff & Winter, 160 Indiana ave.
Thompson & Kregelo, cor. South and Delaware.

Dry Goods, Wholesale.

Crossland & Pee, 42 s. Meridian.
TOUSEY & BYRAM, 70 e. Wash.
Murphy, Kennedy & Co., 42 and 44 e. Washington.

Druggists.

BROWNING & SLOAN, 22 w. Wash. See card, p. 130.
Bryan G. W., 3 Spencer House.
EGNER & WOCHER, 85 e. Wash. See card, p. 70.
Franer J., 185 e. Washington.
Hasket W. J. & Co., 14 w. Wash.
LEE H. H., 12 n. Illinois. See cards pages 122 and 123.
Lowry W. M., 53 Mass. ave.
Senour J. F., 5 Bates House.
SMELSER J. W., 172 e. Wash.
Stewart & Morgan, 40 w. Wash.
Vickers W. B., Odd Fellows Hall.

Dyeing Establishments.

DIXON JAMES W., n. of Washington. See card.
Haef August, 10 s. Penn.

Eating Saloons.

Black Wm. M., cor. St. Clair and Indiana ave.
MASON M., cor. Louisiana and Ill.

Elevator.

SAWYER & HALL, PROP'S PERU ELEVATOR, New Jersey, near Peru Freight Depot. See card, p. 74.

Embroidering.

Leveders Mrs. A. M., 16 s. Illinois.

Engraver.

Ballard Austin, 5 Circle.

Express Co's and Agencies.

Adams, John H. Ohr, agent, 12 e. Washington.
AMERICAN, J. BUTTERFIELD, AGENT, cor. Meridian and Wash. See card, p. 4.
UNION TRANSPORTATION AND INS. CO.'S, FAST FREIGHT LINE, 14 s. Meridian.
United States, J. Butterfield, agent, cor. Meridian and Wash.

Fancy Goods.

ANDERSON GEO. P., 25 s Illinois. See card, p. 100.
Baldwin J. H, 6 E. Wash.
KLOTZ EMIL, NEW YORK BAZARR, 37 e. Wash. See card, p. 46.
MAYER CHAS., 29 w. Wash. See card, p. 98.
Mossler A. I., 75 e. Wash.
NEW YORK BAZARR, EMIL KLATZ, PROP'R, 37 e. Wash. See card, p. 46.
Rothchilds H., 5 Spencer House Block.
Solomon J. & M., Spencer House Square.
WEINBERGER & MULLER, Union Depot. See card, p. 70.
Wilde & Henninger, 71 s. Ill.

Florist.

Wiegand & Co., cor. Kentucky ave. and Miss.

Flour and Feed Stores.

Dunn J. S., 12 s. Penn.
ELLIOTT T. B., cor. Alabama and I. & C. R. R.
ELLIOTT & CLINTON, 19 s. East.
GLAZIER CHAS., 16 s. Meridian.
Heckman C., 266 e. Wash.
MYERS J. D., 8 and 12 s. Pennsylvania. See card, p. 80.
MORGAN T. W., 250 e. Wash.
WEBB & HILL, 85 w. Wash. See card, p. 42.
WINKLE W. F. & CO., 157 e. Wash. See card, p. 58.

Flouring Mills.

Carlisle's Model Mills, Washington, bet. Blake and West.
Capital Mills, J. P. Evans, Prop'r, cor. Market and Canal.

PECKMAN & McARTHUR, BATES' CITY MILLS, 282 e. Wash.

SKILLEN J. & BRO., Wash., bet. Ohio and Blake. See card, p. 68.

Foundries & Machine Shops.

Cox, Lord & Peck, 103 s. Delaware.

EAGLE FOUNDRY, D. ROOT & CO., 130 s. Penn.

REDSTONE, BROS. & CO., s. Delaware, opp. Cincinnati Depot. See card, p. 140.

Hassleman & Vinton, near Union Depot.

SINKER & CO., one square e. of Union Depot. See card, p. 98.

SPRINGER, BARROWS & KING, cor. Kentucky ave. & Miss. See card, p. 74.

WIGGINS & CHANDLER, 262 w. Washington.

Furniture.

(See also Cabinet Makers,)

Adams G. F., 56 e. Washington.

CABINET MAKERS UNION, 97 e. Washington. See card, p. 74.

Heitkam Chas. & Co., 61 e. Wash.

MAROT J. R., 177 e. Wash.

MEYER C. J., 171 e. Wash.

Ramsay J. F., 21 s. Illinois.

Sloan & Burke, 57 w. Wash.

SPIEGEL, THOMS & CO., 73 w. Wash. See card, p. 96.

Furnishing and Piece Goods, Wholesale.

DESSAR, BROS. & CO., Schnull's Block, cor. Meridian and Maryland. See card, p. 94.

Gas and Steam Fitters.

DAVIS J. W. & CO., 96 s. Delaware. See card, p. 106.

Wahannan G., Alabama, bet. Maryland and Virginia ave.

Gents' Furnishing Goods.

Parker R. R., 30 w. Washington.

Thonssen & Lahey, 67 w. Washington.

Grain Dealers.

Bradshaw W. A. & Son, 5 s. Delaware.

Evans J. P. & Co., 98 s. Delaware.

Gallup W. P. & E. P., 74 w. Washington.

Green House and Garden.

LOOMIS WM. H., Woodlawn Green House and Garden, 189 Virginia ave. See card, p. 138 and 139.

Gunsmith.

Wolff R., 17 Kentucky ave.

Gymnasium.

INDIANAPOLIS GYMNASIUM CLUB, rooms 32 s. Meridian.

Grocers.

Brado Thomas, cor. South and East.

Braman A. C., cor. North and Alabama.

Britz Adam, 40 Louisiana.

Breunninger A., cor. Washington and Meridian.

Brinker August, 94 New York.

Brown J. G., 150 n. New Jersey.

Bywater Edward, 226 e. Washington.

CARVIN & RUBLE, EAGLE GROCERY, cor. Indiana ave. and Illinois. See card, p. 44.

Chmitt Geo., 70 s. Delaware.

CITY GROCERY, C. L. HOLMES, 31 w. Washington. See card, p. 120.

Cook Wm., 186 w. Washington.

Danforth & Simpson, 3 n. Pennsylvania.

Diver James, 245 s. Delaware.

Domon Jacob, 138 s. Illinois.

Donelly Francis, 265 s. Delaware.

Draper & Tarlton, 32 n. Illinois.

EATON & FURGASON, Pearl Grocery, 18 s. Meridian. See card, p. 36.

Faught & Woodward, 79 e. Washington.

Feil John, 50 Bluff road.

Gardner Wendel, 183 Indiana ave.

Gear E. & S. H., cor. New Jersey and Virginia ave.

George James, 143 w. Washington.

Gold Adam, National road.

Goodhart B. F., 107 e. Washington.

Harmening C., 205 s. Delaware.

Hill James, 146 w. Washington.

Hinde E. & Co., 155 e. Washington.

HOFMEISTER N. & J., cor. Noble and New Jersey.

HOGSHIER W. R. & Co., 25 w. Washington.

HOHL CHRIST., 77 e. Washington.

HOLMES C. L., 31 w. Washington. See card, p. 120.

ILIFF JOSEPH, 250 e. Washington. See card, p. 112.

Jasper Fred., cor. Delaware and McCarty.

Jenkins A. W. & J., cor. North and Pennsylvania.

Johnson Aaron, Mississippi, near First.

Johnson Wm., cor. Garden and Tennessee.

JORDAN JOHN, 144 w. Washington.

Judson Chas. E., 97 n. Illinois.

Keesee Wm. N., cor. Blake and North.

Kemker C., cor. McCarty and Meridian.

Kepp & Schriver, cor. Massachusetts ave. and Alabama.

Kettenbach & Rentcb, 207 Massachusetts ave.

Klumpp D. F., cor. Washington and Blake.

KNOX JOHN L. & CO., 181 w. Washington.

Koch H. H., cor. South and Noble.

Koller E. H., 165 c. Washington.

Langbein J., 160 e. Washington.

Langenberg H. H., 194 w. Wash.

Lawles Michael, 85 s. Noble.

Lawrence A. V., 133 e. Washington.

Lindsey P. & Co., 39 s. Illinois.

Logan B., 129 w. South.

McGinnis John, 230 e. Washington.

Mann, Seibert & Co., cor. East and Virginia ave.

Martin J. L., 95 Washington.

Middles David, 200 w. Washington.

MILLER & TOMLINSON, 212 e. Washington. See card, p. 136.

MORRIS S. V., 16 and 18 c. Market. See card, p. 114.

MUNSON W. L., 21 n. Alabama.

REESE H. & CO., 91 and 93 w. Washington, and 204 Noble. See card, p. 76.

Reick August, cor. Georgia and Liberty.

Rentsch E., 126 s. Illinois.

Richter Fred., 115 s. Tennessee.

Rittenhouse & Perry, 88 e. Washington.

Robinson A. C., cor. North and Illinois.

Rodewald Henry, 283 s. Delaware.

Ropkoy F., cor. McCarty and Madison ave.

Rosebrock H. H., cor. Virginia ave. and East.

Schott Joseph, 177 e. Washington.

Severn, Goth, Bushman & Co., 247 n. New Jersey.

SIMPSON M. & CO., cor. South and Delaware. See card. p. 72.

Socwell H. M., 190 e. Washington.

SPENCER MILTON, 202 e. Washington. See card, p. 118.

SPOUSEL C., 277 s. Delaware.

Stout F. & Co., 142 w. Washington.

Stout O. B. & Bro., 42 w. Washington.

TARLTON & KEEHN, 8 and 10 s. Meridian.

Thayer & Bro., 220 c. Washington.

Vanhouten & Graham, cor. Market and Illinois.

Walton E. H., cor. Delaware and New York.

Werbe L. F., 185 w. Washington.

White G., 111 w. Washington.

WILGUS G. D., cor. Tennessee and New York.

Williams Chas. C., 3 n. Illinois.

Williams Owen, 134 w. Washington.

Wingate J. F., 27 w. Washington.

Worland W., cor. Del. and Va. ave.

Yaeger C. 215 c. Washington.

Grocers, Wholesale.

Alford, Talbot & Co., 36 e. Wash.

Alvord, Caldwell & Co., 68 e. Wash.

Holland & Son, 72 e. Washington.

Jaycox & Fitzhugh, opp. Union Depot.

Maguire, Jones & Co., 7 and 8 Bates House

SAWYER & STARRET, 13 s. Meridian.

Schnull A. & H., cor. Meridian and Maryland.

WALLACE ANDREW, cor. Del. and Va. ave. See card, p. 20.

Hardware.

FRESE & KROPF, 11 w. Washington. See card, p. 142.

LOYD THOS. A. & CO., 12 w. Washington. See card, p. 82.

Pomeroy, Fry & Co., 24 s. Meridian.

Pottage Benjamin, 76 w. Wash.

SHARE GEORGE K. & CO., 72 w. Wash. See card, back of title.

Sulgrove, Reynolds & Co., 20 w. Washington.

Vajen J. H., 21 w. Washington.

Vonnegut Clemens, 142 e. Wash.

Wilson J. B., 59 w. Washington.
WOOD A. D., 64 e. Washington.

Harness Makers.
BLAIR J. M., 198 w. Washington.

Hats, Caps and Furs.
Baker & McIver, 22 e. Washington.
BAMBERGER H. & CO., 16 e.
Washington.
Brown W. P., 20 Kentucky ave.
DAVIS ISAAC, 15 n. Pennsylvania.
See card, outside cover.
Igale I., 50 s. Illinois.
Wilmot & Thayer, 8 w. Washington.

Hats, Caps, &c., Wholesale.
DONALDSON & CARR, 38 s. Meridian.
Talbott J. M. & Co., 26 s. Meridian.

Hominy Mills.
Hudnut Theodore, Pa., bet. Md. and
South.

Hotels.
BATES HOUSE, J. L. HOLTON,
Prop'r, cor. Ill. and Wash. See
card, p. 128.
CALIFORNIA HOUSE, 136 s. Ill.
See card, p. 90.
Cincinnati House, 124 s. Delaware.
CITY HOTEL, STRICKLAN, Prop.,
s. Ill. See card, p. 60.
COMMERCIAL HOTEL, cor. Ga.
and Illinois.
East Street House, East, bet. Washington and Georgia.
EDWARDS HOUSE, LOUIS EDWARDS, Prop'r, 53 s. Ill. See
card, p. 112.
GRAVEN THOS., Prop'r CENTRAL
HOUSE, 44 s. Meridian.
Hahn Henry, East Street House.
Hamilton T. D., Prop'r Patterson
House, Ala., bet. O. and Market.
LITTLE'S HOTEL, A. R. HYDE,
Prop'r, cor. N. J. and Wash. See
card, p. 58.
MACY HOUSE, W. H. CAMPBELL,
Prop'r, cor. Ill. and Market.
Mason House, B. Mason, prop'r, La.,
opp. Union Depot.
National, David Bender, Prop'r, 217
w. Washington.
Oriental House, Ill., bet. Md. and
Georgia.
Palmer House, cor. Ill. and Wash.
REITZ & BALLWEG, cor. Ill. and
Ga. See card, p. 62.

RAY HOUSE, cor. Del. and South.
SPENCER HOUSE, J. W. CANON,
Prop'r, cor. Ill. and La. See card,
p. 120.
UNION HOUSE, GEO. ILG, Prop'r,
cor. South and Ill. See card, p.
54.

Hub, Spoke and Last Factory.
OSGOOD & SMITH, s. Illinois.

Ice Dealers.
BUTSCH JOSEPH, 48 w. South.
See card, p. 100.
Pitts Geo. W., 78 cor. Vt. and Miss.

**Insurance Companies and
Agencies.**
ÆTNA INS. CO., WM. HENDERSON, ag't, 13 n. Pennsylvania.
DAVIS C. B., 6 Odd Fellows' Hall.
DUNLOP JNO. S., 7 n. Meridian.
EQUITABLE FIRE INS. CO., off. 16
Talbott & New's Block. See card,
p. 110.
FARMERS' AND MERCHANTS'
INS. CO., off. Blackford's Building. See card, outside cover.
GIBSON WM. T., ag't CONN. MUTUAL LIFE INS. CO., 5 Odd Fellows' Hall. See card, p. 110.
HENDERSON WM., Ætna Building. See card, near index.
HOME MUTUAL FIRE INS. CO. OF
INDIANAPOLIS, off. 9 Bates
House Block. See card, front
cover.
INDIANA FIRE INS. CO., off. 5
Odd Fellows' Hall. See card, p.
110.
SINNISSIPPI, J. R. BERRY, Sec'y,
off. 79 e. Wash. See card, p. 88.
LIVERPOOL AND LONDON FIRE
AND LIFE INS. CO., SPANN &
SMITH, ag'ts, cor. Wash. and Pa.
See card, inside front cover.
MARTINDALE & GRUBBS, 4 New
& Talbotts Block.
METROPOLITAN FIRE INS. CO.,
SPANN & SMITH, AGTS., cor.
Wash. and Penn.
NEW YORK LIFE INS. CO., W. J.
WYNN, cor. Wash. and Meridian.
Olin C. C., agent, Equitable Fire
Ins. Co., 16 Talbott & New's
Block.
SINNISSIPPI INS. CO., 79½ o
Wash. See card, p. 88.

UNDERWOOD J. II., GEN. AGT. HOME MUTUAL INS. CO., 64 e. Wash. See card, front cover.
Willetts W. P., 8 n. Penn.
WYNN W. J., s. w. cor. Meridian and Wash.

Institute.

Classical Institute. L. II. Croll, Principal, cor. New York and and Alabama.

Intelligence Office.

WALLACE W. B., 63 e. Wash. See card, p. 32.

Iron Railing.

HAUGH & SCHOWE, 2 n. Delaware. See card, p. 154.

Iron and Steel.

HOLLDAY W. J. & CO., 34 e. Wash

Jewelers.

Bingham W. P. & Co., 50 e. Wash.
BURDICK WM. P., 8 n. Meridian. See card, p. 84.
Craft N. II., 2 Odd Fellows Hall.
DUMONT P. A., 9 s. Meridian. See card, p. 74.
FELLER GEO., 107 e. Wash. See card, p. 30.
FERGUSON C. A., 7 w. Wash. See card, p. 144.
French C. G., 37 w. Wash.
HANCE & TURNER, 9 e. Wash.
Klansner J., 141 w. Wash.
McLene J., under Bates House.
Miller R. A., 51 s. Illinois.
Semmons & Co., 23 s. Ill.
Talbott W. II. & Co., 24 e. Wash.
Waltze W., 64 e. Wash.
Zumbush T., Wash., bet. Delaware and Penn.

Job Printers.

CHANDLER H. C., Hubbard's Block. See card. p. 48.
Downey J. E., Talbott & New's Blok.
Wetmore S. F. & Co., 37 e. Wash.

Justice of the Peace.

Fisher Chas., Yohn's Block.
Kendrick O. II., old post-office.
Sullivan Wm., College Hall.

Lamps and Coal Oil.

Rockey II. S., 7 s. Meridian.

Leather, Hides, Oils, &c.

Fishback J., 28 s. Meridian.
Mooney & Co., 75 s. Meridian.
Yandes & Co., 38 e. Wash.

Liquors Wholesale.

Brinkmeyer J. C. & Co., 82 w. Wash.
CONKLIN & REDMOND, 140 w. Wash. See card, p. 18.
Duncan J. & D., 22 s. Ill.
Elliott C. A. & Co., 32 s. Meridian.
HAHN & ROSE, 11 s. Meridian. See card, p. 66.
Kauffmann S., 209 e. Wash.
Mueller Jno., 256 e. Wash.
Rosenthal A., 38 Louisiana.
Ruschhaupt & Balls, 82 e. Wash.
Schmidt R. & Co., Wash., bet. Delaware and Alabama.

Livery Stables.

ALLEN & STEWART, 12 and 14 e. Pearl. See card, p. 100.
BRINKMAN & RUSCHAUPT, 17 s. Delaware.
Burrows G. W., 14 n. Penn.
GATES, PRAY & CO., e. Market square. See card, p. 72.
HINESLEY WM., Pearl, in rear of Palmer House. See card, p. 108.
Hyde & Bogle, Wash., bet. New Jersey and East.
Landis & Mills, 8 e. Maryland.
MOORHEAD ROBERT I., 25 n. Ill. See card, p. 104.
ORLOPP & TAYLOR, 22 and 24 s. Penn. See card, p. 56.
PEABODY JOHN, 18 e. Maryland. See card, p. 52.
Sullivan J. B., 10 e. Pearl.
Unversaw L. & Co., 11 and 13 w. Pearl.
Wood & Foudray, 10 n. Penn.

Loan Office.

May Edwin, 18½ n. Ills.

Locksmith and Bell Hanger.

Kindle C., 17 Kentucky ave.

Lumber Dealers.

Coburn & Jones, cor. Delaware and New York.
Isgrigg & Brackin, Market, bet. Miss. and Canal.
McCORD & WHEATLEY, 119 s. Delaware. See card, p. 68 and 134.

Marble Workers.

Downey M., 127 e. Wash.
James W. W. & Co., 58 s. Meridian.
Scott & Nicholson, Kentukky ave. near Terre Haute R. R.
Seybold & Ritter, Market, opp. Post-office.
Smith, Ittenboch & Co., cor. Penn. and Merrill.
STOCKINGER J., 173 e. Wash.
Meir W., 13 Virginia ave.
Wilson A. J., 10 n. Delaware.
Wallace W. W., 92 s. Illinois.

Merchants Dispatch.

Clark W. F., agent, cor. Virginia ave. and Alabama.

Merchant Tailors.
(See also *Clothiers*.)

BECKER JACOB, 103 e. Wash.
Clark Wm., 28 Ill.
DESSAR & BROS., 4. e. Wash.
GERSTNER A. J., 158 e. Washington. See card, p. 36.
GRAMLING J. & P., 41 e. Wash. See card, front cover.
Glaser & Bros., 2 Bates House.
GOEPPER F. & CO., 15 e. Wash, See card, p. 78.
HEITKAM G. H., 17 n. Ills. See card, colored leaf.
LENOX E., 15 s. Illinois.
McGINNIS OWEN, 39 e. Washington. See card, p. 90.
Rupp W. F., 105 e. Wash.
Schuldmeir & Rogge, 144 e. Wash.
SCHOLTZ LOUIS, 19 n. Penn. See card, p. 92.

Military Claim Agents.
(See also *Attorneys at Law*.)

Barker T. D., 5 Blackford's Block.
LEATHERS & CARTER, 3 Odd Fellows Hall. See card, outside cover.
McClosky B., 8 w. Wash.
Perrin & Manove, College Hall.
WALKER & McKERNAN, 8 w. Wash. See card, outside front cover.

Millinery.

Baker Mrs. A. & Co., 24 s. Illinois.
Copeland J. W., 8 e. Washington.
Dietrich Mrs., 63 e. Washington.
Doyle Miss J., 18 s. Illinois.
DUNN & FRANCO, 5 n. Meridian. See card, p. 76.

QUIMBY MRS. H. N., 20 s. Illinois.
Thomas Mrs., 46 w. Washington.

Mineral Water.

CLARK PHILO M., 209 e. Wash. See card, p. 64.

Mill Wright.

TAGGART SAMUEL, 94 s. Penn. See card, p. 136.

Music and Piano Dealers.

Benham A. M. & Co., cor. Ill. and Washington.
WILLARD & STOWELL, 4 Bates House. See card, front of book.

Newspapers.

INDIANAPOLIS GAZETTE, daily and weekly, Johnson H. Jordan, editor and prop'r, 14 and 16 s. Meridian.
HERALD & ERA, M. J. Lee, editor, 111 n. Illinois.
INDIANA FREE PRESS, 36 e. Washington.
Indiana School Journal, monthly, 37 e. Washington.
INDIANA STATE SENTINEL, daily and weekly, Elder, Harkness & Bingham, prop'rs, cor. Pearl and Meridian.
INDIANA VOLKSBLATT, 130 e. Washington.
INDIANAPOLIS JOURNAL, daily and weekly, off., Journal Building, cor. Meridian and Circle.

Notary Public.

Beckner S. H., with R. L. Walpool.
Long J. T., 8 w. Washington.
Vandegrift H., 16½ e. Washington.

Ornamental Hair Work.

MAHORNEY J. T., 20 n. Illinois. See card, p. 78.

Optician.

Moses L. W., 50 e. Washington.

House and Sign Painters.

Beale J., room 12 old P. O. Building.
Brown E., 9 Virginia ave.
Fertig Frank, 6 e. Washington.
Hulings J. P., Market, bet. Pa. and Delaware.
KNOTTS NIM. K, 16½ e. Washington. See card, p. 40.
Lanphere James, cor. Washington and Meridian.
RYAN JOHN B., 10 n. Meridian. See card, p. 134.

SINDLINGER JOHN M., 81 e. Washington. See card, p. 82.
SPURGIN & LONG, 6 s. Meridian. See card, p. 46.

Paper Mills.

McLene J. & Co., Wash., on river bank.
Sheets Wm., Market, bet. West and Mississippi.

Patent Medicines.

Frost & Buell, cor. Del. and Md.
Spicer & Henuing, 20 n. Illinois.

Philosophical Instruments.

Steffens Chas. & Co., cor. Meridian and Wash. See card, p. 42.

Photographic Artists

Andrews S. B., opp. Union Depot.
Apple & Thorn, 84 and 86 e. Wash.
Brothers & Schroy, cor. Washington and Meridian.
Bruening E. & J., 6 e. Washington.
CRANE J. D., 19 w. Washington. See card, p. 142.
CRUSIUS MISS CARRIE M., 39 e. Washington. See card, p. 82.
DAVIES & MERRITT, 26 and 28 w. Washington. See card, p. 108.
ELLIOTT J. PERRY, 8 and 10 e. Washington. See card, p. 24.
McCOY & ORR, 33 w. Washington. See card, p. 106.
Miller A. R., 43½ e. Washington.
Morton Lyman, cor. Wash. and Ill.
RUNNION WM., 32½ e. Washington. See card, p. 116.
RYDER P. S., Talbott & New's Block. See card, p. 18.
Smith & Huey, 35½ e. Washington.
Wilson A. R., Meridian, near Union Depot.
Crapo R. C., 17 w. Washington.

Physicians.

Abbett L., 20 Virginia ave.
Backesto J. P., 28½ n. Mississippi.
Bacon E. H., cor. Washington and Meridian.
Barnes H. F., 1 Blake's Block.
Bobbs J. S., 3d floor Harrison's Block.
Boyd J. T., 40 n. Pennsylvania.
Brown & McNab, 7 New & Talbott's Block.
Bullard W. R., 23 s. Meridian.
Burnham N. G., 10 e. Market.

Carter D. E., cor. Tenn. and Wash.
Clarke F. D., 24½ e. Washington.
Cleppinger J. W., 112 n. Delaware.
Dorsey N. J., 46 n. Pennsylvania.
Duzan & Parr, 16 Virginia ave.
Ewing D., 18 Virginia ave.
Fletcher Wm., 67 n. Alabama.
Gall A. D., 22 Virginia ave.
GUSTIN L., off. cor. Ill. and La.
Hervey J. W. M., 123 n. Liberty.
Hillman L. C., 31½ w. Washington.
Howard E. & Son, 52 s. Illinois.
Jameson & Funkhouser, 5 s. Meridian.
Johnson John, cor. Wash. and Ala.
Keiser Dr., 133 Virginia ave.
KITCHEN JNO. M., off. s. w. cor. Washington and Meridian.
Leo E. S., 11 Indiana ave.
McGee R., cor. Ala. and Wash.
Marsh Harmon, Blackford Block.
Mears Geo. W., Meridian and Wash.
MERRILL JOHN F., 156 w. Washington. See card, p. 144.
Miller G. W., 152 s. Illinois.
Newcomer F. S., cor. Va. ave. and Maryland.
Otto Chas., 5 n. Noble.
Rees H., 102 n. East.
Stevens Thaddeus M, Harrison's Block.
Teal N., 5 Blake's Block.
Todd R. N., 10 Virginia ave.
Ware Chas. S., cor. Meridian and Washington.
Ware T. S., cor. Meridian and Wash.
Wiley D., 30 c. Market.
Wright M. H., cor O. and Meridian.

Piano Manufacturer.

TRAEYSER G., Ala., bet. Pearl and Washington. See card, p. 28.

Picture Frames, &c.

LIEBER H., 13 n. Pennsylvania. See card, opp. title.

Planing Mill.

Post, Helwig & Co., cor. New York and Canal.

Plasterer.

Glover G. N. J., 32 n. Pennsylvania.

Plows, &c.

CASE & MARSH, 86 w. Wash.

Plumbing and Gas Fitting.

(*See, also, Gas and Steam Fitters.*)

Dunn J. C. & Co., 24 and 26 Kentucky ave.

Ramsay & Hanning, Pearl, bet. Meridian and Pennsylvania.

Pork Packers.

Coffin B. & Co., 14 s. Meridian.
Coffman & Morton, Blake, near Washington.
FERGUSON J. C., opp. Madison Depot.
PATTISON & CO., Talbott & New's Block.

Produce.

HOLMAN G G., 95 e. Washington.
Lesh L. & A. B., 29 s. Meridian.
Morgan S. C., 95. e Washington.
Neall J. R., 180 e. Washington.
Rush F. P., 81 w. Washington.
SCHOPPENHORST WM., 101 e. Washington. See card, p. 58.
Spann J. R., 93 e. Washington.
Titcomb D., cor. Md. and Va. ave.

Publishers.

BUELL & WILLIAMS, 39 e. Wash.
Hawes & Redfield, 16½ e. Wash.
Perrine C. O., Odd Fellows' Hall.
Streight Col. A. D., Yohn's Block.

Pump Makers.

Childers J. R., 68 s. Delaware.
Hall & Ross, 81 s. Delaware.
Wright & Bro, Md., bet. Va. ave. and Alabama.

Real Estate.

Barker Thos. D., 5 Blackford's Block.
BARNITZ & GRIFFITH, 1 s. Meridian. See card, p. 144.
Casin J. H., 8 w. Washington.
Delzell & Jones, 37 e. Washington.
Duke Jas. & Co., Sentinel Building.
ELDRIDGE JACOB, 31½ w. Wash. See card, p. 50.
Johnson I. E., 4 Blake's Block.
LINDENBOWER WM. H., 30½ w. Washington.
LOVE WM., 1 Talbott & New's Block. See card, p. 78.
McKernan & Pierce, 39½ w. Wash.
McMILLIN & REDFORD, 19 w. Washington. See card, p. 90.
Martin C. M. & Co., 8 e. Wash.
Metzger & Striblen, 6 Odd Fellows' Hall.
Phipps I. N., 36 e. Washington.
Seidensticker & Kappes, Juda's Block.

SPANN & SMITH, cor. Pa. and Wash. See card, inside front cover.
SPICER B. M. & CO., 20½ n. Illinois. See card, p. 136.
STAPP JAS. H., 9 Bates House Block.
Trueblood & Co., 26 w. Wash.
WALKER & McKERNAN, 8 w. Wash. See card, outside front cover.
WILEY & MARTIN, 10 e. Wash. See card, inside back cover.
Wright Chas. A., 30½ w. Wash.

Clothing Renovator.

HARRIS J., 38 s. Illinois. See card, p. 118.

Rolling Mill.

Indianapolis Rolling Mill, Tenn., s. of R. R.

Saddlery and Harness.

ANDRA JOHN & CO., 169 e. Wash. See card, p. 62.
Burt & Cowger, 254 e. Wash.
HERETH JOHN C., 89 e. Washington. See card, p. 34.
HINESLEY A. J. & CO., 34 w. Washington.

Saloons and Restaurants.

See, also, Eating Houses.

ATLANTIC, J. E. GRIDLEY, Prop., Palmer House.
Altman H., 67 s. Illinois.
Balke C., 175 e. Washington.
Bass S., cor. Meridian and Wash.
Bearss C. U., 13 Kentucky ave.
Blaes Nicholas, 48 s. Delaware.
BRILLIANT, JOHN BURNS, Prop., 63 s. Illinois.
Brown A. & Co., 163 e. Wash.
Burke & Shaffer, 3 w. Wash.
Buscher H., 51 e. South.
Bush G. M., Oriental House.
Bush Jacob, 162 w. Washington.
Chapman A. F., 32 s. Illinois.
CHRISTY ALBERT, UNION SALOON, 55 w. South.
City Saloon, 53 s. Illinois.
Coburn, Turner & Co., 15 n. Ill.
CRYSTAL PALACE, E. BECK, Prop., 44 w. Wash. See card, p. 148.
DESCHLER & SCHLOER, ASTOR SALOON, 9 n. Pennsylvania.
Dessar O. H., 212 w. Washington.
Doty & Lee, 107 w. Washington.

Drum & Ramsay, 121 c. Wash.
Emmeneger M., opp. C. H.
Empire, R. Beebe, prop., 23 w. Washington.
Ettinger Gustave, 168 e. Wash.
Eurich & Schoffer, 7 n. Illinois.
Everhart Geo., 278 e. Washington.
Exchange Saloon, 19 and 21 n. Ill.
Fey Randolph, 85 e. Washington.
Frenzel J. T., 85 s. Illinois.
Frick J., Commercial Hotel Saloon.
Ginz & Bro., Little's Hotel Saloon.
GRIDLEY J. E., ATLANTIC SALOON, Palmer House Corner.
HANRAHAN P. G., s. Tennessee.
Hatch Mrs. H., 141 w. Wash.
HEBBLE J. W., 248 c. Washington. See card, p. 62.
HEZEKIAH H. E., 13 n. Illinois.
HOUSE OF LORDS SALOON, J. PEARSON & CO., Props., 78 w. Wash. See card, facing back cover.
HUGELER JOHN, 128 e. Washington. See card, p. 68.
Kissell J. W., 11 n. Illinois.
Laner C., 162 e. Wash.
Lang Louis, 13 e. Wash. See card, opp. title.
McBaker Thos., cor. alley and Pearl.
Magnolia J. Doty, 9 s. Illinois.
Marmon H., 136 w. Wash.
Matthes C., 7 s. Delaware.
Mathewes John, Tenn., bet. Merrill and South.
Mattler & Weaner, 3 and 5 s. Del.
Meikel J. P., 137 w. Maryland.
Monninger C., 164 w. Wash.
MUELLER C. G., cor. East and Washington.
O'CONNOR JOS., 30 s. Ill. See card, front of book.
O'Connel J., 210 w. Wash.
Pattrie John, 222 e. Wash.
PEARSON J. & CO., HOUSE OF LORD'S SALOON, 78 w. Wash. See card, opp. back cover.
Peyton & Line, 65 s. Illinois.
Porter N. F., 49 e. South.
Remman R., 186 e. Wash.
Rhodius G., 27 s. Meridian.
Richter Florence, 1 e. Pearl.
Robinson A., 14½ n. Penn.
Rosenberg & Co., 75 e. Wash.
Rasman C., 119 e. Wash.
Santo E., 36 Louisiana.

Schaub H., 6 w. Wash.
STERN ISRAEL, 14 s. Penn.
Veranda, J. Bussey & Co., Prop's, 36 Louisiana.
Wachtstetter J., 25 s. Meridian.
WASHINGTON HALL, P. FAHRBACH & CO., PROP'S, 78 & 80 w. Wash. See card, p. 54.
Welch & Reighen, under Palmer House.
Youngerman G., cor. Wash. and Delaware.
Zimmer & Co., 138 e. Wash.

Sands' Cream and Stock Ale.

O'CONNER JOS., AGT., 30 s. Ills. See card, front of book.

Sash, doors and Blinds.

BEHYMER D., cor. Benton and Market. See card, p. 130.
BEHYMER S., 47 e. South. See card, p. 114.
Byrkit & Beam, cor. Georgia and Tenn.
Eden & Copeland, 27 e. Market.

Saw Manufacturer.

ATKIN E. C., 155 s. Illinois. See card, opp. contents.

Saw and Planing Mills.

HILL & WINGATE, cor. Georgia and East.
MARSEE J. & SON, rear of Little's Hotel. See card, p. 34.
Off C. & Bro., n. Davidson.

Feed Store.

STILZ J. GEO., 74 e. Wash.

Sewing Machine Agents

BELLIS S., AGENT, FLORENCE SEWING MACHINE, 17 n. Penn.
CLAFLIN C. C., Wheeler & Wilson agency, Journal Building.
Elliott J. F., agent, Singer Sewing Machine, 48 e. Washington.
TURNER WM. H., AGT. GROVER & BAKER, 84 w. Wash. See card, p. 125.

Silver Plater.

Higgins W. B., 8 w. Wash.

Slate and Gravel Roofing.

Zimmerman C., 130 e. Market.

Stamping, Braiding, &c.
HAWKINS MRS. M. A., 5 Yohn's Block. See card, p. 146.

Stone Cutters.
(See also Marble Workers.)
Goddard & Jennings, cor. Market and Tenn.

Stoneware.
Wiles T., 16 s. New Jersey.

Stoves and Tin Ware.
Frankem & Co., 49 and 51 e. Wash.
McOuat R. L., 69 w. Wash.
Munson & Johnson, 66 e. Wash.
Root D. & Co., 66 e. Wash.
TUTEWILER BROS., 182 e. Wash. See card, p. 64.
VOEGTLE & METZGER, 83 e. Wash. See card, p. 38.

Summer Garden.
HUGELE JOHN, 128 e. Washington. See card, p. 68.

Tailors.
Bippus John, 18 n. Penn.
Goodman A., 18 n. Penn.
Hall E. A., 62½ e. Wash.
Kenney Thos., 34 s. West.
McGrath J. C., 8 s. Penn.

Tea Store.
LEE H. H., 14 n. Ills. See card, p. 122 and 123.

Tobacconist.
(See also Cigars and Tobacco.)

Trunks and Valises.
Becker H., 30 w. Wash.

BURTON & SHILLING, 13 s. Ills. See card, p. 86.
MORREY & CO., 27 s. Ills. See card, p. 84.

Undertakers.
Herrmann Jacob, 15 s. Delaware.
Long Matthew, Circle, 1 door e. of Journal Building.
Weaver & Williams, 9 Bates House.

Vinegar Factory.
Porter N. F., 49 e. South.

Wagon Makers.
Baker H., 99 Bluff Road.
Kay Joseph, 205 w. Wash.
Wehling Chas., 166 s. Delaware.

Wall Paper and Window Shades.
ROLL W. H., 16 s. Illinois.
Werden & Co., 26 e. Washington.

Watch Makers.
(See also Jewelers.)

White Lead & Color Works.
DRAKE & MERRYMON, 47 e. South. See card, p. 58.

Wood Turner.
WIEST JOHN, 94 Ft. Wayne ave. See card, p. 86.

Wool Dealers and Wool Manufacturers.
Geisendorff C. E. & Co., Wash., near river bridge.
MERRITT & COUGHLAN, Wash., on river bank.

STREET DIRECTORY.

The leading Streets are named East, West, North and South, taking Meri-
dian Street for one basis, and Washington for the other.   The
Streets printed in Capitals are the most impor-
tant ones in the City.

Agnes, N. and S., N. W. of city.
ALABAMA, N. and S., three blocks E. of Circle.
Ann, from Rolling Mill to McCarty.
Arch, from Jackson to Noble, N. E. of city.
Arizonia, S. of Utah.
Ash, N. of Car Works, N. E. of city.
Anthon, from Rhode Island to Indiana ave.
Burnhill, from North to Davis.
Bates, from Noble to eastern limits, S. of city.
Benton, from Harrison to Central Track, E. of Noble.
Bicking, from Delaware to East, S. of city.
Blackford, from New York to North, three blocks W. of Canal.
Blake, N. and S., from Washington to Ind. ave., near W. Limits.
Bright, from New York to North, N. W. of city.
Broadway, N. of Car Works, N. E. of city.
Buchanan, S. E. of city, three blocks N. of Morris.
Cady, from Harrison to Central Track, E. of Benton.
California, from New York to North, two blocks W. of Canal.
Catharine, from West to Canal, S. of Merrill.
Cedar, Fletcher's Addition, S. E. of city.
Center, from Dunlop to Ellen, N. W. of city.
Charles, from St. Clair to Peru track.
Chatham, from Massachusetts ave. to St. Clair, E. of East.
Cherry, from Fort Wayne ave. to Ash, near Northern boundary.
Christian ave., one block N. of city limits.
Coburn, S. E. of city, one block N. of Morris.
Coe, from Fall Creek to Hiawatha, N. E.
Cottrell, from Georgia to Louisiana, W. of Canal, S. W.
Cross, from Peru Track to city line, N. E.
Curve, from Bellefontaine Car Works, N. E. to city limits.
Decota, from White River to Morris, W. of West.
Davidson, N. and S. E. of Railroad.
Davis, from N. W. city line to Fall Creek.
DELAWARE, N. and S., two blocks E. of Circle.
Douglass, from New York to Michigan, N. W. of city.
Dougherty, S. E. of city, two blocks N. of Morris.
Duncan, from Delaware to New Jersey, continuation of Garden.
Dunlop, from Madison ave. three blocks S. of Morris.
East, N. and S., five blocks E. of Circle.

East Second, W. of city line.
Elizabeth, from Ind. ave. to Blake, N. W. of city.
Elk, Fletcher's Addition, S. E. of city.
Ellen, from North to Indiana ave.
Ellis, from Maryland to S. W. of West.
Elm, from Noble S. E. of Fletcher's Addition.
First, Northern city boundary.
Fifth, five blocks N. of city limits.
Fletcher's ave., Fletcher's Addition, S. E. of city.
Forest Home ave., S of N. W. C. University.
Forest ave., Fletcher's Addition, S. E. of city.
FORT WAYNE AVE., from Nor h running N. E. to city limits.
Fourth, four blocks N. of city limits.
Franklin, from Morris S. two blocks E. of Madison ave.
Garden, from Canal to Delaware, six blocks S. of Circle.
George, from Merrill to Garden, W. of Illinois.
GEORGIA, E. and W., three blocks S. of Circle.
Greer, bet. McCarty and Virginia ave.
Grove, from Virginia ave to city line.
Harris, N. and S., N. W. of city.
Harrison, from Noble to Eastern limits, S. of I. & C. R. R.
Henry, from Canal to Mississippi, S. of South.
Hiawatha, N. and S. W. of City Hospital.
High, from McCarty S., E. of Delaware.
Hosbrook, Fletcher's Addition, S. E. of city.
Howard, North, from First to Seventh, W. of Lafayette Railroad.
Howard South, from Morris S. E. of Madison ave.
Huron, Fletcher's Addition, S. E. of city.
ILLINOIS, N. and S., one block W. of Circle.
INDIANA AVENUE, N. W. Diagonal.
Jackson, N. of Car Works, N. E. of city.
James, N. W. of city.
Japan, from Morris S., three blocks E. of Madison ave.
John, from Peru track to city limits.
Kansas, from Bluff Road to West, S. of city line.
KENTUCKY AVENUE, S. W. Diagonal.
Liberty, N. and S., six blocks E. of Circle.
Lord, from Noble to Eastern limits, S. of I. & C. R. R.
LOUISIANA, E. and W., four blocks S. of Circle.
Loukabee, from East to Liberty, bet. Vermont and New York.
McCarty, from River to Virginia ave., S. of city.
McGill, from Louisiana to South, W. of Mississippi.
McKernan, from Buchanan to Morris, three blocks E. of East.
Madison ave., from South to city line, S. E. Diagonal.
Margaret, S. side City Hospital.
Maria, from Smith to Locke.
MARKET, E. and W., through Circle.
MARYLAND, E. and W., two blocks S. of Circle.
MASSACHUSETTS AVENUE, N. E. Diagonal.
Maxwell, from North to Davis.
Meek, from Noble to Eastern limits, S of Ind. C. R. R
MERIDIAN, N. and S., through Circle.
Merrill, from Kentucky ave. to Virginia ave., seven blocks S. of Circle.
MICHIGAN, E. and W., four blocks n. of Circle.
MICHIGAN ROAD, N. E and S. W., through the city.
Mill from Fifth to Seventh, W. of Howard.
Minerva, N. and S., N. W. of city.
Minnesota, W. of Canal from Morris, S.

MISSISSIPPI, N. and S., three blocks W. of Circle.
MISSOURI, N. and S., along Canal.
Morris, Southern boundary line.
Nebraska, from Madison ave. four blocks S. of Morris.
NEW JERSEY, N. and S., four blocks E. of Circle.
NEW YORK, E. and W., two blocks N. of Circle.
Noble, N. and S., seven blocks E. of Circle.
North ave., N. of N. W. C. University.
NORTH, E. and W., five blocks N. of Circle.
Oak, N. of Car Works, N. E. of city.
OHIO, E. and W., one block N. of Circle.
Orient, from Pennsylvania to Ft. Wayne ave., S. of St. Joseph.
Oxford, from Peru Track to city line.
Patterson, N. and S., N. W. of city.
PENNSYLVANIA, N. and S., one block E. of Circle.
Pine, Fletcher's Addition, S. E. of city.
Pittsfield, continuation of Mill to Lafayette Railroad Track.
Plum, N. of Car Works, N. E. of city.
Powell, from Michigan to North.
Pratt, from Illinois to Ft. Wayne ave., N. of Blind Asylum.
Railroad ave., N. and S., bet. Pennsylvania and S. Delaware.
Railroad Street, N. and S., along Bellefontaine Railroad track.
Ray, from Canal to Railroad, S. of city.
Rhode Island, from Blake to Western limits, N. of city.
St. Clair, from Ind. ave. to Mass. ave., N. of Blind Asylum.
St. Joseph, from Illinois to Ft. Wayne ave., N. of Blind Asylum.
St. Mary, E., from Meridian, Northern city boundary.
School, from South to Virginia ave., W. of Noble.
Second, two blocks N. of city limits.
Seventh, seven blocks N. of city limits.
Short, from Morris to Dougherty, W. of Virginia ave.
Sinker, from Alabama to New Jersey.
Sixth, six blocks N. of city limits.
Smith, from Rhode Island to Indiana ave.
SOUTH, E. and W., five blocks S. of Circle.
TENNESSEE, N. and S., two blocks W. of Circle.
Texas, from Madison ave., W. six blocks S. of Morris.
Third, three blocks, N. of city limits.
VERMONT, E. and W., three blocks N. of Circle.
Vine, from Jackson to Ash, N. E. of city.
VIRGINIA AVENUE, S. E. Diagonal.
Union, from McCarty to Morris, E. of Bluff Road.
University ave., E. of N. W. C. University.
Utah, S. of Wisconsin.
Walnut, from Canal to Massachusetts ave., N. of Blind Asylum.
WASHINGTON, E. and W., one block S. of Circle.
Watters, from McCarty to Virginia ave.
WEST, N. and S., one block W. of Canal.
Western ave., continuation of Fort Wayne ave.
Wilkins, from Canal to Railroad, S. of city.
Willard, from Garden to Merrill, W. of Tennessee.
Williams, bet. McCarty and Virginia ave.
Wilson, from Davis to North.
Winston N. and S., near Eastern limits.
Wisconsin, from Bluff Road to River, S. of Kansas.
Wright, from Buchanan to Morris, two blocks E. of East.
Wyandot.
Wyoming, from Delaware to High, S. of City.

APPENDIX.

STATE GOVERNMENT.

Governor—OLIVER P. MORTON.
Secretary of State—JAMES S. ATHON.
Auditor of State—JOSEPH RESTINE.
Treasurer of State—M. L. BRETT.
Attorney General—OSCAR B. HORD.
Adjutant General—LAZ. NOBLE.

MARION COUNTY OFFICERS.

Clerk—William Wallace.
Sheriff—William Jas. H. Robinson.
Coroner—G. W. Alread.
Treasurer—Geo. F. Meyers.
Auditor—Jacob T. Wright.
Recorder—Wm. J. Elliott.
County Surveyor—O. W. Voorhies.
Commissioners—L. Oreng, D. Vansyoc, Geo. Bruce.
Appraiser of Real Estate—Thos. W. Council.

CITY OFFICERS.

Mayor—JOHN CAVEN.
Clerk—C. S. BUTTERFIELD.
Treasurer—JOSEPH K. ENGLISH.
Civil Engineer—JAMES WOOD.
City Attorney—RICHARD J. RYAN.
Marshal—JOHN UNVERSAW.
Deputy Marshal—JOHN S. RUSSELL.
Assessor—JOHN B. STUMPH.
Street Commissioner—JOHN M. KEMPER.
Chief Fire Engineer—CHARLES RICHMANN.
Market Master—JOHN JACOB WENNER.
City Sealer—JAMES LOUCKS.
City Printer—ELLIS BARNES.
City Sexton—GARRISON W. ALLRED.
Board of Health—{ GEO. W. MEARS, Prest.
JNO. M. GASTON, Sec.
MANSUR H. WRIGHT.

COMMON COUNCIL.

First Ward—Sims A. Colley; P. H. Jameson.
Second Ward—Henry Coburn; Theodore P. Haughey.
Third Ward—H. A. Fletcher; W. C. Thompson.
Fourth Ward—R. B. Emerson; John Blake.
Fiftth Ward—Stephen McNabb; Samuel Lefevre.
Sixth Ward—William Boaz; Austin H. Brown.
Seventh Ward—S. A. Fletcher, Jr.; Chas. Glazier.
Eighth Ward—William Cook; William Allen.
Ninth Ward—Wm. J. Wallace; Joseph Staub.

HEAD-QUARTERS U. S. DEPARTMENT.

Jno. H. Farguhar, Captain, 19th U. S. Infantry, Chief Mustering and Disbursing Officer, Ind.
W. H. Mills, Disbursing Officer.
J. B. Hager, Captain, 14th U. S. Infantry, Mustering and Disbursing Officer, Ind.
H. K. Katcher, Captain, 14th U. S. Infantry, Mustering and Disbursing Officer, Ind.
J. M. Locke, Captain, 14th U. S. Infantry, Mustering and Disbursing Officer, Ind.
W. F. Melbourne, First Lieutenant, 15th U. S. Infantry, Mustering and Disbursing Officer, Ind.
J. F. McElhone, First Lieutenant, 14th U. S. Infantry, Mustering and Disbursing Officer, Ind.
E. R. Craft, Second Lieutenant, 5th U. S. Artillery, Mustering and Disbursing Officer, Ind.
W. O. Douglas, Second Lieutenant, 14th U. S. Infantry, Mustering and Disbursing Officer, Ind.
George S. Browning, Second Lieutenant, 14th U. S. Infantry, Mustering and Disbursing Officer, Ind.

CLERKS IN MUSTERING AND PAY ROLL DEPARTMENT.

D. B. Hunt, residence, 22 West New York Street.
Wm. A. Allen, residence, Little's Hotel.
George Zorger, boards at Tyler's, Virginia Avenue.
D. S. Street, boards, corner Market and Tennessee Sts.
Martin Zorger, boards at Macy House,

CLERKS IN ACCOUNT DEPARTMENT.

James M. Matlock, residence, 81 east South st.
William N. Compton, boards, 21 Delaware st.
W. W. Matlock, residence, 13 School st.
Chauncy Turner, boards, 21 Delaware st.
Robert D'Ewald, residence, cor. n. New Jersey and St. Clair.

INDIANAPOLIS ROLLING MILL COMPANY.

President and Superintendent, John M. Lord.
Manager, John Thomas.
Treasurer, Aquilla Jones.
Secretary, C. B. Parkman, res. 30 s. Tennessee.
Clerk, J. R. Blake.

INDIANAPOLIS CHAMBER OF COMMERCE.

President, T. B. Elliott.
Vice Presidents, W. A. Bradshaw, John M. Lord, S. V. B. Noel.
Directors, John Carlisle, L. W. Hasselman, J. W. Murphy, E. B. Alvord, L. Hills, John Fishback, Fred. P. Rusch, I. Mansur, A. D. Wood, J. D. Pattison.
Secretary, J. Barnard.

INDIANAPOLIS HEBREW BENEVOLENT SOCIETY.

Organized Jan., 1861. Meets every three months for business. Election of officers, semi-annually. The Relief Committee consists of the President, Vice President and one member.

OFFICERS.

President, Solomon Bloom.
Treasurer, David Dessar.
Member of Relief Committee, J. Kahn.

Vice President, Samuel Rosenthal.
Secretary, H. Bamberger.

YOUNG MEN'S LITERARY AND SOCIAL UNION.

Organized December, 1862. Meets every other Sunday for exercises, and the last Wednesday of each month for business. Rooms, third floor next to Harrison's Bank. Election of officers, every three months.

OFFICERS.

President, H. Bamberger.
Secretary, Sol. Rice.
Librarian, Leo Dessar.

Vice President, M. Shelt.
Treasurer, Sol. Bloom.
Committee on Exercises, S. Bernstein, J. B. Dessar, Solomon Moritz.

LOCAL BANKS AND BANKING OFFICES.

BRANCH OF THE BANK OF THE STATE.

Cor. Wash. and Meridian, Yohn's Block ; open from 9 A. M. to 3 P. M. Discount daily. Capital, $233,000.
President, Geo. Tousey.
Cashier, David E. Snyder.

Teller, J. M. Nichol.
Book-keeper, D. M. Taylor.

HARRISON'S BANK.

Location 15 e. Wash. Bank open from 8 A. M. to 4 P. M. Discount daily.

A. & J. S. C. Harrison, *Bankers.* | Samuel W. Watson, *Book-keeper.*

NATIONAL BANK.

Capital, $1,000,000. Location Odd Fellows' Hall, Penn. st.

President, Wm. H. English. | *Cashier,* W. R. Nofsinger.
Vice President, G. W. Riggs. | *Teller,* Lewis Jordan.

INDIANAPOLIS BRANCH BANKING COMPANY.

Location cor. Wash. and Penn.; open from 8 A. M. to 5 P. M. Discount daily.

President, Calvin Fletcher. | *Teller,* E. Sharpe.
Cashier, Thos. H. Sharpe. | *Book-keeper,* J. A. Moore.
Teller, F. A. W. Davis. | *Assistant Book-keeper,* G. Bergner.
Teller, Ingram Fletcher. | *Clerk,* E. Wolfram.

FLETCHER'S BANK.

Location 30 e. Wash.; open from 8 A. M. to 4 P. M. Discount daily. F. M. Churchman, S. A. Fletcher, Proprietors.

CITY BANK.

Location 3 w. Wash.; open daily from 8 A. M. to 4 P. M. Discount daily. Pettibone, Mansur & Co., Proprietors.

FLETCHER, VAJEN & CO.'S BANK.

Location 6 n. Meridian. T. R. Fletcher, J. H. Vajen, J. R. Haugh, Proprietors.

MASONIC.

GRAND COMMANDERY OF INDIANA.

The next Annual Conclave of the Grand Commandery of Knights Templar of the State of Indiana will be held at the Grand Masonic Hall, in the city of Indianapolis, at 2 o'clock P. M., on the first Tuesday (6th day,) of April, 1865.

GRAND OFFICERS.

R. E. Solomon D. Bayless, of Fort Wayne, Grand Commander.
V. D. William Hacker, of Shelbyville, Deputy Grand Commander.
Sir Harvey G. Hazelrigg, of Thornton, Grand Generalissimo.
Sir Austin B. Claypool, of Connersville, Grand Captain General.
Sir Rev. G. C. Beeks, of Fort Wayne, Grand Prelate.
Sir George W. Porter, of New Albany, Grand Senior Warden.
Sir George Vorhis, of Fort Wayne, Grand Junior Warden.
Sir L. B. Stockton, of Lafayette, Grand Standard Bearer.
Sir Augustus W. Murphy, of Lafayette, Grand Sword Bearer.
Sir Charles Fisher, of Indianapolis, Grand Treasurer.
Sir Francis King, of Indianapolis, Grand Recorder.
Sir William W. Clinedenst, of Centerville, Grand Warden.
Sir Henry Colestock, of Indianapolis, Grand Captain Guards.

GRAND COUNCIL R. & S. MASTERS.

The Grand Council of Royal and Select Masters of the State of Indiana, will hold its next Annual Communication at the Grand Masonic Hall, in the city of Indianapolis, at 2 o'clock P. M., on the Tuesday (18th,) preceding the fourth Monday in May, 1865.

GRAND OFFICERS.

M. P. Solomon D. Bayless, of Fort Wayne, Grand Master.
P. Eden H. Davis, of Shelbyville, Deputy Grand Master.
Comp. Thomas Newby, of Cambridge City, T. Ill., Grand Master.
Comp. Joseph Freeman, of Fort Wayne, Grand Conductor of Work.
Comp. John M. Bramwell, of Indianapolis, Grand Capt. of Guards.
Comp. Charles Fisher, of Indianapolis, Grand Treasurer.
Comp. Francis King, of Indianapolis, Grand Recorder.
Comp. Rev. William Pelan, of Connresville, Grand Chaplain.
Comp. Henry Colestock, of Indianapolis, Grand S. and Sentinel.

GRAND R. A. CHAPTER OF INDIANA.

The Grand Chapter of Royal Arch Masons of the State of Indiana, will hold its next Annual Communication at the Grand Masonic Hall, in the city of Indianapolis, at 2 o'clock P. M., on the Wednesday (19th,) preceding the fourth Monday in May, 1865.

GRAND OFFICERS.

M. E. Erastus W. H. Ellis, of Goshen, Grand High Priest.
R. E. Eden H. Davis, of Shelbyville, Deputy Grand High Priest.
R. E. Hugh Hanna, of Wabash, Grand King.
R. E. Thomas Newby, of Cambridge City, Grand Scribe.
E. Charles Fisher, of Indianapolis, Grand Treasurer.
E. Francis King, of Indianapolis, Grand Secretary.
E. Rev. John Leach, of Rolling Prairie, Grand Chaplain.
Comp. Caleb Schmidlapp, of Madison, Grand Capt. of Hosts.
Comp. Wm. Worthington, of Attica, Grand Royal Arch Captain.
Comp. Henry Colestock, of Indianapolis, Grand Guard.

GRAND LODGE F. & A. MASONS OF INDIANA.

The Grand Lodge of Indiana holds its next Annual Communication at the Grand Masonic Hall, in the city of Indianapolis, at 2 o'clock, P. M., on the Tuesday, succeeding the fourth Monday (25th day,) of May, 1864.

GRAND OFFICERS.

M. W. Wm. Hacker, of Shelbyville, Grand Master.
R. W. Harvey G. Hazelrigg, of Lebanon, Deputy Grand Master.
R. W. Wm. J. Millard, Jr., of Millersville, Senior Grand Warden.
R. W. Geo. W. Porter, of New Albany, Junior Grand Warden.
R. W. Chas. Fisher, of Indianapolis, Grand Treasurer.
R. W. Francis King, of Indianapolis, Grand Secretary.
Rev. Bro. John Leach, of Rolling Prairie, Grand Chaplain.
Bro. E. H. M. Berry, of Milroy, Grand Lecturer.
Bro. Joseph A. Woodhull, of Angola, Grand Marshal.
Bro. Caspar Fogel, of Mt. Carmel, Grand Senior Deacon.
Bro. Lyndon A. Smith, of Terre Haute, Grand Junior Deacon.
Bro. Henry Colestock, of Indianapolis, Grand Tyler.

RAPER COMMANDERY, No. 1.

Meets 4th Wednesday of each month, at Masonic Hall.

OFFICERS.

Sir Ephraim Colestock, E. C.
Sir John M. Bramwell, G.
Sir William Sullivan, C. G.
Sir Francis King, P.
Sir Wm. J. Wallace, S. W.
Sir W. P. Noble, J. W.

Sir Samuel Campbell, T.
Sir Charles Fisher, R.
Sir Samuel Delzell, St. B.
Sir John D. Morris, Sw. B.
Sir Joseph Garratt, W.
Sir A. Wilson, Sent.

COUNCIL.

Indianapolis Council, No. 2.

Meets first Monday of each month, at Masonic Hall.

OFFICERS.

John M. Bramwell, T. I. L. L. G. M.
Ephraim Colestock, Dep.
Francis King, P. C. W.
Winston P. Noble, C. G.

Samuel Campbell, T.
Charles Fisher, R.
Abner A. Wilson, S.

CHAPTER.

Indianapolis Chapter, No. 5.

Meets first Friday of each month, at Masonic Hall.

OFFICERS.

John M. Bramwell, H. P.
Ephraim Colestock, K.
Samuel Campbell, Scribe.
Roger Parry, C. H.
Winston P. Noble, P. S.
Jacob King, R. A. C.

James H. Seybold, G. M. 3d V.
Joseph F. Trowbridge, G. M. 2d V.
Francis Farman, G. M. 1st V.
James Sulgrove, T.
Charles Fisher, Sec.
Abner A. Wilson, G.

CENTER LODGE, No. 23.

Meets first Wednesday of each month, at Masonic Hall.

OFFICERS.

William T. Clark, W. M.
Winston P. Noble, S. W.
John C. Conner, J. W.
Isaac H. Roll, T.
Charles Fisher, Sec.

Joseph Solomon, S. D.
Joseph Garratt, J. D.
Henry Colestock, T.
Charles E. Judson and John Mc-
    Grath, Stewards.

OFFICERS OF MARION LODGE, No. 35, FOR 1863–4.

John M. Bramwell, Wor. Master.
Roger Parry, Senior Warden.
George D. Davis, Junior Warden.
James Sulgrove, Treasurer.

Francis King, Secretary.
Joseph F. Trowbridge, Sen. Deacon.
Samuel Campbell, Jun. Deacon.
Abner A. Wilson, Tyler.

A. & A. RITE OF MASONRY.

SERAIAT COUNCIL OF PRINCES OF JERUSALEM.

Edwin A. Davis, M. E. S. P. G. M.
William Wallace, T. G. H. P. S. D.
James M. Tomlinson, M. E. S. G. W.
Theo. P. Haughey, M. E. J. G. W.
John J. Parsons, V. G. K. S. & A.

John C. New, Gr. Treas.
P. G. C. Hunt, Gr. Mast. Cer.
Geo. F. Myer, Gr. Mast. Ent.
John B. Osgood, Tyler.

ADONIRAM LODGE OF PERFECTION.

Meets in their Hall, cor. Meridian and Wash., Yohn's Block.

Edwin A. Davis, T. P. G. M.
William Sullivan, D. G. M.
James M. Tomlinson, S. G. W.
William J. Wallace, J. G. W.
Luther Martin, G. K. of S.

John C. New, G. T.
H. W. Smith, G. S.
John Caven, G. O.
P. G. C. Hunt, G. M. of C.
Theo. P. Haughey, G. C. of G.

ODD FELLOWS.

GRAND LODGE.

Dennis Gregg, M. W. Grand Master, Indianapolis.
John T. Sanders, R. W. D. Grand Master, Jeffersonville.
E. H. Barry, R. W. Grand Secretary, Indianapolis.
T. P. Haughey, R. W. Grand Treasurer.
P. S. Hoffman, R. W. Grand Warden, Madison.
William H. Dixon, Gr. Rep. Gr. L. U. S., Jeffersonville.
J. S. Harvey, Gr. Rep. Gr. L. U. S., Indianapolis.
Joseph McGranahan, Alt. G. Rep. G. L. U. S., Lawrenceburg.
H. D. Scott, Alt. G. Rep. G. L. U. S., Terre Haute.
Rev. Cyrus Nutt, W. Grand Chaplain, Bloomington.
L. A. Burnett, W. Grand Marshal, Terre Haute.
William Shoeneman, W. Grand Conductor, Michigan City.
F. J. Blair, W. Grand Herald, Peru.
John Hunt, W. Grand Guardian, Lawrenceburg.

R. W. GRAND ENCAMPMENT.

Leonidas Sexton, M. W. G. Patriarch, Rushville.
Rev. Cyrus Nutt, M. E. G. High Priest, Bloomington.
Simeon Frasier, R. W. G. Senior Warden, Greenwood.
C. P. Tuley, R. W. G. Junior Warden, Bloomington.
E. H. Barry, R. W. G. Scribe, Indianapolis.
T. P. Haughey, R. W. G. Treasurer, Indianapolis.
Christopher Toler, W. G. Sentinel, Madison.
Jacob T. Williams, Dep. G. Sentinel, Indianapolis.
T. B. McCarty, G. Rep. G. L. U. S., Wabash.
L. M. Campbell, G. Rep. G. L. U. S., Danville.
C. W. Elmore, Alt. G. Rep. G. L. U. S., Crawfordsville.
T. G. Beharrell, Alt. G. Rep. G. L. U. S., Jeffersonville.

PAST GRAND PATRIARCHS.

Christian Bucher, of No. 2.
Isaac H. Taylor, of No. 2.
Daniel Moss, of No. 27.
J. S. Harvey, of No. 5.
Jacob P. Chapman, of No. 5.
Job B. Eldridge, of No. 10.
E. H. Barry, of No. 12.

Lewis Humphreys, of No. 9.
Chris Miller, of No. 6.
J. H. Stailey, of No. 24.
T. B. McCarty, of No. 21.
N. P. Howard, of No. 49.
L. M. Campbell, of No. 47.
D. Ferguson, of No. 50.

PAST GRAND HIGH PRIESTS.

Casper Markle, of No. 11.
W. P. Applegate, of No. 33.
George B. Jocelyn, of No. 1.
Thos. P. Gunnel, of No. 38.
David Ferguson, of No. 50.

R. C. S. Maccoun, of No. 47.
John T. Sanders, of No. 14.
J. A. Moorman, of No. 50.
T. G. Beharrell, of No. 14.

METROPOLITAN ENCAMPMENT. No. 5.

Geo. H. Brinkmeyer, C. P.
James A. Isgrigg, H. P.
Milton S. Huey, S. W.

Samuel Row, J. W.
Charles A. Wright, Scribe.
H. A. Fletcher, Treasurer.

MARION ENCAMPMENT, No. 35.

James H. Brown, C. P.
Paul Sherman, H. P.
Chas. Whipple, S. W.

H. I. Hinesley, J. W.
Eli Fasold, Scribe.
R. C. Stout, Treasurer.

TEUTONIA ENCAMPMENT, No. 57.

T. Ennst Despa, C. P.
Wm. Teckenbrock, H. P.
Fred. Klare, S. W.

Valentine Reinhard, J. W.
Fred. Thoms, Scribe.
Christ. Rarle, Treasurer.

CENTER LODGE, No. 18.

Jas. A. Isgrigg, N. G.
Chas. A. Wright, V. G.
John S. Russell, Secy.

H. A. Fletcher, Treas.
Geo. P. Anderson, Per. Secy.

PHILOXENIAN LODGE, No. 48.

Jos. Ringham, N. G.
Stephen Spencer, V. G.
Geo. Brinkmeyer, Secy.

N. T. Bryam, Treas.
Geo. D. Sterats, Per. Secy.

CAPITAL LODGE, No. 124.

Paul Sherman, N. G.
Jas. H. Brown, V. G.
C. W. Whipple, Secy.

H. J. Hinesley, Treas.
John F. Walleck, Per. Secy.

GERMANIA LODGE, No. 129.

John Schneider, N. G.
Geo. Youngerman, V. G.
Christ. Heckmann, Secy.

Christ. Karle, Treas.
Tobias Bender, Per. Secy.

NORTH MISSOURI
BROAD GUAGE

RAILROAD

The Shortest, Quickest and only all Rail Route from
Indianapolis, via St. Louis, to

ST. JOSEPH,	**COUNCIL BLUFFS,**
ATCHISON,	**OMAHA,**
WESTON,	**NEBRASKA CITY,**
LEAVENWORTH,	**QUINCY, and**
KANSAs CITY,	**HANNIBAL.**

Certain and Close Connections are Made

At Macon City, with the Hannibal and St. Joseph Railroad, Chicago,
Burlington & Iowa Railroad, and all the Railroads of Iowa.

At Iatan, with Steamers which run daily to Leavenworth and Kansas
City.

At Leavenworth, with first class stages to all points in the interior of
Kansas.

Also, at St. Joseph, with Missouri River Packet Company's Line of splendid Steamers, for all points on the Missouri River. Meals and berths
Free.

Arriving at St. Joseph in advance of any other Route via St. Louis.

FARE AS LOW AS BY ANY OTHER ROUTE!

Magnificent Sleeping Cars on all Night Trains.

TICKETS for sale in all Principal Ticket Offices, and at No. 40, under
Planters' House, St. Louis. Where all information can be ob-
tained relative to Routes in Iowa, Kansas and Nebraska.

Be certain your Tickets read, via St. Louis and North Missouri Railroad.

    I. H. STURGEON, President and Superintendent.
    J. H. CONCANNON, General Ticket Agent.
    H. H. SIMMONS, General Traveling Agent.
    R. T. BROWN, Agent, Indianapolis.

21

www.ingramcontent.com/pod-product-compliance
Lightning Source LLC
Chambersburg PA
CBHW031402270326
41929CB00010BA/1288